# Multiagent Scheduling

Alessandro Agnetis • Jean-Charles Billaut •
Stanisław Gawiejnowicz • Dario Pacciarelli •
Ameur Soukhal

# Multiagent Scheduling

## Models and Algorithms

Springer

Alessandro Agnetis
Dipartimento di Ingegneria
dell'Informazione
e Scienze Matematiche
Università di Siena
Siena, Italy

Jean-Charles Billaut
Ameur Soukhal
Laboratoire d'Informatique
Université François Rabelais Tours
Tours, France

Stanisław Gawiejnowicz
Faculty of Mathematics and
Computer Science
Adam Mickiewicz University
Poznań, Poland

Dario Pacciarelli
Dipartimento di Ingegneria
Università Roma Tre
Roma, Italy

ISBN 978-3-642-41879-2 ISBN 978-3-642-41880-8 (eBook)
DOI 10.1007/978-3-642-41880-8
Springer Heidelberg New York Dordrecht London

Library of Congress Control Number: 2014930231



Printed on acid-free paper

Springer is part of Springer Science+Business Media (www.springer.com)

*To Silvia, Walter and Gaia*
*Alessandro Agnetis*
*To my parents*
*Jean-Charles Billaut*
*To Mirosława and Agnieszka*
*Stanisław Gawiejnowicz*
*To my parents*
*Dario Pacciarelli*
*To my parents*
*Ameur Soukhal*

# Preface

Scheduling problems are combinatorial optimization problems in which some activities have to be executed using resources that they need. A feasible allocation of the resources to the activities over time is called a schedule. The quality of a schedule is measured by various optimality criteria that are functions of completion times of the activities and the amounts of resources that have been used. Problems in the construction of different classes of schedules with required properties are considered in the theory of scheduling that originated approximately 60 years ago.

The theory of scheduling is a very active research area containing a great number of scheduling models. Several books (see, e.g., Blazewicz et al. 2007; Brucker 2007 or Pinedo 2008) present classical models of scheduling problems in which all data are described by numbers, and schedules are evaluated by a single optimality criterion. Some other books present more specific models such as scheduling problems in just-in-time manufacturing systems (Jozefowska 2007), scheduling problems when the quality of a schedule is measured by several optimality criteria (T'Kindt and Billaut 2006) or scheduling problems in which job processing times depend on when the jobs are started (Gawiejnowicz 2008).

The book presented to the reader is devoted to multiagent scheduling. Research on this scheduling model was started approximately 10 years ago, after publication of Baker and Smith (2003) and Agnetis et al. (2004), in which two-agent scheduling was introduced. In multiagent scheduling problems, activities share resources but are maintained by two or more agents that use their own optimality criteria. These agents may or may not compete, and the final schedule is evaluated by several optimality criteria. Though multiagent scheduling is intensively studied in view of many applications, it was not presented earlier in a monograph.

This book is organized into six chapters that can be divided into two parts.

The first, introductory part of the book is composed of two chapters. Chapter 1 gives a general introduction to multiagent scheduling, introducing general definitions and notation, several resolution approaches for multicriteria problems and different scenario when considering several agents. Chapter 2 recalls basic elements of complexity theory and resolution methods. Algorithms with performance guarantees, approximation schemes, implicit enumeration algorithms and relaxation techniques are presented.

The second, main part of the book is composed of four chapters. Chapter 3 deals with single machine multiagent scheduling problems with fixed job processing times. Problems presented in the chapter are divided into groups with respect to the optimality criteria used by agents. Chapter 4 concerns single machine scheduling problems with batching constraints. For these problems, jobs of one agent can be gathered into batches that are processed in parallel or in series. Chapter 5 deals with parallel machines environments. Problems with and without preemption are considered. Finally, Chap. 6 deals with variable job processing times; it means scheduling problems where the processing times depend on the job starting times, their positions in schedule or are changing in some interval between a minimum and a maximum value.

In all the chapters, the literature of the subject is reviewed and a lot of problems are presented with complexity results and different resolution methods. In order to make the book as compact and actual as possible, references discussed in the book concern only agent scheduling problems with regular optimality criteria listed in Chap. 1 and published not later than June 30, 2013. The authors also decided to include in the book numerous examples to illustrate the most important aspects of considered problems and to make the contents as clear as possible. Moreover, at the end of Chaps. 3–6, some tables are given that summarize the main results.

The book is intended for researchers and Ph.D. students working in the theory of scheduling and other members of scientific community who are interested in recent scheduling models. Since prerequisites for reading this book are only the basic knowledge of discrete mathematics, algorithmics, complexity theory and a high-level programming language, this book can also serve students of graduate studies.

Multiagent scheduling is still in development. Hence, though the authors made a substantial effort to give the reader a complete presentation of the subject, it is not excluded that some issues or references have been missed. Therefore, the authors will welcome any comments on the book.

Ending, the authors wish to express their gratitude to Christian Rauscher, who on behalf of Springer was responsible for work on this book. Thank you very much, Christian, for your patience and cooperation!

Siena, Italy — Alessandro Agnetis
Tours, France — Jean-Charles Billaut
Poznań, Poland — Stanisław Gawiejnowicz
Roma, Italy — Dario Pacciarelli
Tours, France — Ameur Soukhal

# Contents

# Chapter 1
# Multiagent Scheduling Fundamentals

This chapter gives a general introduction to multicriteria and multiagent scheduling. Basic concepts from the two research areas are presented and a classification of considered problems, illustrating the presentation by examples, is proposed.

The chapter is composed of seven sections. In Sect. 1.1, basic concepts and notions related to multicriteria and multiagent scheduling are introduced. In Sect. 1.2, the main parts of formal statement of any scheduling problem considered in the book are introduced. In Sect. 1.3, we present the possible solution approaches to multiagent scheduling problems. In Sect. 1.4, a classification of multiagent scheduling problems introduces the several scenario that are considered. Notations for multiagent scheduling problems are given in Sect. 1.5. In Sect. 1.6, examples illustrate the introduced concepts and the important notions. The chapter ends by Sect. 1.7 with bibliographic remarks.

## 1.1 Main Concepts and Notions

In this section, we introduce main concepts and notions used in the book. In Sect. 1.1.1 we recall a few definitions of main notions in single- and multiagent scheduling. In Sect. 1.1.2 we give several examples of applications of multiagent scheduling problems. In the book, we use a standard mathematical notation. If a notation is introduced ad hoc, it is clarified at the place of its first appearance. Theorems, lemmas, properties, examples and figures are numbered separately in each chapter. Proofs and examples are ended by box '□' and diamond '◇', respectively. Algorithms are presented in a pseudocode in which standard control statements are used and comments start with symbol '//'.

A. Agnetis et al., *Multiagent Scheduling*, DOI 10.1007/978-3-642-41880-8_1, 

### 1.1.1 *Basic Definitions of Multiagent Scheduling*

Since multiagent scheduling uses the same background and notions as other research domains in the theory of scheduling, we only briefly recall some facts. In the book, by *scheduling* we mean all actions that have to be done in order to determine when each activity of a set is to start and to complete. In the theory of scheduling, the elements of the set are called *jobs* and we will use this name hereafter.

Each job is in competition with the others for the use of time and of *resources* capacity. The resources are understood as everything what is needed for a job for its completion. Therefore, in scheduling we also deal with *allocation of resources* to each job. A *schedule* is determined by a set of start times and of assigned resources, which respect some predefined requirements, called *constraints*, such as arrival times or due dates of jobs, precedence constraints among the jobs, etc.

A problem in which, given some input data, one has to find a schedule is called a *scheduling problem*. A schedule that satisfies all requirements of the considered scheduling problem is called a *feasible schedule*. Unless otherwise stated, we denote feasible schedules by small Greek characters, e.g. $\sigma$, $\pi$, etc.

The quality of a schedule is measured by a function called *optimality criterion* or *objective function* that is generally based on the jobs completion times. Sometimes, for brevity, we call an optimality criterion and objective function as *criterion* and *objective*, respectively.

In multiagent scheduling problems, schedules are evaluated by two or more criteria. In the book, we denote by $f^1(\sigma)$, $f^2(\sigma)$, $\ldots$, $f^K(\sigma)$ the evaluation of $\sigma$ by a criterion $f^1$, $f^2, \ldots, f^K$, respectively. Moreover, we assume that functions $f^k$, where $1 \leq k \leq K$, have to be minimized.

Among all feasible schedules there exists at least one that is *optimal*, i.e. the best one with respect to the applied criteria. There are known different kinds of optimality for multiagent scheduling problems, and the most popular among them are the following two.

**Definition 1.1.** A feasible schedule $\sigma$ is a *strict Pareto optimal* or *strictly nondominated* schedule with respect to the optimality criteria $f^1, f^2, \ldots, f^K$, if there is no feasible schedule $\pi$ such that $f^k(\pi) \leq f^k(\sigma)$ for all $1 \leq k \leq K$, with at least one strict inequality.

The set of all strict Pareto optimal schedules defines the *Pareto set*.

**Definition 1.2.** A feasible schedule $\sigma$ is a *weak Pareto optimal* or *weakly nondominated* schedule with respect to the optimality criteria $f^1, f^2, \ldots, f^K$, if there is no feasible schedule $\pi$ such that $f^k(\pi) < f^k(\sigma)$ for all $1 \leq k \leq K$.

*Remark 1.1.* These definitions are formulated in context of scheduling problems, but they may gain a more general form if we replace word 'schedule' by 'solution'. Hence, throughout the book both the words are used interchangeably if a scheduling problem is discussed.

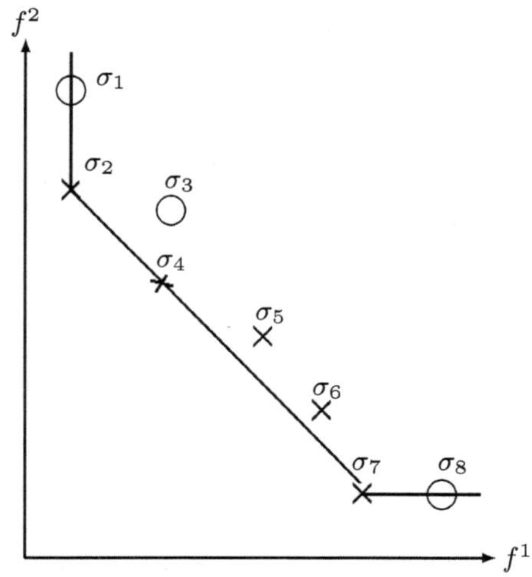


**Fig. 1.1** Strict Pareto solutions vs. weak Pareto solutions

The set of weak Pareto optimal schedules defines the *tradeoff curve*, called also *Pareto curve*. Since this curve may be non convex, we distinguish *supported Pareto optimal schedules* if the solutions are on the convex hull of the Pareto set and the *non supported Pareto optimal schedules* otherwise.

The position of strict and weak Pareto optimal solutions and the notion of supported and non supported Pareto solution are illustrated in Fig. 1.1 for $K = 2$. In the figure, strict Pareto optimal solutions are represented by a cross ($\sigma_2$, $\sigma_4$, $\sigma_5$, $\sigma_6$, $\sigma_7$), while weak Pareto optimal solutions are represented by a circle ($\sigma_1$, $\sigma_3$, $\sigma_8$). Solutions $\sigma_1$, $\sigma_2$, $\sigma_7$ and $\sigma_8$ are supported, while solutions $\sigma_3$, $\sigma_4$, $\sigma_5$ and $\sigma_6$ are non supported.

Notice that given above definitions can be easily extended to the case of more than two optimality criteria. In the following, for simplicity, a *Pareto schedule* will denote a strict Pareto schedule.

## *1.1.2 Multiagent Scheduling Applications*

In the multicriteria scheduling literature, several objective functions are used to measure the performance of a schedule, and all the jobs that are scheduled contribute to each performance measure.

In order to make a distinction between the jobs that will share the same resources, one generally associate a weight to each job. This weight allows us to give more or less importance to a job, in comparison to the others, and helps in scheduling decisions. However, this distinction may not be sufficient.

In some cases, it may happen that some jobs have to be evaluated by a specific performance measure and that other jobs have to be evaluated by another performance measure. This is the subject of *multiagent scheduling*.

In a multiagent scheduling problem, there are several *agents*, each interested in a subset of jobs. Each agent has its own performance measure which depends on the schedule of its jobs only. However, all the jobs have to share common resources, so the problem is to find a schedule of the jobs of all agents, which constitutes a good compromise solution. Below we give several examples of multiagent scheduling problems.

#### 1.1.2.1 Rescheduling Problems

Workshop of Medium Deep Groove Ball Bearings group (Pessan et al. 2008) describes a problem in which the principle objective is the minimization of the total flow time. Some jobs to be scheduled cannot be performed during the day because the production demand exceeds the workshop load. In such a case, the jobs that have not been performed during the day become urgent the next day. These particular jobs receive a deadline and their early production is mandatory. Here, an agent corresponds to the job subset that has to be completed early. Notice that here, all the jobs contribute to the global objective value which is the total flow time.

#### 1.1.2.2 Aircraft Landings

A classical problem in air traffic management is to schedule aircraft landings on a given set of runways, accounting for both safety and quality of service. In *collaborative decision making*, these decisions are made allowing information exchange among the airlines. Each airline is obviously interested in maximizing the satisfaction of its passengers only, which in turn is related to the delay of the corresponding flights. Here, one agent corresponds to one airline, which is interested to a subset of all flights. Notice that because of code sharing, the subsets of flights may not be all disjoint, although the same flight may have different relevance for two airlines.

#### 1.1.2.3 Project Scheduling

In a firm, multiple projects may compete for the usage of shared renewable resources such as people and machinery over time (Knotts et al. 2000). Each project manager is responsible for the performance of a project, and must therefore negotiate the use of the resources with the other managers. In this case, a manager is an agent, the set of activities of one agent contains the tasks of his/her project. Typically, in this case, all sets of activities are disjoint.

#### 1.1.2.4 Railway Scheduling

Brewer and Plott (1996) describe a problem arising in railroad management. The central rail administration sells access to the tracks to private companies, enforcing safety rules according to which an overall timetable is feasible. For example, no two trains can use the same block section at the same time. Hence, a feasible schedule of all trains (jobs) must be devised properly with respect to the objectives of each company (agent). Notice that also in this case, the jobs of agents are disjoint and the agents compete to perform the jobs on shared resources.

#### 1.1.2.5 Cross-Docking Distribution

Multi-agent scheduling problems can be encountered in optimizing product consolidation operations of a cross-docking distribution center. The center receives various products from the suppliers and fulfills demands of these products from the customers, by using a fleet of vehicles of various capacities. A product to be delivered to a customer is a collection of items placed in a standard container, e.g. a box or a pallet. Items intended for specific customers are a priory assigned to specific warehouses and transportation terminals associated with them. Consider customers of the same warehouse. For a planning period, each customer places an order of the required products to be consolidated and delivered by truck of an appropriate capacity. Due to the limited resources of the warehouse, operations on different products are performed sequentially. Each customer takes care of delivery times of its own products by means of specifying an objective function based on the dispatching times of its products. If there are two customers, one of which can specify an upper bound on the value of its objective function, then this situation can be modeled as a problem in which an agent is a customer and a job is a set of operations related to preparing a product from the order of a given customer. Product preparation operations include unloading from the warehouse, labeling, packaging, loading into a truck and documenting of the required number of items.

#### 1.1.2.6 Communication Networks

Competing scheduling problems occur in integrated-services packet-switched networks such as ATM (Asynchronous Transfer Mode) networks, and in soft real-time systems (Peha 1995). Integrated-services networks are networks that carry several traffic types such as voice, video, image transfer, and various kinds of computer data. These different traffic involve different performance objective functions. For example, for most types of computer data, the performance is typically measured in mean queueing delay, which is equivalent to minimizing the weighted total completion time. For voice and video, however, packets that are queued for a too long time will not reach their destination in time for playback and will be lost. It corresponds to minimizing the weighted number of tardy jobs.

In general, in these systems, it is useful to classify jobs in two categories: time-constrained, for jobs which should be processed any time before their deadlines; and non-time-constrained, for jobs which should simply be processed as early as possible. In fact, in any packet-switched network, information carried by the network is first divided into smaller packets. Packets are queued in a buffer at the network access point, awaiting transmission into the network, and a scheduling algorithm orders these packet transmissions.

## 1.2 Multiagent Scheduling Problem Description

In this section, we describe main parts of formal statement of any scheduling problem considered in the book. In Sects. 1.2.1, 1.2.2 and 1.2.3 we describe, respectively, main data concerning job, machine environment and optimality criterion that together compose a scheduling problem formulation.

### *1.2.1 Job Characteristics*

In what follows, we denote by $\mathcal{J}$ the set of jobs, and by $n = |\mathcal{J}|$ the number of jobs. $K$ is the number of agents, i.e., the number of subsets of jobs. In case of two agents, the agents will be denoted by $A$ and $B$ instead of 1 and 2.

$\mathcal{J}^k$ is the subset of agent $k$, and $n_k = |\mathcal{J}^k|$ is the number of jobs in $\mathcal{J}^k$. It may appear in the following that a job belongs to more than one agent. In this case, $\bar{\mathcal{J}}^k$ denotes the jobs that only belong to agent $k$ and $\bar{n}_k = |\bar{\mathcal{J}}^k|$. In the following, a schedule $\sigma$ which is optimal for agent $k$, is denoted by $\sigma^k$ and is called *reference schedule for agent k*. Since we only address regular objective functions, in $\sigma^k$ the jobs of $\mathcal{J}^k$ are scheduled before all other jobs, so the value $f^k(\sigma^k)$ can be computed without considering the jobs of the other agents.

We denote by $J_j$ the job number $j$. When necessary, $J_j^k$ will denote the job number $j$ in subset $\mathcal{J}^k$. Reversely, $\mathcal{J}^{-1}(J_j)$ will denote the agent or the set of agents that own job $J_j$. The main data associated to a job concern its processing time, due date and weight.

The processing time of job $J_j$ ($J_j^k$) we denote by $p_j$ ($p_j^k$). The total processing time of the activities of agent $k$ and the total processing time of all activities will be denoted by $P_k = \sum_{J_j^k \in \mathcal{J}^k} p_j^k$ and $P = \sum_{J_j \in \mathcal{J}} p_j$, respectively. The due date of job $J_j$ ($J_j^k$) we denote by $d_j$ ($d_j^k$). When a due date is associated to a job, at least one performance measure is related to the respect of the due dates. The weight of job $J_j$ ($J_j^k$) we denote by $w_j$ ($w_j^k$).

We will use brackets $[i]$ to denote the job in position $i$ in the sequence. $p_{[i]}$, $d_{[i]}$ and $w_{[i]}$ are respectively the duration, the due date and the weight of the job in position $i$.

Some additional job characteristics may also be considered. Following the three-field notation introduced by Graham et al. (1979), these characteristics are indicated in the $\beta$-field. This field may contain several characteristics, also called *constraints*, and we refer the reader to Brucker (2007) or Blazewicz et al. (2007) for a detailed description of this field. We only mention here the fields that will be considered in the following:

- The release date $r_j$ ($r_j^k$) that means that a job cannot start its processing before this release date,
- $p_j = p$ ($p_j^k = p^k$) in case of *identical* job processing times or *equal length* jobs, if $p = 1$ ($p^k = 1$) we talk about *unitary* processing times,
- $pmtn$ indicates that the preemption of jobs is allowed what means that it is possible to interrupt a job and to resume its processing at a later time, eventually on another machine,
- $prec$ indicates some precedence relations between jobs, given by a directed acyclic graph.

In multiagent scheduling, the particularity is that the job environment may be different for all the agents. Thus, for a formal problem description, the $\beta$-field has to be split between the agents. By default, if there is only one $\beta$-field, it is assumed that the job characteristics are the same for all the jobs.

We illustrate now some job data introduced earlier.

*Example 1.1.* (a) Symbol $r_j^B$ in the $\beta$ field indicates that the jobs of agent $B$ are subject to release dates, whereas it is not the case for the jobs of the other agents. Symbol $r_j$ in the $\beta$ field indicates that the jobs of all agents are subject to release dates.

(b) Notation $pmtn^A; p_j^B = 1$ in the $\beta$ field indicates that the preemption is allowed for the jobs of agent $A$ only and that all the jobs of agent $B$ have unitary processing times.

◇

### 1.2.2 Machine Environment

We denote by $\mathcal{M}$ the set of machines and $m = |\mathcal{M}|$ is the number of machines. The machine number $i$ is denoted by $M_i$. Following the three-field notation, the machine environment is described in the $\alpha$-field by a string of two parameters, $\alpha = \alpha_1\alpha_2$, where $\alpha_1$ denotes the type of machine(s) and $\alpha_2$ is the number of the machines. In case of a single machine $\alpha_1 = \emptyset$ and $\alpha_2 = 1$, otherwise $\alpha_1 \in \{\emptyset, P, Q, R, F, J, O\}$ and $\alpha_2$ is a positive integer. In most of cases, $\alpha_2 \in \{1, 2, 3, m, \emptyset\}$, with $\alpha_2 = m$ when the number of machines is supposed to be known and fixed. $\alpha_2 = \emptyset$ when the number of machines is unknown and it is a parameter of the problem instance. Notice also that not all combinations of $\alpha_1$ and $\alpha_2$ are possible.

If $\alpha_1 \in \{P, Q, R\}$, then jobs have to be scheduled on *parallel machines* and each of the jobs is composed of a single *operation*. If $\alpha_1 = P$, the machines are *identical* and the processing time of a job is the same for all the machines. If $\alpha_1 = Q$, the machines are *uniform* and a coefficient of speed $s_i$ is associated to each machine $M_i$ so that the processing time of a job depends on the performing machine, i.e., $p_{j,i} = \frac{p_j}{s_i}$. If $\alpha_1 = R$, the machines are *unrelated* and the processing time of a job depends on the performing machine, i.e. the speeds are job dependent.

If $\alpha_1 \in \{F, J, O\}$ we deal with a *shop* environment. In this case, to each job $J_j$ is associated a set of $o_j$ operations denoted by $O_{j,1}, O_{j,2}, \ldots O_{j,o_j}$, while to each operation $O_{j,h}$ is associated a performing machine $\mu_{j,h}$ and a processing time $p_{j,h}$. In case of multiagent scheduling, the agent number can be easily introduced in the notation: $o_j^k$, $O_{j,1}^k$, $\mu_{j,h}^k$, etc.

In shop problems, precedence relations among operations of every job $J_j$, $1 \le j \le n$, are in the form of

$$O_{j,1} \prec O_{j,2} \prec \cdots \prec O_{j,o_j},$$

where $O \prec O'$ means that the completion time of operation $O$ precedes the starting time of operation $O'$. It is also assumed that $\mu_{j,h} \neq \mu_{j,h'}$ for $h \neq h'$, $1 \le h, h' \le o_j$. The precedence relations between the operations of a job are not given and are a part of the problem.

The succession of machines required for the processing of a job in a shop problem is called the *routing* of the job. In the general case, when the routings are different, the workshop is called a *jobshop*, denoted by $\alpha_1 = J$. The *flowshop* case is denoted by $\alpha_1 = F$. In this case, the jobs require the $m$ machines in the same order for being processed: $o_j = m$ and $\mu_{j,i} = M_i$, $\forall j, 1 \le j \le n$. If the routings are not specified, we deal with the *openshop* case denoted by $\alpha_1 = O$.

### 1.2.3 Optimality Criteria

Following the three-field notation, the field $\gamma$ contains the expression of the *objective function*, also called *optimality criterion*.

The completion time of a job $J_j$ is denoted by $C_j$. The cost associated to job $J_j$ is a function of its completion time denoted by $f_j(C_j)$. In the multiagent case, we assume that all the jobs associated to an agent contribute to the evaluation for this agent and we denote by $C_j^k$ the completion time of job $J_j^k \in \mathcal{J}^k$ and $f^k$ the objective function related to the jobs of $\mathcal{J}^k$ if it is not job dependent.

The most classical functions $f_j^k$ that are used generally for job $J_j^k \in \mathcal{J}^k$ are the following:

| | |
|---|---|
| the *completion time* | $C_j^k$, |
| the *flow time* | $F_j^k = C_j^k - r_j^k$, |
| the *lateness* | $L_j^k = C_j^k - d_j^k$, |
| the *tardiness* | $T_j^k = \max\left\{C_j^k - d_j^k, 0\right\}$, |
| the *tardiness penalty* | $U_j^k = 1$ if $C_j^k > d_j^k$, 0 otherwise. |

Each function $f_j^k$ leads to four possible objectives:

$$f_{\max}^k = \max_{J_j^k \in \mathcal{J}^k} \left\{f_j^k\right\}, \tag{1.1}$$

$$wf_{\max}^k = \max_{J_j^k \in \mathcal{J}^k} \left\{w_j^k f_j^k\right\}, \tag{1.2}$$

$$\sum f_j^k = \sum_{J_j^k \in \mathcal{J}^k} f_j^k, \tag{1.3}$$

$$\sum w_j^k f_j^k = \sum_{J_j^k \in \mathcal{J}^k} w_j^k f_j^k. \tag{1.4}$$

The most important objective functions are:

the *makespan* $C_{\max}^k$,
the *maximum lateness* $L_{\max}^k$,
the *maximum tardiness* $T_{\max}^k$,
the *total (weighted) completion time* $\sum (w_j^k) C_j^k$,
the *total (weighted) tardiness* $\sum (w_j^k) T_j^k$,
the *(weighted) number of tardy jobs* $\sum (w_j^k) U_j^k$.

For some particular applications, other criteria may be defined, e.g. the *maximum earliness* $E_{\max}^k$, where the *earliness* $E_j^k = \max\left\{d_j^k - C_j^k, 0\right\}$.

All objective functions can be divided into regular and non regular ones. A *regular* objective function is an objective function which is nondecreasing with respect to variables $C_j$. For example, functions $F_j$ and $T_j$ are regular functions, whereas function $E_j$ is not regular. When the objective function is regular, it is always better to shift the jobs to the left, i.e. to schedule the jobs as early as possible. However, in case of a non regular objective function, it may be necessary to introduce idle times in the schedule for having a better solution. In this book, we consider only regular objective functions.

## 1.3 Solution Approaches to Multiagent Scheduling Problems

Multiagent scheduling problems can be solved in a multicriteria context using the following approaches:

- Finding one Pareto optimal schedule,
- Finding the whole set of strict Pareto optimal schedules and
- Counting the number of Pareto optimal schedules.

In case of finding one Pareto optimal schedule, we usually are interested only in the strict Pareto optimal ones. The whole set of Pareto optimal schedules can be obtained by finding strict Pareto optimal schedules one by one and iteratively, or by using population based algorithms. Finally, in counting the number of Pareto optimal schedules, the aim is to count the number of nondominated schedules or to give an approximation of their number.

Several methods exist for finding one of or all the Pareto optimal solutions. These methods are described in details in T'Kindt and Billaut (2006). We report here the most classical approaches used in the multicriteria scheduling literature. The notation is given for $K = 2$ criteria, but they can be easily extended to the general case.

### 1.3.1 *Feasibility Problem*

This approach means that no particular objective function has to be minimized and the problem is to find a feasible solution. We denote the approach by '$-$' in the $\gamma$ field. If we consider the example "Rescheduling Problem" described in Sect. 1.1.2.1, it is possible to consider that the late jobs belong to agent $B$. This agent has to find a feasible schedule, i.e. a schedule where each job satisfies its deadline. For agent $A$, who has the whole set of jobs, the notation of the objective function is $\sum C_j^A$ and suppose that this agent has a goal to reach denoted by $Q$. The constraints that $C_j^A \leq \tilde{d}_j^A$ and $\sum C_j^B \leq Q$ are inserted in the field $\beta$ of the problem notation and the objective function is denoted by '$-$'.

### 1.3.2 *Linear Combination of Criteria*

This method consists in defining a linear combination of objective functions, $\alpha f^A + (1-\alpha) f^B$ if $K = 2$, which has to be minimized. We denote the approach by $\alpha f^A + (1-\alpha) f^B$ in the $\gamma$ field. In case of $K$ agents, the notation becomes $\sum_{k=1}^{K} \alpha_k f^k$.The solutions that can be obtained by this approach constitute a subset of the set of strict Pareto optimal solutions (Geoffrion 1968). In other words, it may be impossible to fix weights to the criteria so that all the Pareto optimal solutions are obtained. This is due to the shape of the tradeoff curve, which can be nonconvex

**Algorithm 1** for the enumeration of Pareto optimal solutions with the $\varepsilon$-constraint approach

$\mathcal{R} := \emptyset$
**for** $Q_2 := ub_2$ **downto** $lb_2$ **step** $\delta_2$ **do**
    **for** $Q_3 := ub_3$ **downto** $lb_3$ **step** $\delta_3$ **do**
        $\vdots$
        **for** $Q_K := ub_K$ **downto** $lb_K$ **step** $\delta_K$ **do**
            $x :=$ lex-min$\{f : f^k(x) \le Q_k, 2 \le k \le K\}$
            **if not** exists $x' \in \mathcal{R}$ such that $f(x') \le f(x)$ **then**
                $\mathcal{R} := \mathcal{R} \cup \{x\}$
            **end if**
        **end for**
        $\vdots$
    **end for**
**end for**
**return** $\mathcal{R}$

for scheduling problems and therefore, the non supported Pareto optimal solutions cannot be returned by such a method.

### *1.3.3 Epsilon-Constraint Approach*

This method is often used in the literature. For example, in case of two objective functions, the first of them is minimized and the other one is bounded. In case of more than two objectives, the scheduling problem becomes: Find $\sigma$, such that $f^1(\sigma)$ is minimized and $f^2(\sigma) \le Q_2, \ldots, f^K(\sigma) \le Q_K$. This method leads to one weak Pareto optimal solution. For obtaining a strict Pareto optimal solution, a symmetric problem has to be solved. In the case of two agents, we denote the approach by putting $f^A$ in the $\gamma$ field and $f^B \le Q$ in the $\beta$ field.

By modifying the vector $Q$ iteratively, it is possible to obtain the whole set of strict Pareto optimal solutions. Notice that several algorithms have been proposed in the literature for improving the implementation of such a process (Laumanns et al. 2006; Mavrotas 2009). Algorithm 1 illustrates this method in the case of $K$ objective functions. The values $\delta_k$ denote the predefined decrement of $Q_k$, $lb_k$ and $ub_k$ denote the bounds for objective function $f^k$ and the function lex-min$(f)$ returns the solution with minimum lexicographic value, i.e. with minimum $f^1$ and then minimum $f^2$, etc.

### *1.3.4 Lexicographic Order*

With this method, an order is defined between the objective functions. The primary objective function is minimized first. Then, a new solution is searched, which

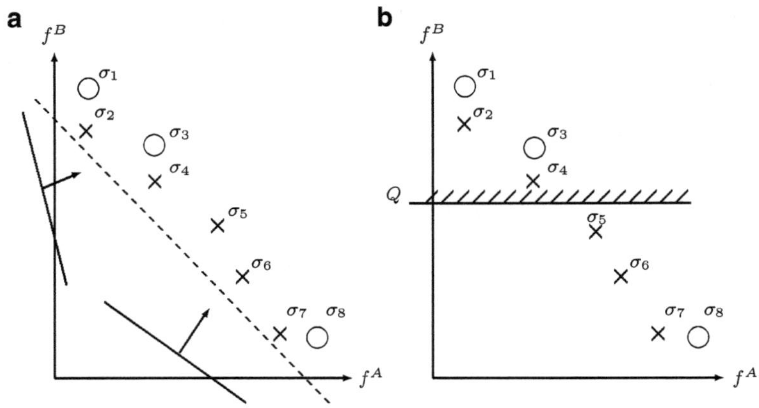


**Fig. 1.2** Linear combination vs. $\epsilon$-constraint approaches

minimizes the second objective function under the constraint that this solution is optimal for the primary objective function, and so on. We denote this approach by $Lex(f^1, f^2, \ldots, f^K)$.

If $\mathcal{S}$ denotes the set of feasible schedules and $f^1$, $f^2$ and $f^3$ are three objective functions to consider in this order, the method consists in finding a sequence $\pi \in \mathcal{S}_3$ with:

$$\mathcal{S}_1 = \left\{\pi \in \mathcal{S} : f^1(\pi) = \min_{\sigma \in \mathcal{S}}\{f^1(\sigma)\}\right\},$$

$$\mathcal{S}_2 = \left\{\pi \in \mathcal{S}_1 : f^2(\pi) = \min_{\sigma \in \mathcal{S}_1}\{f^2(\sigma)\}\right\},$$

$$\mathcal{S}_3 = \left\{\pi \in \mathcal{S}_2 : f^3(\pi) = \min_{\sigma \in \mathcal{S}_2}\{f^3(\sigma)\}\right\}.$$

The linear combination and the $\epsilon$-constraint approach are illustrated in Fig. 1.2 for $K = 2$. The solutions returned by a lexicographic order are $\sigma_1$ if the primary objective is $f^A$ and $\sigma_7$ if the primary objective is $f^B$.

In Fig. 1.2a are depicted the solutions that can be obtained by using a linear combination of criteria are $\sigma_2$ and $\sigma_7$. The dotted line represents the linear combination that allows finding both $\sigma_2$ and $\sigma_7$.

In Fig. 1.2b is depicted solution $\sigma_5$ obtained with the $\varepsilon$-constraint approach with $f^B \le Q$.

### 1.3.5 *Pareto Set Enumeration*

This approach means that we are interested in finding the whole set of strict Pareto optimal solutions. We denote the approach by $\mathcal{P}(f^A, f^B)$ in the $\gamma$ field.

### 1.3.6 Counting

This approach means that our aim is to count the number of strict Pareto optimal solutions. We denote the approach by $\#(f^A, f^B)$ in the $\gamma$ field.

## 1.4 Classification of Multiagent Scheduling Problems

Scheduling problems in which agents (customers, production managers, etc.) have to share the same set(s) of resources are at the frontier of combinatorial optimization and cooperative game theory (Agnetis et al. 2004). The key assumption of our models is that each agent (denoted $A$ and $B$ in case of two agents) has a set of jobs to perform (denoted by $\mathcal{J}^A$ and $\mathcal{J}^B$). The complexity of a multiagent scheduling problem depends on the intersection structure of the job sets $\mathcal{J}^k$. Therefore, we introduce a classification of multiagent problems based on the relationship among the subsets $\mathcal{J}^k$. Below we briefly describe different scenarios of the classification.

### 1.4.1 Competing Agents

In this case, the agents have no job in common, i.e., all jobs in each of the $K$ job sets exclusively belong to one agent. This means that $\mathcal{J}^h \cap \mathcal{J}^k = \emptyset$ for any two agents $h$ and $k$. In this situation, agents purely compete with each other to use system resources. The notation of the COMPETING scenario in the $\beta$-field is 'CO'. Note that in this case the notation of the agents is symmetric, i.e. problems with objective functions $f^A$ and $g^B$ are the same as problems with objective functions $g^A$ and $f^B$.

### 1.4.2 Interfering Sets

In this case, the job sets are nested, and we will always assume that they are numbered so that $\mathcal{J} = \mathcal{J}^1 \supseteq \mathcal{J}^2 \supseteq \ldots \supseteq \mathcal{J}^K$ (in case of two agents we have $\mathcal{J} = \mathcal{J}^A \supseteq \mathcal{J}^B$). The notation of the INTERFERING scenario in the $\beta$-field is 'IN'. Note that this case is asymmetric, e.g., both problems $1|IN|f^A, g^B$ and $1|IN|g^A, f^B$ can be considered, often having different complexity status.

### 1.4.3 Multicriteria Optimization

This is the classical multicriteria scheduling case, i.e., in which $\mathcal{J}^1 = \mathcal{J}^2 = \ldots = \mathcal{J}^K = \mathcal{J}$. The notation of the MULTICRITERIA scenario in the $\beta$-field is 'MU' and the notation in case of two criteria is 'BI' for BICRITERIA.

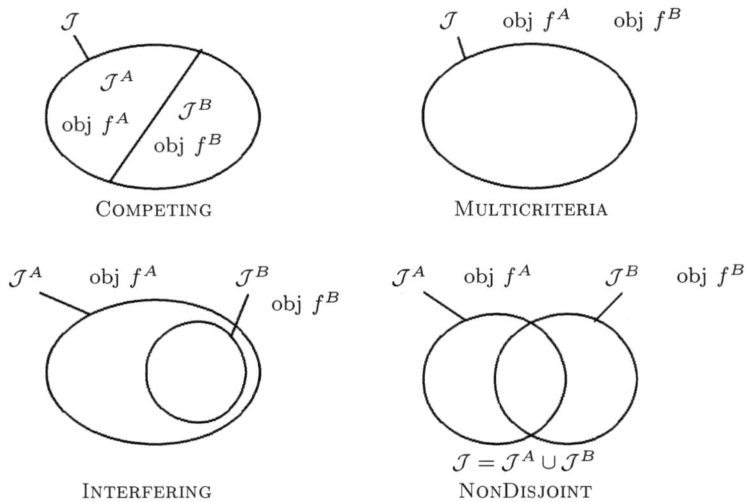


**Fig. 1.3** Possible scenario for multiagent scheduling problems for $K = 2$ agents

### *1.4.4 Nondisjoint Sets*

This is the most general case, in which any two job sets may or may not intersect each other. In this case, the notation $J_j^k$ indicates a job $J_j$ that belongs to $\mathcal{J}^k$ only. The notation for jobs belonging to more than one set is introduced when needed. In the case of $K = 2$ agents, it is assumed that a job in $\mathcal{J}^A \cap \mathcal{J}^B$ has only one possible processing time, whatever the agent it belongs to. However, concerning the other parameters such as due dates or weights, it is assumed that it depends on the agent. Thus, to a given job $J_j \in \mathcal{J}^A \cap \mathcal{J}^B$, can be associated a due date $d_j^A$ and a due date $d_j^B$, $d_j^A \neq d_j^B$. The notation of the NONDISJOINT scenario in the $\beta$-field is 'ND'.

All these cases, for $K = 2$ agents, are illustrated in Fig. 1.3.

## 1.5 Notation of Multiagent Scheduling Problems

It should be apparent from the previous section that multi-agent problems involve multiple issues, which have to be compactly recorded into an appropriate notation to quickly refer to a specific combinatorial problem.

Since it is the most widely used notation tool in scheduling, we will stick as much as possible to the classical $\alpha|\beta|\gamma$ notation of scheduling problems, introduced by Graham et al. (1979); we refer the reader to Blazewicz et al. (2007) for further details on the notation in classical scheduling.

In classical scheduling problems, the field $\alpha$ indicates the machine environment and $\gamma$ the objective function. The field $\beta$ contains all additional features required to completely specify the problem, e.g. the presence of deadlines, release dates, the possibility of preemption etc. In most of our problems, we introduce a new field $\beta_{sc}$ within the field $\beta$, with $\beta_{sc} \in \{CO, IN, BI, MU, ND\}$ that specifies the scenario, i.e., the intersection structure of the job sets $\mathcal{J}^k$.

In this book, we often group the results on the basis of the scheduling criteria adopted. When referring to all problems arising for a given pair $f, g$ (or, more generally, $K$-tuple) of scheduling criteria, we use the following notation

$$\alpha|\beta|f, g$$

The only asymmetric scenario is INTERFERING, since $\mathcal{J}^B \subset \mathcal{J}^A$. In this case we need to distinguish

$$\alpha|IN, \beta|f^A, g^B$$

and

$$\alpha|IN, \beta|g^A, f^B.$$

In a two-agent setting, in general a job $J_j$ may belong to both $\mathcal{J}^A$ and $\mathcal{J}^B$. Hence, if for instance agent B wants to minimize the total weighted completion time, its objective function is denoted by

$$\sum_{J_j \in \mathcal{J}^B} w_j^B C_j.$$

However, in the two-agent COMPETING scenario, in which each job belongs to only one agent, for the sake of clarity we write:

$$\sum_{J_j^B \in \mathcal{J}^B} w_j^B C_j^B.$$

Nonetheless, to keep notation simple, in the $\alpha|\beta|\gamma$ problem description we use the simplified notation $\sum w_j^B C_j^B$ to mean $\sum_{J_j \in \mathcal{J}^B} w_j^B C_j$, in all scenarios. In other words, we tend to use superscripts $A$ and $B$ (or, more generally, $k$) whenever this helps identifying the problem, even if it can result a bit redundant.

*Example 1.2.* Consider the two-agent problem in which agent $A$ wants to minimize the number of tardy jobs and the total weighted completion time for agent $B$ must not exceed a value $Q$. In the NONDISJOINT scenario, the objective functions of the two agents are denoted by

$$\sum_{J_j \in \mathcal{J}^A} U_j \quad \text{and} \quad \sum_{J_j \in \mathcal{J}^B} w_j^B C_j,$$

while, in the COMPETING case, we write:

$$\sum_{J_j^A \in \mathcal{J}^A} U_j^A \quad \text{and} \quad \sum_{J_j^B \in \mathcal{J}^B} w_j^B C_j^B.$$

However, we denote the two corresponding problems as

$$1|ND, \sum w_j^B C_j^B \le Q | \sum U_j^A \quad \text{and} \quad 1|CO, \sum w_j^B C_j^B \le Q | \sum U_j^A$$

◇

If a job $J_j$ only belongs to agent $k$, i.e., $J_j \in \bar{\mathcal{J}}^k$, then it is sometimes convenient to denote its related quantities as $J_j^k$ and $p_j^k$. Also, we tend to use the superscript when considering its completion time.

*Example 1.3.* For instance, if agent $A$ wants to minimize total weighted completion time in the INTERFERING scenario (in which $\mathcal{J}^B \subset \mathcal{J}^A$, so that $\bar{\mathcal{J}}^A = \mathcal{J}^A \setminus \mathcal{J}^B$), we can write the objective function of agent $A$ as:

$$\sum w_j^A C_j^A = \sum_{J_j \in \mathcal{J}^B} w_j^A C_j + \sum_{J_j^A \in \bar{\mathcal{J}}^A} w_j^A C_j^A$$

◇

The notation for multiagent scheduling problems used in the book is summarized in Table 1.1.

## 1.6 Examples of Single- and Multiagent Scheduling Problems

In this section, we illustrate the introduced earlier concepts of Pareto optimal solution, Pareto front, optimality criteria, solution approaches and scenario for multiagent scheduling problems.

We begin with two examples of single-agent scheduling problems.

*Example 1.4.* Problem $1||\sum C_j$ is the problem of scheduling jobs on a single machine such that the sum of completion times is minimized. Let us consider the following 3-job instance:

| $j$ | 1 | 2 | 3 |
|---|---|---|---|
| $p_j$ | 5 | 2 | 1 |

The solution of this problem corresponding to the sequence $(J_2, J_1, J_3)$ is illustrated in Fig. 1.4 and has an objective function value equal to 17. Notice that in this case, with only three jobs, it is easy to evaluate all the possible sequences

**Table 1.1** Summary of multiagent scheduling notation

| Notation of data | |
|---|---|
| $n$ | Total number of jobs |
| $\mathcal{J}^k$ | Subset of jobs of agent $k$ |
| $\bar{\mathcal{J}}^k$ | Subset of jobs that only belong to agent $k$ |
| $\mathcal{J}^{-1}(J_j)$ | (Set of) agent(s) that own $J_j$ |
| $n_k$ ($\bar{n}_k$) | Number of jobs in $\mathcal{J}^k$ ($\bar{\mathcal{J}}^k$) |
| $J_j^k$ | Job $j$ of agent $k$ |
| $p_j^k$ | Processing time of $J_j^k$ |
| $P = \sum_{J_j \in \mathcal{J}} p_j$ | Sum of processing times |
| $P_k = \sum_{J_j \in \mathcal{J}^k} p_j$ | Sum of processing times of jobs of agent $k$ |
| $r_j^k$ | Release date of $J_j^k$ |
| $d_j^k$ | Due date of $J_j^k$ |
| $w_j^k$ | Weight of $J_j^k$ |
| **Notation of variables** | |
| $C_j^k$ | Completion time of $J_j^k$ |
| $F_j^k$ | Flow time of $J_j^k$ |
| $L_j^k$ | Lateness of $J_j^k$ |
| $T_j^k$ | Tardiness of $J_j^k$ |
| $U_j^k$ | Indicator of tardiness of $J_j^k$ |
| **Notation of approaches** | |
| – | Feasibility problem |
| $\alpha f^A + (1-\alpha) f^B$ or $\sum_{k=1}^K \alpha_k f^k$ | Linear combination |
| $f^B \leq Q \| f^A$ or $f^2 \leq Q_2, \dots, f^k \leq Q_k \| f^1$ | Epsilon-constraint |
| $Lex(f^A, f^B)$ or $Lex(f^1, f^2, \dots, f^K)$ | Lexicographic order |
| $\mathcal{P}(f^A, f^B)$ or $\mathcal{P}(f^1, f^2, \dots, f^K)$ | Pareto set enumeration |
| $\#(f^A, f^B)$ or $\#(f^1, f^2, \dots, f^K)$ | Counting |
| **Notation of scenario** | |
| *CO* | COMPETING |
| *IN* | INTERFERING |
| *MU* | MULTICRITERIA |
| *BI* | BICRITERIA |
| *ND* | NONDISJOINT |

(here $n! = 6$) and to find that the optimal solution is sequence $(J_3, J_2, J_1)$ with a value of 12.

◇

*Example 1.5.* Problem $1||L_{\max}$ is a single machine scheduling problem, where jobs have to respect release dates and the objective is to minimize the maximum lateness, which is the maximum difference between the completion time and the due date

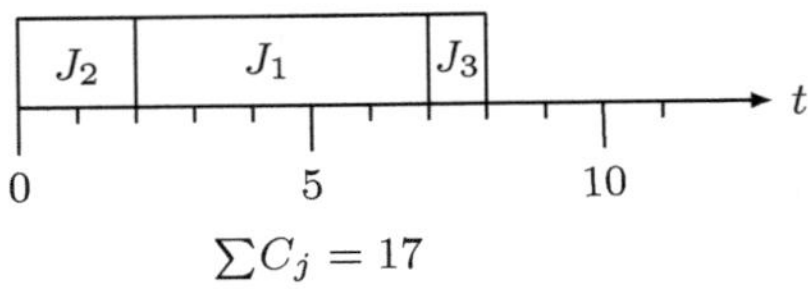


**Fig. 1.4** Solution $(J_2, J_1, J_3)$ for the $1||\sum C_j$ problem

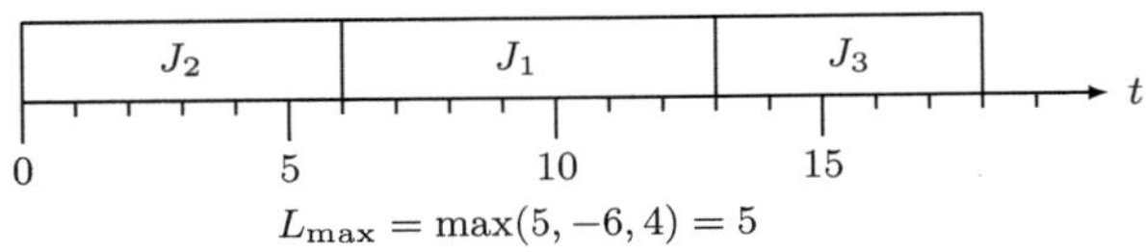


**Fig. 1.5** Solution $(J_2, J_1, J_3)$ for the $1||L_{\max}$ problem

for all the jobs (this value may be negative). Let us consider the following 3-job instance:

| $j$ | 1 | 2 | 3 |
|---|---|---|---|
| $p_j$ | 7 | 6 | 5 |
| $d_j$ | 8 | 12 | 14 |

The solution of this problem corresponding to the sequence $(J_2, J_1, J_3)$ is illustrated in Fig. 1.5 and has an objective function value equal to 5. As for the previous example, a simple enumeration shows that the optimal solution is given by sequence $(J_1, J_2, J_3)$ with a value of 4.

◇

Now, we pass to examples of multiagent scheduling problems.

*Example 1.6.* Notation $1|BI|\sum C_j, L_{\max}$ is used to indicate that we consider a single machine bicriteria scheduling problem where the objective functions are $\sum C_j$ and $L_{\max}$. This notation does not refer to a specific approach.

◇

*Example 1.7.* Problem $1|BI|\mathcal{P}(\sum C_j, L_{\max})$ is a bicriteria scheduling problem, where all the jobs have a processing time and a due date. The problem is to give the list of solutions covering all the strict Pareto optimal solutions. Let us consider the following 6-job instance:

| $j$ | 1 | 2 | 3 | 4 | 5 | 6 |
|---|---|---|---|---|---|---|
| $p_j$ | 5 | 2 | 1 | 7 | 6 | 5 |
| $d_j$ | 30 | 30 | 30 | 8 | 12 | 14 |

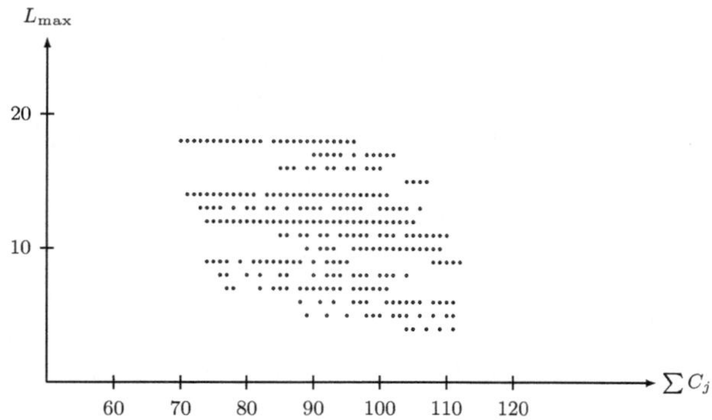


**Fig. 1.6** Set of solutions in the criteria space

**Table 1.2** Whole Pareto set

| $\sigma$ | $\sum C_j(\sigma)$ | $L_{max}(\sigma)$ | $\sigma$ | $\sum C_j(\sigma)$ | $L_{max}(\sigma)$ |
|---|---|---|---|---|---|
| $(J_3, J_2, J_6, J_1, J_5, J_4)$ | 70 | 18 | $(J_3, J_2, J_1, J_6, J_4, J_5)$ | 71 | 14 |
| $(J_3, J_2, J_1, J_5, J_4, J_6)$ | 73 | 13 | $(J_3, J_2, J_6, J_4, J_5, J_1)$ | 74 | 9 |
| $(J_3, J_2, J_1, J_4, J_5, J_6)$ | 74 | 12 | $(J_3, J_2, J_5, J_4, J_6, J_1)$ | 76 | 8 |
| $(J_3, J_2, J_4, J_5, J_6, J_1)$ | 77 | 7 | $(J_2, J_3, J_4, J_5, J_6, J_1)$ | 78 | 7 |
| $(J_3, J_4, J_2, J_5, J_6, J_1)$ | 82 | 7 | $(J_2, J_4, J_3, J_5, J_6, J_1)$ | 84 | 7 |
| $(J_3, J_5, J_4, J_2, J_6, J_1)$ | 85 | 7 | $(J_3, J_6, J_4, J_5, J_2, J_1)$ | 86 | 7 |
| $(J_4, J_3, J_2, J_5, J_6, J_1)$ | 88 | 7 | $(J_3, J_5, J_4, J_6, J_2, J_1)$ | 88 | 6 |
| $(J_3, J_4, J_5, J_6, J_2, J_1)$ | 89 | 5 | $(J_3, J_4, J_5, J_6, J_1, J_2)$ | 92 | 5 |
| $(J_4, J_3, J_5, J_6, J_2, J_1)$ | 95 | 5 | $(J_4, J_3, J_5, J_6, J_1, J_2)$ | 98 | 5 |
| $(J_5, J_4, J_3, J_6, J_2, J_1)$ | 99 | 5 | $(J_4, J_5, J_3, J_6, J_2, J_1)$ | 100 | 5 |
| $(J_5, J_4, J_3, J_6, J_1, J_2)$ | 102 | 5 | $(J_4, J_5, J_3, J_6, J_1, J_2)$ | 103 | 5 |
| $(J_5, J_4, J_6, J_2, J_3, J_1)$ | 104 | 5 | $(J_4, J_5, J_6, J_3, J_2, J_1)$ | 104 | 4 |
| $(J_4, J_5, J_6, J_2, J_3, J_1)$ | 105 | 4 | $(J_4, J_5, J_6, J_3, J_1, J_2)$ | 107 | 4 |
| $(J_4, J_5, J_6, J_2, J_1, J_3)$ | 109 | 4 | $(J_4, J_5, J_6, J_1, J_3, J_2)$ | 111 | 4 |
| $(J_4, J_5, J_6, J_1, J_2, J_3)$ | 112 | 4 | | | |

In the criteria space, the set of all the possibles solutions (here the $n! = 720$ solutions have been enumerated) is represented in Fig. 1.6 (notice that some solutions may have the same vector of criteria $(\sum C_j, L_{max})$).

The Pareto set is composed by the sequences given in Table 1.2 (only one sequence is given per vector $(\sum C_j, L_{max})$).

Among these Pareto optimal sequences, some of them are strict Pareto optimal solutions (sequence $(J_3, J_2, J_1, J_6, J_4, J_5)$ with vector (71,14) or sequence $(J_3, J_2, J_4, J_5, J_6, J_1)$ with vector (77,7) for instance), some of them are weak Pareto optimal solutions (sequence $(J_4, J_3, J_5, J_6, J_2, J_1)$ with vector (95,5) or sequence $(J_4, J_5, J_6, J_2, J_1, J_3)$ with vector (109,4) for instance). Generally, the weak Pareto optimal solutions are not considered as interesting solutions. Notice that sequence $(J_3, J_2, J_1, J_5, J_4, J_6)$ with vector (74,12) and $(J_3, J_5, J_4, J_6, J_2, J_1)$ with vector (88,6) (for instance) are not supported.

◇

*Example 1.8.* Problem $1|BI, \sum C_j \leq Q|L_{\max}$ is to find a sequence of jobs minimizing the maximum lateness but also satisfying the constraint that the sum of completion times is less than or equal to a given value $Q$.

We suppose that the limit for the sum of completion times is $Q = 75$. The maximum value for the sum of completion times could be represented in Fig. 1.6 by a vertical line at abscissa 75, all the vectors being at the right of this line corresponding to forbidden solutions.

It is not difficult to see that one solution which respects the bound on the total completion time and which minimizes the maximum lateness is sequence $(J_3, J_2, J_6, J_4, J_5, J_1)$, with a total completion time of 74 and an $L_{\max}$ value equal to 9.

◇

*Example 1.9.* In problem $1|BI|\alpha \sum C_j + (1-\alpha)L_{\max}$, we search for a sequence of jobs minimizing a linear combination of criteria. This solution belongs to the set of strict Pareto optimal solutions which are given in Table 1.2.

With $\alpha = 0,3$ (we give more importance to the $L_{\max}$), the solution which is returned is sequence $(J_3, J_2, J_4, J_5, J_6, J_1)$ with $\sum C_j = 77$ and $L_{\max} = 7$.

With $\alpha = 0,5$, the best solution is now sequence $(J_3, J_2, J_6, J_4, J_5, J_1)$ with $\sum C_j = 74$ and $L_{\max} = 9$.

We can notice that there is no possible value for $\alpha$ that allow to find sequence $(J_3, J_2, J_5, J_4, J_6, J_1)$ with $\sum C_j = 76$ and $L_{\max} = 8$, even if this solution may be of interest. This is why this sequence is called *non-supported*.

◇

*Example 1.10.* Problem $1|CO, \sum C_j^A \leq Q|L_{\max}^B$ corresponds to a multiagent scheduling problem with two agents in the COMPETING scenario. It means that $\mathcal{J}^A \cap \mathcal{J}^B = \emptyset$. The problem is to find a solution which minimizes the maximum lateness of the jobs of agent $B$, and such that the total completion time of the jobs of agent $A$ do not exceed a given value $Q$. Let us consider the following instance with three jobs per agent.

| | Agent $A$ | | | Agent $B$ | | |
|---|---|---|---|---|---|---|
| $J_j^k$ | $J_1^A$ | $J_2^A$ | $J_3^A$ | $J_1^B$ | $J_2^B$ | $J_3^B$ |
| $p_j^k$ | 5 | 2 | 1 | 7 | 6 | 5 |
| $d_j^k$ | – | – | – | 8 | 12 | 14 |

As an illustration of the evaluation in this case, the sequence $(J_3^A, J_2^A, J_1^B, J_2^B, J_3^B, J_1^A)$ is represented in Fig. 1.7 and evaluated.

In the case of multiagent, the jobs which are taken into account for computing the objective function of one agent are only the jobs of this agent. All the solutions corresponding to the given instance are represented in the criteria space in Fig. 1.8. In this set of solutions, there are only four

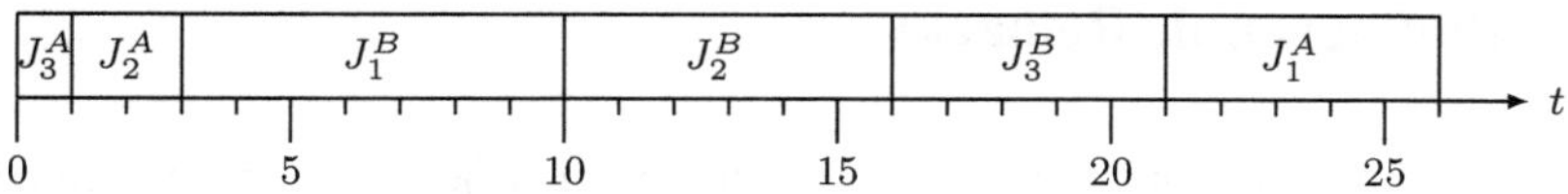


$\sum C_j^A = 26 + 1 + 3 = 30,\ L^B_{\max} = \max\{2, 4, 7\} = 7$

**Fig. 1.7** Solution $(J_3^A, J_2^A, J_1^B, J_2^B, J_3^B, J_1^A)$ for the $1|CO, \sum C_j^A \leq Q|L^B_{\max}$ problem

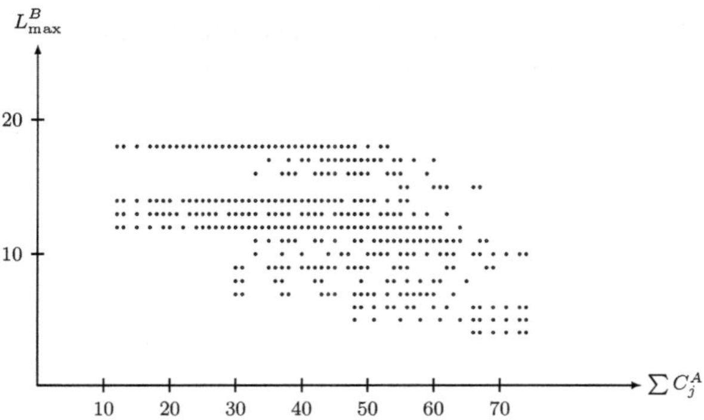


**Fig. 1.8** Set of solutions in the criteria space for the multiagent case

strict Pareto optimal solutions: $(J_3^A, J_2^A, J_1^A, J_1^B, J_2^B, J_3^B)$ with values (12,12), $(J_3^A, J_2^A, J_1^B, J_2^B, J_3^B, J_1^A)$ with values (30,7), $(J_3^A, J_1^B, J_2^B, J_3^B, J_2^A, J_1^A)$ with values (48,5) and $(J_1^B, J_2^B, J_3^B, J_3^A, J_2^A, J_1^A)$ with values (66,4).

If we take for example $Q = 40$, the best solution is given by sequence $(J_3^A, J_2^A, J_1^B, J_2^B, J_3^B, J_1^A)$.

◇

*Example 1.11.* The problem denoted by $1|IN, L^B_{\max} \leq Q|\sum C_j^A$ corresponds to a multiagent scheduling problem with two agents in the INTERFERING scenario. It means that for the evaluation of agent $A$, $\sum C_j^A$ in this case, all the jobs are taken into account. For the evaluation of agent $B$, $L^B_{\max}$ here, only the jobs of agent $B$ are considered.

Let us consider the instance described in Example 1.10 and the sequence $(J_3^A, J_2^A, J_1^B, J_2^B, J_3^B, J_1^A)$ represented in Fig. 1.7. The values of the objective functions for this sequence are $\sum C_j^A = 77$ and $L^B_{\max} = 7$.

For the problem denoted by $1|IN, L^A_{\max} \leq Q|\sum C_j^B$, we need a due date for each job, and the $L_{\max}$ function is evaluated considering all the jobs. If we consider the values reported in Example 1.8, the values of the objective functions for the same sequence are $\sum C_j^B = 47$ and $L^A_{\max} = 7$.

◇

## 1.7 Bibliographic Remarks

The basic concepts and notions of the theory of scheduling are presented in Blazewicz et al. (2007), Brucker (2007) and Pinedo (2008). The three-field notation of scheduling problems has been introduced in the survey (Graham et al. 1979). The descriptions of different extensions to the notation are described in mentioned above monographs.

Problems of scheduling with multiple criteria are discussed in several review papers such as Dileepan and Sen (1988), Lee and Vairaktarakis (1993), Nagar et al. (1995) and Hoogeveen (2005). A more detailed discussion of the topics is given in T'Kindt and Billaut (2006).

# Chapter 2
# Problems, Algorithms and Complexity

In this chapter, the basic notions related to problems, algorithms and complexity are recalled. Some topics related to approximability, problem relaxation and simple reductions between scheduling problems are also discussed.

The chapter is composed of eight sections. Basic notions of complexity theory are recalled in Sect. 2.1, and Sect. 2.2 focus on properties of NP-complete and NP-hard problems. In Sect. 2.3, exact and enumerative algorithms are discussed. In Sects. 2.4 and 2.5, approximation algorithms and approximation schemes are considered. Methods of problems relaxation are presented in Sect. 2.6. Some reductions between scheduling problems are described in Sect. 2.7. The chapter ends by Sect. 2.8 with remarks on references.

## 2.1 Basic Notions of Complexity Theory

A computational problem is a mathematical problem, defined by some parameters and one or more questions, that a computer has to solve, i.e., for which we want to find a *solution*. For solving efficiently a problem, an *algorithm* has to be designed, understood as a finite procedure expressed in terms of predefined *elementary operations*.

The efficiency of an algorithm is given by the amount of resources required to execute it, as time and memory. The most crucial efficiency measure is the *running time* needed by an algorithm for finding a solution for any *instance* of a problem, that is given on the input of the algorithm. This time depends on the size of the input, denoted as $I$. If the input size is $size(I) = n$, it means that $n$ elements are required to describe the problem parameters. The size can be expressed in bytes or bits, but in general it is given informally.

The time required by an algorithm to solve any instance of a problem of size $n$ is a function of $n$, which is called the *algorithm complexity*. The big-O notation

A. Agnetis et al., *Multiagent Scheduling*, DOI 10.1007/978-3-642-41880-8_2,

is commonly used to describe this function. An algorithm for which this function can be bounded from above by a polynomial in $n$ ($O(n)$, $O(n \log n)$, $O(n^2)$, etc.) is called a *polynomial time algorithm*. An algorithm for which this function cannot be bounded by such a polynomial function ($2^n$, $n!$, $n^n$, etc.) is called an *exponential time algorithm*.

A problem which is so hard that no polynomial time algorithm can possibly solve it is called *intractable*.

Algorithms that have running times polynomial in $n$ and the maximum of the elements of the instance, denoted $max(I)$, are called *pseudopolynomial*.

The complexity class of a problem indicates its intrinsic difficulty, and this information is crucial for being able to solve the problem properly. This is the object of the *theory of NP-completeness*, presented in the seminal book of Garey and Johnson (1979).

The Theory of NP-completeness applies on several types of problems. We distinguish the following two main classes of problems:

- *Decision problems* that are defined by a name, an instance, which is a description of all the parameters, and a question for which the answer belongs to the set $\{yes, no\}$,
- *Optimization problems* that are defined by a name, an instance, and in which the aim is to find a solution with minimum value of a given function.

*Example 2.1.* Let us consider the following decision problem, called PARTITION (Garey and Johnson 1979).

PARTITION

Instance: A finite set $A$ of $k$ integers $a_j$, $j = 1, \ldots, k$, such that

$$\sum_{j=1}^{k} a_j = 2E$$

Question: Is there a subset $A' \subseteq A$ such that

$$\sum_{a_j \in A'} a_j = \sum_{a_j \in A \setminus A'} a_j = E?$$

This problem is very important for scheduling theory with fixed (constant) job processing times. ◇

*Example 2.2.* The single machine problem presented in Sect. 1.4 is an optimization problem. Its name is ONEMACHINETOTALCOMPLETIONTIME, denoted by $1||\sum C_j$. An instance is defined by a number $n$ of jobs and a vector $(p_j)_{1 \le j \le n}$ of processing times. The aim is to find a sequence of jobs that minimizes the sum of the completion times. ◇

There exist two main classes of decision problems. The class $\mathcal{P}$ is the class of decision problems that can be solved by a polynomial time algorithm running on a *deterministic* computer in which at any time there may be done at most one action, contrary to non-deterministic computer in which more actions may be done. These problems are said to be 'easy' to solve, in the sense that large instances can possibly be solved in a reasonable computation time. The class $\mathcal{NP}$ is the class of decision problems that can be solved by a polynomial time algorithm running on a *non-deterministic* computer. It is equivalent to say that the class $\mathcal{NP}$ is the class of decision problems for which a response '*yes*' can be verified in polynomial time on a deterministic computer. It is clear that $\mathcal{P} \subset \mathcal{NP}$.

## 2.2 NP-Completeness and NP-Hardness

In the section, we consider basic issues related to NP-completeness and NP-hardness.

### *2.2.1 NP-Completeness*

Some relationships between problems can be established and the principal technique which is used is the *polynomial reduction*, defined as follows.

**Definition 2.1.** We say that a decision problem $P_1$ *polynomially reduces* to a decision problem $P_2$ if and only if there exists a polynomial time algorithm $f$, which can build, from any instance $I_1$ of $P_1$, an instance $I_2 = f(I_1)$ of $P_2$ such that the response to problem $P_1$ for instance $I_1$ is 'yes' if and only if the answer to problem $P_2$ for instance $I_2$ is 'yes'.

If such an algorithm $f$ exists, it proves that any instance of problem $P_1$ can be solved by an algorithm for problem $P_2$. We say that $P_2$ is at least as difficult as $P_1$. If a polynomial time algorithm exists for solving $P_2$, then $P_1$ can also be solved in polynomial time.

The fact that a decision problem $P_1$ polynomially reduces to a decision problem $P_2$ is denoted by $P_1 \propto P_2$.

The next definition introduces an important subclass of the class $\mathcal{NP}$.

**Definition 2.2.** A problem $P$ is *NP-complete* if $P$ belongs to $\mathcal{NP}$ and any problem of $\mathcal{NP}$ polynomially reduces to $P$.

The first problem proven to be NP-complete was SATISFIABILITY problem (Cook 1971).

SATISFIABILITY
Instance: A set $U$ of variables and a collection $C$ of clauses over $U$.
Question: Is there a satisfying truth assignment for $C$?

The NP-complete problems create a subset of $\mathcal{NP}$ and we say that NP-complete problems are the 'difficult' problems of $\mathcal{NP}$. Indeed, let us suppose that an NP-complete problem can be solved in polynomial time. Then, according to Definition 2.1, any problem in $\mathcal{NP}$ can be solved in polynomial time, which implies that $\mathcal{NP} \subset P$ and thus $\mathcal{P} = NP$. Therefore, unless $\mathcal{P} = NP$, the NP-complete problems cannot be solved in polynomial time, which make these problems more 'difficult' that those from the class $\mathcal{P}$.

There exist many NP-complete problems, two examples of such problems are SATISFIABILITY and PARTITION. For more detailed list of NP-complete problems we refer the reader to Garey and Johnson (1979).

The class of NP-complete problems can also be divided into two parts. We distinguish problems that are *NP-complete in the strong sense* and problems that are *NP-complete in the ordinary sense* or in the *weak sense*. For purposes of the book, it is sufficient to state that a problem $P$ is NP-complete in the strong sense if $P$ cannot be solved by a pseudo-polynomial time algorithm, unless $\mathcal{P} = NP$. The NP-complete problems that can be solved by a pseudo-polynomial time algorithm are said to be NP-complete in the ordinary sense. For more detailed discussion of strong and weak NP-complexity, we refer the reader to monographs Garey and Johnson (1979) or Papadimitriou (1994).

### 2.2.2 NP-Hardness

The notion of NP-completeness concerns problems that belong to $\mathcal{NP}$. It has been extended to the problems that are outside $\mathcal{NP}$, for proving that these problems are also hard. Any decision problem $P$, member of $\mathcal{NP}$ or not, to which an NP-complete problem can be transformed, has the property that it cannot be solved in polynomial time, unless $\mathcal{P} = NP$. Therefore, such a problem is called *NP-hard*, i.e. as hard as NP-complete problems.

This definition applies for instance to *search problems* that constitute the third main class of problems, apart decision and optimization ones. A search problem consists in either returning the answer 'no' if the problem has no solution or returning some solution to the problem otherwise. Moreover, this definition applies also to optimization problems.

Let us consider two problems, $P_1$ and $P_2$, and let $A_1$ and $A_2$ be two algorithms for solving these problems, respectively, with the property that $A_1$ calls $A_2$ as a subprogram. If $A_1$ runs in polynomial time if $A_2$ runs in polynomial time, we say that problem $P_1$ is *Turing reducible* to problem $P_2$, denoted by $P_1 \propto_T P_2$. The *Turing reduction* can be used for proving NP-hardness results. Notice that from the above we may deduce that all NP-complete problems are NP-hard.

*Example 2.3.* Let us consider the following decision problem.

> TWO PROCESSORS
> Instance: A set $\mathcal{J}$ of $n$ jobs, $\{p_j\} \in \mathbb{N}, \forall j, 1 \leq j \leq n, Y \in \mathbb{N}$.
> Question: Is there a two-processor schedule for $\mathcal{J}$ such that the jobs complete on both machines not later than $Y$?

We show that this problem is NP-complete by reduction from PARTITION problem. First, we may notice that problem TWO PROCESSORS is in $\mathcal{NP}$, since any response 'yes' can be verified in polynomial time.

Then, considering an arbitrary instance of PARTITION, we define the following instance for problem TWO PROCESSORS: $n = |A|$, $p_j = a_j, \forall j, 1 \leq j \leq n$, $Y = \frac{1}{2}\sum_{a_j \in A} a_j$. This construction can be done in polynomial time. If the answer to PARTITION problem is 'yes', it is sufficient to schedule the jobs of $A'$ on machine $M_1$ and the jobs of $A \backslash A'$ on machine $M_2$ and the makespan of the schedule is exactly equal to $Y$. Therefore, the answer to TWO PROCESSORS is 'yes'. If the answer to TWO PROCESSORS is 'yes', the jobs assigned to $M_1$ and the jobs assigned to $M_2$ constitute a partition of the jobs, each of size $\frac{1}{2}\sum_{a_j \in A} a_j$ and therefore the answer to PARTITION is 'yes'.

Hence, TWO PROCESSORS is NP-complete.

Let us consider now the scheduling problem denoted by $P2||C_{\max}$. This problem can be solved by calling iteratively the algorithm for problem TWO PROCESSORS, by changing the value of $Y$. A binary search can be designed to ensure that the number of calls is bounded by $n$. This method gives a Turing reduction and therefore, $P2||C_{\max}$ is NP-hard and cannot be solved in polynomial time, unless $\mathcal{P} = NP$. ◇

The following NP-complete problems will be used in the following.

> KNAPSACK
> Instance: Two sets of nonnegative integers $\{a_1, a_2, \ldots, a_n\}$ and $\{w_1, w_2, \ldots, w_n\}$ and two integers $b$ and $W$.
> Question: Is there a subset $S \subseteq \{1, 2, \ldots, n\}$ such that
> $$\sum_{i \in S} a_i \leq b \text{ and } \sum_{i \in S} w_i \geq W?$$

3-PARTITION

Instance: An integer $E$, a set $A$ of $3r$ nonnegative integers $\{a_1, a_2, \ldots, a_{3r}\}$, with $E/4 < a_k < E/2, \forall k, 1 \le k \le 3n$,

$$\sum_{k=1}^{3r} a_k = rE$$

Question: Can $A$ be partitioned into $r$ disjoint subsets $A_1, \ldots, A_r$ such that for $1 \le h \le r$,

$$\sum_{k \in A_h} a_k = E?$$

## 2.3 Enumeration and Exact Algorithms

For combinatorial optimization problems, it can be tempting to enumerate the whole set of potential solutions, and to keep the best solution. For example, finding the best sequence of a scheduling problem with $n$ jobs can be done by enumerating the $n!$ possible sequences. Such an enumeration, however, is only possible on current supercomputers and if the value of $n$, in most of the problems, is not greater than, say, 20.

In this section, we describe *enumeration algorithms* and *exact algorithms*. We begin with *implicit enumeration* algorithms based on dynamic programming and branch-and-bound approach. In these cases we explore implicitly the whole set of possible solutions, i.e., we explore only the solutions which can potentially lead to an optimal solution.

### 2.3.1 *Dynamic Programming*

*Dynamic Programming* (DP) is an implicit enumeration method, based on the *Bellman's principle of optimality* (Bellman 1957). The main idea of the DP is that a problem – satisfying certain conditions – can be decomposed into subproblems of the same nature, and the optimal solution of the problem can be obtained from the optimal solutions of the subproblems, by using recursive relations. Each step of the recursion is called a *phase*. The problem is in a given *state* at the beginning of the phase, and after some *decisions*, enters into another state. A *final state* of the DP corresponds to an optimal solution. Depending on the number of states and phases, the running time of a DP algorithm can be polynomial, pseudopolynomial or exponential.

We illustrate application of the DP method with the following problem.

**Problem $1||\sum w_j U_j$**

In the problem, there is a single machine, to each job is associated a due date and a weight and the objective is to minimize the weighted number of tardy jobs. This problem is ordinary NP-hard (Karp 1972). We assume that all jobs are numbered in EDD order. This renumeration can be done in $O(n\log(n))$ time if necessary.

There are $n$ phases in the DP algorithm. A phase $j$ corresponds to job $J_j$, assuming that the first $j-1$ jobs have been scheduled. A state at phase $j$ is $t$, the date at which completes the last early job. A decision at phase $j$ is to schedule job $J_j$ early or tardy.

Let us denote by $F_j(t)$ the minimum cost of scheduling job $J_j$ at phase $j$, assuming that the $j-1$ first jobs are scheduled, and that the last early job completes at time $t$ (Lawler and Moore 1969).

If the decision is that $J_j$ is early (only possible if $t \le d_j$), then $J_j$ does not generate any cost, and the cost is the same as before scheduling $J_j$, when the last early job completed at time $t-p_j$. In this case, $F_j(t) = F_{j-1}(t-p_j)$. If the decision is that $J_j$ is tardy, then $J_j$ generates a cost of $w_j$. In this case, $F_j(t) = F_{j-1}(t)+w_j$.

The recursive relation is given by:

$$F_j(t) = \begin{cases} \min\{F_{j-1}(t-p_j), F_{j-1}(t)+w_j\} & \forall j, 1 \le j \le n, \\ & \forall t, 0 \le t \le d_j \\ F_j(d_j) & \forall j, 1 \le j \le n, \\ & \forall t, d_j+1 \le t \le P \end{cases}$$

with $P = \sum_{j=1}^{n} p_j$.

The initial conditions of the recursion are:

$$\begin{cases} F_0(t) = 0, \quad \forall t \ge 0 \\ F_j(t) = \infty, \ \forall j \in 0,\ldots,n, \forall t < 0 \end{cases}$$

The value of $F_n(P)$ gives the optimal value of the objective function. In order to find the corresponding solution, a backward procedure has to be implemented. This algorithm runs in $O(nP)$ time.

*Example 2.4.* Let us the following 4-job instance of problem $1||\sum w_j U_j$:

| $j$ | 1 | 2 | 3 | 4 |
|---|---|---|---|---|
| $p_j$ | 5 | 2 | 3 | 4 |
| $d_j$ | 8 | 10 | 11 | 12 |
| $w_j$ | 13 | 7 | 5 | 9 |

Details of solution of the problem by the DP are given in Table 2.1. The value of the optimal solution is equal to 5. The corresponding solution can be find by using

**Table 2.1** Solution details of problem $1||\sum w_j U_j$ by dynamic programming

| $t$ | $<0$ | 0 | 1 | 2 | 3 | 4 | 5 | 6 | 7 | 8 | 9 | 10 | 11 | 12 | 13 | 14 |
|---|---|---|---|---|---|---|---|---|---|---|---|---|---|---|---|---|
| $F_0(t)$ | $\infty$ | 0 | 0 | 0 | 0 | 0 | 0 | 0 | 0 | 0 | 0 | 0 | 0 | 0 | 0 | 0 |
| $F_1(t)$ | $\infty$ | 13 | 13 | 13 | 13 | 13 | 0 | 0 | 0 | $\boxed{0}$ | | | | | | |
| $F_2(t)$ | $\infty$ | 20 | 20 | 13 | 13 | 13 | 7 | 7 | 0 | 0 | 0 | $\boxed{0}$ | | | | |
| $F_3(t)$ | $\infty$ | 25 | 25 | 18 | 18 | 18 | 12 | 12 | 5 | 5 | 5 | 0 | $\boxed{0}$ | 0... | | |
| $F_4(t)$ | $\infty$ | 34 | 34 | 27 | 27 | 25 | 21 | 18 | 14 | 14 | 12 | 9 | 5 | $\boxed{5}$ | 5 | 5 |

a backtrack procedure: $F_4(12) = 5$ because it is the minimum between $F_3(12) + 9$ and $F_3(8)$. Therefore, job $J_4$ doesn't generate a cost, and it is an early job. $F_3(8) = 5$ because it is the minimum between $F_2(8) + 5$ and $F_2(5)$. Job $J_3$ generates a cost, this job is tardy. Then, $F_2(8) = 0$, it means that the remaining jobs are early. At the end, the optimal sequence is equal to $(J_1, J_2, J_4, J_3)$. ◇

## 2.3.2 *Branch-and-Bound Algorithms*

Another method of implicit enumeration is used in so-called *branch-and-bound algorithms*. In this case, the enumeration is done by a *tree search procedure*, it means a procedure where the elements are *nodes* of a tree, which are explored in a special order. Each node is equivalent to a state of the DP algorithm and an arc corresponds to a decision. The ending node of an arc is equivalent to a final state of the DP algorithm.

A branch-and-bound procedure is an implicit enumeration method, characterized by two elements: the *branching* and the *bound*. The branching is the way the problem is decomposed. It is related to the definition of nodes and arcs. For example, a branching process can suppose that a sequence for a scheduling problem is developed from the first job to the last job of the schedule. It means that the *root node* of the tree is empty, the *terminal nodes* (leaves of the tree) are complete sequences, and each node is completed by one job in each of its *child nodes*.

Two sorts of *bounds* are considered. For a minimization problem, an *upper bound UB* is generally the value of a feasible solution, therefore greater than or equal to the value of an optimal solution. During the search process, this quantity is the value of the best known solution. A *lower bound LB*$(\sigma)$ is a quantity associated to a node $\sigma$ of the tree. It is an under estimation of the value of the best solution which can be reached from this node, i.e. no feasible solution under this part of the tree has a solution less than this quantity. Therefore, if *LB*$(\sigma) \geq$ *UB*, this part of the tree cannot help improving the best known solution value and there is no need to continue the enumeration of these solutions. Node $\sigma$ is pruned or cutted and we can consider that this part of the tree has been implicitly explored.

The nodes can be explored using several procedures. The three most often used methods to explore the search tree are:

- The *breath first search* – nodes are managed in a *First-In, First-Out* list;
- The *depth first search* – nodes are managed in a *Last-In,First-Out* stack;
- The *best first search* – nodes are sorted in non-decreasing order with respect to their lower bounds.

The algorithm stops when all the nodes have been implicitly explored.

We illustrate the application of the branch-and-bound algorithm with the following problem.

### Problem $1||\sum w_j T_j$

There is a single machine, to each job is associated a due date and a weight and the objective is to minimize the total weighted tardiness. This problem is strongly NP-hard (see Lawler (1977) among others). The upper bound that we consider is the value of the objective function for the EDD sequence. The lower bound at node $\sigma$ is equal to the value of the jobs already scheduled plus the smallest possible cost of the last job scheduled, i.e.

$$LB(\sigma) = \sum_{j \in \sigma} w_j T_j + \min_{j \notin \sigma} \left\{ w_j \max(0, \sum_{k=1}^{n} p_k - d_j) \right\}$$

We assume that the nodes of the tree are explored using the depth first search strategy. We illustrate the application of the branch-and-bound algorithm on the following numerical example.

*Example 2.5.* We consider the problem $1||\sum w_j T_j$ and the following instance:

| $j$ | 1 | 2 | 3 | 4 |
|---|---|---|---|---|
| $p_j$ | 5 | 2 | 3 | 4 |
| $d_j$ | 7 | 8 | 9 | 10 |
| $w_j$ | 1 | 3 | 5 | 8 |

The EDD sequence is $(J_1, J_2, J_3, J_4)$ and the total weighted tardiness is equal to $UB = 37$ (only job $J_4$ is late). The initial lower bound is equal to $LB(\circ) = 7$, where $\circ$ denotes the root node (see Fig. 2.1).

The nodes are created in the following order: 1 ($LB = 18$); 12 ($LB = 25$); 123 ($LB = 37$) is pruned because it cannot improve the solution; 124 ($LB = 33$); 1243 is a leaf with evaluation 33, which allows to update the upper bound ($UB = 33$); 13 ($LB = 18$); 132 ($LB = 38$) is pruned; 134 ($LB = 34$) is pruned; 14 ($LB = 18$); 142

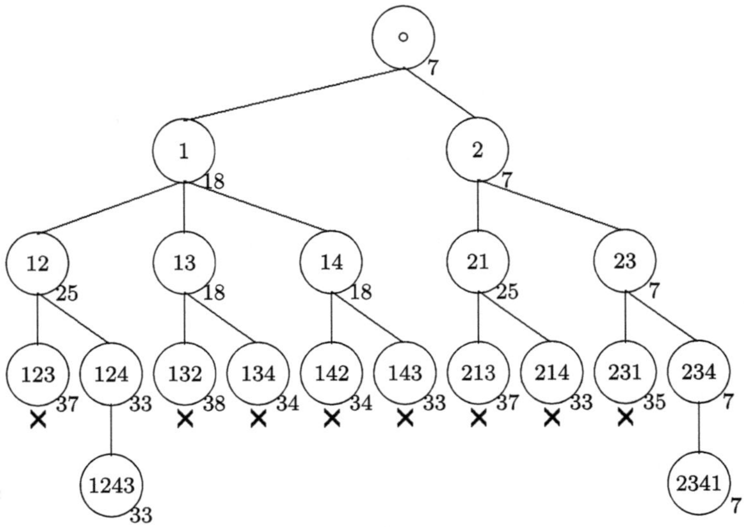


**Fig. 2.1** Search tree for Example 2.5

($LB = 34$) is pruned; 143 ($LB = 33$) is pruned; 2 ($LB = 7$); 21 ($LB = 25$); 213 ($LB = 37$) is pruned; 214 ($LB = 33$); 23 ($LB = 7$); 231 ($LB = 35$) is pruned; 234 ($LB = 7$); 2341 is a leaf with evaluation 7, which allows to update the upper bound ($UB = 7$). The search can stop, this upper bound is equal to the lower bound of the root node, therefore, no better solution can be found.

Solution $(J_2, J_3, J_4, J_1)$ is optimal. ◇

The efficiency of a branch-and-bound algorithm is related to several parameters. The strength of the lower bound is a key point. If the lower bound is strong (near to the optimal), it will allow us to cut a lot of branches. But this efficiency may assume a higher computational complexity and a compromise has to be found between quality and computation time. The size of the search tree is another parameter that has to be considered and the application of some *dominance conditions* in a pre-processing phase can help in decreasing its size. Finally, the search strategy has also an impact on the number of nodes that are explored. For instance, in Example 2.5, the best-first strategy will only explore nodes 2, 23, 234 and 2341.

### 2.3.3 Mathematical Programming Algorithms

*Integer Linear Programming* (ILP) or *Mixed Integer Linear Programming* (MILP) are two variants of *mathematical programming* that sometimes are used for solving scheduling problems. In both cases, first we formulate the problem to be solved in terms of variables, restrictions and functions, and next, using commercial or open source *solvers*, look for solutions. The resolution methods for solving ILP or MILP problems are generic methods using sophisticated variants of branch-and-bound algorithms.

In the section, we describe three basic ways of formulation a scheduling problem using mathematical programming. The models often involve arbitrarily large values called "*big-M*". As we will explain, these models are generally difficult to solve in practice.

#### 2.3.3.1 Positional Variables

We define binary variables $x_{j,k}$ equal to 1 if job $J_j$ is in position $k$ and 0 otherwise. This type of variable can be used when the considered scheduling problem is equivalent to finding a sequence of jobs. Notice that it is not the case for job shop problems of for non-permutation flow shop problems. This sort of model has been introduced in Wagner (1959).

The following constraints insure that there is exactly one job per position and one position per job:

$$\sum_{j=1}^{n} x_{j,k} = 1, \ \forall k, 1 \leq k \leq n$$

$$\sum_{k=1}^{n} x_{j,k} = 1, \ \forall j, 1 \leq j \leq n$$

The processing time, the due date and the release date of the job in position $k$ become variables equal to $p_{[k]} = \sum_{j=1}^{n} p_j x_{j,k}$, $d_{[k]} = \sum_{j=1}^{n} d_j x_{j,k}$ and $r_{[k]} = \sum_{j=1}^{n} r_j x_{j,k}$, respectively. The expression of the completion time of the job in position $k$ is given by:

$$C_{[k]} = \sum_{q=1}^{k} \sum_{j=1}^{n} p_j x_{j,q}$$

For example, let consider the $1||\sum T_j$ problem and let $T_k$ be the tardiness of the job in position $k$. Then, an MILP model for the $1||\sum T_j$ problem is given by:

$$\text{Minimize} \ \sum_{k=1}^{n} T_k \tag{2.1}$$

$$\text{subject to} \ \sum_{j=1}^{n} x_{j,k} = 1, \ \forall k, 1 \leq k \leq n \tag{2.2}$$

$$\sum_{k=1}^{n} x_{j,k} = 1, \ \forall j, 1 \le j \le n \tag{2.3}$$

$$T_k \ge \sum_{q=1}^{k}\sum_{j=1}^{n} p_j x_{j,q} - \sum_{j=1}^{n} d_j x_{j,k}, \ \forall k, 1 \le k \le n \tag{2.4}$$

$$\text{variables} \quad T_k \ge 0, \ \forall k, 1 \le k \le n \tag{2.5}$$

$$x_{j,k} \in \{0,1\}, \ \forall j, 1 \le j \le n, \forall k, 1 \le k \le n \tag{2.6}$$

Notice that using positional variables it is difficult to consider objective functions with weighted functions such as the $\sum w_j T_j$, without using additional *big-M* constraints. Indeed, it is not possible to simply replace in the model $T_k$ by $w_k T_k$, because $w_k$ is also a variable, which makes the model nonlinear.

#### 2.3.3.2 Precedence Variables

We define binary variables $y_{i,j}$ equal to 1 if job $J_i$ precedes job $J_j$ and 0 otherwise. This sort of model has been introduced in Manne (1960) for the job shop scheduling problem. In this case, we generally introduce a continuous variable $C_j$ for the completion time of job $J_j$ and the expression of the disjunctive constraint (only one job at a time on a machine) requires "big-$M$" as follows:

$$C_j \ge C_i + p_j - M(1 - y_{i,j}), \ \forall i, 1 \le i \le n, \forall j, 1 \le j \le n \tag{2.7}$$

$$C_i \ge C_j + p_i - M y_{i,j}, \ \forall i, 1 \le i \le n, \forall j, 1 \le j \le n \tag{2.8}$$

If $J_i$ precedes $J_j$, $y_{i,j} = 1$. In this case, constraints (2.7) ensure that $C_j \ge C_i + p_j$ and constraints (2.8) are deleted because $C_i$ s always greater than $C_j + p_i - M$, with $M$ a big value. If $J_j$ precedes $J_i$, $y_{i,j} = 0$. In this case, constraints (2.7) can be deleted because $C_j$ is always greater than $C_i + p_j - M$ and constraints (2.8) ensure that $C_i \ge C_j + p_i$.

For problem $1||\sum T_j$, we introduce $n$ continuous variables $T_j$ for the tardiness of job $J_j$ and an MILP model is given by:

$$\text{Minimize} \sum_{j=1}^{n} T_j \tag{2.9}$$

$$\text{subject to } C_j \ge C_i + p_j - M(1 - y_{i,j}), \ \forall i, 1 \le i \le n, \forall j, 1 \le j \le n \tag{2.10}$$

$$C_i \ge C_j + p_i - M y_{i,j}, \ \forall i, 1 \le i \le n, \forall j, 1 \le j \le n \tag{2.11}$$

$$T_j \ge C_j - d_j, \ \forall j, 1 \le j \le n \tag{2.12}$$

$$\text{variables } T_j \geq 0, \ \forall j, 1 \leq j \leq n \tag{2.13}$$

$$C_j \geq 0, \ \forall j, 1 \leq j \leq n \tag{2.14}$$

$$y_{i,j} \in \{0, 1\}, \ \forall i, 1 \leq i \leq n, \forall j, 1 \leq j \leq n \tag{2.15}$$

#### 2.3.3.3 Time-Indexed Variables

There are several possible definitions for time-indexed variables (see the initial paper Bowman (1959)). We define binary variables $z_{j,t}$ equal to 1 if job $j$ is being performed at time $t$ and equal to 0 otherwise. Another possibility is to say that it is equal to 1 if job $j$ starts its processing at time $t$.

The disjunctive constraint is simply given by $\sum_{j=1}^{n} z_{j,t} \leq 1$. With such variables, a job can be easily preempted. To prevent this, the following constraints are introduced:

$$p_j \times (z_{j,t} - z_{j,t+1}) + \sum_{t'=t+2}^{T} z_{j,t'} \leq p_j$$

For problem $1||\sum T_j$ we introduce $n$ continuous variables $T_j$ for the tardiness of job $J_j$, $1 \leq j \leq n$ and with $P = \sum_{j=1}^{n} p_j$ an MILP model is given by:

$$\text{Minimize } \sum_{j=1}^{n} T_j \tag{2.16}$$

$$\text{subject to } \sum_{t=0}^{P} z_{j,t} = p_j, \ \forall j \in \{1, \ldots, n\} \tag{2.17}$$

$$\sum_{j=1}^{n} z_{j,t} \leq 1, \ \forall t \in \{1, \ldots, P\} \tag{2.18}$$

$$p_j \times (z_{j,t} - z_{j,t+1}) + \sum_{t'=t+2}^{T} z_{j,t'} \leq p_j,$$

$$\forall j \in \{1, \ldots, n\}, \ \forall t \in \{1, \ldots, P\} \tag{2.19}$$

$$T_j \geq t \times z_{j,t} - d_j, \ \forall j \in \{1, \ldots, n\}, \forall t \in \{1, \ldots, P\} \tag{2.20}$$

$$\text{variables } T_j \geq 0, \ \forall j \in \{1, \ldots, n\} \tag{2.21}$$

$$z_{j,t} \in \{0, 1\}, \ \forall j \in \{1, \ldots, n\}, \ \forall t \in \{1, \ldots, P\} \tag{2.22}$$

This model has a pseudo-polynomial number of variables, depending on the duration $P$ of the schedule.

## 2.4 Approximation Algorithms

An NP-hard problem cannot be solved to optimality by a polynomial time algorithm, unless $\mathcal{P} = \mathcal{NP}$. As we have shown in the previous section, exact resolution methods require a pseudo-polynomial or exponential computation time. However, some polynomial time *approximation algorithms* can be used in order to find *approximate* solutions. Moreover, for many of such algorithms it is possible to give a *performance guarantee* ensuring a certain quality of the solutions the algorithm returns.

In the section, we recall basic definitions and notions related to approximation algorithms, separately for single and multiple objectives.

### *2.4.1 Problems with One Objective Function*

Let us denote by $f^*(I)$ the value of an optimal solution of a given minimization problem, for the instance $I$ and by $H(I)$ the value of the solution returned by the heuristic $H$. Let $\varepsilon > 0$ and set $\rho = \varepsilon + 1$. We say that algorithm $H$ has *a relative performance guarantee* of $\rho$, or that algorithm $H$ is a *$\rho$-approximation algorithm* (or $(1 + \varepsilon)$-approximation algorithm), if for any instance $I$, we have

$$H(I) - f^*(I) \leq \varepsilon f^*(I)$$

or, equivalently,

$$H(I) \leq \rho f^*(I)$$

or, equivalently,

$$\frac{H(I)}{f^*(I)} \leq \rho.$$

We say that $H$ has *an absolute performance guarantee* of $c$, if for any instance $I$, we have:

$$H(I) \leq f^*(I) + c$$

*Example 2.6.* Let us consider the problem $P2||C_{\max}$. We propose algorithm $H$ (see Algorithm 2) to solve this problem. Notice that algorithm $H$ can be applied for an arbitrary number of machines.

We are going to study this algorithm, in order to see if a performance guarantee can be derived.

Let us denote by $J_k$ the last job of the schedule, i.e. the job which gives the maximum completion time of the schedule. We have

**Algorithm 2** for problem $P2||C_{\max}$

```
while there are jobs to be scheduled do
    Schedule the next job on the first available machine
end while
return C_max
```

$$C_{\max}(H) = t_k(H) + p_k,$$

where $C_{\max}(H)$, $p_k$ and $t_k(H)$ denote the makespan of the schedule given by $H$, the duration of job $J_k$ and the starting time of job $J_k$, respectively.

We can establish that the optimal makespan is greater than or equal to the average sum of processing times, i.e.

$$\frac{1}{2}\sum_{j=1}^{n} p_j \leq C^*_{\max},$$

and thus we have

$$\frac{1}{2}(\sum_{j=1}^{n} p_j - p_k) \leq C^*_{\max} - \frac{1}{2}p_k.$$

Because $k$ was assigned to the first available machine, we have

$$t_k(H) \leq \frac{1}{2}(\sum_{j=1}^{n} p_j - p_k).$$

This implies that

$$t_k(H) \leq C^*_{\max} - \frac{1}{2}p_k,$$

and hence

$$C_{\max}(H) \leq C^*_{\max} + p_k - \frac{1}{2}p_k.$$

Because $p_k \leq C^*_{\max}$, we have finally

$$C_{\max}(H) \leq \frac{3}{2}C^*_{\max}.$$

Therefore, we can say that algorithm $H$ is a $\frac{3}{2}$-approximation for $P2||C_{\max}$.

◇

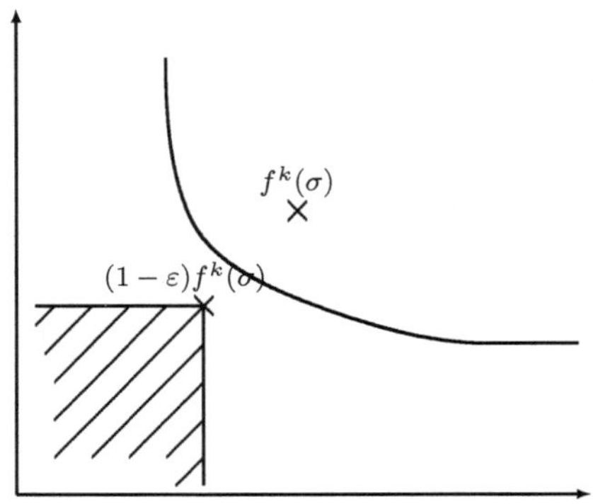


**Fig. 2.2** Illustration of the definition of an approximation algorithm (type I)

## 2.4.2 Problems with Multiple Objective Functions

When the solutions are evaluated by multiple objective functions, several approximation methods can be defined. We refer to Ruzika and Wiecek (2005) and to Zitzler et al. (2008) for a survey on such methods.

Some measures have been proposed, extending the definition of performance guarantee to the case of multiple objectives. We only introduce in this section two basic extensions of the notion of $\varepsilon$-approximation that we call *approximation of type I* and *approximation of type II*.

### 2.4.2.1 Approximation of Type I

In Ehrgott et al. (2011), the authors use the concept of *$\varepsilon$-efficient solution* and *$\varepsilon$-nondominated point* to measure the quality of approximation.

Given a scalar $\varepsilon > 0$, a schedule $\sigma$ and a vector in the objective space $f(\sigma) = (f^1(\sigma), f^2(\sigma), \ldots, f^K(\sigma))$, schedule $\sigma$ is $\varepsilon$-nondominated if there is no other schedule $\pi$ such that $\forall k, 1 \leq k \leq K$,

$$(1+\varepsilon)f^k(\pi) \leq f^k(\sigma).$$

Notice that this is equivalent to say that there is no other schedule $\pi$ such that $\forall k, 1 \leq k \leq K, f^k(\pi) \leq (1-\varepsilon)f^k(\sigma)$.

An algorithm $H$ is called a $(1+\varepsilon)$-approximation if it returns solutions satisfying this condition. This is illustrated in Fig. 2.2 in the case of two criteria.

### 2.4.2.2 Approximation of Type II

Let us denote by $f^{*k}(I)$ the minimal value of objective $f^k$ for instance $I$. The point with coordinates $(f^{*1}(I), f^{*2}(I), \ldots, f^{*K}(I))$ is called the *reference* point for the instance $I$.

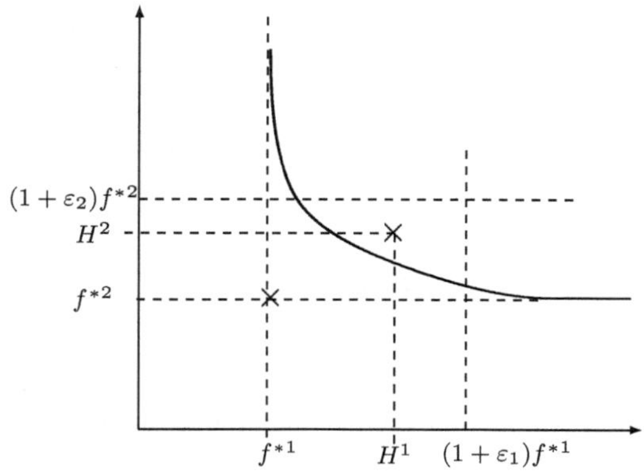


**Fig. 2.3** Illustration of the definition of an approximation algorithm (type II)

Let consider a set of real numbers $(\varepsilon_1, \varepsilon_2, \ldots, \varepsilon_K)$ with $\varepsilon_k > 0$ for any $k$ and set $\beta_k = \varepsilon_k + 1$ for any $k$. We denote by $H$ an algorithm and $H^k(I)$ is the value of the solution returned by algorithm $H$ for the instance $I$ for the function $f^k$.

An algorithm $H$ is called a $(\beta_1, \beta_2, \ldots, \beta_K)$-approximation algorithm iff for any instance $I$,

$$H^k(I) \leq (1 + \varepsilon_k) f^{*k}(I)$$

or

$$\frac{H^k(I)}{f^{*k}(I)} \leq \beta_k, \forall k, 1 \leq k \leq K$$

This definition is illustrated in Fig. 2.3 in the case of two criteria.

## 2.5 Approximation Schemes

An *approximation scheme* is a familly of $(1 + \varepsilon)$-approximation algorithms $H_\varepsilon$, over all $\varepsilon$, $0 < \varepsilon < 1$. A *polynomial-time approximation scheme* (*PTAS*) is an approximation scheme whose time complexity is polynomial in the input size. A *fully polynomial-time approximation scheme* (*FPTAS*) has time complexity that is polynomial in the input size and also polynomial in $\frac{1}{\varepsilon}$ (Schuurman and Woeginger 2011).

These definitions imply that a PTAS may have a time complexity bounded in $O(n^{1/\varepsilon})$, but this is not possible for an FPTAS.

Two types of results can be given in terms of approximation schemes. The first type of result is the proposition of a (fully) polynomial-time approximation scheme. The second type of result is the proof that such an approximation cannot exist unless $\mathcal{P} = \mathcal{NP}$.

Several approaches allow us to obtain an approximation scheme. In the following, we illustrate the technique called *adding structure to the input data* with the $P2||C_{\max}$ problem.

In the following, $C_{\max}(S, I)$ denotes the makespan of solution $S$ for instance $I$.

### 2.5.1 Simplifying

The first step of the technique is called *simplifying* and the aim is to simplify in polynomial time the instance $I$ into another instance $I^{\#}$. The simplification depends on $\varepsilon$ (the closer $\varepsilon$ to zero, the closer $I^{\#}$ to $I$).

For the $P2||C_{\max}$ problem, we introduce the following notations.

$$p_{sum} = \sum_{j=1}^{n} p_j$$

and

$$p_{max} = \max_{j=1}^{n} p_j$$

We denote by $I$ the initial instance and $S^*$ the optimal solution of the problem. We know that:

$$LB = \max(\frac{1}{2} p_{sum}, p_{max}) \leq C_{\max}(S^*, I)$$

For constructing instance $I^{\#}$, we split the jobs into two disjoint sets:

- The big jobs with a processing time greater than $\varepsilon LB$ are not changed,
- If we denote by $\Sigma$ the sum of processing times of all the small jobs, for which the processing time is smaller than or equal to $\varepsilon LB$, we introduce $\lfloor \frac{\Sigma}{\varepsilon LB} \rfloor$ jobs of duration $\varepsilon LB$ in instance $I^{\#}$.

We want to estimate the deviation between $C_{\max}(S^{\#*}, I^{\#})$, the value of the optimal solution of the problem with instance $I^{\#}$ (denoted $S^{\#*}$) and $C_{\max}(S^*, I)$, the optimal solution of the problem with the original instance $I$. We denote by $\Sigma_1$ and $\Sigma_2$ the total processing time of the small jobs on machine $M_1$ and $M_2$ in $S^*$. On machine $M_1$, suppose that we keep unchanged the big jobs and that small jobs are gathered together and replaced by $\lceil \frac{\Sigma_1}{\varepsilon LB} \rceil$ jobs of length $\varepsilon LB$. We do the same on machine $M_2$. It is clear that $\lceil \frac{\Sigma_1}{\varepsilon LB} \rceil + \lceil \frac{\Sigma_2}{\varepsilon LB} \rceil \geq \lfloor \frac{\Sigma}{\varepsilon LB} \rfloor$.

We have an increase of the makespan on $M_1$ at most equal to:

$$\left\lceil \frac{\Sigma_1}{\varepsilon LB} \right\rceil \varepsilon LB - \Sigma_1 \leq \varepsilon LB$$

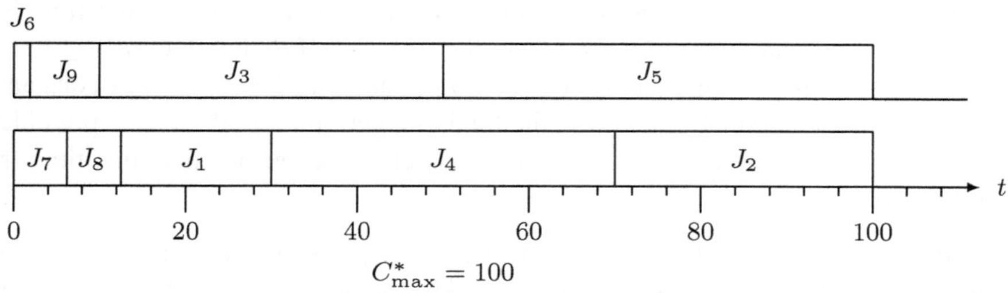


**Fig. 2.4** Optimal solution for the $P2||C_{\max}$ problem

and the same on $M_2$. Therefore, we have $C_{\max}(S^*, I^\#) \geq C_{\max}(S^*, I)$ and $C_{\max}(S^*, I^\#) \leq \varepsilon LB + C_{\max}(S^*, I) \leq \varepsilon C_{\max}(S^*, I) + C_{\max}(S^*, I)$. We deduce that $C_{\max}(S^*, I^\#) \leq (1+\varepsilon)C_{\max}(S^*, I)$. Because $C_{\max}(S^{\#*}, I^\#) \leq C_{\max}(S^*, I^\#)$, we have:

$$C_{\max}(S^{\#*}, I^\#) \leq (1+\varepsilon)C_{\max}(S^*, I)$$

*Example 2.7.* Let us consider the following 9-job instance $I$ of the $P2||C_{\max}$ problem:

| $j$ | 1 | 2 | 3 | 4 | 5 | 6 | 7 | 8 | 9 |
|---|---|---|---|---|---|---|---|---|---|
| $p_j$ | 18 | 30 | 39 | 40 | 50 | 2 | 6 | 6 | 9 |

For this instance, $LB = \max\{100, 50\} = 100$. An optimal solution $S^*$ to this instance has a makespan equal to $C^*_{\max} = 100$ (see Fig. 2.4).

Suppose that we take $\varepsilon = 0.10$. Therefore, jobs $J_6$, $J_7$, $J_8$ and $J_9$ are small jobs and $\sigma = 23$. These small jobs do not belong to $I^\#$ and two dummy jobs of length $\varepsilon LB = 10$ are introduced. The new instance is the following: ◇

| $j$ | 1 | 2 | 3 | 4 | 5 | $6'$ | $7'$ |
|---|---|---|---|---|---|---|---|
| $p_j$ | 18 | 30 | 39 | 40 | 50 | 10 | 10 |

### 2.5.2 Solving

The second step is to solve the problem with the simplified instance in polynomial time.

For the $P2||C_{\max}$ problem, the total processing time has not increased. The total processing time of the small jobs is at most $p_{sum} \leq 2LB$. Each job in $I^\#$ has a processing time greater than or equal to $\varepsilon LB$, thus the total processing time is greater than or equal to $|I^\#|\varepsilon LB$. So $|I^\#|\varepsilon LB \leq p_{sum} \leq 2LB$, and thus $|I^\#| \leq 2/\varepsilon$. So the number of jobs in $I^\#$ only depends on $\varepsilon$, and can be considered constant (it does not depend on $n$). Therefore, the total enumeration of all the $2^{2/\varepsilon}$ possible schedules can be done in "constant" time. It is clear that in practice, this time is strongly related to $\varepsilon$.

*Example 2.8.* An optimal solution to the $P2||C_{\max}$ problem for instance $I^\#$ has a makespan of 100, with jobs $J_4$, $J_5$ and $J_6'$ on $M_1$, the other jobs on $M_2$. ◇

### 2.5.3 Translating Back

The third step of the technique is to translate the optimal solution $S^{\#*}$ for instance $I^\#$ into an approximate solution $S'$ for the original instance $I$.

We denote by $\Sigma_1^\#$ and $\Sigma_2^\#$ the duration of the dummy jobs on $M_1$ and $M_2$ in $S^{\#*}$. We have:

$$\Sigma_1^\# + \Sigma_2^\# = \varepsilon LB \left\lfloor \frac{\Sigma}{\varepsilon LB} \right\rfloor > \Sigma - \varepsilon LB$$

We denote by $C_1^{\#*}$ and $C_2^{\#*}$ the completion time on machine $M_1$ and on machine $M_2$ for solution $S^{\#*}$. We construct a solution $S'$ for instance $I$ as follows. The big jobs are not changed, they keep the same assignment as in $S^{\#*}$. On machine $M_1$, the small jobs are scheduled greedily so that the load does not exceed $C_1^{\#*} + 2\varepsilon LB$. Therefore, if $C_1'$ denotes the completion time of solution $S'$ on machine $M_1$, we have:

$$C_1^{\#*} + 2\varepsilon LB \geq C_1' \geq C_1^{\#*} + \varepsilon LB$$

The unscheduled jobs can be scheduled on machine $M_2$, and the total length of the unscheduled jobs is at most $\Sigma - \Sigma_1^\# - \varepsilon LB < \Sigma_2^\#$. Therefore, the unscheduled small jobs can be put on $M_2$ after the big jobs and complete before $C_2^{\#*}$. We have $C_2' \leq C_2^{\#*}$.

We know that $C_1' \leq C_1^{\#*} + 2\varepsilon LB$ and because $C_1^{\#*} \leq C_{\max}(S^{\#*}, I^\#) \leq (1+\varepsilon)C_{\max}(S^*, I)$, and $LB \leq C_{\max}(S^*, I)$ we have:

$$C_1' \leq (1+3\varepsilon)C_{\max}(S^*, I)$$

Because $C_2' \leq C_2^{\#*} \leq (1+\varepsilon)C_{\max}(S^*, I)$, we deduce finally that:

$$C_{\max}(S', I) \leq (1+3\varepsilon)C_{\max}(S^*, I)$$

*Example 2.9.* Solution $S^\#$ is the following: The jobs $J_4$ to $J_9$ are scheduled on $M_1$, jobs $J_1$ to $J_3$ are scheduled on $M_2$. The makespan is equal to 113. ◇

The complexity of this PTAS is in $O(n + 2^{1/\varepsilon})$.

We refer to the tutorial of Schuurman and Woeginger for a more detailed description of approximation schemes (Schuurman and Woeginger 2011).

## 2.6 Relaxation of Problems

A *relaxation* is a way to simplify the problem. Of course, the optimal solution of the relaxed problem is just an approximated solution of the original problem. In the section, we present two classical relaxation methods, called *linear programming relaxation* and *Lagrangian relaxation*.

### 2.6.1 Linear Programming Relaxation

The linear programming relaxation consists in replacing the integrity constraints of an MILP model by weaker constraints: each binary variable belongs to interval [0,1] and each integer variable may be real. By using this relaxation, also called *linear relaxation*, the NP-hard MILP is transformed into a linear program, i.e. a related problem which can be solved in polynomial time. In case of a minimization problem, the value of the linear relaxation can be used as a lower bound for the corresponding MILP.

*Example 2.10.* To illustrate the relaxation, we consider two integer variables $x$ and $y$ and the following MILP. The advantage with this example is that the constraints can be represented in the plan.

$$\begin{aligned}
&\text{Minimize } Z = x + y \\
&\text{subject to } 11x - 12y \geq -23 \\
&\qquad 6x - 8y \geq -14 \\
&\qquad x \geq 1 \\
&\text{variables } x, y \in \mathbb{N}
\end{aligned}$$

The solution space is represented in Fig. 2.5, where bullets represent the integer solutions.

The solution of the MILP is $x^* = 3$, $y^* = 4$ and $Z^* = 7$ whereas the solution of the linear programming relaxation is $x^* = 1$, $y^* = 2.5$ and $Z^* = 3.5$. For more complex problems, the linear relaxation can be arbitrarily far from the optimal solution of the MILP problem. ◇

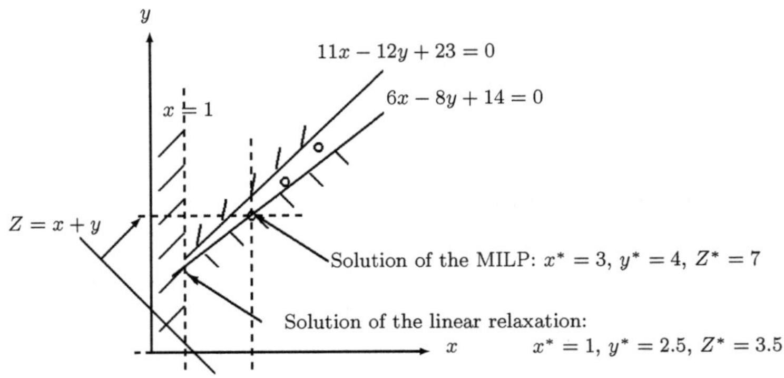


**Fig. 2.5** Solution space for the Example 2.10

The linear relaxation of a model is generally used to provide a global lower bound at the root node of the search tree, but also a local lower bound at any node. The better the relaxation, the better the algorithm convergence.

Notice that the MILP models that use *big-M* formulations are generally difficult to solve, because in this case, the linear relaxation is weak and does not allow to cut branches.

*Example 2.11.* Let consider the model with precedence variables presented in Sect. 2.3.3 from Eqs. (2.9)–(2.15) and consider that the processing times of jobs are comprised between 1 and 100. The completion times are necessarily smaller than $100n$. If $M$ is arbitrarily big, for instance $M = 10^6$, constraints (2.10) and (2.11) are simply canceled in the linear relaxation because always respected, whatever the values of the variables $y_{i,j}$. At the end, the only constraints in the linear relaxation are given by Eq. (2.12) and the value of the objective function of the relaxed linear program is generally equal to 0. Therefore, in case of "big-$M$" formulations, there is a real need to set $M$ as small as possible. ◇

## 2.6.2 Lagrangian Relaxation

Let consider the general formulation of a combinatorial optimization problem ($CO$) with variables $x_j$, $1 \leq j \leq n$.

$$\text{Minimize } cx$$
$$\text{subject to } Ax \geq b$$
$$\text{variables } x \geq 0$$

which is equivalent to:

$$\text{Minimize} \sum_{j=1}^{n} c_j x_j$$

$$\text{subject to} \sum_{j=1}^{n} a_{i,j} x_j \geq b_i, \ \forall i, 1 \leq i \leq m$$

$$\text{variables } x_j \geq 0, \ \forall j, 1 \leq j \leq n$$

This problem is equivalent to its dual version with variables $u_i$, $1 \leq i \leq m$ called *dual*$(CO)$:

$$\text{Maximize} \sum_{i=1}^{m} u_i b_i$$

$$\text{subject to} \sum_{i=1}^{m} u_j a_{j,i} \leq c_j, \ \forall j, 1 \leq j \leq n$$

$$\text{variables } u_i \geq 0, \ \forall i, 1 \leq i \leq m$$

If the variables are integer or binary variables, the problem and its dual version are difficult to solve. The Lagrangian relaxation is a generic technique which is used to compute lower bounds, but it can also be used for obtaining upper bounds. The idea is to relax some constraints in order to make the problem easier to solve. The constraints that are relaxed are put in the objective function, each one multiplied by a parameter called the *Lagrangian multiplier*, that can be viewed as a penalty for violating the constraint.

The Lagrangian version of problem $(CO)$ with all the constraints in the objective function can be formulated by:

$$\text{Minimize } cx + \lambda(b - Ax)$$

$$\text{variables } x \geq 0$$

$$\lambda \geq 0$$

which is equivalent to $L(CO)$:

$$\text{Minimize} \sum_{j=1}^{n} c_j x_j + \sum_{i=1}^{m} \lambda_i (b_i - \sum_{j=1}^{n} a_{i,j} x_j)$$

$$\text{variables } x_j \geq 0, \ \forall j, 1 \leq j \leq n$$

$$\lambda_i \geq 0, \ \forall i, 1 \leq i \leq m$$

We denote by $L(\lambda, x) = cx + \lambda(b - Ax)$ the *Lagrangian function*. We have:

$$L(\lambda, x) = \sum_{j=1}^{n} c_j x_j + \sum_{i=1}^{m} \lambda_i (b_i - \sum_{j=1}^{n} a_{i,j} x_j) \tag{2.23}$$

$$\Leftrightarrow L(\lambda, x) = \sum_{i=1}^{m} \lambda_i b_i - \sum_{j=1}^{n} x_j (\sum_{i=1}^{m} (\lambda_i a_{i,j}) - c_j)$$

The optimal solution of $L(CO)$ is a lower bound of problem $(CO)$. Therefore, the problem is to find a set of variables $\lambda$ so that the optimal solution of $L(CO)$ is as close as possible to the optimal solution of $(CO)$, therefore maximizing $L(CO)$.

This problem is called the *Lagrangian dual* of $(CO)$. The problem is to find the vector $\lambda$ which maximizes $L(\lambda, x)$ for $x \geq 0$, which can be written as follows: Find $\lambda^*$ such that:

$$L(\lambda^*) = \max_{\lambda \geq 0} \left\{ \min_{x \geq 0} \{L(\lambda, x)\} \right\} \tag{2.24}$$

Suppose that $x$ is fixed. Then, $L(\lambda, x)$ is a linear function depending only on $\lambda$. For each possible value of $x$, $\min_{x \geq 0}\{L(\lambda, x)\}$ is a lower envelope of a finite set of linear functions, i.e., a concave, piecewise linear function. The points where this envelope changes its slope are called *breakpoints*. $\lambda^*$ is the value of $\lambda$ for which this envelope reaches its maximal value. This is illustrated by the following example.

*Example 2.12.* To illustrate the Lagrangian relaxation and the envelope of linear functions, we use the following (simple) integer programming problem.

Minimize $Z = x + y$

subject to $3x - 2y \geq 2$

variables $(x, y) \in X$ with $X = \{(0,0), (1,0), (0,1), (1,1), (1,2), (2,1), (2,2)\}$

The Lagrangian function is $L(\lambda, x) = x + y + \lambda(2 - 3x + 2y)$. For each possible value of $(x, y)$, we obtain one linear equation as follows.

$(0,0) : L(\lambda) = 2\lambda$ $\quad (1,0) : L(\lambda) = 1 - \lambda$ $\quad (0,1) : L(\lambda) = 1 + 4\lambda$

$(1,1) : L(\lambda) = 2 + \lambda$ $\quad (1,2) : L(\lambda) = 3 + 3\lambda$ $\quad (2,1) : L(\lambda) = 3 - 2\lambda$

$(2,2) : L(\lambda) = 4$

The dual function is presented in Fig. 2.6, the optimal value of $\lambda$ is equal to $\lambda^* = 1/3$ and the optimal objective value is $L(1/3) = 2/3$. It is clear that the optimal solution of the initial problem is given by $(x, y)^* = (1, 0)$ with an objective value of 1. The difference between the value of the Lagrangian relaxation and the optimal value is called the *duality gap*, equal to 1/3 for this example. ◇

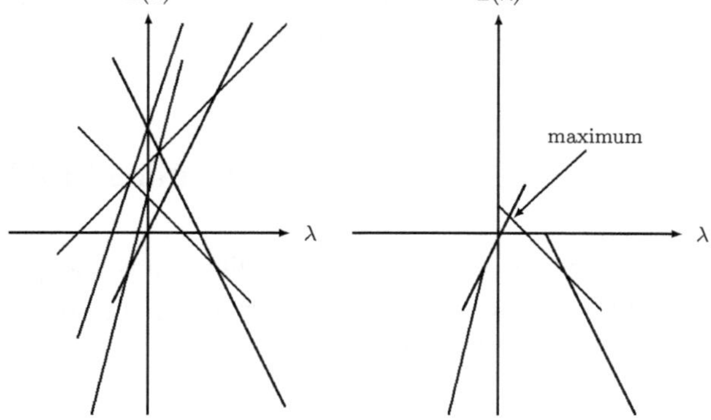


**Fig. 2.6** Dual function

**Algorithm 3** General Lagrangian relaxation

Determine the constraints to relax
Choose an initial value of the dual variables $\lambda^{(0)}$
**for** $i := 1$ **to** $m$ **do**
    Compute $G_i$
**end for**
$UB :=$ HighValue
$LB := -$ HighValue
$k := 0$
**while** stopping condition not met **do**
    Solve $L(CO)$ with $\lambda = \lambda^{(k)}$
    Denote by $x^{(k)}$ the solution
    Denote by $L(\lambda^{(k)})$ the value of $x^{(k)}$
    **if** $x^{(k)}$ is a feasible solution to $(CO)$ **then**
        $UB := \min\{UB, L(\lambda^{(k)})\}$
    **end if**
    Define step size $t^{(k)}$
    **for** $i := 1$ **to** $m$ **do**
        $\lambda_i^{(k+1)} := \lambda_i^{(k)} + t^{(k)} G_i$
    **end for**
    $k := k + 1$
**end while**
**return** the last $L(\lambda^{(k)})$

The Lagrangian relaxation lies in two crucial points: which constraints to relax and how to solve the Lagrangian dual. The *subgradient method* is the most used and generally the best method for solving the problem. Remember the expression of $L(\lambda, x)$ given in Eq. (2.23). We define the subgradient of multiplier $\lambda_i$ by:

$$G_i = \frac{\partial L(\lambda, x)}{\partial \lambda_i} = b_i - \sum_{j=1}^{n} a_{i,j} x_j$$

The general Lagrangian relaxation procedure is depicted in Algorithm 3.

We refer the reader to Geoffrion (1974) and to Van de Velde (1991) for a detailed presentation of the Lagrangian relaxation method.

## 2.7 Complexity of Basic Scheduling Problems

In this section, we give a list of algorithms and problems complexities, which constitute the basic elements in scheduling theory. The elements from the list will be used in the rest of the book.

### *2.7.1 Single Machine Scheduling Problems*

#### 2.7.1.1 Problem $1||L_{\max}$

This problem can be solved optimally by sorting the jobs in their $d_j$ non decreasing order in $O(n\log(n))$ time. This sorting rule is called *EDD* for *Earliest Due Date first* or *Jackson's rule* (Jackson 1955).

#### 2.7.1.2 Problem $1||\sum w_j C_j$

This problem can be solved optimally by sorting the jobs in their $p_j/w_j$ non decreasing order in $O(n\log(n))$ time. This sorting rule is called "WSPT" for *Weighted Shortest Processing time first* or Smith's rule (Smith 1956). This problem can be solved in $O(n\log(n))$ time. Notice that if $w_j = 1$ for all the jobs, the problem becomes the $1||\sum C_j$, which is solved by sorting the jobs in their $p_j$ non decreasing order. In this case, the rule is called "SPT" for *Shortest Processing time first.*

#### 2.7.1.3 Problem $1||\sum U_j$

The problem is to minimize the number of tardy jobs. The Moore-Hodgson's algorithm (Moore 1968), reported in Algorithm 4, returns the best sequence for this problem.

#### 2.7.1.4 Problem $1|prec|f_{\max}$

To each job $J_j$ is associated a non decreasing cost function $f_j(C_j)$ with $C_j$ the completion time of $J_j$. This problem, presented in Lawler (1973), can be solved optimally in $O(n^2)$ time by Algorithm 5. This algorithm builds a solution backward starting by the end of the schedule. At each iteration, there is a job $J_j$ that has

**Algorithm 4** for problem $1||\sum U_j$

Number the jobs so that $d_1 \leq d_2 \leq \cdots \leq d_n$
$S := \emptyset$
$t := 0$
**for** $j := 1$ **to** $n$ **do**
  **if** $t + p_j \leq d_j$ **then**
    $S := S \cup \{J_j\}$
    $t := t + p_j$
  **else**
    Choose as $J_{\max}$ the longest job in $S \cup \{J_j\}$
    $S := S \setminus \{J_{\max}\} \cup \{J_j\}$
    $t := t - p_{\max} + p_j$
  **end if**
**end for**
**return** jobs in $S$ in EDD order, then jobs in $\mathcal{J} \setminus S$ in any order

**Algorithm 5** for problem $1|prec|f_{\max}$

$P := \sum_{j=1}^{n} p_j$
$\mathcal{S} := \{J_j : \Gamma_j = \emptyset\}$
$\sigma := ()$ // initial empty schedule
**while** $\mathcal{S} \neq \emptyset$ **do**
  Choose $J_k \in \mathcal{S}$ such that $f_k(P) = \min_{j \in \mathcal{S}}\{f_j(P)\}$
  Schedule $J_k$ at the end of schedule $\sigma$
  $P := P - p_k$
  Update $\mathcal{S}$
**end while**
**return** $\sigma$

no successors (the set $\gamma_j$ of successors of $J_j$ is empty) with the smallest cost if it completes at time $P$.

#### 2.7.1.5 Problem $1||\sum T_j$

The problem concerns the minimization of the total weighted tardiness with agreeable weights, i.e. $p_i < p_j$ implies $w_i \geq w_j$. This problem has been proved NP-hard in the ordinary sense in Du and Leung (1990).

For the problem, Lawler (1977) proposed a pseudo-polynomial time algorithm. Before we formulate this algorithm, we need some preliminaries.

Let $\pi$ denote an optimal sequence. Let $C_j(\pi)$ denote the completion time of job $J_j$ in sequence $\pi$. We suppose that the jobs are numbered in EDD order. We define arbitrary due dates $d'_j$ such that

$$\min\{d_j, C_j\} \leq d'_j \leq \max\{d_j, C_j\}$$

**Proposition 2.1.** *Any optimal sequence $\pi'$ regarding due dates $d'_j$ is also an optimal sequence regarding due dates $d_j$.*

*Proof.* We denote in the following $T$ the total tardiness regarding due dates $d_j$, $T'$ the total tardiness regarding due dates $d'_j$ and $C_j(\pi')$ the completion time of $J_j$ in $\pi'$. We want to prove that $T(\pi') = T(\pi)$. We know that $T(\pi') \geq T(\pi)$, we have to prove that $T(\pi') \leq T(\pi)$.

We have:

$$T(\pi) - T'(\pi) = \sum_{j=1}^{n} A_j$$

with the following definition of $A_j$:

- If $J_j$ is tardy regarding $d_j$, $C_j > d_j$, then because $d_j \leq d'_j \leq C_j$ we have $A_j = d'_j - d_j$,
- If $J_j$ is early, $C_j \leq d_j$, then $C_j \leq d'_j \leq d_j$ and $A_j = 0$.

Similarly, we have:

$$T(\pi') - T'(\pi') = \sum_{j=1}^{n} B_j$$

with the following definition of $B_j$:

- If $C_j \geq d_j$, we have $d_j \leq d'_j \leq C_j$. There are three possibilities for $C'_j$:

  1. $C'_j \leq d_j$, then $B_j = \max\{0, C'_j - d_j\} + \max\{0, C'_j - d'_j\} = 0$,
  2. $d_j \leq C'_j \leq d'_j$, then $B_j = C'_j - d_j$,
  3. $d'_j \leq C'_j$, then $B_j = C'_j - d_j - C'_j + d'_j = d'_j - d_j$

  Therefore we have $B_j = \max\{0, \min\{C'_j - d_j, d'_j - d_j\}\}$. We can see that $B_j \leq A_j$.
- If $C_j \leq d_j$, we have $C_j \leq d'_j \leq d_j$. Again, three possibilities:

  1. $C'_j \leq d'_j$, then $B_j = 0$,
  2. $d'_j \leq C'_j \leq d_j$, then $B_j = 0 - (C'_j - d'_j)$,
  3. $d'_j \leq C'_j$, then it comes $B_j = -(d_j - d'_j)$.

  Therefore we have $B_j = -\max\{0, \min\{C'_j, d_j\} - d'_j\}$ and again we can see that $B_j \leq A_j$.

In both cases, $A_j \geq B_j$ and thus $\sum_{j=1}^{n} A_j \geq \sum_{j=1}^{n} B_j$. Because $\pi'$ is optimal regarding $d'_j$, we have $T'(\pi') \leq T'(\pi)$ and thus:

$$T'(\pi') + \sum_{j=1}^{n} B_j \leq T'(\pi) + \sum_{j=1}^{n} A_j \Leftrightarrow T(\pi') \leq T(\pi)$$

what is equivalent to inequality $T(\pi') \leq T(\pi)$. □

**Proposition 2.2.** *Let $J_k$ be the job with maximum processing time. There exists a job $J_{j^*}$ with $j^* \geq k$ such that all the jobs in $\{J_1, J_2, \ldots, J_{j^*}\} \setminus \{J_k\}$ are scheduled before $J_k$, the other jobs after $J_k$.*

*Proof.* Let $C'_k$ be the maximum possible completion time of $J_k$ in an optimal sequence. We define the following due dates: $d'_j = d_j$ if $j \neq k$ and $d'_k = \max\{C'_k, d_k\}$. Let $\pi$ be an optimal sequence regarding due dates $d'_j$ and $C_k$ the completion time of $J_k$ in $\pi$. Because the condition $\min\{d_j, C_j\} \leq d'_j \leq \max\{d_j, C_j\}$ of Proposition 2.1 applies, $\pi$ is also optimal regarding due dates $d_j$. Because $C'_k$ is the maximum possible completion time of $J_k$ in an optimal sequence, $C_k \leq C'_k \leq \max\{C'_k, d_k\}$. There is no job $J_j$ before $J_k$ with a greater due date. By choosing $j^*$ as the greater index such that $d_{j^*} \leq d'_k$, then because $d_k \leq d'_k$, $j^* > k$ and the proposition is proved. □

Proposition 2.2 leads to a dynamic programming algorithm, with $O(n^4 p_{\max})$ complexity. A phase $j$ is the number of jobs to schedule. A state at phase $j$ is the subset of jobs to schedule and the start time. A decision at phase $j$ is the job to put in position $k$. We denote by $F_j(\{1,2,\ldots,j\},t)$ the minimum cost of scheduling jobs $J_r$ with $r \in \{1,2,\ldots,j\}$, starting at time $t$.

The recursive relation (see also Pinedo (2008) for a similar presentation of the algorithm) is given by:

$$\begin{aligned} F_j(\{1,2,\ldots,j\},t) = \min_{k \leq r \leq j} \Bigg\{ & F_{r-1}(\{1,2,\ldots,r\} \setminus \{k\},t) \\ & + \max\{0, t + \sum_{\ell=1}^{r} p_\ell - d_k\} \\ & + F_{r-j}(\{r+1, r+2, \ldots, j\}, t + \sum_{\ell=1}^{r} p_\ell) \Bigg\} \end{aligned}$$

with $k$ such that $p_k = \max_{1 \leq \ell \leq j} p_\ell$.

The initial conditions of the recursion are:

$$F_0(\emptyset, t) = 0, \ \forall t$$

$$F_1(\{j\}, t) = \max(0, t + p_j - d_j), \ \forall t, \forall j$$

We search for $F(\{1,2,\ldots,n\},0)$.

#### 2.7.1.6 Problem $1|L_{max} \leq Q|\sum C_j$

In Van Wassenhove and Gelders (1980), the authors consider the problem of enumerating the Pareto solutions for the $1||\sum C_j, T_{max}$ problem. Let consider that $T_{max}$ is bounded by a given quantity $Q$. Then, for any job $j$, one has $T_j \leq Q$ and

**Algorithm 6** for problem $1|L_{max} \leq Q|\sum C_j$

$P := \sum_{j=1}^{n} p_j$
$\mathcal{J} := \{1, 2, \ldots, n\}$
$k := n$
$\sigma := ()$ // initial empty schedule
**while** $k \neq 0$ **do**
  Find index $i$ such that $\tilde{d}_i \geq P$ and $p_i = \max\{p_j : j \in J\}$
  Assign job with index $i$ to position $k$ in $\sigma$
  $P := P - p_j$
  $J := J \setminus \{i\}$
  $k := k - 1$
**end while**
**return** $\sigma$

therefore $C_j \leq Q + d_j$. By defining $\tilde{d}_j = d_j + Q$, the problem is to minimize $\sum C_j$ under the constraints that $C_j \leq \tilde{d}_j$ for any job $J_j$.

The algorithm uses a backward procedure that assigns at each step at the last position, the longest possible job (see Algorithm 6).

The following result can be proved (Lawler 1977).

**Theorem 2.1.** *Problem $1||\sum T_j$ can be solved in $O(n^3 P)$ time.*

## 2.7.2 *Multimachine Scheduling Problems*

### 2.7.2.1 Problem $P||\sum C_j$

The problem with $m = 1$ machine can be solved by sorting the jobs in SPT order (see problem $1||\sum w_j C_j$). It can be proved that this method is also optimal for the $P||\sum C_j$ problem. The jobs are sorted in SPT order. Then, the smallest job is assigned to machine $M_1$, the second to machine $M_2$ and so on until machine $M_m$ and then the $(m+1)$th job to machine $M_1$, the $(m+2)$th job to machine $M_2$, etc. Notice that problems $Q||\sum C_j$ and $R||\sum C_j$ can also be solved in polynomial time. However, problem $P2||\sum w_j C_j$ is ordinary NP-hard and $P||\sum w_j C_j$ is strongly NP-hard.

### 2.7.2.2 Problem $F2||C_{\max}$

This problem is the two-machine flow shop scheduling problem with minimisation of the makespan. It is optimally solved in $O(n \log n)$ time by the Johnson's algorithm (Johnson 1954), presented by Algorithm 7.

**Algorithm 7** for problem $F2||C_{\max}$

1: Let $U := \{J_j / p_{j,1} \leq p_{j,2}\}$
2: Let $V := \{J_j / p_{j,1} > p_{j,2}\}$
3: Sort the jobs of $U$ in non-decreasing order of $p_{j,1}$ values
4: Sort the jobs of $V$ in non-increasing order of $p_{j,2}$ values
5: $\sigma := U|V$ // concatenation of $U$ and $V$
6: **return** $\sigma$

**Table 2.2** Some polynomially solvable scheduling problems

| Problem | Notation | Time complexity | References |
|---|---|---|---|
| Single machine | $1\|\|L_{\max}$ | $O(n \log n)$ | Jackson (1955) |
| | $1\|\|\sum U_j$ | $O(n^2)$ | Moore (1968) |
| | $1\|\|\sum w_j C_j$ | $O(n \log n)$ | Smith (1956) |
| | $1\|prec\|f_{max}$ | $O(n^2)$ | Lawler (1973) |
| Parallel machines | $R\|\|\sum C_j$ | | Horn (1973) and Bruno et al. (1974) |
| Flow shop | $F2\|\|C_{\max}$ | $O(n \log n)$ | Johnson (1954) |

## 2.7.3 Reductions Between Scheduling Problems

We recall in this section the complexity status of some basic scheduling problems. The interested reader can refer to Blazewicz et al. (2007), Brucker (2007) or Pinedo (2008) for a wide overview of scheduling problems. The web site at www.informatik.uni-osnabrueck.de/knust/class/ contains an updated list of complexity status.

Some reductions must be known in order to deduce easily the complexity of some problems. These reductions are also presented.

### 2.7.3.1 Complexity of Basic Scheduling Problems

The complexity of the most classical scheduling problems without preemption is summarized in the following tables. In Table 2.2 we list problems that can be solved in polynomial time. In Table 2.3 we list some NP-hard problems.

### 2.7.3.2 Simple Reductions Between Scheduling Problems

The reductions between problems can be depicted by a graph, called a *reduction graph*. An arc between problem $P_1$ and problem $P_2$ indicates that $P_1 \propto P_2$.

In the theory of scheduling, simple reductions can be established between problems, using several ways. Concerning the machine environment, it is clear that single machine scheduling problems are less complicated than parallel machine problems and less complicated than flow shop scheduling problems, which are less

**Table 2.3** Some NP-hard scheduling problems

| Problem | Notation | References |
|---|---|---|
| Single machine | $1\|\|\sum T_j$ | Lawler (1977) |
| | $1\|\|\sum w_j U_j$ | Lawler and Moore (1969) |
| Parallel machines | $P2\|\|C_{max}$ | Lenstra et al. (1977) |
| | $P\|\|C_{max}$ | Garey and Johnson (1979) |
| | $P2\|r_j\|\sum C_j$ | Simple reduction |
| | $P\|\|\sum w_j C_j$ | Bruno et al. (1974) |
| Flow shop | $F2\|r_j\|C_{\max}$ | Lenstra et al. (1977) |
| | $F2\|\|L_{\max}$ | Lenstra et al. (1977) |
| | $F2\|\|\sum C_j$ | Garey et al. (1976) |
| | $F3\|\|C_{\max}$ | Garey et al. (1976) |

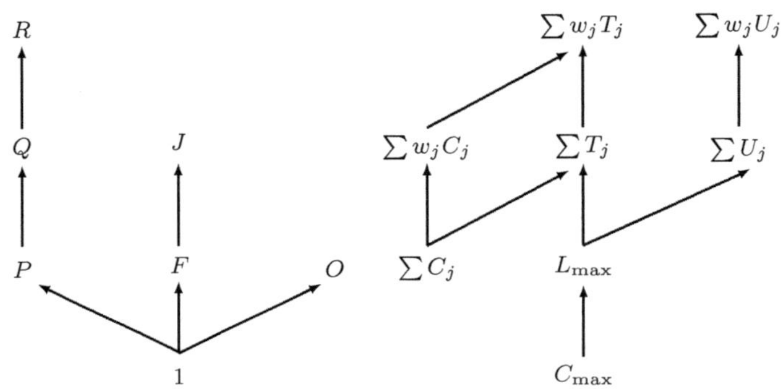


**Fig. 2.7** Simple reductions between problems according to the machine environment and the objective function (Brucker 2007)

complicated than job shop scheduling problems. Considering the constraints, one can say, for instance, that a problem with unitary processing times is less complicated than the same problem with identical processing times, which is less complicated than the one with arbitrary processing times. And simple reductions can also be derived on the objective functions. The reduction trees reported in Fig. 2.7 concern simple reductions between problems according to the machine environments and objective functions.

We can establish general relationships and simple relations among the scenarios which are considered in the multiagent case (see Sect. 1.4).

- MULTICRITERIA is a special case of INTERFERING in which $\mathcal{J}^2 = \mathcal{J}^1 = \mathcal{J}$. Therefore, for the same reasons, we have $\alpha|MU, \beta|\gamma \propto \alpha|IN, \beta|\gamma$.
- INTERFERING is a special case of NONDISJOINT in which $\mathcal{J}^2 \setminus \mathcal{J}^1 = \emptyset$. Therefore, we have $\alpha|IN, \beta|\gamma \propto \alpha|ND, \beta|\gamma$.

These relationships are summarized in Fig. 2.8. Depending on the specific objective functions of the agents, further reductions may hold, as it will be illustrated in detail in the next sections.

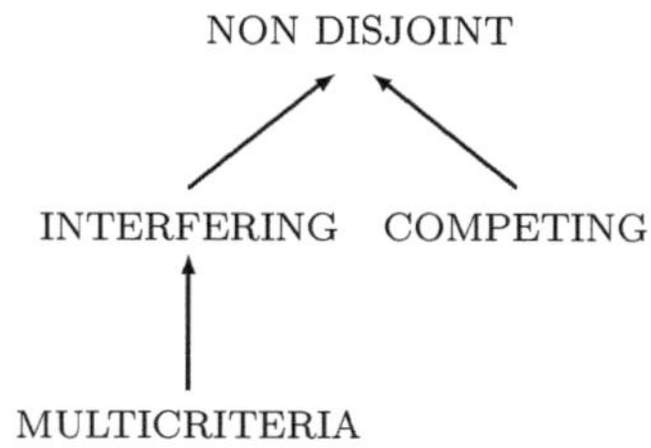


**Fig. 2.8** Simple reductions between scenario in the multiagent case

An important observation concerns the three symmetric scenarios, i.e., COMPETING, NONDISJOINT and MULTICRITERIA. Suppose that, for any of these cases, we have a polynomial algorithm solving $1|\beta_{sc}, f^B \leq Q|g^A$. Then, under the mild assumptions that $g^A$ and $f^B$ are regular, rational-valued and that an upper bound $ub_B$ is known for $f^B$, it turns out that also the symmetric problem $1|\beta_{sc}, g^A \leq R|f^B$ is polynomially solvable. In fact, in order to solve the latter, one can solve a logarithmic ($\log ub_B$) number of instances of $1|\beta_{sc}, f^B \leq Q|g^A$, for various values of $Q$. If $g^{A^*}(q)$ denotes the optimal value of $1|\beta_{sc}, f^B \leq q|g^A$, the value of the optimal solution of $1|\beta_{sc}, g^A \leq R|f^B$ is given by the smallest $q$ for which $g^{A^*}(q) \leq R$.

## 2.8 Bibliographic Remarks

The basic concepts related to problems and algorithms are presented in Knuth (1967–1969), Aho et al. (1974) and Cormen et al. (1994). Models of deterministic and nondeterministic computers are considered in Aho et al. (1974), Hopcroft and Ullman (1979) and Lewis and Papadimitriou (1998). Presentation of the theory of NP-completeness is given in Garey and Johnson (1979) and Papadimitriou (1994). A review of complexity classes other than $\mathcal{P}$ and $\mathcal{NP}$ is presented in Johnson (1990). Enumerative algorithms are considered by Woeginger (2003). Branch-and-bound algorithms and their applications are discussed by Papadimitriou and Steiglitz (1982) and Walukiewicz (1991). Dynamic programming and its applications are studied in Bellman (1957), Bellman and Dreyfus (1962) and Lew and Mauch (2007). Hochbaum (1998), Schuurman and Woeginger (2011) and Vazirani (2003) discuss approximation algorithms and approximation schemes.

# Chapter 3
# Single Machine Problems

This chapter is devoted to single-machine agent scheduling problems. We present most of the results for the case of two agents ($K = 2$), for simplicity and because most of the results found so far in the literature apply to this case. Whenever it is possible, we illustrate how these results can be extended to scenarios with a larger number of agents.

In the chapter, we use the following scheme of presentation of the results. First, at the top level, we categorize the results on the basis of scheduling criteria. Next, for each pair of scheduling objectives, we illustrate the results separately for each solution approach. Finally, for each solution approach, we present the results for the various scenarios.

The chapter is composed of 17 sections. In Sects. 3.1–3.15 we present results concerning scheduling problems with particular pairs of objective functions. First, in Sects. 3.1–3.8, we consider the cases that include one or two objective functions of 'max' type. Next, in Sects. 3.9–3.15, we discuss the cases in which both objective functions are of 'sum' type. We end the chapter with Sects. 3.16 and 3.17 that include, respectively, tables with summary of problems complexities and bibliographic remarks.

## 3.1 Functions $f_{\max}$, $f_{\max}$

In this section, we consider the case in which each job $J_j$ has (in general) two functions associated, namely $f_j^A(C_j)$ and $f_j^B(C_j)$, both of which are supposed to be nondecreasing with $C_j$. The agents $A$ and $B$ are interested in minimizing the maximum value reached by a function $f_j^A$ and $f_j^B$ respectively.

In this case (Fig. 3.1), the reduction NONDISJOINT → BICRITERIA holds, since NONDISJOINT can be seen as a special case of BICRITERIA in which $f_j^k(C_j) = -\infty$ for each job $J_j \in \mathcal{J} \setminus \mathcal{J}^k$, $k \in \{A, B\}$, so the three cases NONDISJOINT, INTERFERING and BICRITERIA collapse into a single case. On the other hand,

A. Agnetis et al., *Multiagent Scheduling*, DOI 10.1007/978-3-642-41880-8_3, 

COMPETING does not. Therefore, in this section, we provide results for NONDISJOINT and COMPETING scenarios.

## 3.1.1 Epsilon-Constraint Approach

### 3.1.1.1 Problem $1|ND, f^B_{\max} \le Q|f^A_{\max}$

We next present an algorithm that solves $1|ND, f^B_{\max} \le Q|f^A_{\max}$, hence the most general scenario. The algorithm has complexity $O(n^2)$, and can be seen as a generalization of the classical Lawler's algorithm (see Algorithm 5, page 49) for the single-agent problem $1|prec|f_{\max}$ with $f_{\max} = \max_{1\le j\le n} f_j(C_j)$. In what follows, therefore, we consider the problem in which agent $A$ wants to minimize $f^A_{\max} = \max_{j\in\mathcal{J}^A} f^A_j(C_j)$ so that $f^B_{\max} = \max_{j\in\mathcal{J}^B} f^B_j(C_j)$ does not exceed $Q$.

Given a schedule $\sigma$ for the overall job set $\mathcal{J} = \mathcal{J}^A \cup \mathcal{J}^B$, we indicate, as usual, with $C_j(\sigma)$ the completion time of the job $J_j$. We next introduce a solution algorithm which can be applied even if precedence constraints may exist among jobs, possibly across the job sets $\mathcal{J}^A$ and $\mathcal{J}^B$. Practical situations in which this can occur include for instance aircraft scheduling problems. An incoming flight may carry some passengers that have to take a certain departing flight, and this introduces a precedence constraint among the jobs, even if they are run by different airlines (agents).

The idea of the algorithm is simple, and consists in building the schedule from right to left, hence first deciding which jobs must be scheduled in the last positions, and then proceeding backwards towards the beginning of the schedule. Since it does not imply any additional complexity, we present the algorithm in the general case in which precedence constraints exist, i.e., for problem $1|ND, prec, f^B_{\max} \le Q|f^A_{\max}$. In what follows, we let $P = \sum_{J_j\in\mathcal{J}} p_j$.

More precisely, the algorithm first decides which is the last job to be processed. Let $L$ be the set of jobs that can be processed last, i.e., $J_j \in L$ if and only if it has no successors in the precedence graph. Thanks to the fact that all functions $f_j$ are regular, we know that whatever the last job, its completion time is $P$. So, if there is a job $J_j \in L$ and $J_j \in \bar{\mathcal{J}}^B = \mathcal{J}^B \setminus \mathcal{J}^A$ such that $f^B_j(P) \le Q$, scheduling it as the last job is certainly the best choice, since this can only favor the remaining jobs. Otherwise, we consider a job $J_h \in L$ for which $f^A_h(P)$ is minimum among the jobs which are either in $\bar{\mathcal{J}}^A = \mathcal{J}^A \setminus \mathcal{J}^B$ or in $\mathcal{J}^A \cap \mathcal{J}^B$ and have $f^B_h(P) \le Q$. Once the last job has been selected, the same procedure is repeated to select the second last job, after $P$ has been decreased by the length of the job in the last position, and $L$ has also been updated accordingly. At the $j$-th iteration of the algorithm, the $j$-th last job is selected, and so on until either all jobs are scheduled or an infeasibility is detected. The latter occurs if only candidates from $\mathcal{J}^B$ are left, and for all of them $f^B_i(P) > Q$.

More formally, consider an instance of the *single-agent* problem $1|prec|f_{\max}$, having job set $\mathcal{J} = \mathcal{J}^A \cup \mathcal{J}^B$, where the objective function is defined as:

$$f_{\max} = \max_{j \in \mathcal{J}} f_j(C_j(\sigma))$$

and for each $t \geq 0$, let

$$f_j(t) = \begin{cases} f_j^A(t) & \text{if } J_j \in \bar{\mathcal{J}}^A \\ f_j^A(t) & \text{if } J_j \in \mathcal{J}^A \cap \mathcal{J}^B \text{ and } f_j^B(t) \leq Q \\ +\infty & \text{if } J_j \in \mathcal{J}^B \text{ and } f_j^B(t) > Q \\ -\infty & \text{if } J_j \in \bar{\mathcal{J}}^B \text{ and } f_j^B(t) \leq Q. \end{cases} \tag{3.1}$$

With these positions, if an optimal schedule $\sigma^*$ for problem $1|prec|f_{\max}$ has finite objective function value $f^*_{\max}$, then $\sigma^*$ is also feasible and optimal for $1|ND, f^B_{\max} \leq Q|f^A_{\max}$, and achieves the same optimal objective function value $f^A_{\max} = f^*_{\max}$. Otherwise, if $f^*_{\max} = \infty$, then no feasible solution exists for the two-agent problem.

In view of the above reduction, Algorithm 8 details Lawler's algorithm for this special case. At each step, $L$ contains the jobs that can be scheduled in the current last position, and $P$ denotes its completion time (the latter equals the total processing time of unscheduled jobs). *Succ*$(j)$ and *Pred*$(j)$ respectively denote the sets of successors and predecessors of $J_j$ in the precedence graph. Under the hypothesis that each $f_j^A(t)$ value can be computed in constant time, Algorithm 8 requires time $O(n^2)$.

#### 3.1.1.2 Problem $1|ND, L^B_{\max} \leq Q|L^A_{\max}$

For some specific agents' cost functions, the analysis seen for problem $1|ND, f^B_{\max} \leq Q|, f^A_{\max}$ can be simplified and, correspondingly, complexity can be decreased. This is in particular the case if $f_{\max} = L_{\max}$. For simplicity we describe the approach omitting precedence constraints, which can however be easily taken into account with no increase in complexity. A simple but useful property of this problem is the following.

**Theorem 3.1.** *There is an optimal solution to problem* $1|ND, L^B_{\max} \leq Q|L^A_{\max}$ *in which the jobs in* $\bar{\mathcal{J}}^A = \mathcal{J}^A \setminus \mathcal{J}^B$ *are scheduled in EDD order, and the jobs in* $\bar{\mathcal{J}}^B = \mathcal{J}^B \setminus \mathcal{J}^A$ *are scheduled in EDD order.*

Note that, when considering the problem $1|ND, L^B_{\max} \leq Q|L^A_{\max}$, each job in $\mathcal{J}^A \cap \mathcal{J}^B$ has length $p_j$ but two distinct (and possibly unrelated) due dates $d_j^A$ and $d_j^B$, respectively for agents $A$ and $B$. As observed by Hoogeveen (1996) for problem $1|BI, L^B_{\max} \leq Q|L^A_{\max}$, also problem $1|ND, L^B_{\max} \leq Q|L^A_{\max}$ can be solved more efficiently than in the case with general $f_{\max}$. More precisely, consider the three sets $\bar{\mathcal{J}}^A$, $\bar{\mathcal{J}}^B$ and $\mathcal{J}^A \cap \mathcal{J}^B$ of size $\bar{n}_A$, $\bar{n}_B$ and $n_{AB}$ respectively. Sort the first two sets

**Algorithm 8** for problem $1|ND, prec, f^B_{\max} \leq Q|f^A_{\max}$

$P := \sum_{j \in \mathcal{J}} p_j$
**for** $j \in \mathcal{J}$ **do**
  Construct the set $L$ of jobs that can be scheduled in the current last position
  Construct the set $Succ(j)$ of successors of job $J_j$
  Construct the set $Pred(j)$ of predecessors of job $J_j$
**end for**
$J_h := \text{argmin}\{f_i(P) : J_i \in L\}$
$f_{\max} := f_h(P)$
**while** $(\mathcal{J} \neq \emptyset)$ **and** $(f_{\max} < \infty)$ **do**
  $C_h(\sigma) := P$
  $P := P - p_h$
  $L := L \setminus \{J_h\}$
  $\mathcal{J} := \mathcal{J} \setminus \{J_h\}$
  **for** $J_j \in Pred(h)$ **do**
    $Succ(j) := Succ(j) \setminus \{J_h\}$
    **if** $Succ(j) = \emptyset$ **then**
      $L := L \cup \{J_j\}$
    **end if**
  **end for**
  Set $J_h := \text{argmin}\{f_i(P) : J_i \in L\}$
  $f_{\max} := \max\{f_{\max}, f_h(P)\}$
**end while**
**return** values $C_h(\sigma)$

in EDD order, while for the third we have two different orderings, with respect to the first and the second set of due dates respectively, call them $EDD_A$ and $EDD_B$. In what follows, suppose that the jobs of $\mathcal{J}^A \cap \mathcal{J}^B$ are numbered according to $EDD_A$. During the execution of Algorithm 8, for a given current value $P$ of the total duration of unscheduled jobs, we have a set of jobs in $\mathcal{J}^A \cap \mathcal{J}^B$ such that $d^B_j + Q \geq P$. These are the *feasible* jobs, i.e., the jobs that can be feasibly scheduled to complete at $P$. Hence, at each step the set of candidates for the last available position in the schedule consists of:

(i) The job having largest due date among unscheduled jobs of $\bar{\mathcal{J}}^A$,
(ii) The job having largest due date among unscheduled jobs of $\bar{\mathcal{J}}^B$, and
(iii) The *feasible* job having largest index (and therefore smallest lateness with respect to $d^A_j$) among unscheduled jobs of $\mathcal{J}^A \cap \mathcal{J}^B$.

To efficiently select the appropriate job in case (iii), we must keep the feasible jobs ordered with respect to their indices (and hence, with respect to $EDD_A$), so that the job having largest index can be extracted in constant time. When a job is scheduled and $P$ is updated, new jobs may be added to the set of feasible jobs, and hence inserted in the ordered list of feasible jobs.

Note that, similar to the algorithm for general $1|ND, f^B_{\max} \leq Q|, f^A_{\max}$, if there is a job $J_j \in \bar{\mathcal{J}}^B$ such that $d^B_j + Q \geq P$, it is certainly convenient to schedule it. Otherwise, we must resort to either the job in $\bar{\mathcal{J}}^A$ having largest due date, or the feasible job in $\mathcal{J}^A \cap \mathcal{J}^B$ having largest due date with respect to $EDD_A$.

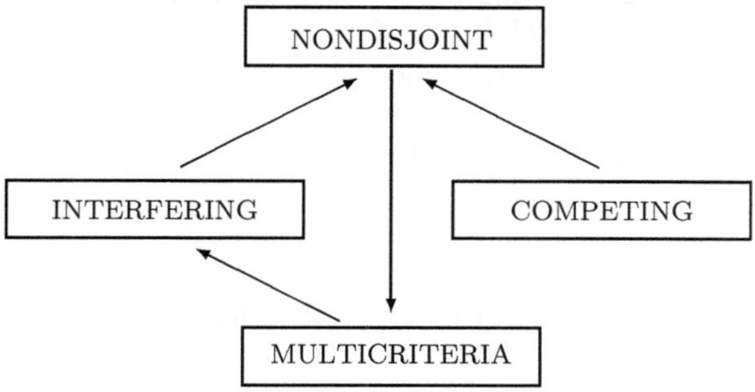


**Fig. 3.1** Reduction graph for $1||f^A_{\max}, f^B_{\max}$

While the jobs from $\bar{\mathcal{J}}^A$ and $\bar{\mathcal{J}}^B$ are considered exactly once during the algorithm, those in $\mathcal{J}^A \cap \mathcal{J}^B$ are also inserted in the ordered list of feasible jobs. The latter operation requires complexity $O(\log n)$, so the overall algorithm complexity is $O(n \log n)$.

In conclusion, we obtain Algorithm 9. In the algorithm, with a slight abuse of notation, we let $h_A$, $h_B$ and $h_{AB}$ be the indices of the currently unscheduled jobs (from $\bar{\mathcal{J}}^A$, $\bar{\mathcal{J}}^B$ and $\mathcal{J}^A \cap \mathcal{J}^B$ respectively) having largest index, and consequently:

- $d_{h_A}$ is the largest due date of the unscheduled jobs from $\bar{\mathcal{J}}^A$
- $d_{h_B}$ is the largest due date of the unscheduled jobs from $\bar{\mathcal{J}}^B$
- $d^A_{h_{AB}}$ is the largest due date (with respect to A) of the unscheduled jobs from $\mathcal{J}^A \cap \mathcal{J}^B$

*Example 3.1.* Let consider the following 6-job instance, where jobs $J_1$ to $J_4$ belong to $\mathcal{J}^A$ and jobs $J_3$ to $J_6$ belong to $\mathcal{J}^B$:

| $J_j$ | $J_1$ | $J_2$ | $J_3$ | $J_4$ | $J_5$ | $J_6$ |
|---|---|---|---|---|---|---|
| $p_j$ | 4 | 2 | 3 | 5 | 7 | 4 |
| $d^A_j$ | 14 | 18 | 19 | 10 | | |
| $d^B_j$ | | | 13 | 16 | 17 | 21 |

We have $\bar{\mathcal{J}}^A = \{1,2\}$, $\bar{n}_A = 2$, $\bar{\mathcal{J}}^B = \{5,6\}$, $\bar{n}_B = 2$ and $\mathcal{J}^A \cap \mathcal{J}^B = \{3,4\}$, $P = 25$. Suppose that we fix $Q = 2$, i.e. we want $L^B_{\max} \leq 2$. The sequence $(J_3, J_4, J_5, J_6, J_1, J_2)$ is represented in Fig. 3.2. The constraint on $L^B_{\max} \leq 2$ is satisfied, but the value of $L^A_{\max} = 9$ is not minimal.

Let us illustrate the execution of Algorithm 9 on this example. At the beginning of the algorithm, no job from $\mathcal{J}^B$ can be feasibly scheduled at the end of the schedule, so we have to schedule the job in $\bar{\mathcal{J}}^A$ having largest due date, i.e., $J_2$. The makespan of unscheduled jobs is therefore $25 - 2 = 23$. Now job $J_6$ from $\bar{\mathcal{J}}^B$ can be scheduled (with a lateness of 2), so the current makespan decreases to 19. This allows scheduling job $J_5$, also from $\bar{\mathcal{J}}^B$ (and also with a lateness of 2). Since the current makespan is now 12, $\mathcal{F}$ becomes non empty, in fact at this point $\mathcal{F} = \{J_3, J_4\}$. Considering $\mathcal{J}^A \cup \mathcal{F}$, the job having largest due date is $J_3$, that can therefore be scheduled to complete at 12. This brings the current makespan to

**Algorithm 9** for problem $1|ND, L_{\max}^B \le Q|L_{\max}^A$

Partition the jobs into the three sets $\bar{\mathcal{J}}^A$ (of size $\bar{n}_A$), $\bar{\mathcal{J}}^B$ (of size $\bar{n}_B$) and $\mathcal{J}^A \cap \mathcal{J}^B$
Sort sets $\bar{\mathcal{J}}^A$ and $\bar{\mathcal{J}}^B$ in EDD order
Sort $\mathcal{J}^A \cap \mathcal{J}^B$ according to $EDD_A$ and $EDD_B$
$\mathcal{J} := \mathcal{J}^A \cup \mathcal{J}^B$
$P := \sum_{j \in \mathcal{J}} p_j$
$h_A := \bar{n}_A$
$h_B := \bar{n}_B$
**if** there exist jobs in $\mathcal{J}^A \cap \mathcal{J}^B$ such that $d_j^B + Q \ge P$ **then**
    Construct the ordered set $\mathcal{F}$ of these jobs
**else**
    $\mathcal{F} := \emptyset$
**end if**
**while** $\mathcal{N} \ne \emptyset$ **do**
    **if** $(h_B > 0)$ **and** $(d_{h_B} + Q \ge P)$ **then**
        $C_{h_B}(\sigma) := P$
        $\mathcal{N} := \mathcal{N} \setminus \{J_{h_B}^B\}$
        $h_B := h_B - 1$
        $P := P - p_{h_B}$
    **else**
        **if** $\mathcal{F} \ne \emptyset$ **then**
            $h_{AB} :=$ largest index of a job in $\mathcal{F}$
        **else**
            $h_{AB} := 0$
        **end if**
        **if** $(h_A > 0)$ **and** $(h_{AB} > 0)$ and $(d_{h_{AB}}^A \ge d_{h_A})$ **then**
            $C_{h_{AB}}(\sigma) := P$
            $\mathcal{N} := \mathcal{N} \setminus \{J_{h_{AB}}\}$
            $\mathcal{F} := \mathcal{F} \setminus \{J_{h_{AB}}\}$
            $P := P - p_{h_{AB}}$
            Update $\mathcal{F}$ by adding all jobs in $\mathcal{J}^A \cap \mathcal{J}^B$ such that $d_j^B + Q \ge P$
        **else**
            **if** $h_A > 0$ **then**
                $C_{h_A}(\sigma) := P$
                $\mathcal{J} := \mathcal{J} \setminus \{J_{h_A}^A\}$
                $h_A := h_A - 1$
                $P := P - p_{h_A}$
            **else**
                **if** $h_B > 0$ **then**
                    **return** 'The problem is infeasible'
                **end if**
            **end if**
        **end if**
    **end if**
**end while**
**return** values $C_{h_A}(\sigma)$, $C_{h_B}(\sigma)$ and $C_{h_{AB}}(\sigma)$

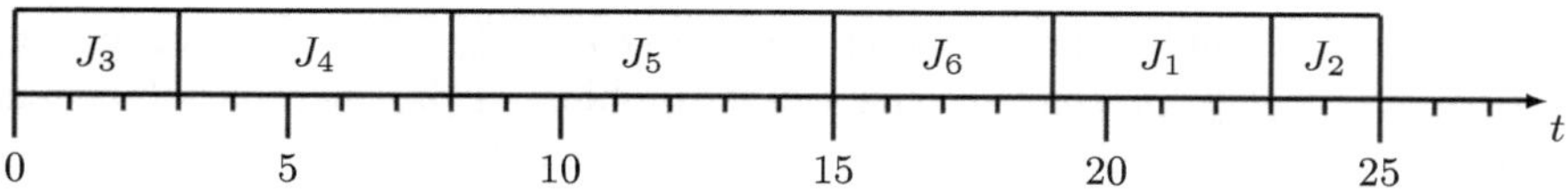


$L^A_{\max} = \max(9, 7, -16, -2) = 9,\ L^B_{\max} = \max(-10, -8, -2, -2) = -2$

**Fig. 3.2** Solution $(J_3, J_4, J_5, J_6, J_1, J_2)$ for problem $1|ND, L^B_{\max} \le Q|L^A_{\max}$

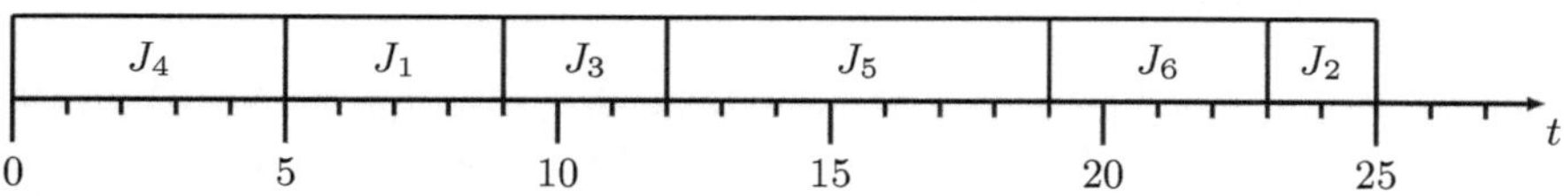


$L^A_{\max} = \max(-5, 7, -7, -5) = 7,\ L^B_{\max} = \max(-1, -11, 2, 2) = 2$

**Fig. 3.3** Optimal solution for problem $1|ND, L^B_{\max} \le Q|L^A_{\max}$

9, so that $J_1$ can be scheduled, and finally $J_4$. In conclusion, the optimal solution represented in Fig. 3.3 is $(J_4, J_1, J_3, J_5, J_6, J_2)$, for which $L^A_{\max} = 7$ (attained by job $J_2$). ◇

#### 3.1.1.3 Problem $1|C^B_{\max} \le Q|C^A_{\max}$

Let us now consider the case in which each agent is interested in minimizing its own makespan. In the COMPETING scenario, the following simple property holds Baker and Smith (2003).

**Proposition 3.1.** *In any Pareto optimal solution to problem* $1|CO, C^B_{\max} \le Q|C^A_{\max}$, *the jobs of each agent are scheduled consecutively.*

In view of this property, $1|CO, C^B_{\max} \le Q|C^A_{\max}$ is trivial. In fact, if $Q < P$, in the optimal schedule the whole set $\mathcal{J}^B$ is scheduled before the whole set $\mathcal{J}^A$, and viceversa if $Q \ge P$. However, if release dates are present, the problem turns out to be NP-hard (Ding and Sun 2010).

**Theorem 3.2.** *Problem* $1|CO, r_j, C^B_{\max} \le Q|C^A_{\max}$ *is NP-hard.*

*Proof.* Given an instance of PARTITION (see definition page 24), define an instance of problem $1|CO, r_j|C^B_{\max} \le Q|C^A_{\max}$ as follows. Agent $A$ has $n$ jobs, of length $a_j$ and release date $r^A_j = 0, \forall j \in \{1, \ldots, n\}$. Agent $B$ has a single job, of length 1, having release date $r^B_1 = R = \frac{1}{2}\sum_j a_j$. A solution such that $C^A_{\max} \le 2R + 1$ and $C^B_{\max} \le R + 1$ exists if and only if the instance of PARTITION is a yes-instance. In fact, in such a solution, the job of agent $B$ must start exactly at time $R$ and complete at $R + 1$. Hence, one has $C^1_{\max} = 2R + 1$ if and only if it is possible to partition all the jobs in $\mathcal{J}^A$ into two sets of length $R$. □

Theorem 3.2 implies the NP-hardness of $1|CO, r_j, f^B_{\max} \leq Q|f^A_{\max}$. Leung et al. (2010) show that the preemptive version of the problem can be solved in polynomial time. Specifically, $1|CO, r_j, pmtn|f^B_{\max} \leq Q|f^A_{\max}$ can be solved in $O(n^2)$, while $1|CO, r_j, pmtn|L^B_{\max} \leq Q|f^A_{\max}$ can be solved in $O(n_A \log n_A + n_B \log n_B)$.

#### 3.1.1.4 Extension to $K$ Agents

The results illustrated so far can be easily extended, even for the NONDISJOINT scenario, to the case of $K$ agents, and each agent $k$ is interested in minimizing an objective function of the form $f^k_{\max} = \max_{J_j \in \mathcal{J}_k} f^k_j$. In what follows, let $\mathcal{J}^{-1}(J_j)$ denote the set of agents that own job $J_j$, i.e.

$$\mathcal{J}^{-1}(J_j) = \{k : J_j \in \mathcal{J}_k\}.$$

Let us first consider the *feasibility* problem (see Sect. 1.3), i.e., given $K$ values $Q_1, Q_2, \ldots, Q_K$, the problem of finding, if it exists, a schedule $\sigma$ such that $f^k_{\max}(\sigma) \leq Q_k, k = 1, \ldots, K$. Since the functions $f^k_j$ are nondecreasing, in order to have $f^k_j(C_j) \leq Q_k$, $C_j$ must not exceed a certain *deadline* $\tilde{d}_j$, defined as

$$\tilde{d}_j = \max\{t | f^k_j(t) \leq Q_k, \;\; k \in \mathcal{J}^{-1}(J_j)\}. \tag{3.2}$$

Assuming to have an explicit expression for the inverse function $(f^k_j(C_j))^{-1}$, $\tilde{d}_j$ can be computed in time $O(K)$. Hence, the feasibility problem consists of finding a schedule $\sigma$ such that $C_j(\sigma) \leq \tilde{d}_j$. Once all values $\tilde{d}_j$ have been computed (in $O(nK)$), we simply order all jobs by nondecreasing values of $\tilde{d}_j$, and schedule them in this order. If no contraint is violated, a feasible schedule is found. Otherwise, no schedule exists for the values $Q_1, Q_2, \ldots, Q_K$. Hence, the feasibility problem $1|ND, f^1_{\max} \leq Q_1, f^2_{\max} \leq Q_2, \ldots, f^K_{\max} \leq Q_K|-$ can be solved in $O(nK + n \log n)$. Notice that the complexity of $1|CO, f^1_{\max} \leq Q_1, f^2_{\max} \leq Q_2, \ldots, f^K_{\max} \leq Q_K|-$ is $O(n \log n)$, since in the COMPETING scenario, each job belongs to exactly one agent and its deadline can be computed in constant time.

Also, the $K$-agent problem $1|ND, f^2_{\max} \leq Q_2, \ldots, f^K_{\max} \leq Q_K|f^1_{\max}$ preserves the complexity of the two-agent case. In fact, notice that we only need to replace, in the positions (3.1), the role of agent $B$ with agents $2, \ldots, K$. More precisely, we let:

$$f_j(t) = \begin{cases} f^1_j(t) & \text{if } \mathcal{N}^{-1}(J_j) \equiv \{1\} \\ f^1_j(t) & \text{if } \mathcal{N}^{-1}(J_j) \supset \{1\} \text{ and } t \leq \tilde{d}_j \\ +\infty & \text{if } \mathcal{N}^{-1}(J_j) \supset \{1\} \text{ and } t > \tilde{d}_j \\ -\infty & \text{if } 1 \notin \mathcal{N}^{-1}(J_j) \text{ and } t \leq \tilde{d}_j. \end{cases}$$

The same complexity considerations done for $1|ND, f^B_{\max} \leq Q|f^A_{\max}$ apply, implying that also in the $K$-agent setting the NONDISJOINT problem can be solved in $O(n^2)$.

## 3.1.2 Computing the Pareto Set

### 3.1.2.1 Problem $1|ND|\mathcal{P}(f^A_{\max}, f^B_{\max})$

Let us now turn to problem $1|ND|\mathcal{P}(f^A_{\max}, f^B_{\max})$. As shown in Sect. 1.3, *each* Pareto optimal solution can be found by solving a logarithmic number of instances of the $\varepsilon$-constraint problem. However, in this case the problem is even easier. In fact, suppose that $F_1$ is the value of the optimal solution of $1|ND, f^B_{\max} \le Q|f^A_{\max}$ for some $Q$. To obtain a Pareto optimal solution, we only need to solve *one* instance of the symmetric problem, i.e., $1|ND, f^A_{\max} \le F_1|f^B_{\max}$. If $F_2$ is the optimal value of such an instance, the pair $(F_1, F_2)$ is Pareto optimal. Similarly, the *next* Pareto optimal solution can be generated by solving $1|ND, f^B_{\max} \le F_2 - \varepsilon|f^A_{\max}$ (for sufficiently small $\varepsilon$) and thereafter one instance of the symmetric problem. In this way, the whole Pareto set can be obtained. Hence, the complexity of this task is essentially related to the size of the Pareto set.

It turns out that the Pareto set has a polynomial number of solutions. This can be shown following an approach originally proposed in Hoogeveen (1996) for problem $1|BI|\mathcal{P}(f^1_{\max}, f^2_{\max})$, which in this case subsumes also problem $1|ND|\mathcal{P}(f^A_{\max}, f^B_{\max})$ (Fig. 3.3).

One Pareto optimal schedule is a reference schedule (defined in Sect. 1.2.1) for agent $A$. This can be found solving an instance of problem $1|ND, f^B_{\max} \le Q|f^A_{\max}$ with $Q = +\infty$. Let $F_1^*$ be the optimal value. The corresponding value $F_2^0$ can be found by solving the symmetric problem $1|ND, f^A_{\max} \le F_1^*|f^B_{\max}$. $(F_1^*, F_2^0)$ is a Pareto optimal pair.

Consecutive Pareto optimal schedules are related by a structural property which allows showing that the Pareto set has polynomial size. Consider a Pareto optimal schedule $\sigma$ having values $(F_1, F_2)$, and consider the *next* Pareto optimal schedule $\sigma'$, of values $(F_1', F_2')$, with $F_2' < F_2$. There must be in $\sigma$ at least one *critical job*, i.e., a job $J_j$ such that $f_j^B(C_j(\sigma)) = F_2$. For each critical job $J_j$ there exists at least one job $J_i$ that precedes $J_j$ in $\sigma$ and follows it in $\sigma'$. More precisely, for each critical job $J_j$ consider the set $\mathcal{J}_j$ of jobs $J_i$ that precede $J_j$ in $\sigma$ and are such that $f_i^2(C_j(\sigma)) < F_2$. Note that $\mathcal{J}_j$ cannot be empty, otherwise one cannot get $F_2' < F_2$. Let now

$$F_1(j) = \min_{J_i \in \mathcal{J}_j} \{f_i^A(C_j(\sigma))\}$$

and consider a job $J_{j^*}$ such that $F_1(j^*) = \max\{F_1(j)\}$ among all critical jobs. It can be shown Hoogeveen (1996) that there can be no Pareto optimal value for agent $A$ between $F_1$ and $F_1(j^*)$, and that if $J_i$ and $J_j$ are such that $f_i^A(C_j(\sigma)) = F_1(j^*)$, in the optimal solution $\sigma'$ to $1|BI, f^B_{\max} \le F_1(j^*)|f^1_{\max}$, $J_i$ completes at $C_{j^*}(\sigma)$. The schedule $\sigma'$ is Pareto optimal if $f_j^B(C_j(\sigma')) < f_j^B(C_j(\sigma))$. Moreover, it can be shown that as we further increase the bound on agent $B$, the same two jobs cannot overtake each other again. As a consequence, going from the ideal solution for agent $A$ to the ideal solution for agent $B$, each pair of jobs can overtake each other at most once, so there are at most $O(n^2)$ Pareto optimal solutions. Since each Pareto optimal point can be found by solving two instances of the $\varepsilon$-constraint problem, and each requires $O(n^2)$ (Sect. 3.1.1), the whole Pareto set can be computed in $O(n^4)$.

#### 3.1.2.2 Problem $1||\mathcal{P}(L^A_{\max}, L^B_{\max})$

It is now interesting to analyze the special case in which both agents want to minimize the maximum lateness. In this case, problem $1|ND|\mathcal{P}(L^A_{\max}, L^B_{\max})$ can be solved in $O(n^3 \log n)$, since each instance of the $\varepsilon$-constraint problem can be solved in $O(n \log n)$ instead of $O(n^2)$.

In turn, problem $1|CO|\mathcal{P}(L^A_{\max}, L^B_{\max})$ can be solved even more efficiently, by exploiting the property in Theorem 3.1. Notice that, in this case $\mathcal{J}^A \cap \mathcal{J}^B = \emptyset$, and hence we can restrict to Pareto optimal solutions in which the jobs of the two agents are EDD-ordered. Given any Pareto optimal solution in the COMPETING scenario, consider the completion time of the job that determines the maximum lateness for agent $A$ (*critical* job), and call such lateness value $y$. As observed in Yuan et al. (2005), if the critical job is $J_u$, such lateness value equals

$$y = \sum_{i=1}^{u} p_i^A + \sum_{i=1}^{v} p_i^B - d_u^A$$

for some $v$, and can therefore assume at most $O(n^2)$ different values. Hence, we can compute a priori (and very simply) all values for $y$, letting $1 \le u \le n_A$ and $0 \le v \le n_B$. For each $y$, we can then solve the corresponding $\varepsilon$-constraint problem $1|CO, L^B_{\max} \le y|L^A_{\max}$, and generate a Pareto optimal solution (Algorithm 10).

Notice that we did not include the sorting phase in Alg. 10, which requires $O(n \log n)$. However, such phase is done once for all, so indeed, after the jobs are sorted, solving problem $1|CO, L^B_{\max} \le y|L^A_{\max}$ only takes $O(n)$ time. Therefore, the problem $1|CO|\mathcal{P}(L^A_{\max}, L^B_{\max})$ can be solved in $O(n^3)$.

*Example 3.2.* To illustrate Algorithm 10, let consider the following 6-job instance, where jobs $J_1^A$ to $J_3^A$ belong to $\mathcal{J}^A$ and jobs $J_1^B$ to $J_3^B$ belong to $\mathcal{J}^B$:

| $J_j^k$ | $J_1^A$ | $J_2^A$ | $J_3^A$ | $J_1^B$ | $J_2^B$ | $J_3^B$ |
|---|---|---|---|---|---|---|
| $p_j$ | 5 | 4 | 2 | 6 | 7 | 4 |
| $d_j$ | 7 | 9 | 16 | 9 | 12 | 17 |

We have $P = 28$, $h_A = n_A = h_B = n_B = 3$. The Pareto optimal solutions for this instance are $S_1$ (for $y = 5$) and $S_2$ (for $y = 9$) represented in Fig. 3.4. With sequence $S_1 = (J_1^B, J_2^B, J_1^A, J_3^B, J_2^A, J_3^A)$, one has $L^A_{\max} = \max(18-7, 26-9, 28-16) = 17$ and $L^B_{\max} = \max(6-9, 13-12, 22-17) = 5 \le y$. With sequence $S_2 = (J_1^A, J_1^B, J_2^B, J_2^A, J_3^B, J_3^A)$, one has $L^A_{\max} = \max(5-7, 22-9, 28-16) = 13$ and $L^B_{\max} = \max(11-9, 18-12, 26-17) = 9 \le y$. $\diamond$

**Algorithm 10** for problem $1|CO, L^B_{\max} \leq y|L^A_{\max}$

$P := \sum_{h \in \mathcal{J}} p_h$
$h_A := n_A$
$h_B := n_B$
**while** $\mathcal{J} \neq \emptyset$ **do**
  **if** $(h_B > 0)$ **and** $(d_{h_B} + h \geq P)$ **then**
    $C_{h_B}(\sigma) := P$
    $\mathcal{J} := \mathcal{J} \setminus \{J_{h_B}\}$
    $h_B := h_B - 1$
    $P := P - p_{h_B}$
  **else**
    **if** $h_A > 0$ **then**
      $C_{h_A}(\sigma) := P$
      $\mathcal{J} := \mathcal{J} \setminus \{J_{h_A}\}$
      $h_A := h_A - 1$
      $P := P - p_{h_A}$
    **else**
      **return** 'The problem is infeasible'
    **end if**
  **end if**
**end while**
**return** values $C_{h_A}(\sigma)$ and $C_{h_B}(\sigma)$

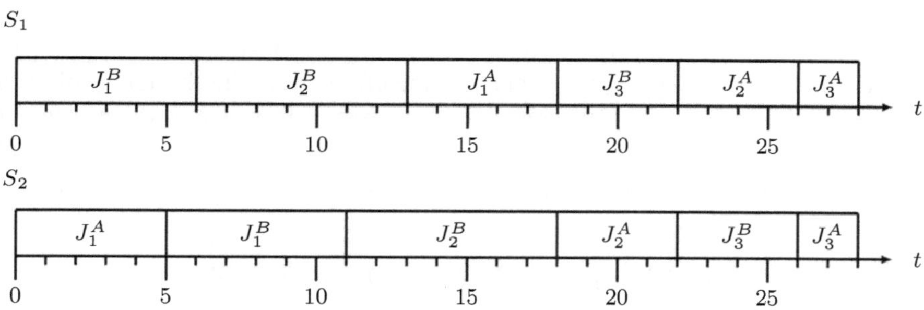


**Fig. 3.4** Optimal solutions for the $1|CO, L^B_{\max} \leq y|L^A_{\max}$ problem with $y = 5$ and $y = 9$

### *3.1.3 Linear Combination*

Let us first consider the $K$-agent, linear combination problem denoted $1|CO|\sum_k \alpha_k f^k_{\max}$. Cheng et al. (2008) have proved that this problem is strongly NP-hard when $K$ is *not* fixed and for general $f^k_{\max}$. In particular, the problem is strongly NP-hard when $f^k_{\max} = \max_{J_j \in \mathcal{J}^k}\{w^k_j C^k_j\}$ for each agent $k$. From the reduction graph in Fig. 3.3, this implies the NP-hardness of all the other scenarios. Notice however that the unweighted problem, i.e., when $f^k_{\max} = \max_{J_j \in \mathcal{J}^k}\{C^k_j\}$, denoted by $1|CO|\sum_k \alpha_k C^k_{\max}$, is indeed very easy. In fact, we can restrict to solutions in which each agent's jobs are performed consecutively, since only the completion time of the last job of an agent contributes to the objective function of that agent (i.e., Proposition 3.1 can be extended to $K$ agents). So, we can indeed aggregate each agent's jobs into a single job of length $P_k = \sum_{J_j \in \mathcal{J}^k} p_j$. The problem is therefore reduced to an instance of the classical, single-agent problem $1||\sum w_j C_j$ in which each job has length $P_k$ and weight $\alpha_k$, and is therefore solved by Smith's rule (see Sect. 2.7.1) in time $O(n + K \log K)$.

Let us turn to problem $1|CO|\sum_k \alpha_k L^k_{\max}$. In the two-agent case, the problem can be solved in $O(n_A n_B n)$ as shown by Yuan et al. (2005). If $K$ is not fixed, Cheng et al. (2008) prove that the problem is at least *binary* NP-hard, and it is open as for strong NP-hardness. However, if $K$ is fixed, the situation is simpler. We next show that the problem $1|CO|\sum_k \alpha_k L^k_{\max}$ can be solved in polynomial time for fixed $K$. In this situation, the same property already stated for the two-agent problem $1|CO, L^B_{\max} \leq Q|L^A_{\max}$ (Theorem 3.1) holds, i.e., we can restrict ourselves to considering solutions in which the jobs of each agent are scheduled in EDD order. As a consequence, in any such solution, the completion time of any job equals the sum of the processing times of the first $u_1, u_2, \ldots, u_K$ jobs for the $K$ agents respectively:

$$\sum_{k=1}^{K} \sum_{j=1}^{u_k} p_j^k$$

Because of this, the number of different values $L^k_{\max}$ can take is at most $\prod_k n_k$. To solve problem $1|CO|\sum_k \alpha_k L^k_{\max}$, one can therefore check the feasibility of each $K$-tuple $(Q_1, Q_2, \cdots, Q_K)$, where each $Q_k$ corresponds to one possible value of $L^k_{\max}$. Such feasibility problem can be solved in $O(n \log n)$, as already discussed in Sect. 3.1.1.4. In conclusion, the optimal value of the objective function is

$$\min \left\{ \sum_{k=1}^{K} \alpha_k Q_k : (Q_1, Q_2, \cdots Q_K) \text{ is feasible} \right\} .$$

Since each $Q_k$ takes at most $\prod_k n_k$ values, the linear combination problem $1|CO|\sum_k \alpha_k L^k_{\max}$ can be solved in $O(n(n_1 n_2 \cdots n_K)^K \log n)$. An open problem is to provide an algorithm for problem $1|CO|\sum_k \alpha_k L^k_{\max}$ having lower complexity.

Indeed, the same approach can be used for the $1|CO|\sum_k \alpha_k f^k_{\max}$ problem, i.e., solving a feasibility problem for each possible $K$-tuple $(Q_1, Q_2, \cdots, Q_K)$. However, since Theorem 3.1 does not apply, the number of $K$-tuples to be tried out is not polynomially bounded, and this indeed results in a pseudopolynomial complexity.

Let us now turn to the NONDISJOINT scenario. The simplest case is the two-agent problem $1|ND|\alpha f^A_{\max} + \beta f^B_{\max}$. Since (see Sect. 3.1.2) the whole Pareto set can be generated in at most $O(n^4)$, this problem can be solved in polynomial time. One only needs to compute the value of the objective function for all Pareto optimal solutions, and select the best. Actually, it is an open problem to determine a more efficient algorithm for the general problem $1|ND|\alpha f_{\max}^A + \beta f_{\max}^B$.

In some special cases, such more efficient algorithm can be devised. For instance, consider the two-agent problem $1|ND|\alpha C_{\max}^A + \beta C_{\max}^B$. It is easy to show that the following property holds.

**Theorem 3.3.** *In any optimal solution to* $1|ND|\alpha C_{\max}^A + \beta C_{\max}^B$*, one of the two following conditions holds:*

1. *First all jobs in* $\mathcal{J}^A$ *are scheduled, followed by* $\bar{\mathcal{J}}^B$
2. *First all jobs in* $\mathcal{J}^B$ *are scheduled, followed by* $\bar{\mathcal{J}}^A$

*Proof.* Let us first rule out the trivial cases $\alpha = 0$ or $\beta = 0$, for which conditions (2) and (1) hold respectively. Hence, $\alpha \neq 0$ and $\beta \neq 0$. Given an optimal schedule $\sigma$, suppose that $C_{\max}^A(\sigma) \leq C_{\max}^B(\sigma)$. In this case, we next show that condition (1) holds. Suppose by contradiction that in $\sigma$ there is a job $J_j \in \bar{\mathcal{J}}^B$ such that $C_j(\sigma) < C_{\max}^A(\sigma)$. This implies that $J_j$ is not the last scheduled job of agent $B$ in $\sigma$. Consider a new schedule $\sigma'$ obtained by postponing $J_j$ so that it completes at $C_{\max}^A(\sigma)$. Therefore, $C_{\max}^A(\sigma') = C_{\max}^A(\sigma) - p_j$, while $C_{\max}^B(\sigma') = C_{\max}^B(\sigma)$. Then $\sigma'$ is strictly better than $\sigma$, a contradiction. A symmetric discussion shows that if $C_{\max}^B(\sigma) \leq C_{\max}^A(\sigma)$, condition (2) holds. □

On the basis of this result, $1|ND|\alpha C_{\max}^A + \beta C_{\max}^B$ can be solved by simply comparing the values of the objective function in the two solutions obtained by scheduling first $\mathcal{J}^A$ or $\mathcal{J}^B$ respectively. (Clearly, scheduling within each set is immaterial.). Theorem 3.3 can be generalized to $K$ agents, by using the very same arguments.

**Theorem 3.4.** *Given any optimal solution* $\sigma$ *to* $1|ND|\sum_k \alpha_k C_{\max}^k$*, there exists an ordering* $k_1, k_2, \ldots, k_K$ *of the* $K$ *agents such that, in* $\sigma$*, first all jobs in* $\mathcal{J}^{k_1}$ *are scheduled, followed by all jobs in* $\mathcal{J}^{k_2} \setminus \mathcal{J}^{k_1}$*, followed by all jobs in* $\mathcal{J}^{k_3} \setminus (\mathcal{J}^{k_1} \cup \mathcal{J}^{k_2})$*,…, followed by all jobs in* $\mathcal{J}^{k_K} \setminus \bigcup_{i=1}^{K-1} \mathcal{J}^{k_i}$*.*

If $K$ is fixed, this theorem allows to devise a polynomial algorithm for $1|ND|\sum_k \alpha_k C_{\max}^k$. In fact, given any ordering $k_1, k_2, \ldots, k_K$ of the $K$ agents, we can build a solution by scheduling the agents as prescribed by Theorem 3.4, i.e., first $\mathcal{J}^{k_1}$, then $\mathcal{J}^{k_2} \setminus \mathcal{J}^{k_1}$, etc. The solution to problem $1|ND|\sum_k \alpha_k C_{\max}^k$ therefore consists in finding the optimal ordering of the agents.

To this aim, one can use the following dynamic programming approach. Let $S$ be any subset of the $K$ agents, and consider the problem restricted to the set $\mathcal{J}(S)$ of jobs belonging to at least one agent of $S$:

$$\mathcal{J}(S) = \bigcup_{k \in S} \mathcal{J}_k$$

and define $T(S)$ as the total processing time of these jobs, i.e.

$$T(S) = \sum_{j \in \mathcal{J}(S)} p_j$$

Let $F(S)$ be the optimal value of the objective function in such restricted problem. If the last completing agent in $S$ is agent $k$, its contribution to the optimal cost is $\alpha_k T(S)$, and the total cost is therefore

$$\alpha_k T(S) + F(S \setminus \{k\}).$$

As a consequence, $F(S)$ can be computed as

$$F(S) = \min_{k \in S}\{\alpha_k T(S) + F(S \setminus \{k\})\} \tag{3.3}$$

The recursive formula (3.3) must be initialized letting $F(\emptyset) = 0$. When $S$ includes all agents ($|S| = K$), we get the last completing agent in the optimal solution as

$$k_K = \arg\min_{k}\{\alpha_k T(S) + F(S \setminus \{k\})\}$$

the second last agent $k_{K-1}$ will be obtained as

$$k_{K-1} = \arg\min_{k}\{\alpha_k T(S \setminus k_K) + F(S \setminus \{k_K, k\})\}$$

and so on, backtracking the whole optimal solution.

Let us now consider complexity issues. Each $T(S)$ can be computed a-priori in $O(n)$. Each $F(S)$ can be computed through Eq. (3.3) in $O(K)$. Since the number of possible agent subsets is $2^K$, the complexity is dominated by the computation of all values $T(S)$, i.e., $O(n2^K)$.

Let us now turn to the case in which $K$ is not fixed. In this case, somewhat surprisingly, the problem turns out to be hard. We employ the following problem, which has been proved strongly NP-hard in Arbib et al. (2003).

**Problem 3.1 (MIN FLOW TIME GRAPH ORDERING (MFTGO)).** Given an undirected graph $G = (V, E)$, let $\rho$ be an ordering of the nodes, and for each $u \in V$ denote by $\rho(u)$ the position of $u$ in the ordering $\rho$. Let $e_i(\rho)$ denote the number of arcs adjacent to the $i$-th node of the ordering $\rho$ that have a position smaller than $i$, i.e., the quantity

$$e_i(\rho) = |\{(u, v) \in E : \rho(u) < \rho(v) = i\}|$$

Given an integer $H$, is there an ordering $\rho$ such that

$$f(\rho) = \sum_{i=1}^{|V|} i\, e_i(\rho) \leq H? \tag{3.4}$$

In the following theorem, we show that MTFGO can be reduced to the decision version of $1|ND|\sum_k \alpha_k C^k_{\max}$, i.e. to the feasibility problem:

$$1|ND, \sum_{k=1}^{K} \alpha_k C^k_{\max} \leq Q|-$$

**Theorem 3.5.** *If $K$ is not fixed, problem $1|ND|\sum_k \alpha_k C^k_{\max}$ is strongly NP-hard, even if all jobs have unit length and each agent owns exactly two jobs.*

*Proof.* Given an instance of MFTGO, we build a corresponding instance of $1|ND, \sum_k \alpha_k C^k_{\max} \leq Q|-$ as follows. There are $K = |E|$ agents and $n = |V|$ jobs. For each node $u \in V$ we define one job, $J_u$. For each edge $(u, v) \in E$, we define one *agent* $A_{uv}$, with corresponding job set $\mathcal{J}_{uv} = \{J_u, J_v\}$. All jobs have unit duration, $p_u = 1$ for all $u$. We denote by $C^{uv}_{\max}$ the makespan of agent $A_{uv}$. Moreover, let $Q = H$ and all $\alpha_{uv} = 1$.

Consider an ordering $\rho$ in MFTGO. As observed, $e_i(\rho)$ is the number of arcs having one endpoint in the $i$-th node of $\rho$ and the other endpoint in a node having a smaller position than $i$ in $\rho$. Such value is multiplied by $i$ to obtain the contribution of the $i$-th node to $f(\rho)$. Now, let us identify the arcs with the agents and the nodes with the jobs. Also, order the jobs in $1|ND, \sum_{k=1}^{K} \alpha_k C^k_{\max} \leq Q|-$ as the nodes in MFTGO, i.e., let $\sigma = \rho$. Then, $e_i(\rho) = e_i(\sigma)$ equals the number of agents who have *both* of their jobs completed when the $i$-th job in $\sigma$ is processed. Since all jobs have unit duration, the $i$-th job is indeed completed at time $i$, i.e., $C^{uv}_{\max} = i$ for all $A_{uv}$ such that $\sigma(u) < \sigma(v) = i$. Therefore, since $\alpha_{uv} = 1$, we can write $\phi(\sigma)$ as

$$\phi(\sigma) = \sum_{uv:(u,v)\in E} C^{uv}_{\max} = \sum_{i=1}^{|V|} i\, e_i(\sigma) \tag{3.5}$$

and hence $\sum_k \alpha_k C^k_{\max} \leq Q$ if and only if (3.4) is verified. □

Concerning the INTERFERING scenario, we observe that, as a consequence of Theorem 3.4, an optimal solution to problem $1|IN|\sum_k \alpha_k C^k_{\max}$ is trivially obtained by sequencing the agents from the innermost to the outermost, i.e., first $\mathcal{J}_K$, then $\mathcal{J}_{K-1} \setminus \mathcal{J}_K$, then $\mathcal{J}_{K-2} \setminus \mathcal{J}_{K-1}, \ldots$, then $\bar{\mathcal{J}}^A$.

All the problems addressed in this section assumed that all jobs are available at the beginning of the schedule. If nonzero release dates are present, even the two-agent problem $1|CO, r_j|\alpha C^A_{\max} + \beta C^B_{\max}$ is NP-hard (Ding and Sun 2010). The proof is almost identical to that of Theorem 3.2, where one defines $\beta >> \alpha$.

## 3.2 Functions $C_{\max}$, $\sum C_j$

In this section we address the first problem in which one agent holds a max-type and the other agent a sum-type objective functions. The simplest such case is when agent $A$ wants to minimize the total completion time, and agent $B$ the makespan

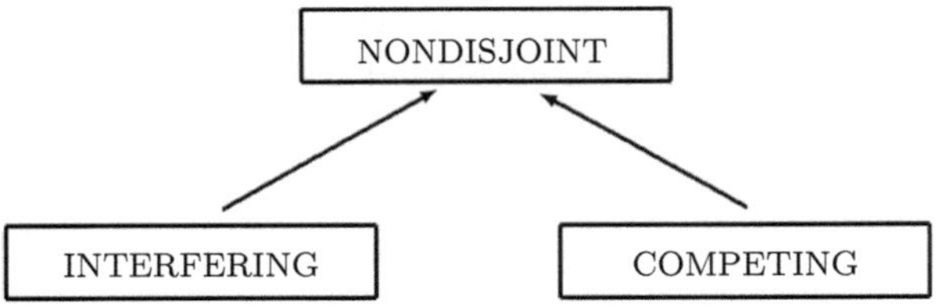


**Fig. 3.5** Reduction graph for $1||\sum C_j, C_{\max}$

of its jobs. Throughout this section, with no loss of generality we can suppose that the jobs in $\bar{\mathcal{J}}^B$ are scheduled consecutively in any Pareto optimal solution. Hence we assume that $\bar{\mathcal{J}}^B$ consists of a *single* job $\bar{J}^B$ of length $\bar{P}_B$, equal to the total processing time of the jobs in $\bar{\mathcal{J}}^B$.

In this case, the reductions in Fig. 3.5 hold. Notice that BICRITERIA is not shown since the $C_{\max}$ criterion is not relevant when applied to all jobs. In what follows we therefore illustrate the results for the NONDISJOINT scenario.

### 3.2.1 Epsilon-Constraint Approach

Let us consider problem $1|ND, C^B_{\max} \le Q|\sum C^A_j$. In what follows, jobs in $\bar{\mathcal{J}}^A$ are numbered in SPT order, are denoted by $J^A_1, J^A_2, \ldots, J^A_{\bar{n}_A}$ and have processing times $p^A_1, p^A_2, \ldots, p^A_{\bar{n}_A}$. A simple pairwise interchange argument allows one to establish the following theorem.

**Theorem 3.6.** *In an optimal solution to problem* $1|ND, C^B_{\max} \le Q|\sum C^A_j$, *jobs in* $\mathcal{J}^A$ *are sequenced in SPT order.*

As a consequence of Theorem 3.6, problem $1|ND, C^B_{\max} \le Q|\sum C^A_j$ can be solved very efficiently. In fact, observe that an optimal solution has the following three-block structure. The first block contains all the jobs in $\mathcal{J}^A \cap \mathcal{J}^B$ as well as the first $j^*$ jobs in $\bar{\mathcal{J}}^A$ sequenced in SPT order. Job $J^A_{j^*}$ is the job such that:

$$\sum_{J_j \in \mathcal{J}^A \cap \mathcal{J}^B} p_i + \sum_{i=1}^{j^*} p^A_i \le Q - \bar{P}_B < \sum_{J_j \in \mathcal{J}^A \cap \mathcal{J}^B} p_i + \sum_{i=1}^{j^*+1} p^A_i \tag{3.6}$$

The second block consists of job $\bar{J}^B$. Finally, the third block contains the remaining jobs in $\bar{\mathcal{J}}^A$, again sequenced in SPT order. Once the jobs in $\mathcal{J}^A$ are sorted in SPT order and the index $j^*$ is computed by the (3.6), the optimal solution is found. The complexity is therefore $O(n_A \log n_A + n_B)$.

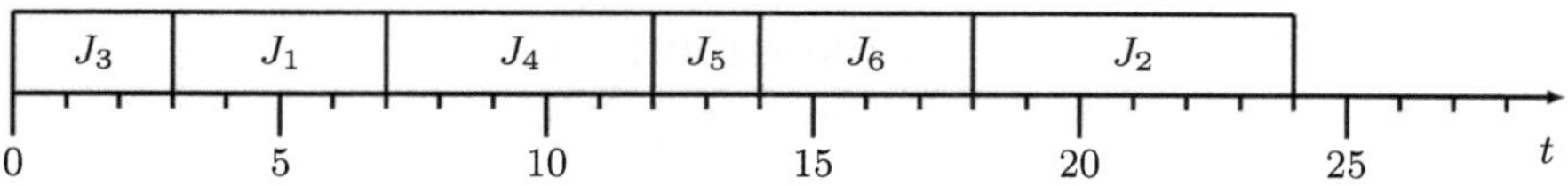


**Fig. 3.6** Solution for problem $1|ND, C^B_{\max} \leq Q|\sum C^A_j$

*Example 3.3.* Let us consider an example with $n = 8$ jobs and the following instance where $\mathcal{J}^A = \{J_1, J_2, J_3, J_4\}$ and $\mathcal{J}^B = \{J_3, J_4, J_5, J_6\}$.

| $J_j$ | $J_1$ | $J_2$ | $J_3$ | $J_4$ | $J_5$ | $J_6$ |
|---|---|---|---|---|---|---|
| $(J^k_j$ | $J^A_2$ | $J^A_4$ | $J^A_1 = J^B_2$ | $J^A_3 = J^B_4$ | $J^B_1$ | $J^B_3)$ |
| $p^A_j$ | 4 | 6 | 3 | 5 | | |
| $p^B_j$ | | | 3 | 5 | 2 | 4 |

If we impose $C^B_{\max} \leq 19$, we will first sequence $J_3$ and then $J_1$ and $J_4$. After these jobs, one has to schedule the remaining jobs of $\bar{\mathcal{J}}^B$, and finally job $J_2$. The solution is represented in Fig. 3.6. We obtain $C^B_{\max} = 18 \leq 19$ and $\sum C^A_j = 3 + 7 + 12 + 24 = 46$. ◇

### 3.2.2 *Computation of the Pareto Set*

Let us turn to problem $1|ND|\mathcal{P}(\sum C_j, C_{\max})$. To generate the whole Pareto set, one may think of starting from a very large $Q$, so that, from (3.6), $j^* = \bar{n}_A$, and decrease it. This yields a reference schedule for agent $A$, in which all jobs of agent $A$ are SPT ordered, followed by $\bar{J}^B$. Decreasing $Q$, this solution remains optimal until $Q$ becomes smaller than

$$\sum_{J_j \in \mathcal{J}^A \cap \mathcal{J}^B} p_j + \sum_{j=1}^{\bar{n}_A} p^A_j - \bar{P}_B$$

At this point, $j^* = \bar{n}_A - 1$, i.e., the new optimal schedule is obtained from the previous one by postponing job $J_{\bar{n}_A}$ after job $\bar{J}^B$.

We can therefore continue decreasing $Q$ in this way, considering that, from (3.6), for each index $h$, $1 \leq h \leq \bar{n}_A - 1$, the optimal schedule is the same for all values of $Q$ such that

$$\sum_{J_j \in \mathcal{J}^A \cap \mathcal{J}^B} p_j + \sum_{j=1}^{h} p^A_j - \bar{P}_B \leq Q < \sum_{J_j \in \mathcal{J}^A \cap \mathcal{J}^B} p^A_i + \sum_{j=1}^{h+1} p^A_j - \bar{P}_B \qquad (3.7)$$

At each new Pareto optimal solution, the only difference between the new and the previous solution is that $\bar{J}^B$ swaps its position with the job $J^A_h \in \bar{\mathcal{J}}^A$ immediately

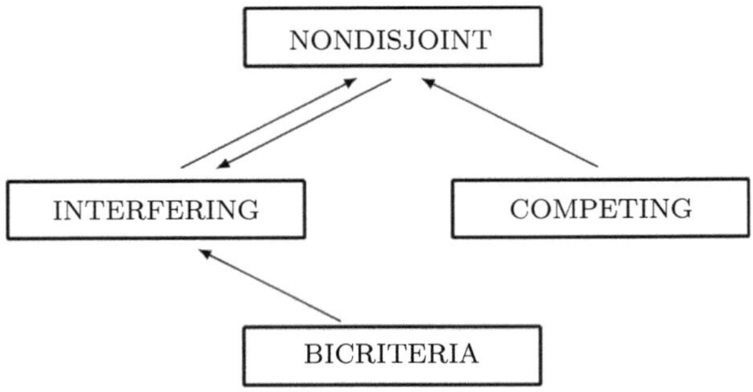


**Fig. 3.7** Reduction graph for $1||f^A_{\max}, \sum C^B_j$

preceding it. Therefore, the new solution can be computed in constant time and we obtain the following result.

**Theorem 3.7.** *There are exactly $\bar{n}_A + 1$ Pareto optimal solutions, that can be computed in $O(n_A \log n_A + n_B)$ time.*

### *3.2.3 Linear Combination*

Problem $1|ND|\alpha \sum C^A_j + \beta C^B_{\max}$ can be obviously solved in time $O(n_A \log n_A + n_B)$, since, from Theorem 3.7, there are only $\bar{n}_A + 1$ Pareto optimal solutions, that can be easily enumerated.

## 3.3 Functions $f_{\max}, \sum C_j$

Now let us turn to the case in which one agent has a general max-type cost function. Notice that in this case, problem $1|ND|f^A_{\max}, \sum C^B_j$ reduces to problem $1|IN|f^A_{\max}, \sum C^B_j$. In fact, in the NONDISJOINT scenario, we can easily extend $\mathcal{J}^A$ to include all jobs, simply by attaching to each job $J_j \in \bar{\mathcal{J}}^B$ a trivial function $f^A_j = -\infty$. Such jobs can be feasibly scheduled in any position and will never contribute to $f^A_{\max}$. The situation is depicted in Fig. 3.7.

Note however that the situation is different if we consider the problem $1|IN|\sum C^A_j, f^B_{\max}$. In this case, INTERFERING reduces to BICRITERIA (see Fig. 3.8).

### *3.3.1 Epsilon-Constraint Approach*

Let us consider the problem $1|ND, f^B_{\max} \le Q|\sum C^A_j$. In the literature, some efficient algorithms have been given for the BICRITERIA scenario (see Hoogeveen and van de Velde 1995) and the COMPETING scenario (see Agnetis et al. 2004). We present

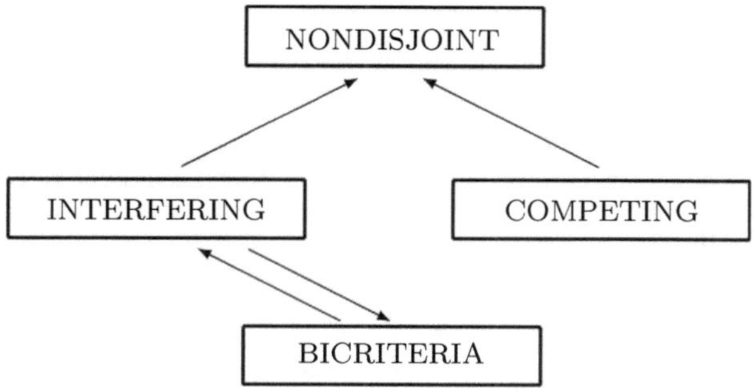


**Fig. 3.8** Reduction graph for $1|IN|\sum C_j^A, f_{\max}^B$

here an algorithm that generalizes both of them to solve the NONDISJOINT case, maintaining the same complexity.

As usual, $P = \sum_{J_j \in \mathcal{J}} p_j$ is the total processing time of all jobs. Similar to what done in Sect. 3.1, let us define a *deadline* $\tilde{d}_j$ for each job $J_j \in \mathcal{J}^B$ so that $f_j^B(C_j) \leq Q$ for $C_j \leq \tilde{d}_j$ and $f_j^B(C_j) > Q$ for $C_j > \tilde{d}_j$. As usual, in the following we suppose that each deadline $\tilde{d}_j$ can be computed in constant time, i.e., that an inverse function is available for each $f_j^B(\cdot)$. If this is not the case, then to determine $\tilde{d}_j$ one must perform a binary search, which may require $O(\log P)$ evaluations of each $f_j^B(\cdot)$.

In order to solve problem $1|f_{\max}^B \leq Q|\sum C_j^A$, we can still adopt a similar reasoning to Lawler's algorithm (Algorithm 5), as follows. We build the schedule from right to left. At the $k$-th iteration, we decide which is the $k$-th last job to be scheduled. Let $t$ denote the total processing time of unscheduled jobs, i.e., the completion time of the next job to be scheduled. The candidates are all jobs in $\bar{\mathcal{J}}^A$ (i.e., jobs that do not have a deadline) and the jobs in $\mathcal{J}^B$ that can complete at $t$ without violating the deadline, i.e., such that $t \leq \tilde{d}_j$.

From the viewpoint of agent $A$, the best candidate is a job from $\bar{\mathcal{J}}^B$. Only if there are no candidates in $\bar{\mathcal{J}}^B$ that can feasibly complete at $t$, we must select the longest job from $\mathcal{J}^A$ that can be feasibly scheduled to complete at $t$. The algorithm proceeds in this way until either all jobs are scheduled, or an infeasibility is detected (because the constraint on $f_{\max}^B$ is too strict).

The procedure is detailed in Algorithm 11, in which we indicate by $L_B$ the set of the jobs in $\bar{\mathcal{J}}^B$ that can be scheduled to complete at the current time $t$, i.e., $L_B = \{J_j \in \bar{\mathcal{J}}^B : t \leq \tilde{d}_j\}$, while $L_A \subseteq \mathcal{J}^A$ is the set of jobs belonging to agent $A$ that can be feasibly scheduled at time $t$, i.e., $L_A = \bar{\mathcal{J}}^A \cup \{J_j \in \mathcal{J}^A \cap \mathcal{J}^B : t \leq \tilde{d}_j\}$.

Algorithm 11 computes the optimal solution in time $O(n \log n)$. In fact, the complexity of the algorithm is dominated by the phase in which the jobs in $\mathcal{J}^A$ are sorted in SPT order and the jobs in $\mathcal{J}^B$ and sorted by nondecreasing deadlines (which we assume can be computed in constant time). Thereafter, at each step the last jobs from the two lists are considered to determine the next job to be scheduled. This is because at the lines 5 and 8 of the algorithm, ties are broken arbitrarily.

**Algorithm 11** for problem $1|ND, f^B_{\max} \leq Q|\sum C^A_j$

1: $L_A := \bar{\mathcal{J}}^A \cup \{J_j \in \mathcal{J}^A \cap \mathcal{J}^B : \tilde{d}_j \geq P\}$
2: $L_B := \{J_j \in \bar{\mathcal{J}}^B : \tilde{d}_j \geq P\}$
3: $t := P$
4: **while** $L_A \cup L_B \neq \emptyset$ **do**
5:    **if** $L_B \neq \emptyset$ **then**
6:       Choose as $J_h$ any job in $L_B$
7:       $L_B := L_B \setminus \{J_h\}$
8:    **else**
9:       Choose as $J_h$ any job such that $p_h = \max\{p_j : J_j \in L_A\}$
10:       $L_A := L_A \setminus \{J_h\}$
11:    **end if**
12:    $C_h(\sigma) := t$
13:    $t := t - p_h$
14:    $L_A := L_A \cup \{J_j \in \mathcal{J}^A \cap \mathcal{J}^B : t \leq \tilde{d}_j < t + p_h\}$
15:    $L_B := L_B \cup \{J_j \in \mathcal{J}^B \setminus \mathcal{J}^A : t \leq \tilde{d}_j < t + p_h\}$
16: **end while**
17: **if** $t > 0$ **then**
18:    **return** 'The problem is infeasible'
19: **else**
20:    **return** values $C_h(\sigma)$
21: **end if**

However, it can be shown that giving a tie-breaking rule for the two above cases, the same algorithm generates a strict Pareto optimal solution. More precisely, at line 5, instead of picking any job in $L_B$, we can decide, in particular, to choose the candidate $J_j \in L_B$ for which $f_j^B(t)$ is minimum. Similarly, at line 8, if there is more than one longest job in $L_A$, we choose one belonging to $\bar{\mathcal{J}}^A$, if any, or else, one from $\mathcal{J}^A \cap \mathcal{J}^B$ for which $f_j^B(t)$ is minimum.

These modifications are shown in Algorithm 12. The only price we have to pay to have a strict Pareto optimal solution is that the overall complexity of the algorithm is now $O(n^2)$, since the selection of the next scheduled job now requires $O(n)$, due to the computation of $f_j^B(t)$. Notice that Algorithm 12, in the BICRITERIA case and when $f^B_{\max} = L^B_{\max}$, is the well-known Van Wassenhove-Gelders algorithm (Van Wassenhove and Gelders 1980).

With minor modifications, Algorithm 11 also solves the $K$-agent problem denoted $1|ND, f^2_{\max} \leq Q_2, f^3_{\max} \leq Q_3, \ldots, f^K_{\max} \leq Q_K|\sum C^1_j$ (with no guarantee of finding a strict Pareto optimal solution) (Agnetis et al. 2007). The only difference is that the role of agent $B$ is now played by the set of agents 2, 3, $\ldots$, $K$. In fact, we can treat all the jobs from $\mathcal{J}^2 \cup \mathcal{J}^3 \cup \ldots \cup \mathcal{J}^K$ as if they belonged to a single agent, and thereafter apply Algorithm 11. The deadline $\tilde{d}_j$ of each job $J_j \in \mathcal{J}^2 \cup \mathcal{J}^3 \cup \ldots \cup \mathcal{J}^K$ can be computed as in (3.2), where $\mathcal{J}^{-1}(J_j)$ is now defined as

$$\mathcal{J}^{-1}(J_j) = \{k : J_j \in \mathcal{J}^k, k \neq 1\}$$

**Algorithm 12** for finding a strict Pareto optimal solution for problem $1|ND|\sum C_j^A, f_{\max}^B$

$L_A := \bar{\mathcal{J}}^A \cup \{J_j \in \mathcal{J}^A \cap \mathcal{J}^B : \tilde{d}_j \geq P\}$
$L_B := \{J_j \in \bar{\mathcal{J}}^B : \tilde{d}_j \geq P\}$
$t := P$
**while** $L_A \cup L_B \neq \emptyset$ **do**
  **if** $L_B \neq \emptyset$ **then**
    Choose as $J_h$ any job such that $f_h^B(t) = \min\{f_j^B(t) : J_j \in L_B\}$
    $L_B := L_B \setminus \{J_h\}$
  **else**
    $A := \{J_k : p_k = \max\{p_j : J_j \in L_1\}\}$
    **if** $A \setminus \mathcal{J}^B \neq \emptyset$ **then**
      Choose as $J_h$ any job from $A \setminus \mathcal{J}^B$
    **else**
      Choose as $J_h$ any job such that $f_h^B(t) = \min\{f_j^B(t) : J_j \in A\}$
      $L_A := L_A \setminus \{J_h\}$
    **end if**
    $C_h(\sigma) := t$
    $t := t - p_h$
    $L_B := L_B \cup \{J_j \in \mathcal{J}^B \setminus \mathcal{J}^A : P \leq \tilde{d}_j < t + p_h\}$
    $L_A := L_A \cup \{J_j \in \mathcal{J}^A \cap \mathcal{J}^B : t \leq \tilde{d}_j < t + p_h\}$
  **end if**
**end while**
**if** $t > 0$ **then**
  **return** 'The problem is infeasible'
**else**
  **return** values $C_h(\sigma)$
**end if**

In conclusion, the deadlines of all jobs can be computed in time $O(nK)$ and the overall complexity then becomes $O(nK + n \log n)$.

Wan et al. (2013) consider the preemptive version of the problem when release dates are present, i.e., $1|CO, r_j, pmtn, f_{\max}^B \leq Q|\sum C_j^A$, and show that it is NP-hard.

### 3.3.2 *Computing the Pareto Set*

Let us now consider problem $1|ND|\mathcal{P}(f_{\max}, \sum C_j)$. For simplicity, and with no loss of generality, we slightly modify the instance of $1|ND|\mathcal{P}(f_{\max}, \sum C_j)$, attaching a dummy function $f_j^B = -\infty$ to each job $J_j \in \bar{\mathcal{J}}^A$. In this way, $\mathcal{J}^B \equiv \mathcal{J}$. We follow a similar approach to Hoogeveen and van de Velde (1995) for problem $1|BI|\mathcal{P}(f_{\max}, \sum C_j)$.

As we have seen in the previous section, a strict Pareto optimal solution can be generated by means of Algorithm 12 in $O(n^2)$. To generate the whole Pareto set, one can employ Algorithm 1, which consists in solving instances of $1|ND, f^B_{\max} \leq Q|\sum C^A_j$ for decreasing values of $Q$. Hence, to determine the complexity of problem $1|ND|\mathcal{P}(f_{\max}, \sum C_j)$, we need to investigate the size of the Pareto set.

Note that the interval of values of interest for $Q$ can be found as follows. First, an upper bound $Q^{UB}$ on the largest value of $f^B_{\max}$ in a strict Pareto optimal solution can be obtained by sequencing all jobs in $\mathcal{J}^A$ in SPT order, followed by the jobs in $\bar{\mathcal{J}}^B$ in any order. Hence, we apply Algorithm 12 to $1|f^B_{\max} \leq Q^{UB}|\sum C^A_j$ and obtain a strict Pareto optimal schedule $\sigma^{SPT}$. Note that it is a reference schedule for agent $A$. Similarly, the minimum value $Q^*_B$ of interest for $Q$ can be found by solving an instance of the single-agent problem $1||f_{\max}$, including all jobs. The corresponding schedule $\sigma^*_B$ is a reference schedule for agent $B$.

Given any schedule $\sigma$, we can associate with any two jobs $J_i$ and $J_j$, an indicator function $\delta_{ij}(\sigma)$ defined as follows:

$$\delta_{ij}(\sigma) = \begin{cases} 1 & \text{if } J_i \in \mathcal{J}^A \text{ precedes } J_j \in \mathcal{J}^A \text{ and } p_i > p_j \\ 1 & \text{if } J_i \in \bar{\mathcal{J}}^B \text{ precedes } J_j \in \mathcal{J}^A \\ 0 & \text{otherwise} \end{cases} \tag{3.8}$$

and we also define

$$\Delta(\sigma) = \sum_{J_i, J_j \in \mathcal{J}} \delta_{ij}(\sigma)$$

Notice that whenever $\delta_{ij}(\sigma) = 1$, jobs $J_i$ and $J_j$ are sequenced in $\sigma$ in reverse order than in $\sigma^{SPT}$. Therefore, we can view $\Delta(\sigma)$ as a "measure" of the distance between schedules $\sigma$ and $\sigma^{SPT}$. More formally, we want to show that $\Delta(\sigma)$ is strictly decreasing as we move across Pareto optimal schedules, going from $\sigma^*_B$ to $\sigma^{SPT}$.

Let us introduce an operation that transforms a schedule into another.

**Definition 3.1.** Operation $move(i, j)$ transforms a schedule $\pi$ in which $J_i$ precedes $J_j$ into a schedule $\sigma$ such that:

(a) If $J_i \in \mathcal{J}^A$, $J_j \in \mathcal{J}^A$ and $p_i \geq p_j$, $\sigma$ is obtained by swapping jobs $J_i$ and $J_j$ in $\pi$

(b) If $J_i \in \bar{\mathcal{J}}^B$, $\sigma$ is obtained by postponing $J_i$ immediately after $J_j$ in $\pi$

Notice that the operation $move(i, j)$ is not defined if $J_i, J_j \in \mathcal{J}^A$ but $p_i < p_j$ or if $J_i \in \mathcal{J}^A$ and $J_j \in \bar{\mathcal{J}}^B$. The following lemma holds for any schedule obtained from another schedule by means of a *move* operation.

In what follows, for ease of notation, we write $\sum C^A_j(\sigma)$ to indicate $\sum_{J_j \in \mathcal{J}^A} C_j(\sigma)$.

**Lemma 3.1.** *If $\sigma$ is obtained from $\pi$ performing* move$(i, j)$, *then either*

- $\Delta(\sigma) < \Delta(\pi)$ *and* $\sum C^A_j(\sigma) < \sum C^A_j(\pi)$, *or*
- $\Delta(\sigma) = \Delta(\pi)$ *and* $\sum C^A_j(\sigma) = \sum C^A_j(\pi)$.

*Proof.* Consider a schedule $\pi$ in which $J_i$ precedes $J_j$. We consider separately cases $a$ and $b$ of Definition 3.1.

In case $a$, $J_i \in \mathcal{J}^A$, $J_j \in \mathcal{J}^A$ and $p_i \geq p_j$. In this case, $\delta_{ij}(\pi) = 0$ if $p_i = p_j$, and $\delta_{ij}(\pi) = 1$ if $p_i > p_j$. The operation *move*$(i, j)$ swaps $J_i$ and $J_j$. Therefore, the difference between $\Delta(\pi)$ and $\Delta(\sigma)$ only depends on $J_i$, $J_j$ and the jobs scheduled between them. Notice that $\delta_{ji}(\sigma) = 0$. If $J_t$ is an arbitrary job scheduled between $J_i$ and $J_j$, it follows from the definition of $\delta$ that $\delta_{it}(\pi) + \delta_{tj}(\pi) \geq \delta_{jt}(\sigma) + \delta_{ti}(\sigma)$. Hence $\Delta(\sigma) \leq \Delta(\pi)$, and the equality holds if and only if $p_i = p_j$, in which case $\sum C_j^A(\sigma) = \sum C_j^A(\pi)$.

Let us now consider case $b$, i.e., $J_i \in \bar{\mathcal{J}}^B$. In this case, the operation *move*$(i, j)$ postpones $J_i$ immediately after $J_j$, yielding $\delta_{ji}(\sigma) = 0$ and also, if $J_t$ is an arbitrary job scheduled between $J_i$ and $J_j$ in $\pi$, $\delta_{ti}(\sigma) = 0$ for all $t$. Since the relative ordering of all other jobs is unchanged, $\Delta(\sigma) \leq \Delta(\pi)$. In particular, $\Delta(\sigma) = \Delta(\pi)$ if and only if only jobs from $\bar{\mathcal{J}}^B$ have been involved, i.e., $J_t \in \bar{\mathcal{J}}^B$ for all $t$. However, in this case no job from $\mathcal{J}^A$ has changed its completion time, and therefore $\sum C_j^A(\sigma) = \sum C_j^A(\pi)$. □

We are now in the position of establishing the key result, which relates Pareto optimal schedules to function $\Delta$.

**Theorem 3.8.** *Consider two arbitrary distinct Pareto optimal schedules $\sigma$ and $\pi$. If we have $\sum C_j^A(\sigma) < \sum C_j^A(\pi)$, then $\Delta(\sigma) < \Delta(\pi)$.*

*Proof.* Since $\sigma$ and $\pi$ are strictly Pareto optimal, $f_{\max}^B(\sigma) > f_{\max}^B(\pi)$. We will show that $\sigma$ can be obtained from schedule $\pi$ by a sequence of *move* operations.

Compare the two schedules $\sigma$ and $\pi$, starting from the end. Suppose that the first difference between the schedules occurs at the $k$-th position; $J_i$ occupies the $k$-th position in $\sigma$, whereas job $J_j$ occupies the $k$-th position in $\pi$. We distinguish three subcases.

1. $J_i \in \mathcal{J}^A$, $J_j \in \mathcal{J}^A$. Since $f_{\max}^B(\sigma) \geq f_{\max}^B(\pi)$, when Algorithm 12 is run with $Q = f_{\max}^B(\sigma)$, both jobs $J_i$ and $J_j$ could be feasibly scheduled in $k$-th position. If $J_i$ is preferred to $J_j$ in $\sigma$, it means that $p_i \geq p_j$. We can then apply *move*$(i, j)$ to $\pi$ and obtain a schedule $\pi'$ in which jobs $J_i$ and $J_j$ are swapped. Note that $C_i(\sigma) = C_i(\pi')$, while all other jobs between $J_i$ and $J_j$ in $\pi'$ have decreased their completion time with respect to $\pi$. Hence, $f_{\max}^B(\sigma) \geq f_{\max}^B(\pi')$.
2. $J_i \in \bar{\mathcal{J}}^B$. Applying *move*$(i, j)$ to $\pi$ we obtain a schedule $\pi'$ in which $J_i$ is moved after $J_j$. Note that $C_i(\sigma) = C_i(\pi')$, while all other jobs between $J_i$ and $J_j$ in $\pi'$ have decreased their completion time with respect to $\pi$. Hence, $f_{\max}^B(\sigma) \geq f_{\max}^B(\pi')$.
3. $J_i \in \mathcal{J}^A$, $J_j \in \bar{\mathcal{J}}^B$. This subcase cannot occur. In fact, since $f_{\max}^B(\sigma) \geq f_{\max}^B(\pi)$, it would have been feasible to select $J_j$ to complete at $C_i(\sigma)$ when running Algorithm 12 with $Q = f_{\max}^B(\sigma)$, and hence, $J_j$ would have been selected instead of $J_i$.

In all cases, we obtain a schedule $\pi'$ which is identical to $\sigma$ for the jobs in $k$-th, $k + 1$-th,..., $n$-th position, and such that $f_{\max}^B(\sigma) \geq f_{\max}^B(\pi')$. Moreover, from Lemma 3.1, $\Delta(\pi') \leq \Delta(\pi)$. The above argument can therefore be repeated replacing $\pi$ with $\pi'$, and so on until we reach schedule $\sigma$. Note that going from $\pi$ to $\sigma$, the values of $\Delta$ are nonincreasing, and since $\sum C_j^A(\sigma) < \sum C_j^A(\pi)$, from Lemma 3.1 at least one move operation causes a strict decrease in $\Delta$, and the thesis follows. □

At this point we are in the position of proving a result on the number of Pareto optimal schedules. In fact, from Theorem 3.8 it turns out that two Pareto optimal solutions must have different values of $\Delta$. We only need therefore to compute the maximum value $\Delta(\sigma)$ can attain, given that the minimum value is $\Delta(\sigma^{SPT}) = 0$. It is easy to verify that the maximum value is attained when, in a reference schedule for agent $B$, all jobs in $\bar{\mathcal{J}}^B$ are sequenced first, followed by jobs in $\mathcal{J}^A$ in LPT order. In this case

$$\Delta = n_A \bar{n}_B + \frac{n_A(n_A - 1)}{2} + 1 \qquad (3.9)$$

and hence there are $O(n^2)$ Pareto optimal solutions. In conclusion, the following result holds.

**Theorem 3.9.** *Problem* $1|ND|\mathcal{P}(f_{\max}, \sum C_j)$ *can be solved in* $O(n^4)$.

Hoogeveen and van de Velde (1995) show that the bound is tight, even in the case of BICRITERIA (for which $n_A = n_B = n$ and $\bar{n}_B = 0$).

It is interesting to observe that the discussion done for two agents does *not* trivially extend to the case of $K$ agents. In fact, consider three agents, one holding $\sum C_j$ and the other two $f_{\max}$. The structure of any strict Pareto optimal solution is such that jobs of $\mathcal{J}^A$ are interleaved with blocks of jobs of $\mathcal{J}^B \cup \mathcal{J}_3$. Depending on how are the latter jobs sequenced within each block, we can get various distinct Pareto optimal solutions. So, even for a fixed position of the jobs in $\mathcal{J}^A$, there can be a large number of Pareto optimal solutions.

### 3.3.3 Linear Combination

As a consequence of the results in Sect. 3.3.2, for two agents the linear combination problem $1|ND|\alpha f_{\max} + \beta \sum C_j$ is solvable in $O(n^4)$, since Algorithm 12 runs in $O(n^2)$ and, from (3.9), there are $O(n^2)$ Pareto optimal solutions.

## 3.4 Functions $\sum w_j C_j$, $C_{\max}$

Let us now consider the situation arising when agent $A$ wants to minimize the *weighted* sum of completion times.

We observe that in this problem, $1|ND, C_{\max}^B \leq Q|\sum w_j^A C_j$ can be seen as a special case of $1|IN, C_{\max}^B \leq Q|\sum w_j^A C_j$ in which all jobs in $\bar{\mathcal{J}}^B$ have

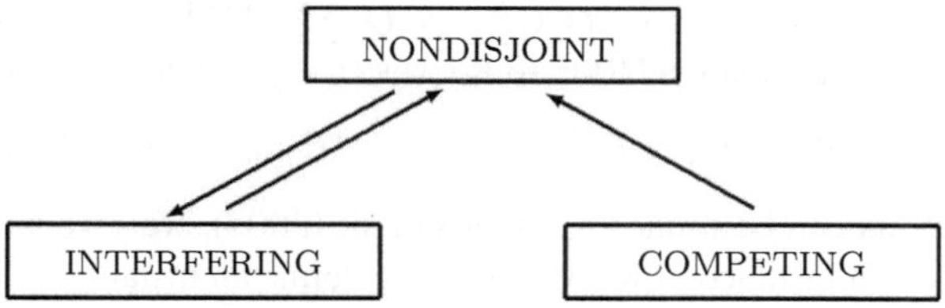


**Fig. 3.9** Reduction graph for $1||\sum w_j C_j, C_{\max}$

$w_j = 0$. (This reduction actually holds, more generally, for $1|IN, f^B_{\max} \le Q|\sum w^A_j C_j$). Obviously, $1|IN, \sum w_j C^B_j \le Q|C^A_{\max}$ reduces to the single-agent problem $1||\sum w_j C_j$, as well as $1|BI, C^B_{\max} \le Q|\sum w_j C^A_j$, so BICRITERIA is not reported in the reduction graph for $1||\sum w_j C_j, C_{\max}$ (Fig. 3.9).

### 3.4.1 *Epsilon-Constraint Approach*

We next address problem $1|CO, C^B_{\max} \le Q|\sum w^A_j C^A_j$, and show that even this special case is NP-hard.

A key result for the unweighted case is that the jobs in $\mathcal{J}^A$ are SPT ordered in any optimal solution (Theorem 3.6). One might think that, similarly, in any optimal solution to $1|CO, C^B_{\max} \le Q|\sum w^A_j C^A_j$, the jobs in $\mathcal{J}^A$ are ordered according to Smith's rule, i.e., by nondecreasing values of the ratios $p^A_j / w^A_j$. Unfortunately, it is easy to show that this is not the case in general. Consider the following example.

*Example 3.4.* Let consider an instance of $1|CO, C^B_{\max} \le Q|\sum w^A_j C^A_j$. Set $\mathcal{J}^A$ contains four jobs $J^A_1, J^A_2, J^A_3, J^A_4$ with processing times and weights below. Set $\mathcal{J}^B$ consists of a single job $J^B_1$ having processing time $p^B_1 = 10$, and let $Q = 20$. The best solution in which the jobs of $\mathcal{J}^A$ are WSPT-ordered is obtained by sequencing the jobs of $\mathcal{J}^A$ by Smith's rule and then inserting $J^2B1$ in the latest feasible position. By doing so, one obtains the sequence $\sigma = \{J^A_1, J^B_1, J^A_2, J^A_3, J^A_4\}$, with $\sum w^A_j C^A_j(\sigma) = 9*6+7*21+4*24+5*28 = 437$. The optimal solution is in turn $\sigma^* = \{J^A_1, J^A_4, J^B_1, J^A_2, J^A_3\}$, with $\sum w^A_j C^A_j(\sigma^*) = 9*6+5*10+7*25+4*28 = 391$. ◇

| $J_j$ | $J^A_1$ | $J^A_2$ | $J^A_3$ | $J^A_4$ | $J^B_1$ |
|---|---|---|---|---|---|
| $p_j$ | 6 | 5 | 3 | 4 | 10 |
| $w^A_j$ | 9 | 7 | 4 | 5 | |

Indeed, we next show that $1|CO, C^B_{\max} \le Q|\sum w^A_j C^A_j$ is binary NP-hard. The reduction uses the well-known NP-hard KNAPSACK problem (see Sect. 2.2.2).

**Theorem 3.10.** *Problem $1|CO, C^B_{\max} \le Q|\sum w^A_j C^A_j$ is binary NP-hard.*

*Proof.* The details can be found in Agnetis et al. (2004), we give here a sketch of the proof. Given an instance of KNAPSACK, we define an instance of $1|CO, C^B_{\max} \le Q|\sum w^A_j C^A_j$ as follows. Agent $A$ has $n$ jobs, having processing times $p^A_i = a_i$ and weights $w^A_i = w_i$, $i = 1, \dots, n$. Agent $B$ has only one *very long* job, having processing time $C = (\sum_{j=1}^n w_j)(\sum_{j=1}^n a_j)$. Also, we set $Q = b + C$. Now, consider a feasible schedule $\sigma$ for $1|CO, C^B_{\max} \le Q|\sum w_j C^A_j$, and let $S$ denote the jobs of $\mathcal{J}^A$ scheduled before $J^B_1$ in $\sigma$. Note that job $J^B_1$ affects the objective function of agent $A$ by the amount

$$\sum_{J_j \in \mathcal{J}^A \setminus S} w_j C$$

Since $C$ is very large, in the optimal solution the total weight of the jobs scheduled after $J^B_1$ is minimum, i.e., the problem consists in maximizing $\sum_{J_j \in S} w_j$. Since such jobs have to be scheduled in the interval $[0, C]$, this is equivalent to solving the original instance of KNAPSACK. □

We next show that $1|ND, C^B_{\max} \le Q|\sum w^A_j C^A_j$ can be solved in pseudo-polynomial time by means of a dynamic programming algorithm. For illustration purposes, we consider *all* jobs in $\mathcal{J}^A$ numbered in WSPT order. Also, we first suppose that $\bar{\mathcal{J}}^B \ne \emptyset$ and later on, we show how to modify the algorithm to account for the case in which $\bar{\mathcal{J}}^B = \emptyset$ (i.e., for the problem $1|IN, C^B_{\max} \le Q|\sum w^A_j C^A_j$).

It is easy to verify that in general the structure of an optimal solution to $1|ND, C^B_{\max} \le Q|\sum w^A_j C^A_j$ consists of three blocks, as follows. The first block contains all jobs in $\mathcal{J}^A \cap \mathcal{J}^B$ plus some jobs from $\bar{\mathcal{J}}^A$, sequenced in WSPT order. The second block is formed by all jobs in $\bar{\mathcal{J}}^B$ (in any order). Finally, the third block contains the remaining jobs from $\bar{\mathcal{J}}^A$, sequenced in WSPT order. Since the jobs in $\bar{\mathcal{J}}^B$ only contribute to $C^B_{\max}$, we can regard them as a single job $J^B_\ell$ of length

$$p^B_\ell = \sum_{J_j \in \bar{\mathcal{J}}^B} p^B_j$$

Note that the completion time of $J^B_\ell$ is $C^B_{\max}$. We adopt a dynamic programming approach described in the following. Let $F(k, t_1, t_2)$ be the optimal value of a subproblem restricted to the first $k$ jobs in $\mathcal{J}^A$ plus job $J^B_\ell$, in which the machine *continuously* works between 0 and $t_1$, it is idle from $t_1$ to $t_2$, and $J^B_\ell$ starts at $t_2$ (Fig. 3.10). Note that this means that each job in $\mathcal{J}^A$ is either processed within 0 and $t_1$, or after $t_2 + p^B_\ell$. In particular, because of the WSPT ordering, in an optimal solution to such restricted problem, either job $J_k \in \mathcal{J}^A$ completes at time $t_1$, or it is

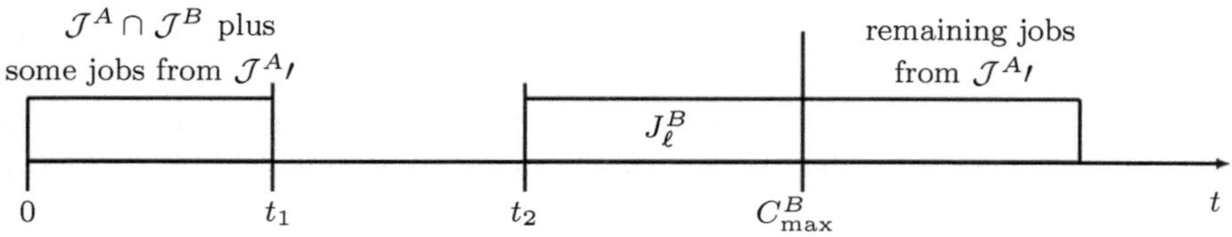


**Fig. 3.10** Illustration of the dynamic programming algorithm for $1|ND, C_{\max}^B \le Q|\sum w_j^A C_j^A$

the last job in the schedule. Clearly, certain boundary conditions must be enforced, namely:

- $F(0, 0, t_2) = 0$
- $F(0, t_1, t_2) = +\infty$ if $t_1 > 0$, since the machine must be working between 0 and $t_1$
- $F(k, t_1, t_2) = +\infty$ if $t_1 < 0$ or $t_1 > t_2$
- $F(k, t_1, t_2) = +\infty$ if $t_2 > Q - p_\ell^B$, since in this case $C_{\max}^B$ would exceed $Q$.

If none of the above boundary conditions hold, the value $F(k, t_1, t_2)$ can be computed by means of a recursive formula. Here we must distinguish two cases, depending on whether (i) $J_k \in \mathcal{J}^A \cap \mathcal{J}^B$ or (ii) $J_k \in \bar{\mathcal{J}}^A$. Let us first consider case (i). $J_k$ can only be scheduled in the first block. Due to WSPT, $J_k$ is the last job of the block, completing at $t_1$, and therefore:

$$F(k, t_1, t_2) = F(k-1, t_1 - p_k^A, t_2) + w_k^A t_1 \tag{3.10}$$

Consider now case (ii). In this case, $J_k$ is scheduled as the last job of either the first or the second block. In the latter case, it completes at time $p_\ell^B + (t_2 - t_1) + \sum_{j=1}^k p_j$, so that:

$$F(k, t_1, t_2) = \min\Big\{F(k-1, t_1 - p_k, t_2) + w_k t_1,$$
$$F(k-1, t_1, t_2) + w_k(p_\ell^B + (t_2 - t_1) + \sum_{j=1}^{k} p_j)\Big\} \tag{3.11}$$

Since the optimal schedule has no idle time, it must be searched among solutions corresponding to values of $F(k, t_1, t_2)$ having $t_1 = t_2$. In conclusion, the optimal value of the total weighted completion time for agent $A$ is

$$\min_{t_1}\{F(n, t_1, t_1)\}$$

So far we assumed $\bar{\mathcal{J}}^B \neq \emptyset$. If $\bar{\mathcal{J}}^B = \emptyset$, we call $J_\ell$ the job in $\mathcal{J}^B$ having smallest ratio $w_j/p_j$ (i.e., the largest index). This job plays the same role that was played by the block $\bar{\mathcal{J}}^B$ in the previous case, and this is why we use the same index $\ell$. In fact, $J_\ell$ is the job scheduled last among the jobs of $\mathcal{J}^B$ in an optimal solution, thus completing at $C_{\max}^B$. However, since now $\bar{\mathcal{J}}^B = \emptyset$, we must pay attention to the fact that $J_\ell$ also contributes to the objective function of agent $A$. Since it starts at $t_2$, its contribution to the objective of agent $A$ is $w_\ell(t_2 + p_\ell)$. In conclusion, when $\bar{\mathcal{J}}^B = \emptyset$, we can apply the same dynamic programming approach (3.10)–(3.11), provided that:

- The job $J_k$ ranges in $\mathcal{J}^A \setminus \{J_\ell\}$,
- $F(0,0,t_2) = w_\ell(t_2 + p_\ell)$.

Let us now turn to complexity issues. Once the jobs in $\mathcal{J}^A$ are ordered, the computation of each value $F(k,t_1,t_2)$ can be done in constant time. Considering that for all $t_1, t_2$ it holds $t_1 \le t_2 \le Q - p_\ell$, we have the following result.

**Theorem 3.11.** *The DP algorithm (3.10)–(3.11) solves problem* $1|ND, C_{\max}^B \le Q|\sum w_j^A C_j^A$ *in* $O(n_A Q^2)$ *time.*

A different exact approach to $1|ND, C_{\max}^B \le Q|\sum w_j^A C_j^A$ exploits the properties of a Lagrangian bound. This is illustrated in the following section.

#### 3.4.1.1 A Lagrangian Bound

In what follows we assume that the problem has a feasible solution (i.e., we assume that $\sum_{J_j \in \mathcal{J}^B} p_j < Q$), and we number the jobs in $\bar{\mathcal{J}}^A$ according to Smith's rule, i.e., for each pair of jobs $J_i^A, J_j^A \in \bar{\mathcal{J}}^A$ such that $i < j$, it holds $p_i^A/w_i^A \le p_j^A/w_j^A$.

Denoting by $\mathcal{S}$ the set of permutations of all jobs in $\mathcal{J}$, we can formulate problem $1|ND, C_{\max}^B \le Q|\sum w_j^A C_j^A$ as follows:

$$\text{Find } z^* = \min_{\sigma} \Big\{ \sum_{J_j \in \mathcal{J}^A} w_j^A C_j(\sigma) \Big\} \tag{3.12}$$

$$\text{subject to } C_{\max}^B(\sigma) \le Q \tag{3.13}$$

$$C_j(\sigma) \le C_{\max}^B(\sigma), \ \forall J_j \in \mathcal{J}^B$$

$$\text{variables } \sigma \in \mathcal{S}$$

Relaxing constraint (3.13) in problem (3.12), we get the Lagrangian problem:

$$L(\lambda) = \min_{\sigma \in \mathcal{S}} \Big\{ \sum_{J_j \in \mathcal{J}^A} w_j^A C_j(\sigma) + \lambda (C_{\max}^B(\sigma) - Q) : \\ C_j(\sigma) \le C_{\max}^B(\sigma), \ J_j \in \mathcal{J}^B \Big\} \tag{3.14}$$

The Lagrangian dual of problem (3.12) is the following:

$$L(\lambda^*) = \max_{\lambda \ge 0} \{L(\lambda)\} \tag{3.15}$$

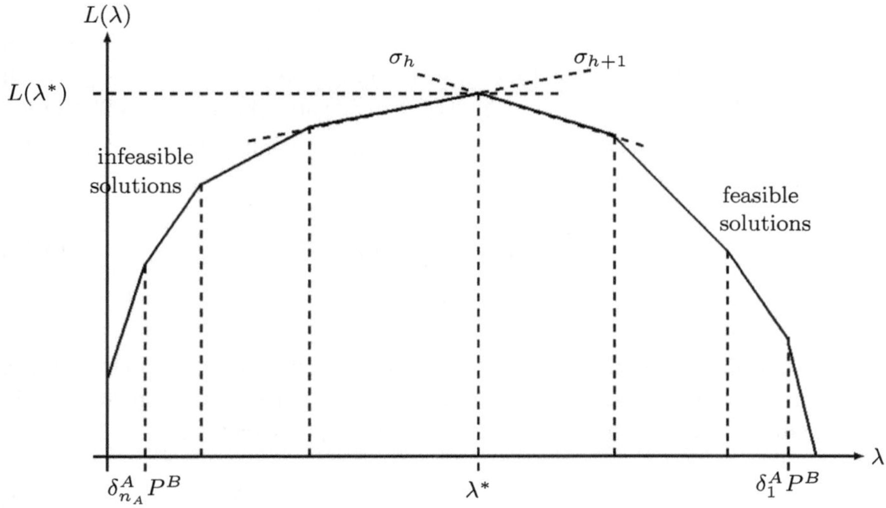


**Fig. 3.11** Lagrangian function $L(\lambda)$

In this section we will see that Problem (3.15) can be solved very efficiently.

As recalled in Sect. 2.6.2, $L(\lambda)$ is a concave piecewise linear function in the variable $\lambda \geq 0$, and the values of $\lambda$ in which the slope of $L(\lambda)$ changes are called breakpoints. Note when $\lambda = 0$, the optimal schedule $\sigma(0)$ to (3.14) is obtained by scheduling all jobs of $\mathcal{J}^A$ in WSPT order, followed by the jobs in $\bar{\mathcal{J}}^B$ in any order. If $L(\lambda)$ is a monotonically nonincreasing function, its maximum is achieved for $\lambda = 0$, which means that the schedule $\sigma(0)$ is feasible, and therefore optimal, for the original problem (in fact, the slope of $L(\lambda)$ implies that $C^B_{\max}(\sigma(0)) \leq Q$). Hence, we rule out this trivial case from further consideration.

In the non-trivial case, the optimal value $\lambda^*$ is obtained at a breakpoint in which the slope of $L(\lambda)$ turns from increasing to non-increasing (see Fig. 3.11). Moreover, for all values of $\lambda$ between two breakpoints, the same schedule $\sigma(\lambda)$ is optimal for the Lagrangian problem (3.14). Therefore, the slope of each segment is given by $(C^B_{\max}(\sigma(\lambda)) - Q)$. In other words, a positive slope corresponds to a solution of the Lagrangian problem (3.14) that is *infeasible* for the original problem (3.12), while a nonpositive slope is corresponds to a *feasible* solution. Notice that in a breakpoint $\bar{\lambda}$, one has two different schedules $\sigma(\bar{\lambda} - \varepsilon)$ and $\sigma(\bar{\lambda} + \varepsilon)$ achieving the same optimal value $L(\bar{\lambda})$ of the Lagrangian problem. Since, for increasing $\lambda$, the quantity $C^B_{\max}(\sigma(\lambda))$ is nonincreasing, the optimal solution $\lambda^*$ of the Lagrangian dual is achieved at a breakpoint in which there are two optimal schedules of the Lagrangian problem (3.14), achieving $L(\lambda^*)$. One of these schedules (the optimal schedule for the Lagrangian problem with $\lambda = \lambda^* - \varepsilon$) is infeasible for (3.12), while the other (the optimal schedule for the Lagrangian problem with $\lambda = \lambda^* + \varepsilon$) is feasible for (3.12). This condition is, in fact, necessary and sufficient for characterizing $\lambda^*$, as we next show.

The Lagrangian problem (3.14) is in the format of the $1|ND|\alpha \sum w_j^A C_j^A + \beta C_{\max}^B$ problem, with $\alpha = 1$ and $\beta = \lambda$. As it will be shown in Sect. 3.4.3, an optimal solution to this problem has the following structure. There is a job $J_h^A \in \bar{\mathcal{J}}^A$ such that first all jobs in $\{J_j^A \in \bar{\mathcal{J}}^A : j \leq h\} \cup (\mathcal{J}^A \cap \mathcal{J}^B)$ are scheduled in WSPT order, then all jobs in $\bar{\mathcal{J}}^B$ (in any order), and finally all the remaining jobs in $\bar{\mathcal{J}}^A$ in WSPT order. Clearly, such schedule is feasible if and only if:

$$\sum_{\substack{J_j^A \in \bar{\mathcal{J}}^A \\ j<h}} p_j + \sum_{J_j \in \mathcal{J}^B} p_j \leq Q \tag{3.16}$$

Recalling that the optimal value $\lambda^*$ for the Lagrangean dual is obtained at a breakpoint in which the slope of $L(\lambda)$ turns from increasing to non-increasing, in order to find $\lambda^*$ one only needs to find the job $J_h^A \in \bar{\mathcal{J}}^A$ such that:

$$\sum_{\substack{J_j^A \in \bar{\mathcal{J}}^A \\ j<h}} p_j + \sum_{J_j \in \mathcal{J}^B} p_j \leq Q < \sum_{\substack{J_j^A \in \bar{\mathcal{J}}^A \\ j \leq h}} p_j + \sum_{J_j \in \mathcal{J}^B} p_j \tag{3.17}$$

Let $\sigma_h$ and $\sigma_h'$ be the two schedules associated with the breakpoint $\lambda^*$. The feasible schedule $\sigma_h'$ is obtained from the infeasible schedule $\sigma_h$ by simply extracting job $J_h^A$ and inserting it immediately after $\mathcal{J}^B$. This way, $C_{\max}^B(\sigma_h') \leq Q$. Since both schedules are optimal for the Lagrangian problem with $\lambda = \lambda^*$, $\lambda^*$ can be simply obtained by solving the equation:

$$\sum_{J_j \in \mathcal{J}^A} w_j^A C_j(\sigma_h) + \lambda^*(C_{\max}^B(\sigma_h) - Q) = \sum_{J_j \in \mathcal{J}^A} w_j^A C_j(\sigma_h') + \lambda^*(C_{\max}^B(\sigma_h') - Q)$$

i.e., observing that $C_{\max}^B(\sigma_h') - C_{\max}^B(\sigma_h) = p_h$,

$$\lambda^* = \frac{\sum_{J_j \in \mathcal{J}^A} w_j^A C_j(\sigma_h') - \sum_{J_j \in \mathcal{J}^A} w_j^A C_j(\sigma_h)}{p_h}$$

Algorithm 13 summarizes the steps necessary for the computation of $\lambda^*$. In Algorithm 13 we assume that problem (3.12) has a feasible solution (i.e., $\sum_{J_j \in \mathcal{J}^B} p_j < Q$) and it is not trivially solvable (i.e., $\sigma(0)$ is infeasible for the original problem (3.12)).

Algorithm 13 can still be used, with minor modifications, even if some jobs of $\bar{\mathcal{J}}^A$ are constrained to precede and some other jobs are constrained to follow the last job in $\mathcal{J}^B$. In Agnetis et al. (2009b), such modified algorithm is used to derive lower bounds at the nodes of the branch-and-bound tree, in an exact approach to the solution of $1|CO, C_{\max}^B \leq Q|\sum w_j^A C_j^A$. In this approach, the branching rule constrains the jobs in $\bar{\mathcal{J}}^A$ to either precede or follow the jobs in $\mathcal{J}^B$ (which, in the COMPETING case, can be treated as a single job).

**Algorithm 13** for the Lagrangean dual of $1|ND|C^B_{\max} \leq Q|\sum w^A_j C_j$

1: $h := \min\{j : J_j \in \bar{\mathcal{J}}^A, \sum_{J_i \in \mathcal{J}^B} p_i + \sum_{\substack{J_i \in \bar{\mathcal{J}}^A \\ i \leq j}} p_i > Q\}$
2: Create schedule $\sigma_h$ by scheduling first all jobs in $\{J_j \in \bar{\mathcal{J}}^A : j \leq h\} \cup (\mathcal{J}^A \cap \mathcal{J}^B)$ in WSPT order, followed by jobs in $\bar{\mathcal{J}}^B$ in any order, and by the remaining jobs in $\bar{\mathcal{J}}^A$ in WSPT order
3: Create schedule $\sigma'_h$ from $\sigma_h$ by moving $J_h$ immediately after the last job in $\mathcal{J}^B$
4: $\lambda^* := \frac{1}{p_h}(\sum_{J_j \in \mathcal{J}^A} w^A_j C_j(\sigma'_h) - \sum_{J_j \in \mathcal{J}^A} w^A_j C_j(\sigma_h))$
5: $L(\lambda^*) := \sum_{J_j \in \mathcal{J}^A} w^A_j C_j(\sigma'_h) + \lambda^*(C^B_{\max}(\sigma'_h) - Q)$
6: **return** $L(\lambda^*)$

### 3.4.2 *Computing the Pareto Set*

Let us now consider the problem of enumerating Pareto optimal solutions. We next show that the number of Pareto optimal solutions is in general not polynomially bounded, even in the COMPETING scenario, problem denoted by $1|CO|\mathcal{P}(\sum w^A_j C^A_j, C^B_{\max})$.

*Example 3.5.* Let consider an instance of $1|CO|\sum w^A_j C^A_j, C^B_{\max}$, in which agent $B$ has a single job $J^B_1$ of unit length, while agent $A$ has $n_A$ jobs. For each job $J_i \in \mathcal{J}^A$ $(i = 1, 2, \ldots, n_A)$, $p^A_i = w^A_i = 2^{i-1}$. We first observe that for every schedule, the quantity

$$C^B_1 + \sum_{i=1}^{n_A} w^A_i C^A_i \qquad (3.18)$$

is constant and does not depend on the schedule. In fact, in (3.18) the completion time of job $J^B_1$ is summed to the other completion times with coefficient 1, which can therefore be regarded as a unit weight. Since $p^B_1 = 1$, we have that $p_j/w_j = 1$ for all jobs, including $J^B_1$, and as a consequence any schedule yields the same value of the sum of (3.18). This value can be computed, for example, by considering the sequence $J^B_1, J^A_1, J^A_2, \ldots, J^A_{n_A}$. In this sequence, the completion time of each job $J^A_i$ is $2^i$, and therefore $C^B_1 + \sum_{i=1}^{n_A} w^A_i C^A_i = 1 + \sum_{i=1}^{n_A} 2^{2i-1}$.

Now, observe that for each integer $x$ from 1 to $2^{n_A}$, there is a subset $S(x)$ of $\mathcal{J}^A$ having total length $x - 1$. Consider the schedule consisting of $S(x)$ followed by $J^2_1$ and thereafter by $\mathcal{J}^A \setminus S(x)$. In this schedule, $C^B_{\max} = x$, and hence $\sum_{i=1}^{n_A} w^A_i C^A_i = 1 + \sum_{i=1}^{n_A} 2^{2i-1} - x$. Clearly, for each $x = 1, \ldots, 2^{n_A}$ we obtain a different Pareto optimal solution. ◇

### 3.4.3 *Linear Combination*

Let us now turn to the linear combination problem. The COMPETING case $1|CO|\alpha \sum w^A_j C^A_j + \beta C^B_{\max}$ is easy. In fact, since all jobs in $\mathcal{J}^B$ are scheduled consecutively in an optimal solution, we can merge them into a single job $J_1^B$ of length $\sum p_j^B$, completing at $C_{\max}^B$. The problem then reduces to an instance of the single-agent problem $1||\sum \tilde{w}_j C_j$ in which $\tilde{w}_j = \alpha w_j^A$ for $J_j \in \mathcal{J}^A$ and $\tilde{w}_j = \beta$ for $J_j = J_1^B$. The complexity is therefore $O(n \log n)$.

We next analyze the INTERFERING case $1|IN|\alpha \sum w_j^A C_j^A + \beta C_{\max}^B$, and then discuss how the approach can be generalized to the NONDISJOINT scenario $1|ND|\alpha \sum w_j^A C_j^A + \beta C_{\max}^B$.

Consider an instance of $1|IN|\alpha \sum w_j^A C_j^A + \beta C_{\max}^B$ (remember that $\mathcal{J}^B \subseteq \mathcal{J}^A$). In what follows, we assume that the jobs in $\mathcal{J}^B$ are numbered in WSPT order from $J_1$ to $J_{n_B}$ and that the jobs in $\bar{\mathcal{J}}^A$ are numbered in WSPT order from $J_{n_B+1}$ to $J_{n_A}$. Observe that $J_{n_B}$ is the last scheduled job from $\mathcal{J}^B$ in an optimal solution, so that its completion time equals $C_{\max}^B$. In what follows we let

$$W_j = \sum_{h=j}^{n_B} w_h^A \tag{3.19}$$

$$P_j = \sum_{h=j}^{n_B} p_h$$

The values $W_j$ and $P_j$ represent the total weight and, respectively, total processing time of the last $(n_B - j + 1)$ jobs of $\mathcal{J}^B$ in the WSPT order.

**Theorem 3.12.** *In an optimal solution $\sigma$ for problem $1|IN|\alpha \sum w_j^A C_j^A + \beta C_{\max}^B$,*

1. *All jobs scheduled up to $J_{n_B}$ (including $J_{n_B}$) are in WSPT order*
2. *All jobs scheduled after $J_{n_B}$ are in WSPT order*
3. *All jobs in $\bar{\mathcal{J}}^A$ are in WSPT order throughout the schedule.*

*Proof.* A simple interchange argument allows to establish points 1 and 2. We next prove point 3.

Given an optimal schedule $\sigma$, let $J_j \in \bar{\mathcal{J}}^A$ be the job following $J_{n_B}$ in $\sigma$. Let $J_k$ be the last job in $\bar{\mathcal{J}}^A$ before $J_{n_B}$. Between $J_k$ and $J_{n_B}$ there are in general other jobs from $\mathcal{J}^B$, all consecutively scheduled. Let $J_f$ be the first such job. Now consider the block of jobs $[J_f, \ldots, J_{n_B}]$ (all belonging to $\mathcal{J}^B$), having total processing time $P_f$ and total weight $W_f$, and let $\sigma'$ be a schedule obtained from $\sigma$ by moving $J_k$ after $J_{n_B}$. Going from $\sigma$ to $\sigma'$, the completion time of $J_k$ increases by $P_f$, while the completion time of each job in the block decreases by $p_k$. The difference between the objective 1values of $\sigma'$ and $\sigma$ is therefore

$$\alpha w_k^A P_f - (\alpha W_f + \beta) p_k$$

Since $\sigma$ is optimal, such difference must be nonnegative, i.e.:

$$\frac{p_k}{\alpha w_k^A} \leq \frac{P_f}{\alpha W_f + \beta} \tag{3.20}$$

Similarly, consider a schedule $\sigma''$ obtained from $\sigma$ by moving $J_j$ before $J_f$. Going from $\sigma$ to $\sigma''$, the completion time of $J_j$ decreases by $P_f$, while the completion time of each job in the block increases by $p_j$. The difference between the two objective values is therefore

$$(\alpha W_f + \beta) p_j - \alpha w_j^A P_f$$

again, since $\sigma$ is optimal, it must hold:

$$\frac{P_f}{\alpha W_f + \beta} \le \frac{p_j}{\alpha w_j^A} \tag{3.21}$$

and hence, from (3.20) and (3.21),

$$\frac{p_k}{\alpha w_k^A} \le \frac{P_f}{\alpha W_f + \beta} \le \frac{p_j}{\alpha w_j^A} \tag{3.22}$$

which shows that also the jobs in $\bar{\mathcal{J}}^A$ are WSPT ordered throughout the whole schedule. □

Theorem 3.12 completely describes the structure of an optimal solution. In fact, all we need to decide is the position of $J_{n_B}$ within the jobs of $\bar{\mathcal{J}}^A$, ordered by WSPT. This allows to solve $1|IN|\alpha \sum w_j^A C_j^A + \beta C_{\max}^B$ by means of the following simple algorithm, in which we let $f(\sigma) = \alpha \sum_{j \in \mathcal{J}^A} w_j^A C_j^A(\sigma) + \beta C_{\max}^B(\sigma)$.

Let $\sigma_0$ be the schedule in which all jobs of $\mathcal{J}^B$ (in WSPT order) precede all jobs of $\bar{\mathcal{J}}^A$ (in WSPT order), and let $\sigma_1$ be the schedule obtained from $\sigma_0$ inserting job $J_{n_B+1}$ between $J_1$ and $J_{n_B}$ according to WSPT. Now let $\sigma_i$ $(i = 2 \ldots \bar{n}_A)$ be the schedule obtained from $\sigma_{i-1}$ inserting job $J_{n_B+i}$ between $J_{n_B+i-1}$ and $J_{n_B}$, according to WSPT. If $J_f$ denotes the job of $\mathcal{J}^B$ that immediately follows $J_{n_B+i}$ in $\sigma_i$, the value of $f(\sigma_i)$ can be computed as:

$$f(\sigma_i) = f(\sigma_{i-1}) + \alpha(W_f p_{n_B+i} - w_{n_B+i}^A P_f) + \beta p_{n_B+1} \tag{3.23}$$

Once all values $f(\sigma_i)$ are computed, one simply needs to pick the best. The procedure is summarized in Algorithm 14, in which $\bar{\mathcal{J}}^A$ and $\mathcal{J}^B$ are supposed WSPT-ordered, and where "|" indicates the concatenation of two subsequences.

**Theorem 3.13.** *Given the WSPT-ordered sets $\bar{\mathcal{J}}^A$ and $\mathcal{J}^B$, Algorithm 14 correctly solves problem $1|ND|\alpha \sum w_j^A C_j^A + \beta C_{\max}^B$ in $O(n)$. If $\bar{\mathcal{J}}^A$ and $\mathcal{J}^B$ are not ordered, the complexity is $O(n \log n)$.*

*Proof.* Theorem 3.12 specifies the structure of an optimal schedule. Schedules $\sigma_0, \sigma_1, \ldots, \sigma_{n'_A}$ are the only schedules having such structure. Since Algorithm 14 selects the best among them, its correctness follows. Note that if $p_{n_B+i}/w_{n_B+i}^A > p_{n_B}/w_{n_B}^A$, schedule $\sigma_i$ (and hence also $\sigma_{i+1}, \ldots, \sigma_{\bar{n}_A}$) is certainly worse than $\sigma_{i-1}$, so one can avoid generating it (line 6 in Algorithm 14).

**Algorithm 14** for problem $1|IN|\alpha \sum_{j \in \mathcal{J}^A} w_j^A C_j^A + \beta C_{\max}^B$

1: $\sigma_X := \mathcal{J}^B$
2: $\sigma_Y := \bar{\mathcal{J}}^A$
3: Compute all values $W_j$, $P_j$ via (3.19)
4: $\sigma_0 := \sigma_X | \sigma_Y$
5: $\sigma^* := \sigma_0$
6: **for** $i = 1$ **to** $\bar{n}_A$ **do**
7:   **if** $p_{n_B+i}/w_i^A \leq p_{n_B}/w_{n_B}^A$ **then**
8:     Remove $J_{n_B+i}$ from $\sigma_Y$
9:     **if** $i = 1$ **then**
10:       Insert $J_{n_B+1}$ between $J_1$ and $J_{n_B}$ in $\sigma_X$, according to WSPT
11:     **else**
12:       Insert $J_{n_B+i}$ between $J_{n_B+i-1}$ and $J_{n_B}$ in $\sigma_X$, according to WSPT
13:     **end if**
14:     Choose as $J_f$ the job in $\mathcal{J}^B$ following $J_{n_B+i}$
15:     $\sigma_i := \sigma_X | \sigma_Y$
16:     $f(\sigma_i) := f(\sigma_{i-1}) + \alpha(W_f p_{n_B+i} - w_{n_B+i}^A P_f) + \beta p_{n_B+i}$
17:     **if** $f(\sigma_i) < f(\sigma^*)$ **then**
18:       $\sigma^* := \sigma_i$
19:     **end if**
20:   **end if**
21: **end for**
22: **return** final schedule

Turning to complexity issues, we observe the following two facts.

- Considering that $W_j = W_{j+1} + w_j^A$ and $P_j = P_{j+1} + p_j$, at line 2 all these values can be computed in $O(n_B)$.
- The main cycle of Algorithm 14 is executed $\bar{n}_A$ times. In order to correctly insert job $J_{n_B+i}$ in $\sigma_X$ (lines 9 and 11), and hence find $J_f$, $\sigma_X$ is scanned starting from $J_{n_B+i-1}$, so that all jobs of $\mathcal{J}^B$ are considered at most once throughout the whole algorithm. Hence, the complexity of the whole cycle is $O(\bar{n}_A + n_B)$.

Considering that, at line 15, each $f(\sigma_i)$ can be computed in constant time through (3.23), and that $\bar{n}_A + n_B = n$, we conclude that, once the two sets $\bar{\mathcal{J}}^A$ and $\mathcal{J}^B$ are WSPT-ordered, the optimal schedule can be found in $O(n)$. Hence, if $\bar{\mathcal{J}}^A$ and $\mathcal{J}^B$ are not ordered, the whole complexity is dominated by the sorting phase, $O(n \log n)$. □

Finally, we observe that $1|ND|\alpha \sum w_j^A C_j^A + \beta C_{\max}^B$ can be easily reduced to $1|IN|\alpha \sum w_j^A C_j^A + \beta C_{\max}^B$. Simply, all the jobs in $\bar{\mathcal{J}}^B$ (which only contribute to $C_{\max}^B$) can be scheduled contiguously, and therefore behave as a *single* job of $\mathcal{J}^B$ of length given by the sum of their processing times, *and weight zero*. Actually, the same approach can be used to solve the $K$-agent case in $O(n \log n)$, in which $H$ agents hold the weighted sum of completion times, and the other $K - H$ the maximum completion time.

### 3.4.4 Approximation

Here we report on some approximation results for $1|ND, C^B_{\max} \le Q|\sum w^A_j C^A_j$. We refer to the basic concepts about approximation introduced in Sect. 2.4.2, more specifically we make use of the type II approximation concept. First of all, we recall that the schedule $\sigma'_h$ produced by Algorithm 13 in Sect. 3.4.1.1 solves the Lagrangean dual and is feasible for $1|ND, C^B_{\max} \le Q|\sum w^A_j C^A_j$. One may therefore question how good is $\sigma'_h$ for the two agents. In what follows, recall that the jobs of $\bar{\mathcal{J}}^A$ are numbered in WSPT order, and $h$ is such that

$$h = \min\{j : J^A_j \in \bar{\mathcal{J}}^A, P_B + \sum_{\substack{J^A_i \in \bar{\mathcal{J}}^A \\ i \le j}} p_i > Q\}$$

Also, we recall that $P_B$ and $\bar{P}_B$ denote the total processing time of the jobs in $\mathcal{J}^B$ and $\bar{\mathcal{J}}^B$ respectively. In particular, the quality of a schedule for agent $k$ can be expressed with respect to a *reference schedule* $\sigma^k$ (Sect. 1.2.1) for that agent. From the viewpoint of agent $B$, since $\sigma'_h$ is feasible, $C^B_{\max}(\sigma'_h) \le Q$, while in the reference schedule $\sigma^B$, obviously $C^B_{\max}(\sigma^B) = P_B$. Hence, letting $\beta_B = Q/P_B$, the schedule is $\beta_B$-approximate for agent $B$.

Let us now consider agent $A$, for which the reference schedule $\sigma^A$ is obtained sequencing all jobs in $\mathcal{J}^A$ in WSPT order. For each job in $\mathcal{J}^A$, we next compare $C_j(\sigma'_h)$ with $C_j(\sigma^A)$. If $J_j \in \mathcal{J}^A \cap \mathcal{J}^B$, $C_j(\sigma'_h) \le C_j(\sigma^A)$, since all jobs preceding $J_j$ in $\sigma'_h$ certainly precede it also in the reference schedule $\sigma^A$ (while viceversa may not be true). Consider now $J_j \in \bar{\mathcal{J}}^A$. If $j < h$, i.e., $C_j(\sigma^A) \le Q - \bar{P}_B$, then its completion time is the same as in the reference schedule, $C_j(\sigma'_h) = C_j(\sigma^A)$. If $j \ge h$, $C_j(\sigma'_h) = C_j(\sigma^A) + \bar{P}_B$. Since, by (3.16),

$$C_j(\sigma^A) > Q - \bar{P}_B$$

one has

$$\frac{C_j(\sigma'_h)}{C_j(\sigma^A)} = 1 + \frac{\bar{P}_B}{C_j(\sigma^A)} < 1 + \frac{\bar{P}_B}{Q - \bar{P}_B} = \frac{Q}{Q - \bar{P}_B}$$

so that, in conclusion, the following result is proved.

**Theorem 3.14.** *The feasible schedule $\sigma'_h$ found by Algorithm 13, that solves the Lagrangean dual of problem $1|ND, C^B_{\max} \le Q|\sum w^A_j C^A_j$, is $(\beta_1, \beta_2)$-approximate, where*

$$\beta_1 = \frac{Q}{Q - \bar{P}_B}$$

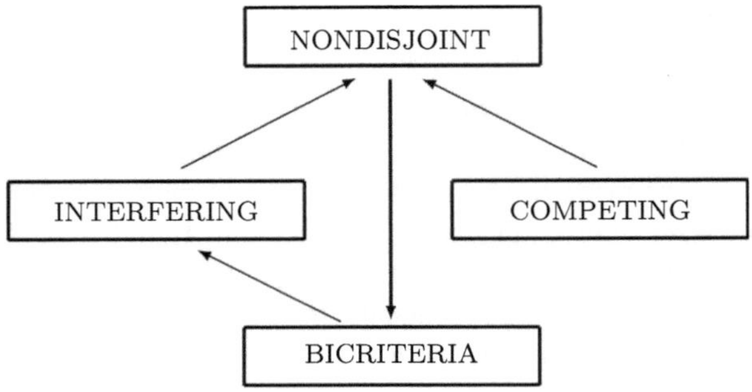


**Fig. 3.12** Reduction graph for $1||\sum w_j C_j, L_{\max}$

*and*

$$\beta_2 = \frac{Q}{P_B}.$$

Finally, another approximation result has been given for the COMPETING case $1|CO, C^B_{\max} \leq Q|\sum w^A_j C^A_j$. For this case, a strongly polynomial FPTAS is provided in Kellerer and Strusevich (2010). It is based on a quadratic knapsack formulation of the problem, and has complexity $O(n^6/\varepsilon^3)$.

## 3.5 Functions $\sum w_j C_j, L_{\max}$

In this case, NONDISJOINT is a special case of BICRITERIA. In fact, if we attach a due date $d_j = +\infty$ to all jobs in $\bar{\mathcal{J}}^A$, one can incorporate them in $\mathcal{J}^B$. Similarly, one can define a weight $w_j = 0$ for all jobs in $\bar{\mathcal{J}}^B$, and hence incorporate them in $\bar{\mathcal{J}}^A$. We therefore obtain the reduction graph in Fig. 3.12.

### *3.5.1 Epsilon-Constraint Approach*

Throughout this section we focus on the COMPETING scenario. We suppose that the jobs in $\mathcal{J}^A$ are numbered according to non-decreasing $p^A_j/w^A_j$ (WSPT order), and jobs in $\mathcal{J}^B$ are numbered according to non-decreasing due dates (EDD order).

Let us consider the problem $1|CO, L^B_{\max} \leq Q|\sum w^A_j C^A_j$. We observe that it strictly generalizes $1|CO, C^B_{\max} \leq Q|\sum w^A_j C^A_j$, since the latter can be seen as a special case of the former in which all jobs belonging to agent $B$ have due date $d^B_j = 0$.

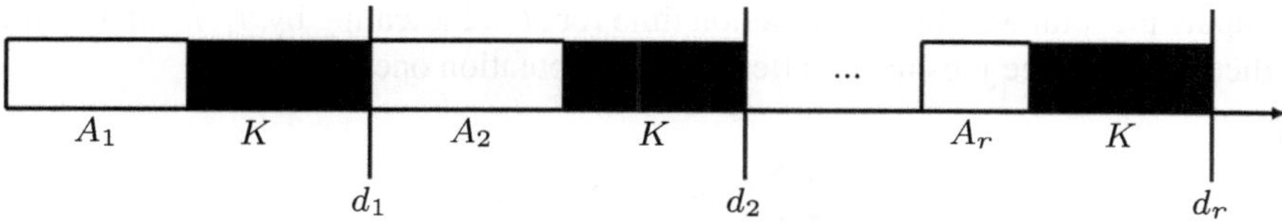


**Fig. 3.13** Schedule in the NP-hardness proof for $1|CO, L^B_{\max} \le Q|\sum w^A_j C^A_j$

While problem $1|CO, C^B_{\max} \le Q|\sum w^A_j C^A_j$ is binary NP-hard, problem $1|CO, L^B_{\max} \le Q|\sum w^A_j C^A_j$ is strongly NP-hard.

As observed in Cheng et al. (2008), this result is a consequence of a result in Lawler (1977). In fact, Lawler showed that problem $1||\sum w_j T_j$ is strongly NP-hard. In the reduction, an instance of $1||\sum w_j T_j$ is defined in which the job set is partitioned into two subsets. The jobs in the first subset have due date equal to zero, and therefore their completion time coincides with their tardiness. The jobs in the second subset have a very large weight, so that, in any feasible solution, none of them is ever tardy. Therefore, the total weighted tardiness indeed equals the total weighted completion time of the first subset so that no job of the second set is late. Identifying the two subsets with $\mathcal{J}^A$ and $\mathcal{J}^B$ respectively, this implies that $1|CO, L^B_{\max} \le Q|\sum w^A_j C^A_j$ is strongly NP-hard.

However, a direct proof of this result is given by Tuong (2009). Such proof will be useful also later on (Theorem 3.17). We make use of the strongly NP-complete problem 3-PARTITION (see Sect. 2.2.2).

**Theorem 3.15.** *Problem* $1|CO, L^B_{\max} \le Q|\sum w^A_j C^A_j$ *is strongly NP-hard.*

*Proof.* Given an instance of 3-PARTITION, we build an instance of problem $1|CO, L^B_{\max} \le Q|\sum w^A_j C^A_j$ as follows. Set $\mathcal{J}^A$ consists of $3r$ jobs, having $p^A_i = w^A_i = a_i$, $i = 1, \ldots, 3r$. Let now $K$ be a very large integer, say $K > E^2$. Set $\mathcal{J}^B$ consists of $r$ jobs, $J^B_1, J^B_2, \ldots, J^B_r$ with $p^B_j = K$ and $d^B_j = j(K + E)$ for $j = 1, \ldots, r$. Moreover, let $Q = 0$. We want to show that the instance of 3-PARTITION has a solution if and only if there is a feasible schedule such that

$$\sum_{j=1}^{3r} w^A_j C^A_j \le \sum_{i=1}^{3r}\sum_{j=1}^{3r} p^A_i p^A_j + KEr(r-1)/2 \tag{3.24}$$

We first illustrate the key idea, and then work out the details. In the instance of $1|CO, L^B_{\max} \le Q|\sum w^A_j C^A_j$, the jobs of $\mathcal{J}^B$ are very long. Therefore, it is convenient to process each of them as close as possible to its due date. This leaves $r$ intervals of length $E$. If and only if it is possible to perfectly fill these intervals with triples of jobs from $\mathcal{J}^A$, then the instance of 3-PARTITION is a yes-instance (see Fig. 3.13).

(Only if.) First observe that if there is a 3-PARTITION, then we can schedule the jobs so that each job in $\mathcal{J}^B$ completes at its due date, and we can schedule the triple of jobs in $\mathcal{J}^A$ corresponding to each set $A_h$ between two jobs of $\mathcal{J}^B$. Let us now compute the total weighted completion time for $\mathcal{J}^A$. Indicating by $h_1, h_2$ and $h_3$ the indices of the three jobs in $A_k$, after some computation one gets:

$$\begin{aligned}\sum_{j=1}^{3r} w_j^A C_j^A &= \sum_{i=1}^{3r}\sum_{j=1}^{3r} p_i^A p_j^A + \sum_{h=1}^{r-1}(hK(p_{h_1}^A + p_{h_2}^A + p_{h_3}^A)) \\ &= \sum_{i=1}^{3r}\sum_{j=1}^{3r} p_i^A p_j^A + KE\sum_{h=1}^{r-1} h \\ &= \sum_{i=1}^{3r}\sum_{j=1}^{3r} p_i^A p_j^A + KEr(r-1)/2 \qquad (3.25)\end{aligned}$$

(If.) Suppose now that a feasible schedule $\sigma$ exists such that (3.24) is satisfied. Let $G_h$ be the set of jobs of $\mathcal{J}^A$ scheduled consecutively between the $(h-1)$-th and the $h$-th job of $\mathcal{J}^B$ in $\sigma$, and let $p(G_h)$ denote their total length. It is easy to see that the value of the total weighted completion time for agent $A$ is given by:

$$\sum_{j=1}^{3r} w_j^A C_j^A(\sigma) = \sum_{i=1}^{3r}\sum_{j=1}^{3r} p_i^A p_j^A + \sum_{h=1}^{r}(h-1)Kp(G_h) \qquad (3.26)$$

where $p(G_1) + p(G_2) + \ldots + p(G_r) = rE$. Moreover, due to the constraint on maximum lateness, and recalling that $d_h^B = h(E+K)$, the total length of the jobs from $\mathcal{J}^A$ scheduled before $d_h^B$ cannot exceed $hE$.

Now, in order to obtain a lower bound on $\sum_{j=1}^{3r} w_j^A C_j^A(\sigma)$, we can therefore find $r$ values for $p(G_h)$, $h = 1, \ldots, r$ that minimize the function $\sum_{h=1}^{r}(h-1)p(G_h)$, subject to the constraints

$$\begin{aligned}&p(G_1) \le E \\ &p(G_1) + p(G_2) \le 2E \\ &\vdots \\ &p(G_1) + p(G_2) + \ldots + p(G_h) \le hE \\ &\vdots \\ &p(G_1) + p(G_2) + \ldots + p(G_{r-1}) \le (r-1)E \\ &p(G_1) + p(G_2) + \ldots + p(G_{r-1}) + p(G_r) = rE\end{aligned}$$

it is easy to check that the minimizer is $p(G_h) = E$, $h = 1, \ldots, r$, so that we get the lower bound

$$\sum_{j=1}^{3r} w_j^A C_j^A(\sigma) \ge \sum_{i=1}^{3r}\sum_{j=1}^{3r} p_i^A p_j^A + KEr(r-1)/2 \qquad (3.27)$$

hence, from (3.24), $\sigma$ satisfies (3.24) at equality. But this can only occur if $p(G_h) = E$ for all $h$, i.e., if the instance of 3-PARTITION is a yes-instance. □

As a consequence of this result, in view of the reduction graph in Fig. 3.12, all problems are strongly NP-hard, and one is led to consider effective solution approaches. As we have already seen for $1|ND, C_{\max}^B \leq Q|\sum w_j^A C_j^A$, also in this case a viable approach is to pursue lower bounds by means of a Lagrangian relaxation of the problem. It turns out that even in this case the Lagrangian dual can be solved very efficiently, and the quality of the bound is sufficient to solve instances of the problem of reasonable size. We next illustrate this approach for COMPETING. Details can be found in Agnetis et al. (2009b).

#### 3.5.1.1 The Lagrangian Approach for $1|CO, L_{\max}^B \leq Q|\sum w_j^A C_j^A$

To start with, let us perform a "shaving" of the due dates of the jobs in $\mathcal{J}^B$. Let $\bar{d}_{n_B} = d_{n_B}^2$ and recursively, for $j = (n_B - 1), \ldots 1$, let $\bar{d}_j = \min\{d_j^2, \bar{d}_{j+1} - p_{j+1}^2\}$. For each job in $\mathcal{J}^B$ we define a *shifted due date* $Q_j = \bar{d}_j + Q$, for which the following holds

$$Q_j \leq Q_{j+1} - p_{j+1}^2 \qquad j = 1, \ldots, n_B - 1 \tag{3.28}$$

With no loss of generality, from now on we regard $Q_j$ as a deadline for job $J_j^B$. Note that, with no loss of generality, we can always assume that the jobs in $\mathcal{J}^B$ are scheduled in EDD order in an optimal solution, and hence formulate problem $1|CO, L_{\max}^B \leq Q|\sum w_j^A C_j^A$ as:

$$\text{Find } z^* = \min_{\sigma} \sum_{j=1}^{n_A} w_j^A C_j^A(\sigma) \tag{3.29}$$

$$\begin{aligned} \text{subject to } C_1^B(\sigma) &\leq Q_1 \\ C_2^B(\sigma) &\leq Q_2 \\ &\vdots \\ C_{n_B}^B(\sigma) &\leq Q_{n_B} \end{aligned}$$

Relaxing the $n_B$ constraints on the completion times of the jobs in $\mathcal{J}^B$ in (3.29), we get the *Lagrangian problem*:

$$L(\lambda) = \min_{\sigma} \left\{ \sum_{i=1}^{n_A} w_i^A C_i^A(\sigma) + \sum_{j=1}^{n_B} \lambda_j (C_j^B(\sigma) - Q_j) \right\} \tag{3.30}$$

and the corresponding *Lagrangian dual*:

$$\bar{L}(\lambda^*) = \max_{\lambda \geq 0} \left\{ \min_{\sigma} \left\{ \sum_{i=1}^{n_A} w_i^A C_i^A(\sigma) + \sum_{j=1}^{n_B} \lambda_j (C_j^B(\sigma) - Q_j) \right\} \right\} \tag{3.31}$$

A key role is played by the ratios between the weight of a job in (3.30) and its processing time (Smith's ratio). Notice that for jobs in $\mathcal{J}^A$ such ratio is given by:

$$\delta_i^A = w_i^A / p_i^A$$

and is therefore part of problem input. For jobs in $\mathcal{J}^B$,

$$\delta_j^B = \lambda_j / p_j^B$$

and it therefore depends on the vector of Lagrangian multipliers. We denote with $\delta^A$, $\delta^B$ and $\delta$ the vectors $(\delta_1^A, \ldots, \delta_{n_A}^A)$, $(\delta_1^B, \ldots, \delta_{n_B}^B)$ and $(\delta_1^A, \ldots, \delta_{n_A}^A, \delta_1^B, \ldots, \delta_{n_B}^B)$ respectively. We can rewrite the Lagrangian problem (3.31) as:

$$L(\delta^B) = \min_{\sigma \in \mathcal{S}} \left\{ \sum_{i=1}^{n_A} \delta_i^A p_i^A C_i^A(\sigma) + \sum_{j=1}^{n_B} \delta_j^B p_j^B (C_j^B(\sigma) - Q_j) \right\} \tag{3.32}$$

Note that in (3.32) only the $\delta_j^B$ are variables, whereas the $\delta_i^A$ are given. The dual problem (3.31) becomes

$$L(\delta^{B^*}) = \max_{\delta^B \geq 0} \{L(\delta^B)\} \tag{3.33}$$

#### 3.5.1.2 The Algorithm for the Lagrangian Dual

For convenience of exposition, we introduce a (long) dummy job, $J_{n_A+1}^A$, such that $p_{n_A+1}^A = Q_{n_B}$ and $w_{n_A+1}^A = 0$. Clearly, such job will be always scheduled last in an optimal solution to (3.29) and (3.32). We next consider the *Lagrangian Dual Algorithm* (*LDA*) for (3.33).

The algorithm is fairly simple. The schedule is built from left to right. At each step, either a job $J_i^A \in \mathcal{J}^A$ or a job $J_j^B \in \mathcal{J}^B$ is scheduled. In the latter case, a value is assigned to $\delta_j^B$. In particular, the algorithm considers the current makespan $T$ augmented by $p_i^A$, where $J_i^A$ is the first unscheduled job from $\mathcal{J}^A$, and the latest start time for the first unscheduled job $J_j^B$ from $\mathcal{J}^B$, i.e., $Q_j - p_j^B$. If such latest start time falls between $T$ and $T + p_i^A$, then $J_j^B$ is scheduled, and receives the value $\delta_i^A$. Otherwise, $J_i^A$ is scheduled. This goes on until all jobs are scheduled, as reported in Algorithm 15.

We denote with $\sigma_{LDA}^*$ and $\delta_{LDA}^B$ the schedule and, respectively, the values of the Smith's ratios of jobs in $\mathcal{J}^B$ produced by LDA. We also denote with $\mathcal{J}_i^B$ the set of the jobs in $\mathcal{J}^B$ whose $\delta_j^B$ is set equal to $\delta_i^A$, and call *cluster* $\mathcal{J}_i$ the set

**Algorithm 15** (LDA) for the Lagrangian dual of $1|CO, L^B_{\max} \leq Q|\sum w^A_i C^A_i$

$i := 1$
$j := 1$
$T := 0$
**while** $i \leq n_A + 1$ **do**
    **while** $(T + p^A_i > Q_j - p^B_j)$ **and** $(j \leq n_B)$ **do**
        $\delta^B_j := \delta^A_i$
        Schedule $J^B_j$
        $T := T + p^B_j$
        $j := j + 1$
    **end while**
    Schedule $J^A_i$
    $T := T + p^A_i$
    $i := i + 1$
**end while**
**return** final schedule

$\mathcal{J}^B_i \cup \{J^A_i\}$. Note that the jobs in $\mathcal{J}^B$ belonging to the same cluster are scheduled consecutively, followed by the corresponding job $J^A_i \in \mathcal{J}^A$ at the end of the cluster. In the remainder of this section, we show that LDA optimally solves problem (3.33). To this aim, we first need to establish some preliminary results.

**Proposition 3.2.** *If (3.29) is feasible then, for each* $J^B_j$,

*(a)* $Q_j - C^B_j(\sigma^*_{LDA}) \geq 0$ *and*
*(b)* $Q_j - C^B_j(\sigma^*_{LDA}) < p^A_i$, *where* $\mathcal{J}_i$ *is the cluster* $J^B_j$ *belongs to.*

*Proof.* For the sake of simplicity, in this proof we omit $\sigma^*_{LDA}$ from the completion times notation (so we write $C^B_j$ for $C^B_j(\sigma^*_{LDA})$). We prove the thesis by induction. From the feasibility of (3.29) immediately follows that $Q_1 - p^B_1 \geq 0$. Then $J^B_1$ will be scheduled starting at time $T = \sum_{k=1}^{i-1} p^A_k$, where $i$ is such that $T \leq Q_1 - p^B_1 < T + p^A_i$ ($T = 0$ if $i = 1$). Hence, $C^B_1 = T + p^B_1 \leq Q^B_1$, proving (a) for $j = 1$, and $Q_1 - C^B_1 = Q_1 - T - p^B_1 < p^A_i$, proving (b) for $j = 1$.

Now, suppose that (a) and (b) hold for job $J^B_j$. Note that, after $J^B_j$ has been scheduled, $T$ is set equal to $C^B_j$. Two cases can occur:

(i) $C^B_j + p^A_i > Q_{j+1} - p^B_{j+1}$. In this case $J^B_{j+1}$ is scheduled immediately after the end of $J^B_j$, and

$$\begin{aligned} C^B_{j+1} &= C^B_j + p^B_{j+1} \\ &\leq Q_j + p^B_{j+1} && \text{by the induction hypothesis} \\ &\leq Q_{j+1} && \text{for (3.28)} \end{aligned}$$

proving (a). Moreover, $Q_{j+1} - C^B_{j+1} = Q_{j+1} - C^B_j - p^B_{j+1} < p^A_i$, proving (b). (Note that, in particular, for cluster $\mathcal{J}_{n_A+1}$ this holds because $p^A_{n_A+1} = Q_{n_B}$.)

(ii) $C_j^B + p_i^A \leq Q_{j+1} - p_{j+1}^B$. In this case, after the end of job $J_j^B$, the jobs $J_i^A, \ldots, J_{i'}^A$ will be consecutively scheduled, being $i'$ such that

$$C_j^B + \sum_{k=i}^{i'-1} p_k^A \leq Q_{j+1} - p_{j+1}^B < C_j^B + \sum_{k=i}^{i'} p_k^A$$

Then $J_{j+1}^B$ is scheduled to start at the end of $J_{i'-1}^B$, and so

$$C_{j+1}^B = C_j^B + \sum_{k=i}^{i'-1} p_k^A + p_{j+1}^B \leq Q_{j+1},$$

proving (a). Moreover,

$$Q_{j+1} - C_{j+1}^B = Q_{j+1} - C_j^B - \sum_{k=i}^{i'-1} p_k^A - p_j^B < p_{i'}^A,$$

proving (b) (again, for $\mathcal{J}_{n_A+1}$ this holds because $p_{n_A+1}^A = Q_{n_B}$).

This completes the proof. □

Note that schedule $\sigma_{LDA}^*$ is feasible as a consequence of $(a)$.

The following is a well known general property that holds for all scheduling problems, and can be easily proved by a simple pairwise interchange argument.

**Proposition 3.3.** *Let $\sigma$ be a single-machine schedule of the jobs $\{J_1, \ldots, J_n\}$ with durations $\{p_1, \ldots, p_n\}$, and let $\mathcal{I} \subseteq \{J_1, \ldots, J_n\}$ be a subset of consecutively scheduled jobs. The quantity*

$$\sum_{J_i \in \mathcal{I}} p_i C_i(\sigma) \tag{3.34}$$

*does not depend on the ordering of the jobs in $\mathcal{I}$.*

**Lemma 3.2.** *Given $\sigma_{LDA}^*$ and any cluster $\mathcal{J}_i$, let $\tilde{\sigma}$ be any schedule obtained from $\sigma_{LDA}^*$ by arbitrarily reordering the jobs within cluster $\mathcal{J}_i$. Also, denote with $J_{\pi_1}^B, \ldots, J_{\pi_{\ell-1}}^B, J_{\pi_\ell}^A, J_{\pi_{\ell+1}}^B, \ldots, J_{\pi_{|\mathcal{J}_i|}}^B$ the jobs of $\mathcal{J}_i$, ordered according to their position in the schedule $\tilde{\sigma}$. Then*

$$\sum_{k=1}^{h} p_{\pi_k}^B (C_{\pi_k}^B(\tilde{\sigma}) - Q_{\pi_k}) \leq 0 \qquad \forall h = 1, \ldots, \ell - 1 \tag{3.35}$$

$$\sum_{k=h}^{|\mathcal{J}_i|} p_{\pi_k}^B (C_{\pi_k}^B(\tilde{\sigma}) - Q_{\pi_k}) > 0 \qquad \forall h = \ell + 1, \ldots, |\mathcal{J}_i| \tag{3.36}$$

*Proof.* Let $\bar{\sigma}$ be the schedule obtained reordering the jobs of $\sigma^*_{LDA}$ within cluster $\mathcal{J}_i$ as follows: schedule in EDD order the jobs $J^B_{\pi_1}, \ldots, J^B_{\pi_{\ell-1}}$, then schedule $J^A_i$, then schedule in EDD order the jobs $J^B_{\pi_{\ell+1}}, \ldots, J^B_{\pi_{|\mathcal{J}_i|}}$. Note that $C^B_{\pi_k}(\bar{\sigma}) \le C^B_{\pi_k}(\sigma^*_{LDA})$ for any $k < \ell$. Then, from Proposition 3.2(a), it follows that $C^B_{\pi_k}(\bar{\sigma}) - Q_{\pi_k} \le C^B_{\pi_k}(\sigma^*_{LDA}) - Q_{\pi_k} \le 0$ for any $k < \ell$. Symmetrically, $C^B_{\pi_k}(\bar{\sigma}) \ge C^B_{\pi_k}(\sigma^*_{LDA}) + p^A_i$ for any $k > \ell$, and from Proposition 3.2(b) it follows that $C^B_{\pi_k}(\bar{\sigma}) - Q_{\pi_k} \ge C^B_{\pi_k}(\sigma^*_{LDA}) - Q_{\pi_k} + p^A_i > 0$ for any $k > \ell$. Hence, for schedule $\bar{\sigma}$ it holds

$$\sum_{k=1}^{h} p^B_{\pi_k}(C^B_{\pi_k}(\bar{\sigma}) - Q_{\pi_k}) \le 0 \qquad \forall h = 1, \ldots, \ell - 1 \tag{3.37}$$

$$\sum_{k=h}^{|\mathcal{J}_i|} p^B_{\pi_k}(C^B_{\pi_k}(\bar{\sigma}) - Q_{\pi_k}) > 0 \qquad \forall h = \ell + 1, \ldots, |\mathcal{J}_i| \tag{3.38}$$

Any schedule $\tilde{\sigma}$ differs from $\bar{\sigma}$ only in the order of the jobs of $\mathcal{J}^B$ within the two blocks, before and after $J^A_i$ respectively. Then, in view of Proposition 3.3, the thesis holds. □

We are now in the position of proving the correctness of Algorithm LDA.

**Theorem 3.16.** *Algorithm LDA correctly solves the Lagrangian dual problem (3.33) in $O(n)$.*

*Proof.* We first show that the vector $\delta^2_{LDA}$ of Smith's ratios produced by the algorithm LDA is optimal for (3.33). Due to the concavity of $L(\delta^B)$ (Sect. 2.6.2), it is sufficient to prove that $\delta^B_{LDA}$ is locally optimal. To this aim, let us consider an arbitrary perturbed vector $\delta^B_{LDA} + \varepsilon\Delta$, where $\Delta$ is an arbitrary real vector with $n_B$ components and $\varepsilon > 0$ is small enough to preserve relative ordering, i.e., if $\delta^B_h > \delta^B_k$, then $\delta^B_h + \varepsilon\Delta_h > \delta^B_k + \varepsilon\Delta_k$. By resequencing all jobs by the Smith's rule, we obtain an optimal schedule $\tilde{\sigma}$ for the Lagrangian problem (3.32) in which the jobs that belong to the same cluster in $\sigma^*_{LDA}$ are still sequenced consecutively (in nonincreasing order of $\Delta_j$). The value of the perturbed Lagrangian function can be expressed as a summation over all clusters:

$$L(\delta^B_{LDA} + \varepsilon\Delta) = \sum_{i=1}^{n_A}\left(\delta^A_i p^A_i C^A_i(\tilde{\sigma}) + \sum_{J^B_j \in \mathcal{J}^B_i}\left(\delta^B_j + \varepsilon\Delta_j\right) p^B_j (C^B_j(\tilde{\sigma}) - Q_j)\right)$$

$$= \underbrace{\sum_{i=1}^{n_A} \delta^A_i \left(p^A_i C^A_i(\tilde{\sigma}) + \sum_{J^B_j \in \mathcal{J}^B_i} p^B_j (C^B_j(\tilde{\sigma}) - Q_j)\right)}_{\#1}$$

$$+ \underbrace{\varepsilon \sum_{i=1}^{n_A}\left(\sum_{J^B_j \in \mathcal{J}^B_i} \Delta_j p^B_j (C^B_j(\tilde{\sigma}) - Q_j)\right)}_{\#2}$$

From Proposition 3.3, it follows that the term #1 is equal to the unperturbed value, $L(\delta^B_{LDA})$. So, the variation of the Lagrangian function is given by the term #2. We next show that all terms in square brackets in the summation #2 are non-positive. Each of such terms can be split into two parts, taking into account the jobs in $\mathcal{J}^B$ for which $\Delta_j > 0$ and $\Delta_j < 0$ respectively. Note that the jobs in $\mathcal{J}^B$ for which $\Delta_j$ is strictly positive are scheduled before $J_i^A$ in $\tilde{\sigma}$ and the jobs in $\mathcal{J}^B$ for which $\Delta_j$ is strictly negative are scheduled after $J_i^A$ in $\tilde{\sigma}$.

$$L(\delta^B_{LDA} + \varepsilon\Delta) - L(\delta^B_{LDA}) = \varepsilon \sum_{i=1}^{n_A} \Bigg( \sum_{\substack{J_j^B \in \mathcal{J}_i^B \\ \Delta_j > 0}} \Delta_j p_j^B (C_j^B(\tilde{\sigma}) - Q_j) + \sum_{\substack{J_j^B \in \mathcal{J}_i^B \\ \Delta_j < 0}} \Delta_j p_j^B (C_j^B(\tilde{\sigma}) - Q_j) \Bigg) \quad (3.39)$$

For any cluster $\mathcal{J}_i$, denote with $J^B_{\pi_1}, \ldots, J^A_{\pi_\ell}, \ldots, J^B_{\pi_{|\mathcal{J}_i|}}$ the jobs belonging to $\mathcal{J}_i$, ordered according to their position in the schedule $\tilde{\sigma}$ (i.e., by nonincreasing values of $\Delta_j$). Letting $\Delta_{\pi_\ell} = 0$ for uniformity of notation, the two summations for $\Delta_j > 0$ and $\Delta_j < 0$ in (3.39) can be respectively rewritten as

$$\sum_{k=1}^{\ell-1} \Delta_{\pi_k} p^B_{\pi_k} (C^B_{\pi_k}(\tilde{\sigma}) - Q_{\pi_k}) = \sum_{h=1}^{\ell-1} \underbrace{(\Delta_{\pi_h} - \Delta_{\pi_{h+1}})}_{\#1} \underbrace{\sum_{k=1}^{h} p^B_{\pi_k} (C^B_{\pi_k}(\tilde{\sigma}) - Q_{\pi_k})}_{\#2} \quad (3.40)$$

$$\sum_{k=\ell+1}^{|\mathcal{J}_i|} \Delta_{\pi_k} p^B_{\pi_k} (C^B_{\pi_k}(\tilde{\sigma}) - Q_{\pi_k}) = \sum_{h=\ell+1}^{|\mathcal{J}_i|} \underbrace{(\Delta_{\pi_h} - \Delta_{\pi_{h-1}})}_{\#1} \underbrace{\sum_{k=h}^{|\mathcal{J}_i|} p^B_{\pi_k} (C^B_{\pi_k}(\tilde{\sigma}) - Q_{\pi_k})}_{\#2} \quad (3.41)$$

Since $\Delta_{\pi_h} \geq \Delta_{\pi_{h+1}}$, all the coefficients #1 in (3.40) are non-negative, and from Lemma 3.2, all the terms #2 in (3.40) are non-positive. Similarly, all the coefficients #1 in (3.41) are non-positive, while from Lemma 3.2 all the terms #2 in (3.41) are strictly positive. Then $L(\delta^B_{LDA} + \varepsilon\Delta) - L(\delta_{LDA})$, being the sum of non-positive terms, is non-positive, which implies that $L(\delta^B_{LDA})$ is a local maximum.

As for the complexity of LDA, we observe that each job is considered exactly once throughout the algorithm. Assuming that the jobs in $\mathcal{J}^A$ have preliminarily been ordered according to WSPT and jobs in $\mathcal{J}^B$ according to EDD, the thesis follows. □

*Example 3.6.* Let consider an instance of $1|CO, L^B_{\max} \le Q|\sum w_i^A C_i^A$, with the following data, in which the values $Q_j$ are shifted due dates.

| $J_j^k$ | $J_1^A$ | $J_2^A$ | $J_3^A$ | $J_1^B$ | $J_2^B$ | $J_3^B$ |
|---|---|---|---|---|---|---|
| $p_j^k$ | 1 | 4 | 3 | 3 | 2 | 2 |
| $w_j^k$ | 4 | 10 | 3 | | | |
| $\delta_j^A$ | 4 | 2.5 | 1 | | | |
| $Q_j$ | | | | 6 | 9 | 13 |

Algorithm LDA schedules $J_1^A$ first, completing at $T = 1$. The latest start time of job $J_1^B$ is $Q_1 - p_1^B = 6 - 3 = 3$, larger than $T$. Then, we schedule the second job from $\mathcal{J}^A$, i.e., $J_2^A$, and $T = 5$. Since $5 > 3$, we assign to $\delta_1^B$ the same Smith's ratio value of the last scheduled job from $\mathcal{J}^A$, i.e., $\delta_1^B = \delta_2^A = 2.5$. Hence, we schedule job $J_1^B$ and update $T$ to 8. Considering now job $J_2^B$, its latest start time is $Q_2 - p_2^B = 9 - 2 = 7$. Again, being it smaller than the current value of $T$, we also set $\delta_2^B = 2.5$, schedule $J_2^B$ and increase $T$ to 10. Now $Q_3 - p_3^B = 11 > 10$, so job $J_3^A$ is scheduled, to complete at 13. Since $13 > 11$, job $J_3^B$ gets $\delta_3^B = \delta_3^A = 1$. In conclusion, an optimal solution of the Lagrangian dual is given by

$$\{J_1^A\}\{J_2^A, J_1^B, J_2^B\}\{J_3^A, J_3^B\}$$

where we highlighted the three clusters. The corresponding value of the bound is 117. In this example, it can be seen that the optimal solution is

$$\{J_1^B, J_2^A, J_2^B, J_1^A, J_3^B, J_3^A\}$$

having value 155. ◇

Note that LDA computes a bound at the root node of the enumeration tree. If a set of branching constraints is added, LDA has to be suitably adapted. In particular, an effective branching strategy in this case consists in fixing the jobs in $\mathcal{J}^A$ from left to right. Details and computational experiments can be found in Agnetis et al. (2009b).

### 3.5.2 Computing the Pareto Set

Since $1|CO, L^B_{\max} \le Q|\sum w_j^A C_j^A$ generalizes $1|CO, C^B_{\max} \le Q|\sum w_j^A C_j^A$, the result in Sect. 3.4.2 applies, so also in this case there can be a nonpolynomial number of Pareto optimal solutions.

### 3.5.3 Linear Combination

Now consider $1|CO|\alpha \sum w_j^A C_j^A + \beta L_{\max}^B$. As stated by Baker and Smith (2003), the problem is strongly NP-hard. In fact, the NP-hardness of this problem can be shown by slightly modifying the construction in the proof of Theorem 3.15.

**Theorem 3.17.** *Problem* $1|CO|\alpha \sum w_j^A C_j^A + \beta L_{\max}^B$ *is strongly NP-hard.*

*Proof.* Given an instance of 3-PARTITION, we build an instance of problem $1|CO|\alpha \sum w_j^A C_j^A + \beta L_{\max}^B$ as in Theorem 3.15, with the only addition of a dummy job $J_{r+1}^B$ to $\mathcal{J}^B$ having $p_{r+1}^B = d_{r+1}^B = 0$. The presence of such job ensures that $L_{\max}^B \geq 0$. Moreover, let $\alpha = 1$ and $\beta$ a sufficiently large number, to ensure that in a yes-instance of $1||\alpha \sum w_j^A C_j^A + \beta L_{\max}^B$, no job from $\mathcal{J}^B$ completes late. With these positions, the same proof of Theorem 3.15 shows that the instance of 3-PARTITION has a solution if and only if there is a feasible schedule such that

$$\alpha \sum_{j=1}^{3r} w_j^A C_j^A + \beta L_{\max}^B \leq \sum_{i=1}^{3r} \sum_{j=1}^{3r} p_i^A p_j^A + KEr(r-1)/2.$$

□

## 3.6 Functions $\sum w_j C_j$, $f_{\max}$

This setting is clearly a generalization of $1||\sum w_j C_j, L_{\max}$, hence the same NP-hardness results hold.

For the linear combination approach, Nong et al. (2011) provide a PTAS for the case in which $f_{\max}^A = \max w_j^A C_j^A$. Actually, their scheme is polynomial only for fixed $n_A$, since it has time complexity which grows exponentially with $n_A$.

Moreover, they give a 2-approximation algorithm for the same problem. This exploits a well-known result by Queyranne (1993) concerning the convex hull $\mathcal{Q}$ of all feasible completion time vectors $\{C_j^A, C_j^B\}$ in a single-machine scheduling problem. In particular, the algorithm consists in minimizing the function $U + \sum_{J_j \in \mathcal{J}^B} w_j^B C_j^B$, over the points of $\mathcal{Q}$ such that $U \geq w_j^A C_j^A$ for all $J_j^A \in \mathcal{J}^A$. This LP can be solved in polynomial time using the ellipsoid algorithm. Let $C_j^{LP}$ denote the value of $C_j$ in the optimal solution of the LP. Nong et al. show that sequencing the jobs by increasing values of $C_j^{LP}$, one obtains a 2-approximate schedule.

## 3.7 Functions $\sum U_j$, $f_{\max}$

Let us now turn to the case in which agent $A$ wants to minimize the total number of tardy jobs, while agent $B$ holds a general max-type objective function.

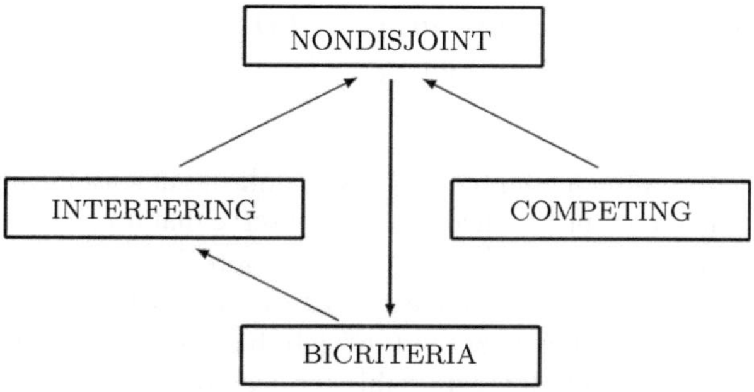


**Fig. 3.14** Reduction graph for $1||\sum U_j, f_{\max}$

As in Sect. 3.5, also in this case NonDisjoint → BiCriteria. In fact, if we attach a due date $d_j = +\infty$ to all jobs in $\bar{\mathcal{J}}^B$ (which only contribute to $f^B_{\max}$), one can incorporate them in $\mathcal{J}^A$. Similarly, one can set $f_j = -\infty$ for $j \in \mathcal{J}^A$ (since these jobs only contribute to the number of tardy jobs), and hence incorporate them in $\bar{\mathcal{J}}^B$. We therefore have the situation of Fig. 3.14.

## *3.7.1 Epsilon-Constraint Approach*

In this section we consider the problem $1|CO, f^B_{\max} \leq Q|\sum U^A_j$. As we will see, this problem can be solved in $O(n \log n)$ by a suitable generalization of Moore's algorithm (Sect. 2.7.1) (Agnetis et al. 2004).

As in Sect. 3.1, we define a *deadline* $\tilde{d}^B_k$ for each job $J^B_k \in \mathcal{J}^B$ such that $f^B_k(C^B_k) \leq Q$ for $C^B_k \leq \tilde{d}^B_k$ and $f^B_k(C^B_k) > Q$ for $C^B_k > \tilde{d}^B_k$. In what follows, we call the *latest start time* (denoted $LS_k$) of job $J^B_k$ the maximum value the starting time of $J^B_k$ can attain in a feasible schedule (i.e., a schedule respecting all deadlines). The values $LS_k$ can be computed as follows. Order the jobs of $\mathcal{J}^B$ in nondecreasing order of deadline. Start from the last job, $J^B_{n_B}$, and schedule such job to start at time $\tilde{d}^B_{n_B} - p^B_{n_B}$. Continue backwards, letting $LS_k := \min\{\tilde{d}^B_k, LS_{k+1}\} - p^B_k$, for all $k = n_B - 1, \ldots, 1$. Clearly, if job $J^B_k$ starts after time $LS_k$, at least one job in $\mathcal{J}^B$ violates its deadline, i.e., $f^B_{\max} > Q$.

Consider now, for each job $J^B_k \in \mathcal{J}^B$, the latest processing interval $[LS_k, \tilde{d}^B_k]$. Let $I = \cup_{k=1}^{n_B}[LS_k, \tilde{d}^B_k]$. Set $I$ consists of a number $\beta \leq n_B$ of intervals, $I_{1,h_1}, I_{h_1,h_2}, \ldots, I_{h_{\beta-1},n_B}$, call them *reserved intervals*. Each reserved interval $I_{u,v}$ ranges from $LS_u$ to $\tilde{d}^B_v$. Note that, by construction, the length $||I_{u,v}||$ of interval $I_{u,v}$ equals $\tilde{d}^B_v - LS_u = \sum_{k=u}^{v} p^B_k$. We say that jobs $J^B_u, J^B_{u+1}, \ldots, J^B_v$ are *associated with* $I_{u,v}$.

Consider now problem $1|CO, pmtn, f^B_{\max} \leq Q|\sum U^A_j$, i.e., the preemptive variant of $1|CO, f^B_{\max} \leq Q|\sum U^A_j$.

**Lemma 3.3.** *Given an optimal solution to* $1|CO, pmtn, f^B_{\max} \le Q|\sum U^A_j$*, there exists an optimal solution to problem* $1|CO, f^B_{\max} \le Q|\sum U^A_j$ *with the same number of late jobs from* $\mathcal{J}^A$.

*Proof.* Clearly, the optimal nonpreemptive schedule has at least the number of tardy jobs of an optimal preemptive schedule. Now observe that if in an optimal schedule $\sigma^*$ for $1|CO, pmtn, f^B_{\max} \le Q|\sum U^A_j$ there is a job $J_i$ (of any agent), ending at $C_i$, which is preempted at least once, we can always schedule the whole $J_i$ in interval $[C_i - p_i, C_i]$, moving other (parts of) jobs backwards, without increasing the completion time of any job. Repeating this for each preempted job, we eventually obtain a nonpreemptive solution having a number of tardy jobs not greater than $\sigma^*$, and the proof follows. □

**Lemma 3.4.** *There exists an optimal solution to the* $1|CO, pmtn, f^B_{\max} \le Q|\sum U^A_j$ *problem in which each job from* $\mathcal{J}^B$ *is nonpreemptively scheduled in the reserved interval it is associated with.*

*Proof.* In an optimal solution to $1|CO, pmtn, f^B_{\max} \le Q|\sum U^A_j$, all the jobs from $\mathcal{J}^B$ associated with an interval $I_{u,v}$ complete within $\tilde{d}^B_v$. Hence, if we move all the pieces of $J^B_u, J^B_{u+1}, \ldots, J^B_v$ to exactly fit the interval $I_{u,v}$, we obtain a solution in which the completion time of no job from $\mathcal{J}^A$ has increased, since we only moved pieces of such jobs backwards. □

Lemma 3.4 allows one to fix the position of the jobs from $\mathcal{J}^B$ in an optimal solution to $1|CO, pmtn, f^B_{\max} \le Q|\sum U^A_j$. The schedule of the jobs from $\mathcal{J}^A$ can then be found by solving an auxiliary instance of the well-known single-agent, nonpreemptive problem $1||\sum U_j$, solvable by Moore's algorithm (see Chap. 2.7.1). Given an instance of $1|CO, pmtn, f^B_{\max} \le Q|\sum U^A_j$, the auxiliary instance includes the jobs from $\mathcal{J}^A$ only, with modified due dates as follows. For each job $J^A_h$, if $d^A_h$ falls outside of any reserved interval, we subtract from $d^A_h$ the total length of all the reserved intervals preceding $d^A_h$, i.e., we define the modified due date $D^A_h$ of job $J^A_h$ as:

$$D^A_h = d^A_h - \sum_{u,v:\tilde{d}^B_v \le d^A_h} ||I_{u,v}|| \tag{3.42}$$

If $d^A_h$ falls within the reserved interval $I_{p,q}$, we do the same, but instead of $d^A_h$ we use the left extreme of $I_{p,q}$:

$$D^A_h = LS_p - \sum_{u,v:\tilde{d}^B_v < d^A_h} ||I_{u,v}|| \tag{3.43}$$

We can now prove the main result of this section.

**Algorithm 16** for problem $1|CO, f^B_{\max} \le Q|\sum U^A_j$

**for** $J^B_k \in \mathcal{J}^B$ **do**
  Compute deadlines $D^B_k$
**end for**
Arrange all jobs in $\mathcal{J}^B$ in non-decreasing order of deadlines $D^B_k$
$LS_{n_B} := \tilde{d}^B_{n_B}$
**for** $k := n_B - 1$ **downto** 1 **do**
  $LS_k := \min\{\tilde{d}^B_k, LS_{k+1}\}$
**end for**
Compute reserved intervals $I_{1,h_1}, I_{h_1,h_2}, \ldots, I_{h_{\beta-1},n_B}$ and associated job sets from $\mathcal{J}^B$
**for** $J^A_h \in J^A$ **do**
  **if** $d^A_h \in I_{p,q}$ for some $p, q$ **then**
    $D^A_h := LS_p - \sum_{u,v:\tilde{d}^B_v \le d^A_h} ||I_{u,v}||$
  **else**
    $D^A_h := d^A_h - \sum_{u,v:\tilde{d}^B_v \le d^A_h} ||I_{u,v}|$
  **end if**
**end for**
Solve an instance of problem $1||\sum U^A_j$ with due dates $D^A_h$
Denote by $\sigma$ the optimal schedule
Insert in $\sigma$ the jobs from $\mathcal{J}^B$ in the corresponding reserved intervals, producing an optimal schedule $\sigma'$ for problem $1|CO, pmtn, f^B_{\max} \le Q|\sum U^A_j$
Consolidate preempted jobs from $\mathcal{J}^A$ by moving the jobs from $\mathcal{J}^B$ backwards, constructing an optimal schedule $\sigma''$ for problem $1|CO, f^B_{\max} \le Q|\sum U^A_j$
**return** $\sigma''$

**Theorem 3.18.** *Problem $1|CO, f^B_{\max} \le Q|\sum U^A_j$ can be solved in $O(n_A \log n_A + n_B \log n_B)$ time.*

*Proof.* Given a schedule $\sigma$ for the auxiliary instance of $1||\sum U^A_j$, it is possible to define a solution $\sigma'$ to $1|CO, pmtn, f^B_{\max} \le Q|\sum U^A_j$ by re-inserting the reserved intervals (with the associated jobs from $\mathcal{J}^B$) in the schedule, one at a time, from the first to the last, every time shifting everything forward. Each reinsertion can possibly preempt one job from $\mathcal{J}^A$. From the definition of the modified due dates in the auxiliary instance, it follows immediately that each job from $\mathcal{J}^A$ is early in $\sigma'$ if and only if it is early in $\sigma$. Hence, from an optimal solution to the auxiliary instance we obtain an optimal solution to $1|CO, pmtn, f^B_{\max} \le Q|\sum U^A_j$. Applying Lemma 3.3, we can obtain an optimal solution to $1|CO, f^B_{\max} \le Q|\sum U^A_j$ by rearranging the jobs from $\mathcal{J}^A$ that had been preempted during the reinsertion phase. Let us now turn to complexity issues. The jobs from $\mathcal{J}^B$ are ordered first; the complexity for this is $O(n_B \log n_B)$. Then, the computation of the reserved intervals takes time $O(n_B)$. The auxiliary instance can be defined in time $O(n_A)$ and solved in time $O(n_A \log n_A)$ by Moore's algorithm. The optimal solution to $1|CO, pmtn, f^B_{\max} \le Q|\sum U^A_j$ can be reconstructed in time $O(n_A + n_B)$. Finally, the optimal solution to $1|CO, f^B_{\max} \le Q|\sum U^A_j$ is obtained in time $O(n_A + n_B)$. The overall complexity is therefore dominated by the ordering steps and the theorem follows. □

The polynomiality result for the two-agent problem $1|CO, f^B_{\max} \le Q|\sum U^A_j$ can be generalized to the case with $K$ agents in which $p$ agents hold an objective function $f_{\max}$ and $K-p$ hold $\sum U_j$ (Agnetis et al. 2007). In fact, the $p$ agents holding $f_{\max}$ are essentially treated as a single agent, since the only relevant information of each job is its deadline. In the wake of Lemma 3.4 and Theorem 3.18, the problem reduces to an instance of a problem with $K-p$ agents, each interested in minimizing the number of tardy jobs. This can be solved by dynamic programming, suitably modifying the algorithm that will be shown in Sect. 3.14.1.1.

On the basis of the above results, the COMPETING case appears indeed significantly easier than the other cases. In fact, we next show that the problem $1|BI, L^B_{\max} \le Q|\sum U^A_j$ is NP-hard, and as a consequence so are also $1|IN, L^B_{\max} \le Q|\sum U^A_j$, $1|IN, \sum U^B_j \le Q|f^A_{\max}$ and $1|ND, L^B_{\max} \le Q|\sum U^A_j$.

A result by Lawler (1982) establishes the (ordinary) NP-hardness of the following single-agent, single-machine problem (denoted by $1|d_j, \tilde{d}_j|\sum U_j$). A set of $n$ jobs is given, each having processing time $p_j$, due date $d_j$ and deadline $\tilde{d}_j$. A schedule is feasible if all deadlines are respected. The problem consists in finding the feasible schedule that minimizes the number of tardy jobs (with respect to due dates). To see why this result implies the NP-hardness of $1|BI, L^B_{\max} \le Q|\sum U^A_j$, just suppose that for each $J_j \in \mathcal{J}$ we let $d^A_j = d_j, d^B_j = \tilde{d}_j$ and $Q = 0$. Finding an optimal solution for $1|d_j, \tilde{d}_j|\sum U_j$ is then equivalent to finding an optimal solution to $1|BI, L^B_{\max} \le 0|\sum U^A_j$.

Notice that in the above observation it is of critical importance to assume that deadlines and due dates are independent of each other. A different problem is when the maximum tardiness of a job is computed with respect to the *same* due date used to compute the number of tardy jobs. In other words, $1|BI, d^A_j = d^B_j, T^B_{\max} \le Q|\sum U^A_j$ consists in minimizing the number of tardy jobs when none of them is allowed to have a tardiness larger than $Q$. The complexity of this problem still stands out as one of the most prominent open issues in theoretical scheduling (Huo et al. 2007a).

In spite of the above results, we note that the complexity of problems $1|IN, C^B_{\max} \le Q|\sum U^A_j$ and $1|ND, C^B_{\max} \le Q|\sum U^A_j$ is still open.

Leung et al. (2010) address the problem in the COMPETING scenario with the addition of release dates and preemption, i.e., $1|CO, r_j, pmtn, f^B_{\max} \le Q|\sum U^A_j$. They provide an algorithm of complexity $O(n^7)$, which exploits an algorithm by Lawler (1990) for the (weighted) single-agent problem $1|r_j, pmtn|\sum w_j U_j$. In the unweighted case, the complexity of Lawler's algorithm is $O(n^5)$. In what follows, we show that also the two-agent problem can be solved in $O(n^5)$, by combining the decomposition approach of Algorithm 16 with the unweighted version of Lawler's algorithm.

Similar to what already done for problem $1|CO, f^B_{\max} \le Q|\sum U^A_j$, for each $J^B_k \in \mathcal{J}^B$ we compute a deadline $\tilde{d}^B_k$ such that, as usual, $f^B_k(C^B_k) \le Q$ for $C^B_k \le \tilde{d}^B_k$ and $f^B_k(C^B_k) > Q$ for $C^B_k > \tilde{d}^B_k$. Next, for the jobs in $\mathcal{J}^B$ we define a set of reserved intervals. These can be computed by reversing the time axis, viewing the deadlines as release dates and scheduling the jobs according to the preemptive earliest-due-date rule (where the earliest due date corresponds indeed to the latest release date). In the reserved interval $I_{p,q}$, the jobs $J_p^B, J_{p+1}^B, \ldots, J_q^B$ are entirely (preemptively) scheduled. We let $S(I_{p,q})$ and $F(I_{p,q})$ denote the start time and finish time of the interval $I_{p,q}$ respectively. When doing so, if a job cannot be entirely scheduled between its release and due date, the instance of $1|CO, f_{\max}^B \le Q|\sum U_j^A$ is infeasible.

Thereafter, the jobs of $\mathcal{J}^A$ are to be scheduled. To this aim, we define an auxiliary instance of the single-agent problem $1|r_j, pmtn|\sum U_j$ in which only the jobs of agent $A$ appear, with suitably defined release and due dates. Precisely, if $r_h^A$ or $d_h^A$ fall outside a reserved interval, similarly to (3.42) we define

$$R_h^A = r_h^A - \sum_{u,v:F(I_{u,v}) \le r_h^A} ||I_{u,v}|| \tag{3.44}$$

$$D_h^A = d_h^A - \sum_{u,v:F(I_{u,v}) \le d_h^A} ||I_{u,v}|| \tag{3.45}$$

whereas, if they fall within reserved interval $I_{p,q}$, similarly to (3.43) we define

$$R_h^A = S(I_{p,q}) - \sum_{u,v:F(I_{u,v}) \le r_h^A} ||I_{u,v}|| \tag{3.46}$$

$$D_h^A = S(I_{p,q}) - \sum_{u,v:F(I_{u,v}) \le d_h^A} ||I_{u,v}|| \tag{3.47}$$

In conclusion, the problem can be solved by Algorithm 17.

### 3.7.2 *Computing the Pareto Set and Linear Combination*

Obviously, if agent $A$ holds $\sum U_j^A$, there are $O(n_A)$ Pareto optimal solutions. Hence, in the COMPETING scenario, in view of Theorem 3.18, problems $1|CO|\mathcal{P}(\sum U_j^A, f_{\max}^B)$ and $1|CO|\alpha \sum U_j^A + \beta f_{\max}^B$ can be solved in polynomial time. In view of view of the observation in Sect. 2.7.3, also the $\varepsilon$-constraint problem $1|CO, f_{\max}^B \le Q|\sum U_j^A$ can be solved in polynomial time and hence the problem of finding a single single Pareto optimal solution, namely $O(n \log n \log UB)$, where $UB$ is an upper bound on $f_{\max}^B$. consequence, $1|CO|\mathcal{P}(\sum U_j^A, f_{\max}^B)$ and $1|CO|\alpha \sum U_j^A + \beta f_{\max}^B$ can both be solved in $O(n_A n \log n \log UB)$ time. However, the complexity of the corresponding problems in INTERFERING and NONDISJOINT scenarios is still open, even for $f_{\max} = C_{\max}$.

Similarly, the complexity of the linear combination problem is open in the $K$-agent case ($K$ fixed), even in the COMPETING scenario, when some agents hold $C_{\max}$ and others $\sum U_j$. However, when the number of agents holding $C_{\max}$

**Algorithm 17** for problem $1|CO, r_j, pmtn, f^B_{\max} \leq Q|\sum U^A_j$

**for** $J^B_k \in \mathcal{J}^B$ **do**
    Compute deadlines $\tilde{d}^B_k$
**end for**
Arrange all jobs in $\mathcal{J}^B$ in non-decreasing order of deadlines $\tilde{d}^B_k$
Compute reserved intervals $I_{1,h_1}, I_{h_1,h_2}, \ldots, I_{h_{\beta-1},n_B}$ and associated job sets from $\mathcal{J}^B$
**for** $J^A_h \in \mathcal{J}^A$ **do**
    **if** $d^A_h \in I_{p,q}$ for some $p, q$ **then**
        $D^A_h := S(I_{p,q}) - \sum_{u,v:F(I_{u,v})\leq d^A_h} ||I_{u,v}||$
    **else**
        $D^A_h := d^A_h - \sum_{u,v:F(I_{u,v})\leq d^A_h} ||I_{u,v}||$
    **end if**
    **if** $r^A_h \in I_{p,q}$ for some $p, q$ **then**
        $R^A_h := S(I_{p,q}) - \sum_{u,v:F(I_{u,v})\leq r^A_h} ||I_{u,v}||$
    **else**
        $R^A_h := r^A_h - \sum_{u,v:F(I_{u,v})\leq r^A_h} ||I_{u,v}||$
    **end if**
**end for**
Solve an instance of problem $1|r_j, pmtn|\sum U^A_j$ with release dates $R^A_h$ and due dates $D^A_h$
Denote by $\sigma$ the obtained optimal schedule
Insert in $\sigma$ the jobs from $\mathcal{J}^B$ in the corresponding reserved intervals, producing an optimal schedule $\sigma'$ for problem $1|CO, r_j, pmtn, f^B_{\max} \leq Q|\sum U^A_j$
**return** $\sigma'$

is not fixed, the problem is strongly NP-hard. In fact, one can easily reduce $1|CO|\alpha \sum w^A_j C^A_j + \beta \sum U^B_j$ (which is shown to be strongly NP-hard in Sect. 3.13.2) to $1|CO|\sum_{k=1}^{K-1} \alpha_k C^k_{\max} + \alpha_K \sum U^K_j$, in which $K = n_A + 1$, there is one agent (holding a single job) for each original job of $J^A$, $\alpha_k = w^A_k$ for $k = 1, \ldots, K-1$ and $\alpha_K = \beta$.

## 3.8 Functions $\sum T_j$, $f_{\max}$

As in the previous section, NONDISJOINT $\rightarrow$ BICRITERIA, setting a very large due date $d_j = \infty$ for all jobs in $\mathcal{J}^B$ and $f_j = -\infty$ for $J_j \in \mathcal{J}^A$ (Fig. 3.15).

### *3.8.1 Epsilon-Constraint Approach*

Note that even the simplest scenario for problem $1|CO, f^B_{\max} \leq Q|\sum T^A_j$ is at least NP-hard, since so is the classical single-agent problem $1||\sum T_j$ (Du and Leung 1990). In fact, a pseudopolynomial pseudopolynomial algorithm can be given for $1|CO, f^B_{\max} \leq Q|\sum T^A_j$ (Leung et al. 2010). Such algorithm exploits the construction presented in Sect. 3.7.1. Also here, for each job $J^B_j \in \mathcal{J}^B$ we compute a deadline $D^B_j$ such that if $C^B_j > D^B_j$, then $F^B_j(C^B_j) > Q$. Hence, we

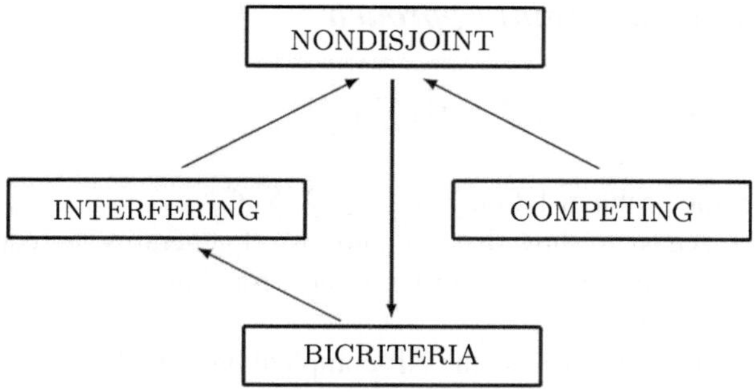


**Fig. 3.15** Reduction graph for $1||\sum T_j^A, f_{\max}^B$

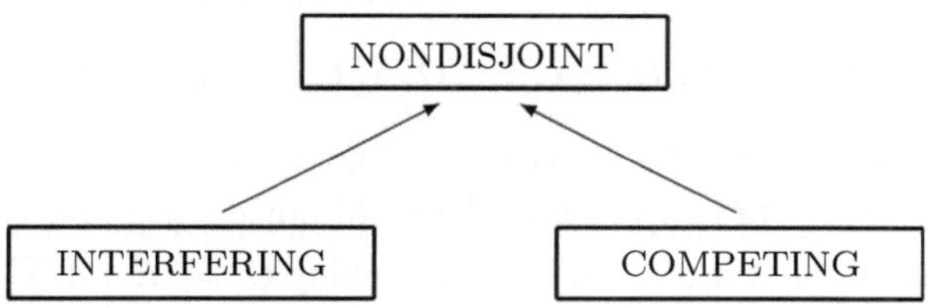


**Fig. 3.16** Reduction graph for $1||\sum C_j, \sum C_j$

can compute a set of reserved intervals for the jobs in $\mathcal{J}^B$. The reserved intervals are used to define an instance of the single-agent problem $1||\sum T_j$ in which only jobs in $\mathcal{J}^A$ appear. In this instance, the due dates of the jobs are modified to account for the reserved intervals, using relations (3.42) and (3.43). By applying the same arguments of Lemma 3.4 (page 104) and Theorem 3.18 (page 104), it can be shown that the optimal solution to this instance of $1||\sum T_j$ allows to derive an optimal solution to the original problem. Hence, in view of algorithm (Lawler 1977) for problem $1||\sum T_j$ (Theorem 2.1 in Sect. 2.7.1), letting $P$ denote the total processing time of all jobs, the following results holds.

**Theorem 3.19.** *Problem* $1|CO, f_{\max}^B \leq Q|\sum T_j^A$ *can be solved in time* $O(n_A^4 P + n_B \log n_B)$.

Notice that the term $O(n_B \log n_B)$ in the complexity is due to the computation of reserved intervals, which only involves jobs of $\mathcal{J}^B$.

## 3.9 Functions $\sum C_j, \sum C_j$

Let us now turn to problems in which both objective functions are of sum-type. The simplest such case is when the two functions are the sum of completion times. In this case, no further reductions hold in general besides those in Fig. 2.8. Since BICRITERIA does not make sense in this case, we get Fig. 3.16.

## 3.9.1 Epsilon-Constraint Approach

### 3.9.1.1 Problem $1|CO, \sum C_j^B \leq Q|\sum C_j^A$

Let us consider the problem $1|CO, \sum C_j^B \leq Q|\sum C_j^A$.

First of all, it is easy to show that, with no loss of generality, we can suppose that both agents order their jobs in SPT order. Hence, for simplicity we number the jobs of each agent accordingly.

In the following proof, we use the NP-complete problem PARTITION (Sect. 2.1). With no loss of generality we assume that the $k$ integers in the instance of PARTITION are all different. For the sake of simplicity, we number the $k$ integers in increasing order, i.e., $a_1 < a_2 < \ldots < a_k$. Remember that $\sum_{j=1}^{k} a_j = E$.

**Theorem 3.20.** *Problem $1|CO, \sum C_j^B \leq Q|\sum C_j^A$ is binary NP-hard.*

*Proof.* Given an instance of PARTITION, define an instance of $1|CO, \sum C_j^B \leq Q|\sum C_j^A$ as follows. The two job sets $\mathcal{J}^A$ and $\mathcal{J}^B$ are identical, and each contains $k$ jobs, having length $p_i = a_i, i = 1, 2, \ldots, k$. Letting $Q = 3E + 2(\sum_{i=1}^{k}(k-i)p_i)$, we want to establish whether there is a schedule $\sigma$ such that $\sum C_j^A(\sigma) \leq Q$ and $\sum C_j^B(\sigma) \leq Q$.

Consider any schedule $\sigma$ in which the jobs are sequenced in SPT order. Such a schedule has the following structure: the two jobs of length $p_1$ are scheduled first, followed by the two jobs of length $p_2$, ..., followed by the two jobs of length $p_k$. Note that there exist exactly $2^k$ SPT schedules, obtained by choosing in all possible ways the agent who has the precedence in a pair of jobs having the same length. Also, note that the sum of the two agents' objective functions, i.e., the quantity $\sum C_j^A + \sum C_j^B$ is the same for all SPT schedules, and it equals $T = 6E + 4\sum_{i=1}^{k}(k-i)p_i$. Note that $Q = T/2$.

Now let us consider the cost of an SPT schedule for each agent. We denote by $J[i]$ the pair of jobs $J_i^A$ and $J_i^B$ (both of length $p_i$). Given an SPT schedule, the notation $A \prec_i B$ means that in this schedule $J_i^A$ precedes $J_i^B$ in $J[i]$. Given an SPT schedule, observe that the contribution to the total completion time of the jobs in $J[1]$ is $p_1$ for one agent and $2p_1$ for the other, the contribution of the jobs in $J[2]$ is $2p_1+p_2$ for one agent and $2p_1+2p_2$ for the other, etc., the contribution of the jobs in $J[h]$ is $2p_1+2p_2+\ldots+2p_{h-1}+p_h$ for one agent and $2p_1+2p_2+\ldots+2p_{h-1}+2p_h$ for the other. Hence, in a given SPT schedule, the contribution of $J[h]$ to $\sum C_j^A$ can be obtained by adding to $2p_1 + 2p_2 + \ldots + 2p_{h-1} + p_h$ either 0 or $p_h$, depending on whether agent $A$ precedes agent $B$ in $J[h]$ or viceversa, for each $h = 1, \ldots, k$. For agent $B$ the opposite holds, i.e., if $B \prec_i A$, then the value $p_h$ is added to the objective function of agent $A$. Given an SPT schedule, let $x(0, p_h) = 0$ if $A \prec_h B$ and $x(0, p_h) = p_h$ if $B \prec_h A$ in the solution, and let $x = \sum_{h=1}^{k} x(0, p_h)$. Hence, in any SPT schedule, the total completion time for agent $A$ is:

$$\begin{aligned} & p_1 + x(0, p_1) \\ & +2p_1 + p_2 + x(0, p_2) \\ & +2p_1 + 2p_2 + p_3 + x(0, p_3) \\ & \vdots \\ & +2p_1 + 2p_2 + \cdots + 2p_{h-1} + p_h + x(0, p_h) \\ & \vdots \\ & +2p_1 + 2p_2 + \cdots + 2p_{k-1} + p_k + x(0, p_k) \\ & = 2E + 2(\sum_{i=1}^{k}(k-i)p_i) + x \end{aligned} \tag{3.48}$$

whereas for agent $B$ the total completion time equals

$$2E + 2(\sum_{i=1}^{k}(k-i)p_i) + (2B - x). \tag{3.49}$$

We next call *feasible* a schedule $\sigma$ such that $\sum C_j^A(\sigma) \leq T/2$ and $\sum C_j^B(\sigma) \leq T/2$. We want to show that a schedule $\sigma$ is feasible, then it is an SPT schedule.

Suppose in fact that a feasible schedule $\sigma'$ exists that is *not* SPT. Then, there must be at least two consecutive jobs in $\sigma'$, say $J_i^A$ and $J_\ell^B$, such that $J_i^A$ precedes $J_\ell^B$ and $p_i > p_\ell$. Now if we swap the two jobs, we obtain a new schedule $\sigma''$ such that $\sum C_j^A(\sigma'') = \sum C_j^A(\sigma') + p_\ell$ and $\sum C_j^B(\sigma'') = \sum C_j^B(\sigma') - p_i$. Since $p_i > p_\ell$, one has $\sum C_j^A(\sigma') + \sum C_j^B(\sigma') > \sum C_j^A(\sigma'') + \sum C_j^B(\sigma'')$, i.e., the *overall* total completion time $\sum C_j^A + \sum C_j^B$ has decreased of the amount $p_i - p_\ell$. So, each job of $\mathcal{J}^B$ following a *longer* job of $\mathcal{J}^A$ can be swapped with it, hence decreasing the overall total completion time of the solution. This can be repeated until no such pair of jobs exists. A symmetrical discussion could be done for each job $J_v^A \in \mathcal{J}^A$ following a longer job $J_u^B \in \mathcal{J}^B$. This time, if we swap them, the agent $A$ gains $p_u$ and the agent $B$ loses $p_v$, and so the overall total completion time of the solution decreases by $p_u - p_v$. By repeatedly applying the above swaps, we eventually find an SPT solution $\sigma''$. However, since the solution we started with, $\sigma'$, was feasible, the overall total completion time of $\sigma''$ cannot exceed $T = 6E + 4\sum_{i=1}^{k}(k-i)p_i$. At each swap, the overall total completion time of the solution actually decreased. However, we ended up with an SPT schedule, whose weight is exactly $6E + 4\sum_{i=1}^{k}(k-i)p_i$, a contradiction. Therefore only SPT schedules can be feasible. For a schedule to be feasible, the total completion time for each agent must be $T/2$. Recalling the expressions (3.48) and (3.49) of the completion times for the two agents in an SPT solution, we observe that a feasible solution may exist if and only if $x = E$, i.e., if and only if there is a solution to the instance of PARTITION. □

#### 3.9.1.2 Problem $1|IN, \sum C_j^B \leq Q|\sum C_j^A$

Now let us consider $1|IN, \sum C_j^B \leq Q|\sum C_j^A$. The following properties can be easily established by a pairwise interchange argument

**Lemma 3.5.** *Given a feasible instance of problem* $1|IN, \sum C_j^B \leq Q|\sum C_j^A$, *there is always an optimal solution such that:*

- *All jobs in* $\bar{\mathcal{J}}^A$ *are ordered in SPT*
- *All jobs in* $\mathcal{J}^B$ *are ordered in SPT*
- *If* $p_i < p_j$, $J_i \in \mathcal{J}^B$ *and* $J_j \in \bar{\mathcal{J}}^A$, *then* $J_i$ *precedes* $J_j$

Note that this lemma does *not* imply that a job in $\bar{\mathcal{J}}^A$ must precede a longer job in $\mathcal{J}^B$. One can deduce the following result (Tuong et al. 2012).

**Theorem 3.21.** *Problem* $1|IN, \sum C_j^B \leq Q|\sum C_j^A$ *is binary NP-hard.*

*Proof.* Let $\mathcal{J}^B \subset \mathcal{J}$. Given an instance of PARTITION, in which we suppose that $a_1 < a_2 < \cdots < a_k$, we define an instance of $1|IN, \sum C_j^B \leq Q|\sum C_j^A$ in a similar way as in Theorem 3.20, but with some relevant differences. Consider the two disjoint job sets $\bar{\mathcal{J}}^A$ and $\mathcal{J}^B$. For each integer $a_i$ in the instance of PARTITION, we define a pair of jobs, namely job $J_{2i-1} \in \bar{\mathcal{J}}^A$ of length $p_{2i-1} = Ma_i$ and $J_{2i} \in \mathcal{J}^B$ of length $p_{2i} = \alpha M a_i$, where $\alpha = 1 + 1/M$, and $M$ is a sufficiently large integer that guarantees that $p_{2i} < p_{2i+1}$ and all processing times are integer. To this aim, one can choose any integer $M$ such that

$$M \geq \max_{i=1}^{k-1} \left\{ \frac{a_i}{a_{i+1} - a_i} \right\}$$

Note that the jobs are numbered in SPT order, and there is a single SPT schedule $J_1, J_2, \ldots, J_{2k}$. Note that the SPT schedule is the best possible schedule for agent $A$. We let $X_A$ and $X_B$ be the costs for the two agents of the SPT sequence:

$$X_A = M \sum_{j=1}^{k} (a_j + a_j(1+\alpha)(2(k-j)+1)) \tag{3.50}$$

$$X_B = M \sum_{j=1}^{k} a_j(1+\alpha)(k-j+1) \tag{3.51}$$

We then address the question of whether there exists a schedule such that the cost to agent $A$ is at most $X_A + (\alpha - 1)ME$ and the cost to agent $B$ is at most $X_B - ME$. We call *feasible* such a schedule if it exists. We next show that a feasible schedule exists if and only if the instance of PARTITION is a yes-instance. We observe that if, in the SPT sequence, we swap jobs $J_{2i-1} \in \bar{\mathcal{J}}^A$ and $J_{2i} \in \mathcal{J}^B$, the cost of agent $B$ reduces by $p_{2i-1} = Ma_i$ while the cost of agent $A$ increases by $p_{2i} - p_{2i-1} = (\alpha - 1)Ma_i$.

Given a yes instance $(A', A \setminus A')$ of PARTITION, we build a schedule as follows. We start from the SPT sequence and, for each $a_i \in A'$, we swap jobs $J_{2i-1} \in \bar{\mathcal{J}}^A$ and $J_{2i} \in \mathcal{J}^B$. The cost for the two agents in the resulting schedule is therefore:

$$\text{agent } A\text{: } X_A + \sum_{a_i \in A'} (\alpha - 1)Ma_i = X_A + (\alpha - 1)ME$$

$$\text{agent } B\text{: } X_B - \sum_{a_i \in A'} Ma_i = X_B - ME.$$

i.e., the obtained schedule is feasible.

Viceversa, consider a feasible schedule $\sigma$. Lemma 3.5 implies that there is a feasible schedule obtained from the SPT schedule by swapping jobs $J_{2i-1}$ and $J_{2i}$ for a subset $\hat{A} \subseteq \{a_1, a_2, \ldots, a_k\}$. Since $\sigma$ is obtained from the SPT sequence by swapping jobs $J_{2i}$ and $J_{2i-1}$ for each $a_i \in \hat{A}$ and the cost for the two agents is:

$$\text{agent } A\text{: } X_A + \sum_{a_i \in \hat{A}} (\alpha - 1)Ma_i \leq X_1 + (\alpha - 1)ME \tag{3.52}$$

$$\text{agent } B\text{: } X_B - \sum_{a_i \in \hat{A}} Ma_i \leq X_2 - ME. \tag{3.53}$$

From (3.52), $\sum_{a_i \in \hat{A}} a_i \leq E$, while from (3.53), $\sum_{a_i \in \hat{A}} a_i \geq E$. Hence $\sum_{a_i \in \hat{A}} a_i = E$ and we can build a solution to PARTITION letting $a_i \in A'$ if and only if $a_i \in \hat{A}$. □

#### 3.9.1.3 Problem $1|ND, \sum C_j^B \leq Q|\sum C_j^A$

In view of these two NP-hardness results, one is led to question whether the problems are weakly or strongly NP-hard. We next show that the most general problem, i.e., $1|ND, \sum C_j^B \leq Q|\sum C_j^A$ can be solved by a pseudopolynomial dynamic-programming algorithm. In what follows we will consider the three disjoint sets $\bar{\mathcal{J}}^A$, $\bar{\mathcal{J}}^B$ and $\mathcal{J}^A \cap \mathcal{J}^B$, and assume that the jobs are numbered in SPT order within each of these three sets. In fact, it is easy to prove (by a simple pairwise interchange argument) that in any optimal solution to problem $1|ND, \sum C_j^B \leq Q|\sum C_j^A$, the jobs are SPT ordered within each set.

We denote by $A(i, j, h)$ the set consisting of the first $i$ jobs of $\bar{\mathcal{J}}^A$, the first $j$ jobs of $\bar{\mathcal{J}}^B$ and the first $h$ jobs of $\mathcal{J}^A \cap \mathcal{J}^B$. Here we denote as $J_t^{AB}$ the $t$-th job of $\mathcal{J}^A \cap \mathcal{J}^B$ and $n_{AB} = |\mathcal{J}^A \cap \mathcal{J}^B|$. Let $P(i, j, h)$ be the sum of the processing times of the jobs in $A(i, j, h)$. Let $F(i, j, h, q)$ denote the value of an optimal solution to the instance of $1|ND, \sum C_j^B \leq q|\sum C_j^A$ in which only jobs from $A(i, j, h)$ are considered, with $q \leq Q$. In an optimal solution to this problem, the last job is either $J_i^A$, $J_j^B$, or $J_h^{AB}$. In the first case, the contribution of the last job to the objective function is given by $P(i, j, h)$, and this must be added to the optimal solution up to that point. In the second case, the completion time of $J_j^B$ is $P(i, j, h)$. In the third case, the completion time of $J_h^{AB}$ is $P(i, j, h)$, and this quantity must be added to the objective function. Therefore we can define the following dynamic programming formula:

$$F(i,j,h,q) = \min\{ \; F(i-1,j,h,q) + P(i,j,h); \quad F(i,j-1,h,q-P(i,j,h)); \quad F(i,j,h-1,q-P(i,j,h)) + P(i,j,h)\} \tag{3.54}$$

Formula (3.54) must be suitably initialized, by setting $F(0,0,0,q) = 0$ for all $q = 0, \ldots, Q$ and $F(i,j,h,q) = +\infty$ for $q < 0$.

Note that $F(\bar{n}_A, \bar{n}_B, n_{AB}, Q)$ gives the optimal solution value. Since each quantity $F(i,j,h,q)$ can be computed in constant time, the following theorem holds.

**Theorem 3.22.** *Problem* $1|ND, \sum C_j^B \leq Q|\sum C_j^A$ *can be solved in* $O(\bar{n}_A \bar{n}_B n_{AB} Q)$ *time.*

The pseudopolynomial algorithm can in principle be extended to any number $K$ of agents, each holding $\sum C_j^k$ as objective function. The recursive formula (3.54) must consider all possible subsets of $K$ agents, since a job may contribute to the cost of any subset of objective functions. Since in this case the number of possible job subsets is $2^K - 1$, one would get a complexity of $O(n^{2^K-1} Q_2 \ldots Q_K)$. Though such complexity grows rapidly with $K$, it shows that the problem is still solvable in pseudopolynomial time for a *fixed* number of agents. Of course, in many cases some of these subsets may be empty. In particular, for both COMPETING and INTERFERING one has only $K$ disjoint subsets. For COMPETING these subsets coincide with $\mathcal{J}^1, \mathcal{J}^2, \ldots, \mathcal{J}^K$, and in the INTERFERING case, the subsets are $\bar{\mathcal{J}}^1 = \mathcal{J}^1 \backslash \mathcal{J}^2, \mathcal{J}^2 \backslash \mathcal{J}^3$, etc., $\mathcal{J}^{K-1} \backslash \mathcal{J}^K, \mathcal{J}^K$. Therefore in both these scenarios the problem is solvable by formula (3.54) in $O(n^K Q_2 \ldots Q_K)$. However, all $K$-agent problems are open as for strong NP-hardness if $K$ is not fixed.

## 3.9.2 Computing the Pareto Set

### 3.9.2.1 Problem $1||\mathcal{P}(\sum C_j^A, \sum C_j^B)$

We next address problem $1||\mathcal{P}(\sum C_j^A, \sum C_j^B)$. Even in the COMPETING scenario, we show that the size of the Pareto set may not be polynomial.

*Example 3.7.* Let consider an instance of problem $1|CO|\mathcal{P}(\sum C_j^A, \sum C_j^B)$ in which the sets $\mathcal{J}^A$ and $\mathcal{J}^B$ are identical. Each set consists of $k$ jobs of size

$p_0 = 1, p_1 = 2, p_2 = 4, p_3 = 8, \ldots, p_{k-1} = 2^{k-1}$. Consider now a subset of all possible schedules, namely those in which the two jobs of length $p_0$ are scheduled first, then the two jobs of length $p_1$, the two of length $p_2$ etc. Let $\sigma$ be one such schedule. In $\sigma$, for each pair of jobs having equal length, either the job of agent $A$ or of agent $B$ is scheduled first. Call $\mathcal{N}^A$ the set of job pair indices in which the job of $\mathcal{J}^A$ precedes the job of $\mathcal{J}^B$ having the same length in $\sigma$, and $\mathcal{N}^B$ the set of pair indices in which the opposite holds in $\sigma$. Consider job $J_h^A$. If it is scheduled before $J_h^B$, its contribution to the cost function of Agent 1 is $2^h + 2(2^h - 1)$, otherwise it is $2(2^h) + 2(2^h - 1)$. Hence, the total completion time for the Agent 1 is given by

$$\sum_{J_h \in \mathcal{J}^A} C_h^A = \sum_{h \in \mathcal{N}^A} (2^{h+1} + 2^h - 2) + \sum_{h \in \mathcal{N}^B} (2^{h+2} - 2) \tag{3.55}$$

$$= \sum_{h \in \mathcal{N}^A} (3(2^h) - 2) + \sum_{h \in \mathcal{N}^B} (4(2^h) - 2) \tag{3.56}$$

$$= \sum_{h=0}^{k-1} 3(2^h) - 2k + \sum_{h \in \mathcal{N}^B} 2^h \tag{3.57}$$

Note that only the last term in expression (3.57) depends on the actual schedule $\sigma$. This expression shows that the quantity $\sum_{J_h \in \mathcal{J}^A} C_h^A$ may attain $2^k$ different values, one for each possible set $\mathcal{N}^B$. Symmetrically, the same analysis for Agent 2 yields

$$\sum_{J_h \in \mathcal{J}^B} C_h^B = \sum_{h=0}^{k-1} 3(2^h) - 2k + \sum_{h \in \mathcal{N}^A} 2^h. \tag{3.58}$$

Since obviously $\sum_{h \in \mathcal{N}^A} 2^h + \sum_{h \in \mathcal{N}^B} 2^h = 2^k - 1$, for each choice of the set $\mathcal{N}^A$ we find a Pareto optimal solution. Hence, the size of the Pareto set is $2^k$. ◇

## *3.9.3 Linear Combination*

### 3.9.3.1 Problem $1|ND|\alpha \sum C_j^A + \beta \sum C_j^B$

The linear combination problem $1|ND|\alpha \sum C_j^A + \beta \sum C_j^B$ can be solved in $O(n \log n)$ by the Smith's rule. In fact, it is equivalent to an instance of the single-agent problem $1||\sum w_j C_j$ in which:

$$w_j = \alpha \quad \text{for } j \in \bar{\mathcal{J}}^A$$
$$w_j = \beta \quad \text{for } j \in \bar{\mathcal{J}}^B$$
$$w_j = \alpha + \beta \quad \text{for } j \in \mathcal{J}^A \cap \mathcal{J}^B.$$

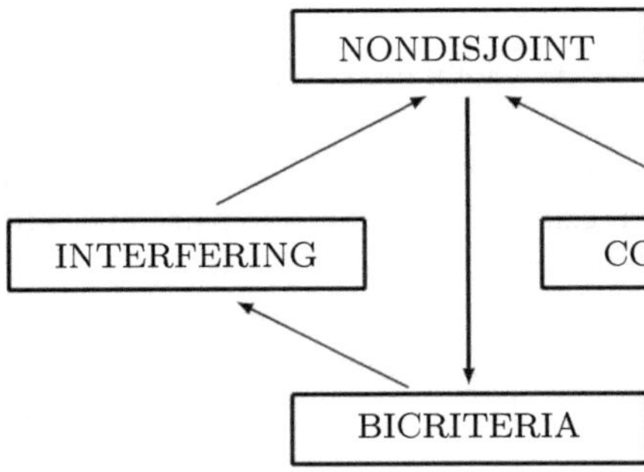


**Fig. 3.17** Reduction graph for $1||\sum w_j C_j, \sum w_j C_j$

## 3.10 Functions $\sum w_j C_j, \sum w_j C_j$

Let us now turn to the more general problem in which both agents want to minimize the weighted sum of the completion times of their respective jobs. This is actually one of the scenarios that has received most attention in the literature.

In this case, NONDISJOINT $\rightarrow$ BICRITERIA. In fact, it is a special case of BICRITERIA in which we simply set $w_j^B = 0$ if $J_j \notin \mathcal{J}^B$ and $w_j^A = 0$ if $J_j \notin \mathcal{J}^A$. We have therefore the reduction graph of Fig. 3.17.

### *3.10.1 Epsilon-Constraint Approach*

We next show that problem $1|CO, \sum w_j^B C_j^B \le Q|\sum w_j^A C_j^A$ is strongly NP-hard. In view of the reduction graph in Fig. 3.17, this implies the strong NP-hardness of the other cases, including $1|BI, \sum w_j^B C_j \le Q|\sum w_j^A C_j$. To the best of our knowledge, so far only the binary NP-hardness of the BICRITERIA problem $1|BI, \sum w_j^B C_j \le Q|\sum w_j^A C_j$ had been established (Hoogeveen 2005).

**Theorem 3.23.** *Problem* $1|CO, \sum w_j^B C_j^B \le Q|\sum w_j^A C_j^A$ *is strongly NP-hard.*

*Proof.* Given an instance of 3-PARTITION, we build an instance of problem $1|CO, \sum w_j^B C_j^B \le Q|\sum w_j^A C_j^A$ as follows. Set $\mathcal{J}^A$ consists of $3r$ jobs, having $p_i^A = w_i^A = a_i$, $i = 1, \ldots, 3r$. Set $\mathcal{J}^B$ consists of $r$ jobs, $J_1^B, J_2^B, \ldots, J_r^B$ with $p_j^B = E$ and $w_j^B = E^{3(r-j)}$ for $j = 1, \ldots, r$. We want to show that the instance of 3-PARTITION has a solution if and only if there is a schedule such that, for the objective functions of the two agents, one has:

$$\sum_{j=1}^{3r} w_j^A C_j^A \le \sum_{i,j} p_i^A p_j^A + \frac{r(r-1)}{2} E^2 = Y_A \tag{3.59}$$

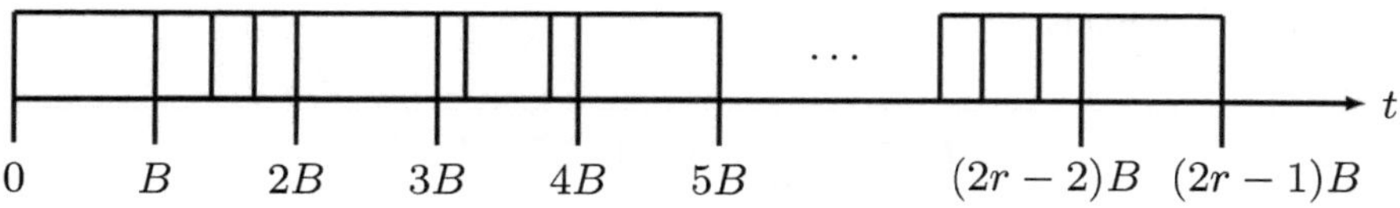

**Fig. 3.18** Schedule in the NP-hardness proof for $1|CO, \sum w_j^B C_j^B \leq Q|\sum w_j^A C_j^A$

and

$$\sum_{j=1}^{r} w_j^B C_j^B \leq \sum_{j=1}^{r} (2j-1)E^{3(r-j)+1} = Y_B \tag{3.60}$$

The key idea is similar to the one used in Theorem 3.15. In the instance of $1|CO, \sum w_j^B C_j^B \leq Q|\sum w_j^A C_j^A$, the jobs of $\mathcal{J}^B$ have "large" weights. In particular, their weights and the value $Y_B$ are defined in such a way that job $J_j^B$ cannot complete after $(2j-1)E$, for each $j = 1, \ldots, r$. On the other hand, in order for agent $A$ not to exceed $Y_A$, it is convenient to process each $J_j^B$ as close as possible to $(2j-1)E$. This leaves $r$ intervals of length $E$. If and only if it is possible to perfectly fill these intervals with triples of jobs from $\mathcal{J}^A$, then the instance of 3-PARTITION is a yes-instance (see Fig. 3.18).

(Only if.) First observe that if there is a 3-PARTITION, then we can schedule the jobs so that each job in $\mathcal{J}^B$ completes at $(2j-1)E$, and we can schedule the triple of jobs in $\mathcal{J}^A$ corresponding to each set $A_h$ between two jobs of $\mathcal{J}^B$. Let us now compute the total weighted completion time for $\mathcal{J}^A$. Indicating by $h_1, h_2$ and $h_3$ the indices of the three jobs in $A_k$, after some computation one gets:

$$\sum w_j^A C_j^A = \sum_{i=1}^{3r} \sum_{j=1}^{3r} p_i^A p_j^A + \sum_{h=1}^{r} (hE(p_{h_1}^A + p_{h_2}^A + p_{h_3}^A))$$

$$= \sum_{i=1}^{3r} \sum_{j=1}^{3r} p_i^A p_j^A + \frac{r(r+1)}{2} E^2 = Y_A \tag{3.61}$$

Similarly,

$$\sum_{j=1}^{r} w_j^B C_j^B = \sum_{j=1}^{r} (2j-1)E^{3(r-j)+1} = Y_B$$

So, the schedule is feasible.

(If.) Suppose now that a feasible schedule $\sigma$ exists such that (3.59) and (3.60) are satisfied. We claim that in $\sigma$ the first job of $\mathcal{J}^B$, i.e., $J_1^B$, cannot complete after $E$. In fact, in this case its completion time would be

$$w_1^B C_1^B \leq (E+1)E^{3r-3}$$

since $E \geq 3$, it holds

$$E^{3r-3} > \sum_{j=2}^{r}(2j-1)E^{3r-3j+1}$$

and this implies that the total weighted completion time for agent $B$ would exceed $Y_B$, hence contradicting the fact that $\sigma$ is feasible. So, the first job $J_1^B$ of $\mathcal{J}^B$ must complete at time $E$ (i.e., it starts at time 0). By a very similar argument, one can show that $J_2^B$ cannot complete after $3E$, and so on, so that $J_j^B$ does not complete after $(2j-1)E$.

Now let $G_h$ be the set of jobs of $\mathcal{J}^A$ scheduled consecutively between $J_h^B$ and $J_{h+1}^B$ in $\sigma$ for $h = 1, \ldots, r-1$, while $G_r$ denotes the jobs of $\mathcal{J}^A$ scheduled after $J_r^B$. Let $p(G_h)$ denote the total length of the jobs in $G_h$. It is easy to see that the value of the total weighted completion time for agent $A$ is given by:

$$\sum_{j=1}^{3r} w_j^A C_j^A(\sigma) = \sum_{i=1}^{3r}\sum_{j=1}^{3r} p_i^A p_j^A + \sum_{h=1}^{r} hEp(G_h) \tag{3.62}$$

Since, from the previous discussion, job $J_h^B$ cannot complete after $(2h-1)E$, the total length of the jobs from $\mathcal{J}^A$ scheduled before time $(2h-1)E$ cannot exceed $(h-1)E$. Now, in order to obtain a lower bound on $\sum_{j=1}^{3r} w_j^A C_j^A(\sigma)$, we can reason exactly as in the proof of Theorem 3.15, and compute $r$ figures for $p(G_h)$, $h = 1, \ldots, r$ that minimize the function $\sum_{h=1}^{r} hp(G_h)$. It is easy to verify that the minimizer is $p(G_h) = E$, $h = 1, \ldots, r$, so that we get the lower bound:

$$\sum_{j=1}^{3r} w_j^A C_j^A(\sigma) \geq \sum_{i=1}^{3r}\sum_{j=1}^{3r} p_i^A p_j^A + \frac{r(r+1)}{2}E^2 \tag{3.63}$$

since $\sigma$ is feasible, both (3.59) and (3.63) hold, and therefore

$$\sum_{j=1}^{3r} w_j^A C_j^A(\sigma) = Y_A \tag{3.64}$$

but this can only occur if $p(G_h) = E$ for all $h$, i.e., if the instance of 3-PARTITION is a yes-instance. □

#### 3.10.1.1 Problem $1|BI, \sum w_j^B C_j^B \leq Q|\sum w_j^A C_j^A$

As we have already seen for problem $1|ND, C_{\max}^B \leq Q|\sum w_j^A C_j^A$ and $1|CO, L_{\max}^B \leq Q|\sum w_j^A C_j^A$, also in this case a viable approach to build an exact algorithm is to pursue lower bounds by means of a Lagrangian relaxation of the problem. It turns out that even in this case the Lagrangian dual can be solved very efficiently, and the quality of the bound is sufficient to solve instances of the problem of reasonable size. We next illustrate this approach for $1|BI, \sum w_j^B C_j^B \leq Q|\sum w_j^A C_j^A$ (since the other scenarios can be reduced to it setting the appropriate weights to zero), and give an efficient algorithm to solve the Lagrangian dual. In what follows, we let $\delta_i^A$ and $\delta_j^B$ denote the ratios $w_i^A/p_i$ and $w_j^B/p_j$ respectively. Recalling (Sect. 3.4.1.1) that $\mathcal{S}$ denotes the set of all job permutations, the original problem is

$$z^* = \min_{\sigma \in \mathcal{S}} \left\{ \sum_{i=1}^{n} w_i^A C_i(\sigma) : \sum_{j=1}^{n} w_j^B C_j(\sigma) \leq Q \right\} \tag{3.65}$$

Relaxing the constraint on the jobs of agent $B$ in (3.65), we get the Lagrangian problem:

$$L(\lambda) = \min_{\sigma \in \mathcal{S}} \left\{ \sum_{i=1}^{n} w_i^A C_i(\sigma) + \lambda \left( \sum_{j=1}^{n} w_j^B C_j(\sigma) - Q \right) \right\} \tag{3.66}$$

Note that for each value of $\lambda \geq 0$, the problem (3.66) is in the format of a classical, single-agent problem $1||\sum \tilde{w}_j C_j$, in which the weights are defined as $\tilde{w}_h = w_h^A + \lambda w_h^B$. The optimal schedule $\sigma(\lambda)$ for this problem can be found by the Smith's rule, i.e., scheduling the jobs in non-increasing order of their ratios $\delta_h^A + \lambda \delta_h^B$. For each $\lambda$, the solution of (3.66) is a lower bound for the original problem. The Lagrangian dual is therefore:

$$L(\lambda^*) = \max_{\lambda \geq 0} \left\{ \min_{\sigma \in \mathcal{S}} \left\{ \sum_{i=1}^{n} w_i^A C_i(\sigma) + \lambda \Big( \sum_{j=1}^{n} w_j^B C_j(\sigma) - Q \Big) \right\} \right\} \tag{3.67}$$

Recall that $L(\lambda)$ is a concave, piecewise linear function (see Fig. 3.19), and that the *breakpoints* of $L(\lambda)$ are the values of $\lambda$ in which the slope of $L(\lambda)$ changes. For all values of $\lambda$ between two consecutive breakpoints, the optimal schedule for (3.66) remains the same. If $\bar{\lambda}$ is not a breakpoint, the slope of $L(\lambda)$ in $\bar{\lambda}$ is

$$\sum_{j=1}^{n} w_j^B C_j \left(\sigma(\bar{\lambda})\right) - Q \tag{3.68}$$

which represents the violation of the constraint $\sum_{j=1}^{n} w_j^B C_j\ (\sigma) \leq Q$ in (3.65). If $\bar{\lambda}$ is a breakpoint, then, for sufficiently small $\varepsilon > 0$, the schedules $\sigma(\bar{\lambda} - \varepsilon)$ and $\sigma(\bar{\lambda} + \varepsilon)$ are obtained one from the other simply swapping the jobs of all adjacent pairs $(J_i, J_j)$ for which

$$\delta_i^A + \bar{\lambda}\delta_i^B = \delta_j^A + \bar{\lambda}\delta_j^B. \tag{3.69}$$

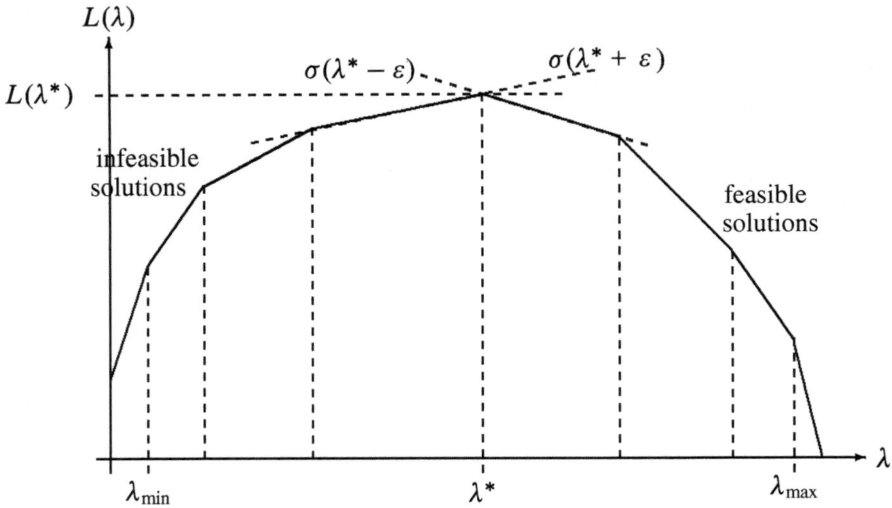


**Fig. 3.19** Shape of Lagrangian function

Note that there is at least one such pair. Both schedules $\sigma(\bar{\lambda} - \varepsilon)$ and $\sigma(\bar{\lambda} + \varepsilon)$ are optimal for problem (3.66), with $\lambda = \bar{\lambda}$. Notice that if, for some pair $(J_i, J_j)$, $\delta_i^A = \delta_j^A$, then for any $\lambda$, the job having higher ratio for Agent 2 will be sequenced first in $\sigma(\lambda)$. Symmetrically, if $\delta_i^B = \delta_j^B$, their relative ordering in $\sigma(\lambda)$ is decided by the ratios $\delta_i^A$ and $\delta_j^A$. Hence, any breakpoint in $L(\lambda)$ is associated with two jobs $(J_i, J_j)$ such that $\delta_i^A \neq \delta_j^A$ and $\delta_i^B \neq \delta_j^B$. Now, with no loss of generality suppose that $\delta_i^A > \delta_j^A$, i.e., for Agent 1 job $J_i$ has a higher priority than $J_j$. If also $\delta_i^B > \delta_j^B$, then for no $\lambda \geq 0$ one has that (3.69) holds. Therefore, in this case, for any $\lambda$, $J_i$ will always precede $J_j$ in $\sigma(\lambda)$. If, on the other hand, $\delta_i^B < \delta_j^B$, then $J_i$ precedes $J_j$ in $\sigma(\lambda)$ for $\lambda < \bar{\lambda}$, and $J_i$ follows $J_j$ for $\lambda > \bar{\lambda}$, where $\bar{\lambda}$ is given by (3.69). In conclusion, as $\lambda$ goes from 0 to $\infty$, any two jobs overtake each other at most once (see Fig. 3.20). As a consequence, the overall set $\Lambda$ of breakpoints is given by:

$$\Lambda = \left\{ \frac{\delta_i^A - \delta_j^A}{\delta_j^B - \delta_i^B} : \delta_i^A > \delta_j^A, \delta_j^B > \delta_i^B, i, j = 1, \ldots, n \right\}$$

and the total number of breakpoints cannot exceed $n(n-1)/2$.

The maximum $L(\lambda^*)$ is attained in the breakpoint $\lambda^*$ in which the slope of $L(\lambda)$ switches from positive to non-positive, and therefore schedule $\sigma(\lambda^* + \varepsilon)$ is feasible for (3.65). The breakpoint $\lambda^*$ can be efficiently found as follows.

First compute the set $\Lambda$ and sort it by nondecreasing values. Then, compute the schedule $\sigma(\infty)$ obtained by ordering the jobs by nonincreasing ratios $\delta_i^B$. This coincides with $\sigma(\lambda)$ for sufficiently large $\lambda$. As $\lambda$ decreases, the same schedule $\sigma(\infty)$ remains optimal until the largest breakpoint $\bar{\lambda} \in \Lambda$ is encountered, i.e., $\sigma(\bar{\lambda}) \equiv \sigma(\infty)$. The schedule $\sigma(\bar{\lambda} - \varepsilon)$ can be generated from $\sigma(\bar{\lambda})$ by simply

| | | | | | | | | | | | | |
|---|---|---|---|---|---|---|---|---|---|---|---|---|
| $\lambda \in [\lambda_{k-1},\lambda_k]$ | $J_1^B$ | $J_2^B$ | $J_3^B$ | $J_4^B$ | $J_5^B$ | $J_6^B$ | $J_1^A$ | $J_2^A$ | $J_3^A$ | $J_4^A$ | $J_5^A$ | $J_6^A$ |
| $\lambda \in [\lambda_{k-2},\lambda_k - 1]$ | $J_1^B$ | $J_2^B$ | $J_3^B$ | $J_4^B$ | $J_5^B$ | $J_1^A$ | $J_6^B$ | $J_2^A$ | $J_3^A$ | $J_4^A$ | $J_5^A$ | $J_6^A$ |
| $\lambda \in [\lambda_{k-3},\lambda_k - 2]$ | $J_1^B$ | $J_2^B$ | $J_3^B$ | $J_4^B$ | $J_1^A$ | $J_5^B$ | $J_6^B$ | $J_2^A$ | $J_3^A$ | $J_4^A$ | $J_5^A$ | $J_6^A$ |
| $\lambda \in [\lambda_{k-4},\lambda_k - 3]$ | $J_1^B$ | $J_2^B$ | $J_3^B$ | $J_4^B$ | $J_1^A$ | $J_5^B$ | $J_2^A$ | $J_6^B$ | $J_3^A$ | $J_4^A$ | $J_5^A$ | $J_6^A$ |

| | | | | | | | | | | | | |
|---|---|---|---|---|---|---|---|---|---|---|---|---|
| $\lambda \in [\lambda_3,\lambda_4]$ | $J_1^A$ | $J_2^A$ | $J_3^A$ | $J_4^A$ | $J_1^B$ | $J_5^A$ | $J_2^B$ | $J_6^A$ | $J_3^B$ | $J_4^B$ | $J_5^B$ | $J_6^B$ |
| $\lambda \in [\lambda_2,\lambda_3]$ | $J_1^A$ | $J_2^A$ | $J_3^A$ | $J_4^A$ | $J_1^B$ | $J_5^A$ | $J_6^A$ | $J_2^B$ | $J_3^B$ | $J_4^B$ | $J_5^B$ | $J_6^B$ |
| $\lambda \in [\lambda_1,\lambda_2]$ | $J_1^A$ | $J_2^A$ | $J_3^A$ | $J_4^A$ | $J_5^A$ | $J_1^B$ | $J_6^A$ | $J_2^B$ | $J_3^B$ | $J_4^B$ | $J_5^B$ | $J_6^B$ |
| $\lambda \in [\lambda_0,\lambda_1]$ | $J_1^A$ | $J_2^A$ | $J_3^A$ | $J_4^A$ | $J_5^A$ | $J_6^A$ | $J_1^B$ | $J_2^B$ | $J_3^B$ | $J_4^B$ | $J_5^B$ | $J_6^B$ |

**Fig. 3.20** Optimal schedules for problem (3.66) for decreasing values of $\lambda$, where $\lambda_0 = \lambda_{min}$ and $\lambda_k = \lambda_{\max}$

swapping all job pairs $J_i, J_j$ such that $(\delta_i^A - \delta_j^A)/(\delta_j^B - \delta_i^B) = \bar{\lambda}$. As $\lambda$ further decreases, the schedule $\sigma(\bar{\lambda}-\varepsilon)$ remains optimal up to the second largest breakpoint, and the same argument applies. At each breakpoint, the value of (3.68) can be updated by computing the contribution of each swap in constant time. The optimal breakpoint $\lambda^*$ is the first value for which the slope (3.68) computed in $\lambda^* - \varepsilon$ is positive. Since the overall number of swaps cannot exceed $n(n-1)/2$, the complexity is dominated by the ordering of the breakpoints, and the following theorem holds.

**Theorem 3.24.** *The Lagrangian dual of problem* $1|BI, \sum w_j^B C_j^B \leq Q|\sum w_i^A C_i^A$ *can be solved in* $O(n^2 \log n)$.

This result can be slightly refined for $1|CO, \sum w_j^B C_j^B \leq Q|\sum w_j^A C_j^A$. In this case, it can be shown that the total number of breakpoints cannot exceed $n_A n_B$. Details can be found in Agnetis et al. (2009b), where it is also shown how the Lagrangian bound can be embedded in a branch-and-bound scheme for $1|CO, \sum w_j^B C_j^B \leq Q|\sum w_j^A C_j^A$.

### 3.10.2 Approximation

In this section we present an approximation result concerning problem $1|CO|\sum w_j^A C_j^A, \sum w_j^B C_j^B$. In what follows we refer to the concept of $(\beta_A, \beta_B)$-approximation schedule, introduced in Sect. 2.4.2 as type II approximation. Also, we assume that the jobs of each agent are numbered in WSPT order. For each agent $k$, $k \in \{A, B\}$, consider the *reference schedule* $\sigma^k$ (Sect. 1.2.1), and let $\tau_j^k$ denote the completion time of job $J_j^k$ in such schedule. Note that this is simply the sum of the processing

**Algorithm 18** Approximation for $1|CO|\sum w_j^A C_j^A, \sum w_j^B C_j^B$

1: Construct the reference schedule $\sigma^A$ via WSPT
2: $\tau_j^A := C_j^A(\sigma^A)$
3: Construct the reference schedule $\sigma^B$ via WSPT
4: $\tau_j^B := C_j^B(\sigma^B)$
5: Schedule all jobs in non-decreasing order of $\beta_i \tau_j^i$ values
6: **return** $\tilde{\sigma}$

times of the first $j$ jobs of agent $k$. For the sake of clarity, in this section we let $Q_k^*$ denote the optimal value of the objective function of agent $k$ in its reference schedule $\sigma^k$. This is a lower bound to the cost agent $k$ will pay in any two-agent feasible schedule.

Suppose we want to find a $(\beta_A, \beta_B)$-approximation schedule for given $\beta_A > 1$ and $\beta_B > 1$. This can be achieved by the simple Algorithm 18, as long as the following condition holds:

$$\frac{1}{\beta_A} + \frac{1}{\beta_B} = 1 \tag{3.70}$$

As shown in Algorithm 18, the algorithm consists in computing the two reference schedules, multiplying each $\tau_j^A$ by $\beta_A$ and each $\tau_j^B$ by $\beta_B$, and then scheduling the jobs by nondecreasing values of $\beta_k \tau_j^k$. We call $\tilde{\sigma}$ the schedule produced. Lee et al. (2009) proved the following result.

**Theorem 3.25.** *Given $\beta_A > 1$ and $\beta_B > 1$ satisfying (3.70), Algorithm 18 produces a $(\beta_A, \beta_B)$-approximation schedule.*

*Proof.* The proposition holds if we show that in the schedule $\tilde{\sigma}$, the completion time of each job $C_j^k(\tilde{\sigma})$ does not exceed $\beta_k \tau_j^k$. The proof is by induction on the number of jobs. At the beginning of the algorithm, the job with smallest $\beta_k \tau_j^k$ is scheduled first. In this case, $C_1^k(\tilde{\sigma}) = \tau_1^k$ and since $\beta_k > 1$, the thesis obviously holds.

Now consider that $p$ jobs from $\mathcal{J}^A$ and $q$ jobs from $\mathcal{J}^B$ have been scheduled so far. By the inductive hypothesis, $C_j^k(\tilde{\sigma}) \leq \beta_k \tau_j^k$ for all jobs scheduled so far, and suppose that the next job in the list is from $\mathcal{J}^A$, i.e., job $J_{p+1}^A$ (a symmetric discussion holds if it is from $\mathcal{J}^B$). Since the algorithm schedules the jobs by nondecreasing $\beta_k \tau_j^k$, one has that

$$\beta_B \tau_q^B \leq \beta_A \tau_{p+1}^A. \tag{3.71}$$

Now let us consider the completion time of $J_{p+1}^A$. Recalling that $\tau_p^A$ and $\tau_q^B$ equal the total processing time of scheduled jobs from $\mathcal{J}^A$ and $\mathcal{J}^B$ respectively, one has

$$C_{p+1}^A(\tilde{\sigma}) = \tau_q^B + \tau_{p+1}^A.$$

From (3.71),

$$C^A_{p+1}(\tilde{\sigma}) \le \frac{\beta_A}{\beta_B}\tau^A_{p+1} + \tau^A_{p+1} = \beta_A\left(\frac{1}{\beta_A} + \frac{1}{\beta_B}\right)\tau^A_{p+1},$$

and hence, from (3.70), $C^A_{p+1}(\sigma_A) \le \beta_1 \tau^A_{p+1}$ and the thesis holds. □

This theorem has interesting implications on the $\varepsilon$-constraint problem, since it allows to establish a relationship between the optimal value of $1|CO, \sum w^B_j C^B_j \le Q|\sum w^A_j C^A_j$ for a given $Q$ and the value of the reference schedule of agent $A$. To this aim, consider an instance of $1|CO, \sum w^B_j C^B_j \le Q|\sum w^A_j C^A_j$. For the problem to be feasible, clearly $Q$ must be at least $Q^*_B$. Consider now the optimal schedule $\bar{\sigma}$ for $1|CO, \sum w^B_j C^B_j \le Q|\sum w^A_j C^A_j$. The value of the optimal solution for agent $A$ cannot be worse than what agent $A$ could attain by Algorithm 18. Expressing $Q$ as $Q = \beta_B Q^*_B$, from (3.70) one has:

$$\sum_{j=1}^{n_A} w^A_j C^A_j(\bar{\sigma}) \le \frac{\beta_B}{\beta_B - 1} Q^*_A$$

This allows to express the tradeoff between the two agents with respect to the ideal values $Q^*_A$ and $Q^*_B$. For instance, if we allow that agent $B$ pays up to 1.5 times its ideal cost, the cost to agent $A$ will certainly not exceed 3 times its ideal cost.

For illustration purposes, we presented Theorem 3.25 for $K = 2$, but Lee et al. (2009) indeed established the result for any number $K$ of agents, given that:

$$\frac{1}{\beta_1} + \frac{1}{\beta_2} + \ldots, + \frac{1}{\beta_K} = 1. \tag{3.72}$$

*Example 3.8.* Let us consider a three-agent instance, in which all jobs have unit weight and unit length. Each of the three agents owns four jobs. We want to find a $(\beta_1, \beta_2, \beta_3)$-approximation schedule, in which $\beta_1 = \beta_2 = \beta_3 = 3$, so that Eq. (3.72) holds. Clearly, the reference schedules $\sigma^1$, $\sigma^2$, $\sigma^3$ have values $Q^*_1 = Q^*_2 = Q^*_3 = 10$. When applying Algorithm 18, we obtain the following vectors of modified completion times:

$$\{\beta_1 \tau^A_j\} = \{3,\ 6,\ 9,\ 12\}$$

$$\{\beta_2 \tau^B_j\} = \{3,\ 6,\ 9,\ 12\}$$

$$\{\beta_3 \tau^3_j\} = \{3,\ 6,\ 9,\ 12\}$$

Since ties can be broken arbitrarily, suppose we always break them in favor of agent 1 and then agent 2, so that we obtain the schedule

$$\sigma_A = \{J^1_1, J^2_1, J^3_1, J^1_2, J^2_2, J^3_2, J^1_3, J^2_3, J^3_3, J^1_4, J^2_4, J^3_4\}$$

and

$$f^1(\sigma_A) = 1 + 4 + 7 + 10 = 22$$
$$f^2(\sigma_A) = 2 + 5 + 8 + 11 = 26$$
$$f^3(\sigma_A) = 3 + 6 + 9 + 12 = 30$$

we observe that

$$f^1(\sigma_A) = 22 < 30 = \beta_1 Q_1^*,$$
$$f^2(\sigma_A) = 26 < 30 = \beta_2 Q_2^*,$$
$$f^3(\sigma_A) = 30 = \beta_3 Q_3^*.$$

If we consider the same type of instance, in which each agent owns $n/3$ identical unit time jobs, with arbitrary $n$, we get, for each agent $k$,

$$Q_k^* = n(n+3)/18 \tag{3.73}$$

and, always solving the ties in favor of agent 1 and then 2,

$$f^1(\sigma_A) = n(n-1)/6$$
$$f^2(\sigma_A) = n(n+1)/6$$
$$f^3(\sigma_A) = n(n+3)/6$$

Hence, for each agent $k$,

$$\lim_{n\to\infty} \frac{f^k(\sigma_A)}{Q_k^*} = 3 = \beta_k$$

and this shows that the bound is indeed tight. ◇

As shown in Saule and Trystram (2009) and Lee et al. (2009), it turns out that the simple Algorithm 18 is the *best possible*, i.e., if $(\beta_1, \beta_2, \ldots, \beta_K)$ satisfies (3.72), there cannot exist an approximation algorithm yielding a strictly better approximation than $(\beta_1, \beta_2, \ldots, \beta_K)$. We next show such tightness result considering again Example 3.8. In this example the *sum* of the three agents' costs is independent of the actual schedule (since all schedules are SPT in this case), and equals

$$\frac{n(n+1)}{2}, \tag{3.74}$$

while the value of the reference schedule for each agent is given by (3.73). Now suppose that we perfectly divide the cost (3.74) among the three agents. In this case, the cost to each agent would be

$$\frac{n(n+1)}{6} \tag{3.75}$$

and therefore, the ratio between (3.75) and (3.73) is

$$\frac{3(n+1)}{n+3}$$

which approaches 3 as $n \to \infty$. This means that *no algorithm* can ensure to find a $(\beta_1, \beta_2, \beta_3)$-approximation schedule strictly better than $(3,3,3)$-approximation.

It is interesting to observe that Angel et al. (2005) give a fairly sophisticated (2,2)-approximation algorithm for the more general scenario $1|BI, \sum w_j^B C_j^B \le Q|\sum w_j^A C_j^A$.

Finally, let us apply the above considerations to the two-agent problem $1|CO, C_{\max}^B \le Q|\sum w_j^A C_j^A$ (Sect. 3.4.1), which can indeed be viewed as a special case of $1|CO, \sum w_j^B C_j^B \le Q|\sum w_j^A C_j^A$, in which, with no loss of generality, agent $B$ only has *one* job of length $P_B$ and weight 1. Observing that in this case $Q_B^* = P_B$, one has that any feasible solution to $1|CO, C_{\max}^B \le Q|\sum_j w_j^A C_j$ is $\beta_2$-approximate, where

$$\beta_B = \frac{Q}{P_B} \tag{3.76}$$

and hence, from (3.70), the best possible approximation for agent $A$ is:

$$\beta_A = \frac{Q}{Q - P_2}. \tag{3.77}$$

We can compare these expressions with those in Theorem 3.14. When applied to the COMPETING scenario, one has $\bar{P}_B = P_B$, and we retrieve exactly (3.76) and (3.77), thus showing that the optimal feasible schedule for the Lagrangean dual provides the same approximation.

Moreover, notice that in the general NONDISJOINT scenario, $\bar{P}_2 \le P_2$, and as a consequence, the $(\beta_A, \beta_B)$-approximation provided by Theorem 3.14 may be such that

$$\frac{1}{\beta_A} + \frac{1}{\beta_B} > 1. \tag{3.78}$$

Note that this does not contradict the tightness result above, since $1|ND, C_{\max}^B \le Q|\sum w_j^A C_j$ is *not* a special case of $1|ND, \sum w_j^B C_j \le Q|\sum w_j^A C_j$. In other words, (3.78) shows that $1|ND, C_{\max}^B \le Q|\sum w_j^A C_j$ can be better approximated than $1|CO, C_{\max}^B \le Q|\sum w_j^A C_j$.

We conclude this section on approximation observing that, since problem $1|CO, \sum w_j^B C_j \le Q|\sum w_j^A C_j$ is strongly NP-hard (see Theorem 3.23), no FPTAS is likely to exist. In Levin and Woeginger (2006) the authors give a PTAS for problem $1|BI, \sum w_j^B C_j^B \leq Q|\sum w_j^A C_j^A$, of complexity $O(n^2 \log^2 n(\log\log WP)n^{3/\varepsilon}(2/\varepsilon)!(2/\varepsilon)^{1/\varepsilon})$.

### 3.10.3 Computing the Pareto Set

In view of the result established in Sect. 3.9.2, in the worst case the size of the Pareto set can be exponential.

### 3.10.4 Linear Combination

Problem $1|ND|\alpha \sum w_j^A C_j + \beta \sum w_j^B C_j$ is easily solved in $O(n \log n)$ by the Smith's rule (indeed, so does even the $K$-agent problem $1|ND|\sum \alpha_k \sum w_j^k C_j$). Notice that this fact has been exploited by the Lagrangian approach to the $\varepsilon$ constraint problem, where the weights of the jobs in $\mathcal{J}^B$ are simply multiplied by $\lambda$ (Sect. 3.10.1).

## 3.11 Functions $\sum U_j, \sum C_j$

Let us now consider the case in which one agent wants to minimize total (unweighted) completion time and the other wants to minimize the number of tardy jobs.

The reduction graphs for this case reflect the asymmetry of the problem. In fact, the scenario $1|IN|\sum C_j^A, \sum U_j^B$ reduces to $1|BI|\sum C_j^A, \sum U_j^B$, by simply associating a very large due date to the jobs of $\bar{\mathcal{J}}^A$. This yields the reduction graph in Fig. 3.21. Similarly, the scenario $1|ND|\sum U_j^A, \sum C_j^B$ reduces to $1|IN|\sum U_j^A, \sum C_j^B$ associating a very large due date to the jobs of $\mathcal{J}^B$ (see Fig. 3.22).

### 3.11.1 Epsilon-Constraint Approach

Problems $1|CO, \sum C_j^B \leq Q|\sum U_j^A$ and $1|BI, \sum U_j^B \leq Q|\sum C_j^A$ have been proved NP-hard in Leung et al. (2010) and Huo et al. (2007b) respectively. In view of the reduction graphs in Figs. 3.21 and 3.22, these NP-hardness results imply the NP-hardness of all other scenarios. A pseudopolynomial algorithm having complexity $O(n_A n_B^2 P_B)$ has been proposed in Ng et al. (2006) for problem $1|CO, \sum U_j^B \leq Q|\sum C_j^A$.

In Meiners and Torng (2007), the authors address the problem in which the jobs have release dates and preemptions are allowed, i.e., problem $1|CO, r_j, prmt, \sum C_j^B \leq Q|\sum U_j^A$. They show that even if $|\mathcal{J}^A| = 1$, the problem is NP-

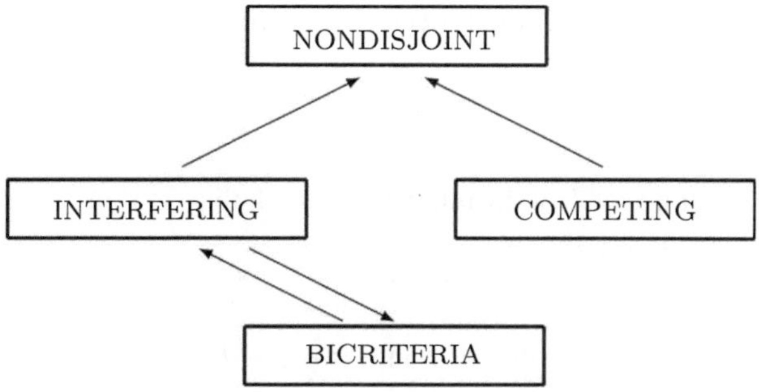


**Fig. 3.21** Reduction graph for $1||\sum C_j^A, \sum U_j^B$

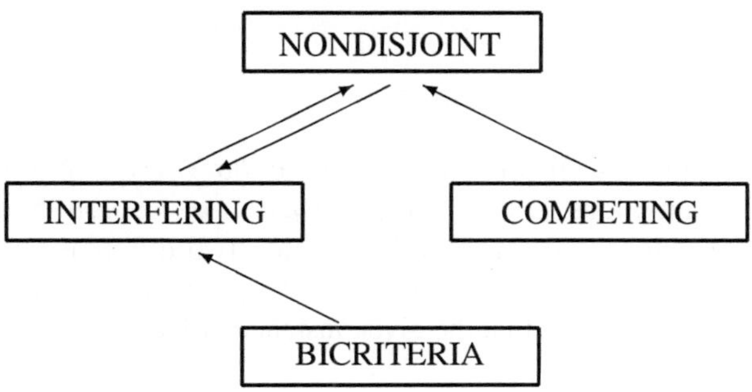


**Fig. 3.22** Reduction graph for $1||\sum U_j^A, \sum C_j^B$

hard. Moreover, they consider the lexicographic approach for the weighted problem $1|CO, r_j, pmtn|Lex(\sum w_j^A U_j^A, \sum C_j^B)$, and give a polynomial time algorithm for the special case in which all jobs have unit length (in which case, preemption is indeed immaterial).

### *3.11.2 Computing the Pareto Set*

In all scenarios, as the cost function of agent $k$ is the number of tardy jobs, there are at most $n_k + 1$ Pareto optimal solutions. Incidentally, we observe that this is one of the few cases in which the Pareto set is polynomially bounded, but the $\varepsilon$-constraint problem is hard.

### *3.11.3 Linear Combination*

Turning to problem $1|CO|\alpha \sum U_j^A + \beta \sum C_j^B$, it has been proved to be NP-hard by Choi et al. (2009).

The proof uses a variant of the PARTITION problem:

EVEN-ODD PARTITION
Instance: A finite set $I$ of $2n$ integers $a_j$, such that

$$\sum_{j=1}^{k} a_j = 2E$$

Question: Is there a partition of $I$ into two sets $I_1$ and $I_2$, such that

$$\sum_{a_j \in I_1} a_j = \sum_{a_j \in I_2} a_j = E$$

where $I_1$ and $I_2$ each contains exactly one element from $\{a_{2i-1}, a_{2i}\}$?

**Theorem 3.26.** *The problem* $1|CO|\alpha \sum U_j^A + \beta \sum C_j^B$ *is NP-hard.*

*Proof.* We reduce EVEN-ODD PARTITION to $1|CO|\alpha \sum U_j^A + \beta \sum C_j^B$. We make the following assumptions. Let $\sigma_i = a_{2i} - a_{2i-1}$, $i = 1, \ldots, n$. Notice that since each pair of integers, $a_{2i}, a_{2i-1}$ must be put into two different sets, we can add a constant $c_i$ to each pair without changing the problem instance. By carefully choosing $c_i$, we may assume that the given instance of Even-Odd Partition satisfies the following properties:

1. $a_1 > (2n+2)\max\{\sigma_1, \ldots, \sigma_n\}$
2. $a_{2i-1} > \sum_{j=1}^{2i-2} a_j$
3. $a_i/j$ is integer

If this is not true, we can multiply each $a_i$ by $n!$ without changing the problem instance. Note that although the numbers $a_i$ may become exponential, the size of the binary input remains polynomial.

Now given an instance of the EVEN-ODD PARTITION problem, we create the instance of $1|CO|\alpha \sum C_j^A + \beta \sum U_j^B$ as follows. There are $2n$ "P-jobs", each of which corresponds to an integer in the EVEN-ODD PARTITION instance, and a large "R-job" for Agent B. There are $n$ "Q-jobs" for Agent A. The processing times and due dates of these jobs are shown in the following table.

| Job | Processing time | Due date |
|---|---|---|
| $P_{2i-1}$ | $a_{2i-1} (= p_{2i-1})$ | $\sum_{k=1}^{i-1} p_{2k} + \sum_{k=1}^{i-1} x_k + p_{2i-1}$ |
| $P_{2i}$ | $a_{2i} + (l_i - 1)\sigma_i \; (= p_{2i})$ | $\sum_{k=1}^{i-1} p_{2k} + \sum_{k=1}^{i} x_k + p_{2i}$ |
| $R$ | $L$ | $\sum_{i=1}^{n} x_i + [E + \frac{1}{2}\sum_{i=1}^{n}(l_i - 1)\sigma_i] + L$ |
| $Q_i$ | $x_i$ | |

where:

- $L$ is an integer larger than $2E$
- $x_1 = 1$, $x_i = \frac{n-i+1}{n-i+2}a_{2i-3}$ for $i = 2, \ldots, n-1$ and $x_n = \frac{1}{2}a_{2n-3} + a_{2n-5}$. Note that $x_1 < x_2 <, \ldots, < x_n$ and they are all integers
- $l_i\sigma_i = \frac{1}{n-i+1}a_{2i-1}$ for $i = 1, \ldots, n-1$. Note that by the third of the above assumptions, $l_i\sigma_i$ is integer.

Also, let

$$TC = \sum_{i=1}^{n}(n-i)[a_{2i} + (l_i - 1)\sigma_i] + \sum_{i=1}^{n}(n-i+1)x_i + \frac{1}{2}\sum_{i=1}^{n} l_i\sigma_i$$

and finally, let $\alpha = \varepsilon$ and $\beta = 1 - \varepsilon$, where $\varepsilon$ is a very small, positive value. The problem consists in determining whether there exists a schedule such that the objective function value is at most $\varepsilon TC + (1-\varepsilon)n$.

In the instance of EVEN-ODD PARTITION, without loss of generality, we can assume that

$$a_1 \geq 2 \text{ and } a_{2i-1} - \sum_{j=1}^{2i-2} a_j \geq 2$$

First of all we claim that in the instance of $1|CO|\alpha \sum C_j^A + \beta \sum U_j^B$, there should exist at least $n$ tardy jobs of agent B in all schedules. In fact, consider two jobs of agent B of length $p_{2i-1}$ and $p_{2i}$. Then,

$$p_{2i-1} + p_{2i} = a_{2i-1} + a_{2i}$$

and

$$d_{2i} = \sum_{k=1}^{i-1} p_{2k} + \sum_{k=1}^{i} x_k + p_{2i} = \sum_{k=1}^{i-1} \frac{n-k+2}{n-k+1}a_{2k-1} + x_1$$

$$+ \sum_{k=2}^{i} \frac{n-k+1}{n-k+2}a_{2k-3} + p_{2i} = 1 + \sum_{k=2}^{i}\left(\frac{n-k+3}{n-k+2} + \frac{n-k+1}{n-k+2}\right)a_{2k-3} + p_{2i}$$

$$= 1 + 2\sum_{k=2}^{i} a_{2k-3} + p_{2i}$$

In case $i = 1$, since $a_1 \geq 2$,

$$p_1 + p_2 - d_2 = a_1 + a_2 - (x_1 + a_2) = a_1 - 1 > 0$$

In case $i > 1$, since $a_{2i-1} > \sum_{k=1}^{2i-2} a_k$ and $a_{2k} - a_{2k-1} > 0$,

$$p_{2i-1} + p_{2i} - d_{2i} = a_{2i-1} - (1 + 2\sum_{k=2}^{i} a_{2k-3}) > \sum_{k=1}^{2i-2} a_k - (1 + 2\sum_{k=2}^{i} a_{2k-3})$$

$$= \sum_{k=1}^{i-1}(a_{2k} - a_{2k-1}) - 1 \geq 0$$

These two cases imply that one job among $2i-1$ and $2i$ should be tardy. Thus, there should be at least $n$ tardy jobs of Agent B in all schedules and the claim is proved.

Because of this claim and the small value of $\varepsilon$, there exists an optimal schedule with $n$ tardy jobs of agent B. Moreover, it can be shown (Leung et al. 2010) that the lower bound to total completion time for agent A is $TC$, and that a schedule attaining such a bound exists if and only if there exists a partition $I_1, I_2$ in the instance of EVEN-ODD PARTITION. This completes the proof. □

## 3.12 Functions $\sum T_j, \sum C_j$

Now let us turn to the case in which one agent wants to minimize the total unweighted completion time and the other wants to minimize the total tardiness.

It is easy to see that in this case the same reduction graphs of Figs. 3.22 and 3.21 hold, where $\sum T_j$ replaces $\sum U_j$. The scenario $1|IN|\sum C_j^A, \sum T_j^B$ reduces to $1|BI|\sum C_j^B, \sum T_j^A$, by simply associating a very large due date to the jobs of $\bar{\mathcal{J}}^A$, while $1|CO|\sum T_j^A, \sum C_j^B$ reduces to $1|IN|\sum T_j^A, \sum C_j^B$, associating a very large due date to the jobs of $\mathcal{J}^B$.

In Leung et al. (2010) the authors give a pseudopolynomial algorithm for problem $1|CO, \sum C_j^B \leq Q|\sum T_j^A$, which combines the ideas developed in Agnetis et al. (2004) with the pseudo-polynomial time algorithm by Lawler for $1||\sum T_j$ (Sect. 2.7.1). The following result holds:

**Theorem 3.27.** *Problem* $1|CO, \sum C_j^B \leq Q|\sum T_j^A$ *can be solved in* $O(n_A^4 n_B^2 Q (P_1 + P_2))$ *time.*

## 3.13 Functions $\sum w_j C_j, \sum U_j$

For this case, one has the reduction graph in Fig. 3.23. In fact, problem $1|ND|\sum w_j^A C_j^A, \sum U_j^B$ reduces to $1|BI|\sum w_j^A C_j^A, \sum U_j^B$, by assigning a weight $w_j = 0$ to each $j \in \bar{\mathcal{J}}^B$ and setting a very large due date $d_j$ to each $j \in \bar{\mathcal{J}}^A$.

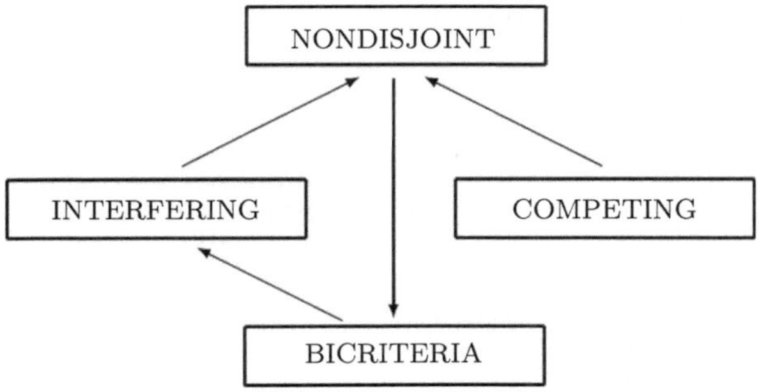


**Fig. 3.23** Reduction graph for $1||\sum w_j C_j, \sum U_j$

### 3.13.1 *Epsilon-Constraint Approach*

As observed by Ng et al. (2006), a consequence of a result in Lawler (1977) is that problem $1|CO, \sum U_j^B \leq Q|\sum w_j^A C_j^A$ is strongly NP-hard. This implies the NP-hardness of the $\varepsilon$-constraint problem in all other scenarios.

### 3.13.2 *Linear Combination*

For what concerns the problem $1|CO|\alpha \sum w_j^A C_j^A + \beta \sum U_j^B$, it is strongly NP-hard. In fact, since (Lawler 1977) the problem $1|CO, L_{\max}^B \leq 0|\sum w_j^A C_j^A$ is strongly NP-hard, so is also $1|CO, \sum U_j^B = 0|\sum w_j^A C_j^A$. The latter problem can be reduced to $1|CO|\alpha \sum w_j^A C_j^A + \beta \sum U_j^B$ just by setting a very large $\beta$.

In view of the reduction graph of Fig. 3.23, also all other scenarios are strongly NP-hard.

## 3.14 Functions $\sum U_j, \sum U_j$

In this section we turn to the case in which both agents want to minimize the total number of tardy jobs. It is well-known that in the single-agent case, $1||\sum U_j$ is solved by Moore's algorithm (Sect. 2.7.1). When we address this problem in the two-agent, NONDISJOINT setting, we must make an important distinction on whether:

(i) A job $J_i \in \mathcal{J}^A \cap \mathcal{J}^B$ has the same due date for both agents (we write $d_j^A = d_j^B$ in the $\beta$ field of the problem notation to refer to this case)
(ii) A job $J_i \in \mathcal{J}^A \cap \mathcal{J}^B$ may have different due dates for the two agents.

In case (i), the reduction graph in Fig. 3.24 holds. In this case, the BICRITERIA setting makes no sense, and, as we will see, all problems in the NONDISJOINT scenario can be solved in polynomial time.

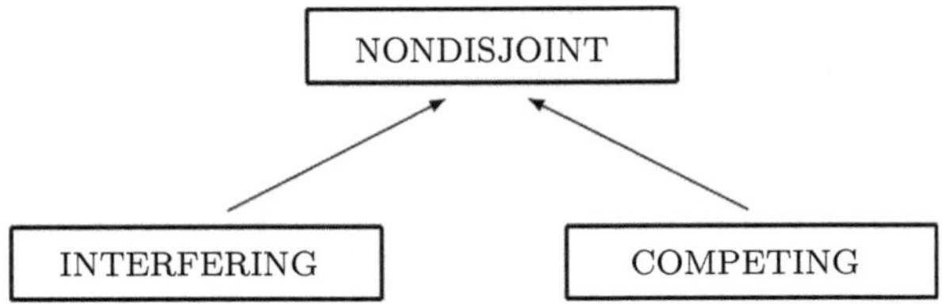


**Fig. 3.24** Reduction graph for $1|d_j^A = d_j^B|\sum U_j^A, \sum U_j^B$ when the common jobs have the same due dates for both agents

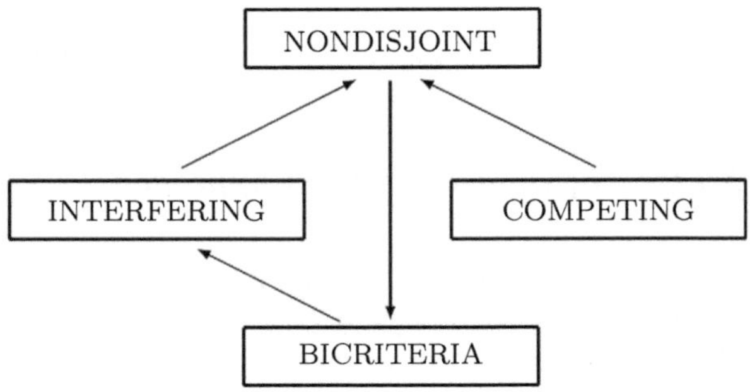


**Fig. 3.25** Reduction graph for $1||\sum U_j^A, \sum U_j^B$ when the common jobs may have different due dates for both agents

In case (ii), the reduction graph in Fig. 3.25 holds. Actually, in this case the COMPETING scenario is the same as with a single due date, since there are no jobs in common between the two agents. However, we will see that all problems in the remaining scenarios are hard.

## *3.14.1 Epsilon-Constraint Approach*

### 3.14.1.1 Problem $1|ND, d_j^A = d_j^B, \sum U_j^B \le Q|\sum U_j^A$

Let us start by considering problem $1|ND, d_j^A = d_j^B, \sum U_j^B \le Q|\sum U_j^A$ when the two agents apply the same due date to common jobs. We show that this problem can be efficiently solved by dynamic programming. The following lemma relates to the structure of an optimal schedule.

**Lemma 3.6.** *There is an optimal schedule $\sigma^*$ for problem $1|ND, d_j^A = d_j^B, \sum U_j^B \le Q|\sum U_j^A$ in which all the late jobs are scheduled consecutively at the end of the schedule, and all the early jobs are scheduled consecutively in Earliest Due Date (EDD) order at the beginning of the schedule.*

*Proof.* Consider an optimal schedule $\sigma^*$ and move all the late jobs to the end of the schedule, thus obtaining a new schedule $\sigma'$. Clearly, $\sum U_j^A(\sigma') \le \sum U_j^A(\sigma^*)$, since we are moving backward the early jobs. Consider now all the early jobs in $\sigma'$, that are sequenced consecutively at the beginning of the schedule, and resequence them in EDD order. This does not increase the number of late jobs, thus completing the proof. □

In the remaining part of this section we assume that the jobs in $\mathcal{J}$ are globally numbered from $J_1$ to $J_n$ in EDD order.

We next illustrate a recursion relation that can be exploited to design a polynomial time dynamic programming algorithm for $1|ND, d_j^A = d_j^B, \sum U_j^B \le Q|\sum U_j^A$.

Let $C(i,h,k)$ be the minimum completion time of the last early job in a partial schedule of the job set $\{J_1,\ldots,J_i\}$ in which agent $A$ has at most $h$ late jobs and agent $B$ at most $k$ late jobs. By definition, we set $C(i,h,k) = +\infty$ if no such schedule exists. The following relations hold.

*Boundary Conditions:*

$$C(0,h,k) = 0, \quad \text{for all } h \ge 0, k \ge 0$$
$$C(i,h,k) = +\infty, \quad \text{if } i < 0 \text{ or } h < 0 \text{ or } k < 0.$$

*Recursion Relation:*

$$f(i,h,k) = \begin{cases} +\infty & \text{if } C(i-1,h,k) + p_i > d_i \\ 0 & \text{otherwise.} \end{cases}$$

$$C(i,h,k) =$$
$$\begin{cases} \min\{C(i-1,h,k) + p_i + f(i,h,k); C(i-1,h-1,k)\} & \text{if } J_i \in \bar{\mathcal{J}}^A \\ \min\{C(i-1,h,k) + p_i + f(i,h,k); C(i-1,h,k-1)\} & \text{if } J_i \in \bar{\mathcal{J}}^B \\ \min\{C(i-1,h,k) + p_i + f(i,h,k); C(i-1,h-1,k-1)\} & \text{if } J_i \in \mathcal{J}^A \cap \mathcal{J}^B \end{cases}$$

In all three subcases of the recursion relation, the first term refers to job $J_i$ being scheduled on time. If this occurs, the makespan increases by $p_i$. The second term equals the makespan when $J_i$ is late. This term is slightly different depending on the subset $J_i$ belongs to.

**Lemma 3.7.** *If $C(i,h,k)$ is finite, then it is the minimum completion time of the last early job over all feasible schedules for the job set $\{J_1,\ldots,J_i\}$, with at most $h$ late jobs for agent $A$ and $k$ for agent $B$. If $C(i,h,k) = +\infty$, then there is no such feasible schedule.*

*Proof.* The proof is by induction on $i$. Clearly the property holds for $i = 1$, for any $h,k = 1,\ldots,n$. Now, assume that the property holds until $(i-1)$. We will show that the property holds also for $i$ and for any $h,k$.

Let $\sigma$ be a schedule for the job set $\{J_1,\ldots,J_i\}$, such that the completion time $\tau$ of the last early job in $\sigma$ is minimum among all feasible schedules with at most $h$ late jobs for agent $A$ and $k$ for agent $B$. If $J_i$ is early in $\sigma$ then, again from the inductive hypothesis, $\tau = C(i-1,h,k) + p_i$. If $J_i$ is late in $\sigma$, we consider three subcases.

1. If $J_i$ only belongs to agent $A$, from the inductive hypothesis, $\tau = C(i-1, h-1, k)$. If $C(i-1, h-1, k) = +\infty$, there can be no feasible schedule of $\{J_1, \ldots, J_i\}$ with at most $h$ and $k$ late jobs for the two agents respectively, and the algorithm sets $C(i, h, k) = +\infty$.
2. The argument is symmetrical if $J_i$ only belongs to agent $B$, so that $\tau = C(i-1, h, k-1)$ and the schedule attaining $C(i, j, k)$ is infeasible if $C(i-1, h, k-1) = +\infty$.
3. Finally, consider the case in which $J_i$ belongs to both agents. Now, from the inductive hypothesis, $\tau = C(i-1, h-1, k-1)$.

In all three cases, the recursion relation correctly chooses the smallest between the two quantities. □

**Theorem 3.28.** *The value* $h^* = \min\{h : C(n, h, Q) < +\infty\}$ *is an optimal solution value to problem* $1|ND, d_j^A = d_j^B, \sum U_j^B \leq Q|\sum U_j^A$*, and it can be computed in time* $O(n^3)$.

*Proof.* Suppose that an optimal schedule $\sigma$ for $1|ND, d_j^A = d_j^B, \sum U_j^B \leq Q|\sum U_j^A$ exists in which $\sum U_j^A(\sigma) = \tilde{h} < h^*$. In this case, by definition of $h^*$, it must hold $C(n, \tilde{h}, Q) = +\infty$. On the other hand, since $\tilde{h} < h^*$, in $\sigma$ there is at least one early job for agent $A$. Without loss of generality, we can assume that $\sigma$ has the structure illustrated in Lemma 3.6, and let $J_\ell$ be the last scheduled early job in $\sigma$. From Lemma 3.7, $C_\ell(\sigma)$ cannot be smaller than the minimum completion time of an early job, i.e., $C_\ell(\sigma) \geq C(n, \tilde{h}, Q)$. But since $C(n, \tilde{h}, Q) = +\infty$, this is a contradiction. Therefore, $h^*$ is the optimal value for $1|ND, d_j^A = d_j^B, \sum U_j^B \leq Q|\sum U_j^A$.

Let us now turn to complexity. Computing each $C(i, h, k)$ requires constant time. Since $h, k \leq n$, computing all of them requires $O(n^3)$ time. The quantity $h^*$ can be computed $O(n)$ time, and therefore the thesis holds. □

The dynamic programming approach can be extended to any number $K$ of agents, each holding $\sum U_j^k$ as objective function ($k = 1, \ldots, K$). In this case, $C(i, h_1, h_2, \ldots, h_K)$ will denote the smallest completion time of the last early job in a schedule of the first $i$ jobs, in which at most $h_j$ jobs are late for agent $k$, $k = 1, \ldots, K$. Although job $J_i$ can contribute to the number of late jobs of all the agents it belongs to, the computation of $C(i, h_1, h_2, \ldots, h_K)$ can still be done in constant time, since it only involves the comparison between two quantities. Therefore, the $K$-agent problem in the NONDISJOINT scenario can be solved in $O(n^{K+1})$. The complexity status of the $\varepsilon$-constraint problem in all scenarios when $K$ is not fixed is still open (Cheng et al. 2006).

The dynamic programming approach can also be extended to the problem with release dates, as long as these are *agreeable*, i.e., $d_i < d_j$ if and only if $r_i < r_j$. In fact, assuming with no loss of generality that $d_i \geq r_i + p_i$ for each $J_i$, the algorithm can still be applied, provided that the recursion relation is modified as follows:

$$C(i,h,k) =$$

$$\begin{cases} \min\{\max\{C(i-1,h,k), r_i\} + p_i + f(i,h,k);\ C(i-1,h-1,k)\} \\ \qquad\qquad\qquad\qquad \text{if } J_i \in \bar{\mathcal{J}}^A \\ \min\{\max\{C(i-1,h,k), r_i\} + p_i + f(i,h,k);\ C(i-1,h,k-1)\} \\ \qquad\qquad\qquad\qquad \text{if } J_i \in \bar{\mathcal{J}}^B \\ \min\{\max\{C(i-1,h,k), r_i\} + p_i + f(i,h,k);\ C(i-1,h-1,k-1)\} \\ \qquad\qquad\qquad\qquad \text{if } J_i \in \mathcal{J}^A \cap \mathcal{J}^B \end{cases}$$

In conclusion, the following result holds.

**Theorem 3.29.** *An optimal solution value to problem* $1|ND, r_j, d_j^A = d_j^B, \sum U_j^B \leq Q|\sum U_j^A$ *when release and due dates are agreeable can be computed in time* $O(n^3)$.

#### 3.14.1.2 Problem $1|ND, \sum U_j^B \leq Q|\sum U_j^A$

Let us now consider the case in which a job belonging to $\mathcal{J}^A \cap \mathcal{J}^B$ may have distinct due dates for the two agents. The problem $1|BI, \sum U_j^A \leq Q|\sum U_j^B$ is binary NP-hard. In fact, it reduces to the single-agent problem $1|d_j, \tilde{d}_j|\sum U_j$, which has already been recalled in Sect. 3.7.1, and that was proved binary NP-hard by Lawler (1982). In fact, $1|d_j, \tilde{d}_j|\sum U_j$ is a special case of $1|BI, \sum U_j^A \leq Q|\sum U_j^B$ in which deadlines $\tilde{d}_j$ play the role of due dates for agent $B$, and $Q = 0$. As a consequence, in view of Fig. 3.25, also $1|IN, \sum U_j^B \leq Q|\sum U_j^A$ and $1|ND, \sum U_j^A \leq Q|\sum U_j^B$ are NP-hard.

### *3.14.2 Computing the Pareto Set and Linear Combination*

From Lemma 3.7, it follows that a schedule with $h$ late jobs from $\mathcal{J}^A$ and $k$ late jobs from $\mathcal{J}^B$ is Pareto optimal if $C(n,h,k)$ is finite, while $C(n,h-1,k)$ and $C(n,h,k-1)$ are both infinite. The proof of Theorem 3.28 shows that all values $C(n,h,k)$ can be computed in $O(n^3)$. Hence, one can conclude the following.

**Theorem 3.30.** *The problem* $1|ND, d_j^A = d_j^B|\mathcal{P}(\sum U_j^A, \sum U_j^B)$ *and the problem* $1|ND, d_j^A = d_j^B|\alpha \sum U_j^A + \beta \sum U_j^B$ *can both be solved in* $O(n^3)$.

A corollary of this theorem is that problem $1|CO|\mathcal{P}(\sum U_j^A, \sum U_j^B)$ and problem $1|CO|\alpha \sum U_j^A + \beta \sum U_j^B$ can also be solved in $O(n^3)$.

Turning to the more general case in which the due dates of common jobs may be distinct for the two agents, we have the following result:

**Theorem 3.31.** *The problem* $1|BI, \alpha \sum U_j^A + \beta \sum U_j^B \leq Q|-$ *is NP-complete.*

*Proof.* Membership in NP is obvious. Given a feasibility instance of the single-agent problem $1|d_j, \tilde{d}_j, \sum U_j \leq Q|-$, we can define a feasibility instance $1|BI, \alpha \sum U_j^A + \beta \sum U_j^B \leq Q|-$. The due dates $d_j$ are the due dates of the jobs for agent $A$, while deadlines $\tilde{d}_j$ play the role of due dates for agent $B$. Let also $\alpha = 1$ and $\beta = Q + 1$. Hence, in a feasible instance for the BICRITERIA problem, no job can be tardy with respect to $\tilde{d}_j$, and therefore there is a schedule with at most $Q$ tardy jobs with respect to $d_j$ if and only if the original instance of the single-agent problem is feasible. □

The above result implies the NP-hardness of $1|IN|\alpha \sum U_j^A + \beta \sum U_j^B$ and $1|ND|\alpha \sum U_j^A + \beta \sum U_j^B$.

## 3.15 Functions $\sum w_j U_j, \sum w_j U_j$

The classical, single-agent problem $1||\sum w_j U_j$ is well-known to be binary NP-hard (Lawler and Moore 1969). This obviously implies that all multi-agent problems in this scenario are at least binary NP-hard. As in the previous section, also here we distinguish the two cases in which common jobs have the same due date for the two agents, and, respectively, have different due dates.

### *3.15.1 Epsilon-Constraint Approach*

#### 3.15.1.1 Common Jobs Have the Same Due Date

Let us consider the general $K$-agent setting (Fig. 3.26). When the jobs belonging to more than one set $\mathcal{J}^k$ have the same due date for all the sets they belong to, one can still assume that all jobs are numbered in EDD order. Cheng et al. (2006) show that the algorithm in Sect. 3.14.1.1 can be easily generalized to solve the $K$-agent problem $1|CO, \sum w_j^2 U_j^2 \leq Q_2, \ldots, \sum w_j^K U_j^K \leq Q_K|\sum w_j^1 U_j^1$. Here we report the algorithm for the general, multi-criteria case $1|MU, d_j^k = d_j, \sum w_j^2 U_j^2 \leq Q_2, \ldots, \sum w_j^K U_j^K \leq Q_K|\sum w_j^1 U_j^1$.

Let $C(i, X_1, X_2, \ldots, X_K)$ be the minimum completion time of the last early job in a partial schedule of the job set $\{J_1, \ldots, J_i\}$ in which $\sum w_j^k U_j \leq X_k$, $k = 1, \ldots, K$ and we set $C(i, X_1, X_2, \ldots, X_K) = +\infty$ if no such schedule exists. The following relations hold:

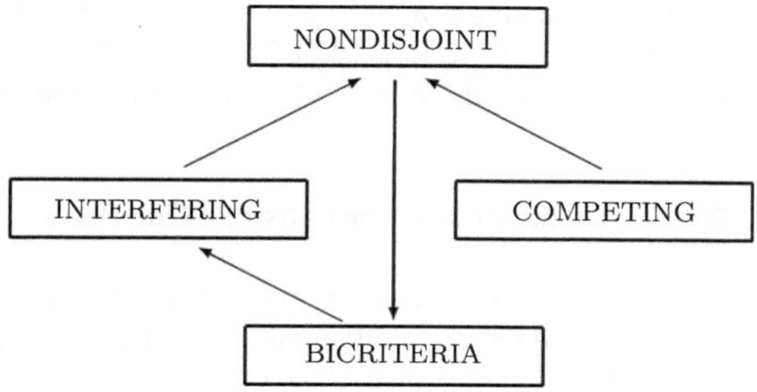


**Fig. 3.26** Reduction graph for $1|d_j^k = d_j|\sum w_j U_j, \sum w_j U_j$

*Boundary Conditions:*

$$C(0, X_1, X_2, \dots, X_K) = 0, \text{ for all } X_k \geq 0$$
$$C(i, X_1, X_2, \dots, X_K) = +\infty, \text{ if } i < 0 \text{ or some } X_k < 0.$$

*Recursion Relation:*

$$f(i, X_1, X_2, \dots, X_K) = \begin{cases} +\infty & \text{if } C(i-1, X_1, X_2, \dots, X_K) + p_i > d_i \\ 0 & \text{otherwise.} \end{cases}$$

$$C(i, X_1, X_2, \dots, X_K) = \min \Big\{ C(i-1, X_1, X_2, \dots, X_K) + p_i + f(i, X_1, X_2, \dots, X_K); \; C(i-1, X_1 - w_i^1, X_2 - w_i^2, \dots, X_K - w_i^K) \Big\}$$

In the recursion relation, the first term refers to job $J_i$ being scheduled on time. If this occurs, the makespan of early jobs increases by $p_i$. The second term equals the makespan of early jobs when $J_i$ is late. An analogous result to Theorem 3.28 can be easily established.

**Theorem 3.32.** *The value* $z^* = \min\{z : C(n, z, Q_2, \dots, Q_K) < +\infty\}$ *is an optimal solution value to* $1|MU, d_j^k = d_j, \sum w_j^2 U_j^2 \leq Q_2, \dots, \sum w_j^K U_j^K \leq Q_K|\sum w_j^1 U_j^1$*, and it can be computed in time* $O(nW_1 Q_2 \dots Q_K)$*, where* $W_1 = \sum w_j^1$.

Cheng et al. (2006) provide an FPTAS for problem $1|CO, \sum w_j^2 U_j^2 \leq Q_2, \dots, \sum w_j^K U_j^K \leq Q_K|\sum w_j^1 U_j^1$ for fixed $K$. Also, similar considerations to those of Sect. 3.14.1.1 can be done for what concerns the problem with release dates, which can therefore be solved in pseudopolynomial time if release and due dates are agreeable.

When the number $K$ of agents is not fixed, they show that the problem $1|CO, \sum w_j^2 U_j^2 \leq Q_2, \dots, \sum w_j^K U_j^K \leq Q_K | \sum w_j^1 U_j^1$ is strongly NP-hard. Figure 3.25 implies the strong NP-hardness of all the other scenarios.

#### 3.15.1.2 Common Jobs Have Distinct Due Dates

Here we limit ourselves to observing that when the same job may have distinct due dates, the dynamic programming algorithm of Sect. 3.15.1.1 no longer holds in general, since a unique EDD ordering of the jobs may not exist. Problem $1|ND, \sum w_j^B U_j^B \leq Q_B | \sum w_j^A U_j^A$ is in fact open as for strong NP-hardness.

## *3.15.2 Computing the Pareto Set*

We next address the problem of determining the size of the Pareto set. For simplicity we refer to the COMPETING scenario with two agents, i.e., to problem $1|CO|\mathcal{P}(\sum w_j^A U_j^A, \sum w_j^B U_j^B)$. By means of a similar construction to Example 3.7, we show that the size of the Pareto set may not be polynomial, even if all jobs have the same due date.

*Example 3.9.* Let consider an instance of $1|CO|\mathcal{P}(\sum w_j^A U_j^A, \sum w_j^B U_j^B)$ in which the sets $\mathcal{J}^A$ and $\mathcal{J}^B$ are identical. Each set consists of $h$ jobs of size and weight $p_0 = w_0 = 1, p_1 = w_1 = 2, p_2 = w_2 = 4, p_3 = w_3 = 8, \dots, p_{h-1} = w_{h-1} = 2^{h-1}$. All jobs have the same due date, $d = 2^h - 1$. Notice that, in this example, for any schedule the sum of the two agents' objectives cannot be smaller than $2^h - 1$. Hence, any schedule for which this sum equals $2^h - 1$ is Pareto optimal. One such schedule can be obtained as follows. For each pair of jobs of equal size, schedule the job of one (arbitrary) agent between 0 and $d$ (i.e., early) and the job of the other agent after $d$ (i.e., tardy). By doing so, the makespan of the early jobs is exactly $d$. Hence, if the cost to agent $A$ is $x$, the cost to agent $B$ is $2^h - 1 - x$. For each value of $x$ such that $0 \leq x \leq 2^h - 1$, we get a distinct Pareto optimal schedule. Hence, there are at least $2^h$ Pareto optimal solutions. ◇

## 3.16 Tables

This section summarizes the complexity results presented in this chapter in 13 tables. Tables 3.1–3.5 present the results in the COMPETING scenario, Tables 3.6–3.9 present the results in the NONDISJOINT scenario, Tables 3.10 and 3.11 concern the INTERFERING scenario and Tables 3.12 and 3.13 concern the BICRITERIA scenario.

**Table 3.1** Complexity of two-agent, $\varepsilon$-constraint COMPETING problems

| Problem | Complexity | Section | Page |
|---|---|---|---|
| $1\|CO, C^B_{\max} \leq Q\|C^A_{\max}$ | $O(n)$ | 3.1.1.3 | 63 |
| $1\|CO, L^B_{\max} \leq Q\|L^A_{\max}$ | $O(n \log n)$ | 3.1.1.2 | 59 |
| $1\|CO, prec, f^B_{\max} \leq Q\|f^A_{\max}$ | $O(n^2)$ | 3.1.1 | 58 |
| $1\|CO, C^B_{\max} \leq Q\|\sum C^A_j$ | $O(n_A \log n_A + n_B)$ | 3.2.1 | 72 |
| $1\|CO, f^B_{\max} \leq Q\|\sum C^A_j$ | $O(n \log n)$ | 3.3.1 | 74 |
| $1\|CO, C^B_{\max} \leq Q\|\sum w^A_j C^A_j$ | bNPH, $O(n_A Q^2)$ | 3.4.1 | 81 |
| $1\|CO, L^B_{\max} \leq Q\|\sum w^A_j C^A_j$ | sNPH | 3.5.1 | 92 |
| $1\|CO, f^B_{\max} \leq Q\|\sum U^A_j$ | $O(n_A \log n_A + n_B \log n_B)$ | 3.7.1 | 103 |
| $1\|CO, f^B_{\max} \leq Q\|\sum T^A_j$ | bNPH, $O(n_A^4 P + n_B \log n_B)$ | 3.8 | 108 |
| $1\|CO, \sum C^B_j \leq Q\|\sum C^A_j$ | bNPH, $O(n_A n_B Q)$ | 3.9.1 | 110 |
| $1\|CO, \sum w^B_j C^B_j \leq Q\|\sum w^A_j C^A_j$ | sNPH | 3.10.1 | 116 |
| $1\|CO, \sum C^B_j \leq Q\|\sum U^A_j$ | bNPH | 3.11.1 | 126 |
| $1\|CO, \sum C^B_j \leq Q\|\sum T^A_j$ | bNPH, $O(n_A^4 n_B^2 QP)$ | 3.12 | 130 |
| $1\|CO, \sum w^B_j C^B_j \leq Q\|\sum U^A_j$ | sNPH | 3.13.1 | 131 |
| $1\|CO, \sum U^B_j \leq Q\|\sum U^A_j$ | $O(n^3)$ | 3.14.1.1 | 132 |
| $1\|CO, \sum w^B_j U^B_j \leq Q\|\sum w^A_j U^A_j$ | bNPH, $O(nW^2)$ | 3.15.1.1 | 136 |
| $1\|CO, r_j, pmtn, f^B_{\max} \leq Q\|f^A_{\max}$ | $O(n^2)$ | 3.1.1 | 63 |
| $1\|CO, r_j, pmtn, L^B_{\max} \leq Q\|L^A_{\max}$ | $O(n_A \log n_A + n_B \log n_B)$ | 3.1.1 | 63 |
| $1\|CO, r_j, pmtn, f^B_{\max} \leq Q\|\sum C^A_j$ | bNPH | 3.3.1 | 77 |
| $1\|CO, r_j, pmtn, f^B_{\max} \leq Q\|\sum U^A_j$ | $O(n^5)$ | 3.7.1 | 106 |
| $1\|CO, r_j, pmtn, \sum C^B_j \leq Q\|\sum U^A_j$ | bNPH | 3.11.1 | 126 |

'bNPH' for *binary NP-hard*
'sNPH' for *strongly NP-hard*

**Table 3.2** Complexity of two-agent, linear combination COMPETING problems

| Problem | Complexity | Section | Page |
|---|---|---|---|
| $1\|CO\|\alpha C^A_{\max} + \beta C^B_{\max}$ | $O(n)$ | 3.1.3 | 67 |
| $1\|CO\|\alpha L^A_{\max} + \beta L^B_{\max}$ | $O(n^3)$ | 3.1.3 | 67 |
| $1\|CO\|\alpha f^A_{\max} + \beta f^B_{\max}$ | $O(n^4)$ | 3.1.3 | 67 |
| $1\|CO\|\alpha \sum C^A_j + \beta C^B_{\max}$ | $O(n_A \log n_A)$ | 3.2.3 | 74 |
| $1\|CO\|\alpha \sum C^A_j + \beta f^B_{\max}$ | $O(n^4)$ | 3.3.3 | 80 |
| $1\|CO\|\alpha \sum w^A_j C^A_j + \beta C^B_{\max}$ | $O(n \log n)$ | 3.4.3 | 87 |
| $1\|CO\|\alpha \sum w^A_j C^A_j + \beta L^B_{\max}$ | sNPH | 3.5.3 | 102 |
| $1\|CO\|\alpha \sum w^A_j C^A_j + \beta f^B_{\max}$ | sNPH | 3.5.3 | 102 |
| $1\|CO\|\alpha \sum U^A_j + \beta f^B_{\max}$ | $O(n_A n \log n \log UB)$ | 3.7.2 | 107 |
| $1\|CO\|\alpha \sum C^A_j + \beta \sum C^B_j$ | $O(n \log n)$ | 3.9.3 | 115 |
| $1\|CO\|\alpha \sum w^A_j C^A_j + \beta \sum w^B_j C^B_j$ | $O(n \log n)$ | 3.10.4 | 126 |
| $1\|CO\|\alpha \sum C^A_j + \beta \sum U^B_j$ | bNPH | 3.11.3 | 127 |
| $1\|CO\|\alpha \sum w^A_j C^A_j + \beta \sum U^B_j$ | sNPH | 3.13.2 | 131 |
| $1\|CO\|\alpha \sum U^A_j + \beta \sum U^B_j$ | $O(n^3)$ | 3.14.2 | 135 |
| $1\|CO\|\alpha \sum w^A_j U^A_j + \beta \sum w^B_j U^B_j$ | NP-hard | 3.15 | 136 |

'bNPH' for *binary NP-hard*
'sNPH' for *strongly NP-hard*

**Table 3.3** Complexity of two-agent, Pareto optimality COMPETING problems

| Problem | Complexity | Size | Section | Page |
|---|---|---|---|---|
| $1\|CO\|\mathcal{P}(C^A_{\max}, C^B_{\max})$ | $O(n)$ | 2 | 3.1.1.3 | 63 |
| $1\|CO\|\mathcal{P}(L^A_{\max}, L^B_{\max})$ | $O(n^3)$ | $O(n^2)$ | 3.1.2.2 | 66 |
| $1\|CO\|\mathcal{P}(f^A_{\max}, f^B_{\max})$ | $O(n^4)$ | $O(n_A n_B)$ | 3.1.2 | 65 |
| $1\|CO\|\mathcal{P}(\sum C^A_j, C^B_{\max})$ | $O(n_A \log n_A)$ | $O(n_A)$ | 3.2.2 | 73 |
| $1\|CO\|\mathcal{P}(f^A_{\max}, \sum C^B_j)$ | $O(n^4)$ | $O(n_A n_B)$ | 3.3.2 | 77 |
| $1\|CO\|\mathcal{P}(C^A_{\max}, \sum w^B_j C^B_j)$ | | Nonpolynomial | 3.4.2 | 87 |
| $1\|CO\|\mathcal{P}(L^A_{\max}, \sum w^B_j C^B_j)$ | | Nonpolynomial | 3.4.2 | 87 |
| $1\|CO\|\mathcal{P}(\sum U^A_j, f^B_{\max})$ | $O(n_A n \log n \log UB)$ | $O(n_A)$ | 3.7.2 | 107 |
| $1\|CO\|\mathcal{P}(\sum C^A_j, \sum C^B_j)$ | | Nonpolynomial | 3.9.2 | 114 |
| $1\|CO\|\mathcal{P}(\sum w^A_j C^A_j, \sum w^B_j C^B_j)$ | | Nonpolynomial | 3.9.2 | 114 |
| $1\|CO\|\mathcal{P}(\sum U^A_j, \sum U^B_j)$ | $O(n^3)$ | $O(n)$ | 3.14.2 | 135 |

**Table 3.4** Complexity of $K$-agent COMPETING problems, $K$ fixed. We let $U = \max_j\{f_j(P)\}$ and $\bar{Q} = \max_{2\leq k\leq K}\{Q_k\}$

| Problem | Complexity | Section | Page |
|---|---|---|---|
| $1\|CO, f^2_{\max} \leq Q_2, \dots, f^K_{\max} \leq Q_K\|f^1_{\max}$ | $O(\min\{n^2, n \log n \log U\})$ | 3.1.1.4 | 64 |
| $1\|CO, f^1_{\max} \leq Q_1, f^2_{\max} \leq Q_2, \dots, f^K_{\max} \leq Q_K\|-$ | $O(n \log n)$ | 3.1.1.4 | 64 |
| $1\|CO, f^2_{\max} \leq Q_2, \dots, f^K_{\max} \leq Q_K\|\sum C^1_j$ | $O(n \log n)$ | 3.3.1 | 74 |
| $1\|CO, \sum U^2_j \leq Q_2, \dots, \sum U^K_j \leq Q_K\|\sum U^1_j$ | $O(n^{K+1})$ | 3.14.1.1 | 132 |
| $1\|CO, \sum w^2_j U^2_j \leq Q_2, \dots, \sum w^K_j U^K_j \leq Q_K\|\sum w^1_j U^1_j$ | bNPH, $O(n W_1 Q_2 \dots Q_K)$ | 3.15.1.1 | 136 |
| $1\|CO, \sum C^2_j \leq Q_2, \dots, \sum C^K_j \leq Q_K\|\sum C^1_j$ | bNPH, $O(n^K \bar{Q}^{K-1})$ | 3.9.1.3 | 114 |
| $1\|CO\|\sum \alpha_k C^k_{\max}$ | $O(n)$ | 3.1.3 | 67 |
| $1\|CO\|\sum \alpha_k L^k_{\max}$ | $O(n^{2K+1})$ | 3.1.3 | 67 |
| $1\|CO\|\sum_{k=1}^{K-1} \alpha_k C^k_{\max} + \alpha_K(\sum w^K_j C^K_j)$ | $O(n \log n)$ | 3.4.3 | 87 |
| $1\|CO\|\sum_{k=1}^{K-1} \alpha_k C^k_{\max} + \alpha_K(\sum_j U^K_j)$ | Open | 3.7.2 | 107 |
| $1\|CO\|\sum_{k=1}^{K-1} \alpha_k(\sum_j w^k_j C^k_j) + \alpha_K C^K_{\max}$ | $O(n \log n)$ | 3.4.3 | 87 |
| $1\|CO\|\sum_k \alpha_k(\sum w^k_j C^k_j)$ | $O(n \log n)$ | 3.10.4 | 126 |
| $1\|CO\|\sum_{k=1}^{K-1} \alpha_k(\sum_j w^k_j C^k_j) + \alpha_K \sum U^K_j$ | sNPH | 3.13.2 | 131 |
| $1\|CO\|\sum_{k=1}^{K-1} \alpha_k(\sum_j U^k_j) + \alpha_K C^K_{\max}$ | Open | 3.7.2 | 107 |
| $1\|CO\|\sum_{k=1}^{K-1} \alpha_k(\sum_j U^k_j) + \alpha_K(\sum_j w^K_j C^K_j)$ | sNPH | 3.13.2 | 131 |
| $1\|CO\|\sum_k \alpha_k(\sum_j U^k_j)$ | $O(n^{K+1})$ | 3.14.2 | 135 |

'bNPH' for *binary NP-hard*
'sNPH' for *strongly NP-hard*

Tables 3.1, 3.6, 3.10 and 3.12 deal with the $\varepsilon$-constraint approach. Tables 3.2, 3.7, 3.11 and 3.13 deal with the linear combination approach. Table 3.3 deals with the enumeration of the Pareto set. Tables 3.4, 3.5, 3.8 and 3.9 concern the $K$-agent case.

**Table 3.5** Complexity of $K$-agent COMPETING problems, $K$ not fixed. We let $U$ denote $\max_j\{f_j(P)\}$

| Problem | Complexity | Section | Page |
|---|---|---|---|
| $1\|CO, f^2_{\max} \le Q_2, \ldots, f^K_{\max} \le Q_K\|f^1_{\max}$ | $O(\min\{n^2 + nK,$ $n \log n \log U\}$ | 3.1.1.4 | 65 |
| $1\|CO, f^1_{\max} \le Q_1, f^2_{\max} \le Q_2, \ldots, f^K_{\max} \le Q_K\|-$ | $O(n \log n)$ | 3.1.1.4 | 65 |
| $1\|CO, f^2_{\max} \le Q_2, \ldots, f^K_{\max} \le Q_K\|\sum C^1_j$ | $O(n \log n)$ | 3.3.1 | 74 |
| $1\|CO, \sum U^2_j \le Q_2, \ldots, \sum U^K_j \le Q_K\|\sum U^1_j$ | Open | 3.14.1.1 | 132 |
| $1\|CO, \sum w^2_j U^2_j \le Q_2, \ldots, \sum w^K_j U^K_j \le Q_K\|\sum w^1_j U^1_j$ | sNPH | 3.15.1.1 | 136 |
| $1\|CO, \sum C^2_j \le Q_2, \ldots, \sum C^K_j \le Q_K\|\sum C^1_j$ | bNPH* | 3.9.1 | 110 |
| $1\|CO\|\sum \alpha_k C^k_{\max}$ | $O(n + K \log K)$ | 3.1.3 | 67 |
| $1\|CO\|\sum \alpha_k L^k_{\max}$ | bNPh* | 3.1.3 | 67 |
| $1\|CO\|\sum_{k=1}^{K-1} \alpha_k C^k_{\max} + \alpha_K(\sum_j w^K_j C^K_j)$ | $O(n \log n)$ | 3.4.3 | 87 |
| $1\|CO\|\sum_{k=1}^{K-1} \alpha_k C^k_{\max} + \alpha_K(\sum_j U^K_j)$ | sNPH | 3.7.2 | 107 |
| $1\|CO\|\sum_{k=1}^{K-1} \alpha_k(\sum_j w^k_j C^k_j) + \alpha_K C^K_{\max}$ | $O(n \log n)$ | 3.4.3 | 87 |
| $1\|CO\|\sum_k \alpha_k(\sum_j w^k_j C^k_j)$ | $O(n \log n)$ | 3.10.4 | 126 |
| $1\|CO\|\sum_{k=1}^{K-1} \alpha_k(\sum_j w^k_j C^k_j) + \alpha_K \sum_j U^K_j$ | sNPH | 3.13.2 | 131 |
| $1\|CO\|\sum_{k=1}^{K-1} \alpha_k(\sum_j U^k_j) + \alpha_K C^K_{\max}$ | bNPH | 3.14.2 | 136 |
| $1\|CO\|\sum_{k=1}^{K-1} \alpha_k(\sum_j U^k_j) + \alpha_K(\sum_j w^K_j C^K_j)$ | sNPH | 3.13.2 | 131 |
| $1\|CO\|\sum_k \alpha_k(\sum_j U^k_j)$ | bNPH | 3.14.2 | 135 |

'bNPH' for *binary NP-hard*
'sNPH' for *strongly NP-hard*
'bNPH*' for *binary NP-hard*, open as for strong NP-hardness

## 3.17 Bibliographic Remarks

This chapter has covered most of the literature on single-machine multi-agent problems. Actually, several papers are coming out on this topic, mainly devoted to developing exact and heuristic approaches for hard problems. We briefly point out some of the most recent papers.

A few paper consider tardiness-related objective functions. In particular, Lee et al. (2012) address problem $1|CO, r_j, T^B_{\max} \le Q|\sum T^A_j$, Wu (2013) addresses problem $1|CO, T^B_{\max} \le 0|\sum T^A_j$ and Yin et al. (2012c) address problem $1|CO, r_j, L^B_{\max} \le Q|\sum T^A_j$. In each of these papers a branch-and-bound algorithm and various meta-heuristic algorithms are proposed. Wu et al. (2013a) address problem $1|CO, r_j, \sum C^B_j \le Q|\sum C^A_j$ and show that it is strongly NP-hard. They also provide an exact algorithm and various meta-heuristic algorithms. For problem $1|CO, r_j, L^B_{\max} \le Q|\sum w^A_j C^A_j$, Cheng et al. (2013) propose a branch-and-bound algorithm and a simulated annealing algorithm.

Khowala et al. (2009) propose a heuristic approach for generating Pareto optimal solutions of the problem $1|CO|\mathcal{P}(\sum U^A_j, \sum C^B_j)$.

**Table 3.6** Complexity of two-agent, $\varepsilon$-constraint NONDISJOINT problems

| Problem | Complexity | Section | Page |
|---|---|---|---|
| $1\|ND, C^B_{\max} \leq Q\|C^A_{\max}$ | $O(n)$ | 3.1.1.3 | 63 |
| $1\|ND, L^B_{\max} \leq Q\|L^A_{\max}$ | $O(n \log n)$ | 3.1.1.2 | 59 |
| $1\|ND, prec, f^B_{\max} \leq Q\|f^A_{\max}$ | $O(n^2)$ | 3.1.1.1 | 58 |
| $1\|ND, C^B_{\max} \leq Q\|\sum C^A_j$ | $O(n_A \log n_A)$ | 3.2.1 | 72 |
| $1\|ND, f^B_{\max} \leq Q\|\sum C^A_j$ | $O(n \log n)$ | 3.3.1 | 74 |
| $1\|ND, C^B_{\max} \leq Q\|\sum w^A_j C^A_j$ | bNPH, $O(n_A Q^2)$ | 3.4.1 | 81 |
| $1\|ND, L^B_{\max} \leq Q\|\sum w^A_j C^A_j$ | sNPH | 3.5.1 | 92 |
| $1\|ND, C^B_{\max} \leq Q\|\sum U^A_j$ | Open | 3.7.1 | 103 |
| $1\|ND, L^B_{\max} \leq Q\|\sum U^A_j$ | bNPH | 3.7.1 | 103 |
| $1\|ND, C^B_{\max} \leq Q\|\sum T^A_j$ | bNPH | 3.8.1 | 108 |
| $1\|ND, \sum C^B_j \leq Q\|\sum C^A_j$ | bNPH, $O(n^3 Q)$ | 3.9.1 | 110 |
| $1\|ND, \sum w^B_j C^B_j \leq Q\|\sum w^A_j C^A_j$ | sNPH | 3.10.1 | 116 |
| $1\|ND, \sum C^B_j \leq Q\|\sum U^A_j$ | bNPH | 3.11.1 | 126 |
| $1\|ND, \sum C^B_j \leq Q\|\sum T^A_j$ | bNPH | 3.12 | 130 |
| $1\|ND, \sum w^B_j C^B_j \leq Q\|\sum U^A_j$ | sNPH | 3.7.2 | 107 |
| $1\|ND, d^A_j = d^B_j, \sum U^B_j \leq Q\|\sum U^A_j$ | $O(n^3)$ | 3.14.1.1 | 132 |
| $1\|ND, \sum U^B_j \leq Q\|\sum U^A_j$ | bNPH | 3.14.1.2 | 135 |
| $1\|ND, d^A_j = d^B_j, \sum w^B_j U^B_j \leq Q\|\sum w^A_j U^A_j$ | bNPH, $O(n W_A Q)$ | 3.15.1.1 | 136 |
| $1\|ND, \sum w^B_j U^B_j \leq Q\|\sum w^A_j U^A_j$ | bNPH* | 3.15.1.2 | 138 |

'bNPH' for *binary NP-hard*
'bNPH*' for *binary NP-hard*, open as for strong NP-hardness
'sNPH' for *strongly NP-hard*

**Table 3.7** Complexity of two-agent, linear combination NONDISJOINT problems

| Problem | Complexity | Section | Page |
|---|---|---|---|
| $1\|ND\|\alpha C^A_{\max} + \beta C^B_{\max}$ | $O(n)$ | 3.1.3 | 67 |
| $1\|ND\|\alpha f^A_{\max} + \beta f^B_{\max}$ | $O(n^4)$ | 3.1.3 | 67 |
| $1\|ND\|\alpha \sum C^A_j + \beta C^B_{\max}$ | $O(n_A \log n_A)$ | 3.2.3 | 74 |
| $1\|ND\|\alpha \sum C^A_j + \beta f^B_{\max}$ | $O(n^4)$ | 3.3.3 | 80 |
| $1\|ND\|\alpha \sum w^A_j C^A_j + \beta C^B_{\max}$ | $O(n \log n)$ | 3.4.3 | 87 |
| $1\|ND\|\alpha \sum w^A_j C^A_j + \beta L^B_{\max}$ | sNPH | 3.5.3 | 102 |
| $1\|ND\|\alpha \sum C^A_j + \beta \sum C^B_j$ | $O(n \log n)$ | 3.9.3 | 115 |
| $1\|ND\|\alpha \sum w^A_j C^A_j + \beta \sum w^B_j C^B_j$ | $O(n \log n)$ | 3.10.4 | 126 |
| $1\|ND\|\alpha \sum C^A_j + \beta \sum U^B_j$ | bNPH | 3.11.3 | 127 |
| $1\|ND\|\alpha \sum w^A_j C^A_j + \beta \sum U^B_j$ | sNPH | 3.13.2 | 131 |
| $1\|ND, d^A_j = d^B_j\|\alpha \sum U^A_j + \beta \sum U^B_j$ | $O(n^3)$ | 3.14.2 | 135 |
| $1\|ND\|\alpha \sum U^A_j + \beta \sum U^B_j$ | bNPH | 3.14.2 | 135 |

'bNPH' for *binary NP-hard*
'sNPH' for *strongly NP-hard*

**Table 3.8** Complexity of $K$-agent, NONDISJOINT problems, $K$ fixed. $\bar{Q}$ denotes $\max_{2\le k\le K}\{Q_k\}$

| Problem | Complexity | Section | Page |
|---|---|---|---|
| $1\|ND, f^2_{\max} \le Q_2, \ldots, f^K_{\max} \le Q_K\|f^1_{\max}$ | $O(n^2)$ | 3.1.1.4 | 65 |
| $1\|ND, f^2_{\max} \le Q_2, \ldots, f^K_{\max} \le Q_K\|\sum_j C^1_j$ | $O(n \log n)$ | 3.3.1 | 74 |
| $1\|ND, \sum C^2_j \le Q_2, \ldots, \sum C^K_j \le Q_K\|\sum C^1_j$ | bNPH, $O(n^{2^K-1}\bar{Q}^{K-1})$ | 3.9.1 | 110 |
| $1\|ND, d^k_j = d_j, \sum U^2_j \le Q_2, \ldots, \sum U^K_j \le Q_K\|\sum U^1_j$ | $O(n^{K+1})$ | 3.14.1.1 | 132 |
| $1\|ND, d^k_j = d_j, \sum w^2_j U^2_j \le Q_2, \ldots, \sum w^K_j U^K_j \le Q_K\|\sum w^1_j U^1_j$ | bNPH, $O(nW_1 Q_2 \ldots Q_K)$ | 3.15.1.1 | 136 |
| $1\|ND\|\sum \alpha_k C^k_{\max}$ | $O(n2^K)$ | 3.1.3 | 67 |
| $1\|ND\|\sum_{k=1}^{K-1} \alpha_k(\sum_j w^k_j C^k_j) + \alpha_K C^K_{\max}$ | $O(n \log n)$ | 3.4.3 | 90 |
| $1\|ND\|\sum_k \alpha_k(\sum_j w^k_j C^k_j)$ | $O(n \log n)$ | 3.10.4 | 126 |
| $1\|ND\|\sum_{k=1}^{K-1} \alpha_k(\sum_j w^k_j C^k_j) + \alpha_K \sum_j U^K_j$ | sNPH | 3.13.2 | 131 |
| $1\|ND\|\sum_{k=1}^{K-1} \alpha_k(\sum_j U^k_j) + (\sum_j w^K_j C^K_j)$ | sNPH | 3.13.2 | 131 |
| $1\|ND, d^k_j = d_j\|\sum_k \alpha_k(\sum_j U^k_j)$ | $O(n^{K+1})$ | 3.14.2 | 135 |

'bNPH' for *binary NP-hard*
'sNPH' for *strongly NP-hard*

**Table 3.9** Complexity of $K$-agent, NONDISJOINT problems, $K$ not fixed

| Problem | Complexity | Section | Page |
|---|---|---|---|
| $1\|ND, f^2_{\max} \le Q_2, \ldots, f^K_{\max} \le Q_K\|f^1_{\max}$ | $O(n^2 + nK)$ | 3.1.1.4 | 65 |
| $1\|ND, f^2_{\max} \le Q_2, \ldots, f^K_{\max} \le Q_K\|\sum C^1_j$ | $O(n \log n + nK)$ | 3.3.1 | 74 |
| $1\|ND, \sum C^2_j \le Q_2, \ldots, \sum C^K_j \le Q_K\|\sum C^1_j$ | bNPH* | 3.9.1 | 110 |
| $1\|ND, d^k_j = d_j, \sum U^2_j \le Q_2, \ldots, \sum U^K_j \le Q_K\|\sum U^1_j$ | Open | 3.14.1.1 | 132 |
| $1\|ND, d^k_j = d_j, \sum w^2_j U^2_j \le Q_2, \ldots, \sum w^K_j U^K_j \le Q_K\|\sum w^1_j U^1_j$ | sNPH | 3.15.1.1 | 136 |
| $1\|ND\|\sum \alpha_k C^k_{\max}$ | sNPH | 3.1.3 | 67 |
| $1\|ND\|\sum_{k=1}^{K-1} \alpha_k C^k_{\max} + \alpha_K(\sum_j w^K_j C^K_j)$ | sNPH | 3.1.3 | 67 |
| $1\|ND\|\sum_{k=1}^{K-1} \alpha_k C^k_{\max} + \alpha_K(\sum_j U^K_j)$ | sNPH | 3.13.2 | 131 |
| $1\|ND\|\sum_{k=1}^{K-1} \alpha_k(\sum_j w^k_j C^k_j) + \alpha_K C^K_{\max}$ | $O(nK + n \log n)$ | 3.4.3 | 90 |
| $1\|ND\|\sum_k \alpha_k(\sum_j w^k_j C^k_j)$ | $O(nK + n \log n)$ | 3.10.4 | 126 |
| $1\|ND\|\sum_{k=1}^{K-1} \alpha_k(\sum_j w^k_j C^k_j) + \alpha_K \sum_j U^K_j$ | sNPH | 3.13.2 | 131 |
| $1\|ND\|\sum_{k=1}^{K-1} \alpha_k(\sum_j U^k_j) + \alpha_K C^K_{\max}$ | NP-hard | 3.14.2 | 135 |
| $1\|ND\|\sum_{k=1}^{K-1} \alpha_k(\sum_j U^k_j) + \alpha_K(\sum_j w^K_j C^K_j)$ | sNPH | 3.13.2 | 131 |
| $1\|ND\|\sum_k \alpha_k(\sum_j U^k_j)$ | NP-hard | 3.14.2 | 135 |

'bNPH' for *binary NP-hard*
'bNPH*' for *binary NP-hard*, open as for strong NP-hardness
'sNPH' for *strongly NP-hard*

**Table 3.10** Complexity of two-agent, $\varepsilon$-constraint INTERFERING problems

| Problem | Complexity | Section | Page |
|---|---|---|---|
| $1\|IN, L^B_{\max} \le Q\|L^A_{\max}$ | $O(n \log n)$ | 3.1.1.2 | 59 |
| $1\|IN, prec, f^B_{\max} \le Q\|f^A_{\max}$ | $O(n^2)$ | 3.1.1 | 58 |
| $1\|IN, f^B_{\max} \le Q\|\sum C^A_j$ | $O(n \log n)$ | 3.3.1 | 74 |
| $1\|IN, C^B_{\max} \le Q\|\sum w^A_j C^A_j$ | bNPH, $O(nQ^2)$ | 3.4.1 | 81 |
| $1\|IN, L^B_{\max} \le Q\|\sum w^A_j C^A_j$ | sNPH | 3.5.1 | 92 |
| $1\|IN, C^B_{\max} \le Q\|\sum U^A_j$ | Open | 3.7.1 | 103 |
| $1\|IN, L^B_{\max} \le Q\|\sum U^A_j$ | bNPH | 3.7.1 | 103 |
| $1\|IN, C^B_{\max} \le Q\|\sum T^A_j$ | bNPH | 3.8.1 | 108 |
| $1\|IN, \sum C^B_j \le Q\|\sum C^A_j$ | bNPH, $O(n^2 Q)$ | 3.9.1 | 110 |
| $1\|IN, \sum w^B_j C^B_j \le Q\|\sum w^A_j C^A_j$ | sNPH | 3.10.1 | 116 |
| $1\|IN, \sum C^B_j \le Q\|\sum U^A_j$ | bNPH | 3.11.1 | 126 |
| $1\|IN, \sum U^B_j \le Q\|\sum C^A_j$ | bNPH | 3.11.1 | 126 |
| $1\|IN, \sum C^B_j \le Q\|\sum T^A_j$ | bNPH | 3.12 | 130 |
| $1\|IN, \sum w^B_j C^B_j \le Q\|\sum U^A_j$ | sNPH | 3.13.1 | 131 |
| $1\|IN, d^A_j = d^B_j, \sum U^B_j \le Q\|\sum U^A_j$ | $O(n^3)$ | 3.14.1.1 | 132 |
| $1\|IN, \sum U^B_j \le Q\|\sum U^A_j$ | bNPH | 3.14.2 | 135 |
| $1\|IN, \sum w^B_j U^B_j \le Q\|\sum w^A_j U^A_j$ | bNPH, $O(nW_A Q)$ | 3.15.1.2 | 138 |

'bNPH' for *binary NP-hard*
'sNPH' for *strongly NP-hard*

**Table 3.11** Complexity of two-agent, linear combination INTERFERING problems

| Problem | Complexity | Section | Page |
|---|---|---|---|
| $1\|IN\|\alpha f^A_{\max} + \beta f^B_{\max}$ | $O(n^4)$ | 3.1.3 | 67 |
| $1\|IN\|\alpha \sum C^A_j + \beta C^B_{\max}$ | $O(n \log n)$ | 3.2.3 | 74 |
| $1\|IN\|\alpha \sum C^A_j + \beta f^B_{\max}$ | $O(n^4)$ | 3.3.3 | 80 |
| $1\|IN\|\alpha \sum w^A_j C^A_j + \beta C^B_{\max}$ | $O(n \log n)$ | 3.4.3 | 87 |
| $1\|IN\|\alpha \sum w^A_j C^A_j + \beta L^B_{\max}$ | sNPH | 3.5.3 | 102 |
| $1\|IN\|\alpha \sum C^A_j + \beta \sum C^B_j$ | $O(n \log n)$ | 3.9.3 | 115 |
| $1\|IN\|\alpha \sum w^A_j C^A_j + \beta \sum w^B_j C^B_j$ | $O(n \log n)$ | 3.10.4 | 126 |
| $1\|IN\|\alpha \sum C^A_j + \beta \sum U^B_j$ | bNPH | 3.11.3 | 127 |
| $1\|IN\|\alpha \sum w^A_j C^A_j + \beta \sum U^B_j$ | sNPH | 3.13.2 | 131 |
| $1\|IN, d^A_j = d^B_j\|\alpha \sum U^A_j + \beta \sum U^B_j$ | $O(n^3)$ | 3.14.2 | 135 |
| $1\|IN\|\alpha \sum U^A_j + \beta \sum U^B_j$ | bNPH | 3.14.2 | 135 |

'bNPH' for *binary NP-hard*
'sNPH' for *strongly NP-hard*

Yin et al. (2012a) analyze the complexity of the linear combination approach for various COMPETING, two-agent due date assignment problems, i.e., problems in which due dates must be assigned to individual jobs.

While throughout this book we consider regular cost functions, it is worth noticing that in Mor and Mosheiov (2010) two-agent problems in the COMPETING scenario have been analyzed in which the agents cost functions depending on job earliness (and hence are non regular).

**Table 3.12** Complexity of two-agent, $\varepsilon$-constraint BICRITERIA problems

| Problem | Complexity | Section | Page |
|---|---|---|---|
| $1\|BI, L^B_{\max} \le Q\|L^A_{\max}$ | $O(n \log n)$ | 3.1.1.2 | 59 |
| $1\|BI, prec, f^B_{\max} \le Q\|f^A_{\max}$ | $O(n^2)$ | 3.1.1 | 74 |
| $1\|BI, f^B_{\max} \le Q\|\sum C^A_j$ | $O(n \log n)$ | 3.3.1 | 74 |
| $1\|BI, L^B_{\max} \le Q\|\sum w^A_j C^A_j$ | sNPH | 3.5.1 | 92 |
| $1\|BI, L^B_{\max} \le Q\|\sum U^A_j$ | bNPH | 3.7.1 | 103 |
| $1\|BI, d^A_j = d^B_j, T^B_{\max} \le Q\|\sum U^A_j$ | Open | 3.7.1 | 103 |
| $1\|BI, L^B_{\max} \le Q\|\sum T^A_j$ | bNPH | 3.8.1 | 108 |
| $1\|BI, \sum w^B_j C^B_j \le Q\|\sum w^A_j C^A_j$ | sNPH | 3.10.1 | 116 |
| $1\|BI, \sum C^B_j \le Q\|\sum U^A_j$ | bNPH | 3.11.1 | 126 |
| $1\|BI, \sum C^B_j \le Q\|\sum T^A_j$ | bNPH | 3.12 | 130 |
| $1\|BI, \sum w^B_j C^B_j \le Q\|\sum U^A_j$ | sNPH | 3.13.1 | 131 |
| $1\|BI, d^A_j = d^B_j, \sum U^B_j \le Q\|\sum U^A_j$ | $O(n^3)$ | 3.14.1.1 | 132 |
| $1\|BI, \sum U^B_j \le Q\|\sum U^A_j$ | bNPH | 3.14.1.2 | 135 |
| $1\|BI, \sum w^B_j U^B_j \le Q\|\sum w^A_j U^A_j$ | bNPH | 3.15.1.2 | 138 |

'bNPH' for *binary NP-hard*
'sNPH' for *strongly NP-hard*

**Table 3.13** Complexity of two-agent, linear combination BICRITERIA problems

| Problem | Complexity | Section | Page |
|---|---|---|---|
| $1\|BI\|\alpha f^A_{\max} + \beta f^B_{\max}$ | $O(n^4)$ | 3.1.3 | 67 |
| $1\|BI\|\alpha \sum C^A_j + \beta f^B_{\max}$ | $O(n^4)$ | 3.3.3 | 80 |
| $1\|BI\|\alpha \sum w^A_j C^A_j + \beta L^B_{\max}$ | Strongly NP-hard | 3.5.3 | 102 |
| $1\|BI\|\alpha \sum w^A_j C^A_j + \beta \sum w^B_j C^B_j$ | $O(n \log n)$ | 3.10.4 | 126 |
| $1\|BI\|\alpha \sum w^A_j C^A_j + \beta \sum U^B_j$ | Strongly NP-hard | 3.13.2 | 131 |
| $1\|BI\|\alpha \sum U^A_j + \beta \sum U^B_j$ | Binary NP-hard | 3.14.2 | 135 |

Finally, we want to briefly mention that recently attempts have started to analyze multi-agent scheduling problems through game-theoretical concepts. In Agnetis et al. (2009a), the concept of Nash bargaining solution is applied to the two-agent setting $1|CO|\sum w^A_j C^A_j, \sum w^B_j C^B_j$, showing the hardness of its determination. Moreover, in Agnetis et al. (2013) the situation is addressed in which two agents submit their jobs one at a time, and each time the shortest is selected for processing. Depending on an agent's objective function, the problem of deciding the best submission sequence may turn out to be easy or hard.

# Chapter 4
# Batching Scheduling Problems

In this chapter, we consider batching scheduling problems in the context of agent scheduling. The main feature of these problems is the partition of the set of jobs into a number of subsets of jobs called *batches*.

The chapter is composed of five sections. In Sect. 4.1, we introduce basic definitions and notions of batching scheduling. In Sects. 4.2 and 4.3 we discuss two-agent $s$-batching and two-agent $p$-batching problems, respectively. We end the chapter with Sects. 4.4 and 4.5 including, respectively, complexity tables and bibliographic remarks.

## 4.1 Introduction

In batching scheduling problems, the set of jobs is partitioned into a number of subsets of jobs called batches. For each subset, jobs are executed jointly on the same machine in a 'compact' time interval. It means that the starting time of all the jobs in a given batch is given by the starting time of the first job in the batch and the completion time of all the jobs in the batch is equal to the completion time of the last job. A setup time is generally required before starting the execution of a batch. This setup time is supposed to be independent of the jobs and to each batch of a given agent is associated a constant batch setup time. The computation of the duration of a batch depends on the problem type. More precisely, two types of batching scheduling problems are distinguished in the literature, depending on the type of machine. We distinguish *serial batching machines* (jobs are processed in sequence) and *parallel batching machines* (jobs are processed in parallel) respectively denoted by $s - batch$ and $p - batch$.

In this chapter, we review multiagent batching scheduling problems in which jobs from different agents cannot be assigned to the same batch, i.e., one processing batch can only contain jobs from one specific agent. In the literature, we say that the agents are *incompatible* or *non compatible*. Some papers in the literature also

A. Agnetis et al., *Multiagent Scheduling*, DOI 10.1007/978-3-642-41880-8_4,

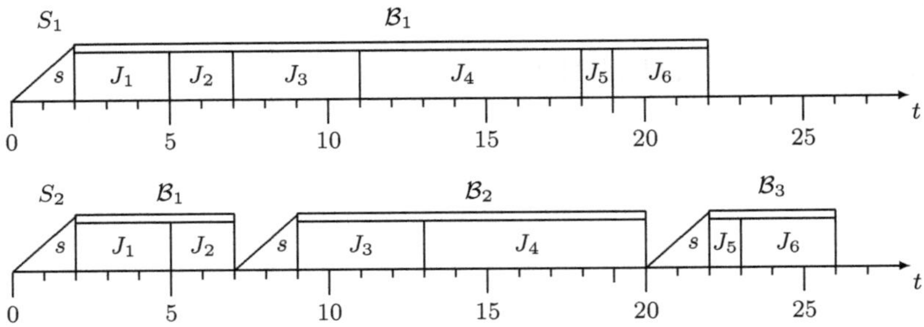


**Fig. 4.1** Two schedules for a serial batching problem

consider the case where agents are *compatible* (Fan et al. 2013; Li and Yuan 2012; Sabouni and Jolai 2010) but these papers are not referred here.

A serial batching machine processes the jobs of one batch sequentially and the length of each batch is equal to the sum of the job processing times in the batch, plus a setup time. According to the three-field notation of scheduling problems, this is generally noted by "$s - batch$" in the $\beta$-field.

A parallel batching machine processes the jobs of one batch in parallel and the length of each batch is equal to the maximum of the job processing times in the batch, plus a setup time. According to the three-field notation of scheduling problems, this is generally noted by "$p - batch$" in the $\beta$-field.

For both types of batching models, the capacity of the batching machine can be *bounded* or *unbounded*. If there is a limit on the size of a batch, the machine is bounded. Otherwise, it is unbounded. A scheduling decision for the batching machine deals with the composition of the batches and their sequencing.

*Example 4.1.* For the serial batching case, let consider the following instance with $n = 6$ jobs:

| $J_j$ | $J_1$ | $J_2$ | $J_3$ | $J_4$ | $J_5$ | $J_6$ |
|---|---|---|---|---|---|---|
| $p_j$ | 3 | 2 | 4 | 7 | 1 | 3 |
| $d_j$ | 9 | 11 | 13 | 14 | 18 | 19 |

We assume that $s = 2$ is the setup time. Two schedules $S_1$ and $S_2$ are represented in Fig. 4.1 with only one batch in $S_1$ and three batches in $S_2$ (the setup time before a batch is represented by a triangle). The schedules are evaluated as follows: $C_{\max}(S_1) = 22$, $C_{\max}(S_2) = 26$, $\sum C_j(S_1) = 132$ (all jobs complete at time 22), $\sum C_j(S_2) = 106$ (jobs $J_1$ and $J_2$ complete at time 7, jobs $J_3$ and $J_4$ complete at time 20, and jobs $J_5$ and $J_6$ complete at time 26), $L_{\max}(S_1) = \max(22 - 9, 22 - 11, 22 - 13, 22 - 14, 22 - 18, 22 - 19) = 13$, and $L_{\max}(S_2) = \max(7 - 9, 7 - 11, 20 - 13, 20 - 14, 26 - 18, 26 - 19) = 7$. ◇

*Example 4.2.* For the parallel batching case, let consider the same instance as in Example 4.1 with $n = 6$ jobs. In this case, we do not consider setup times because

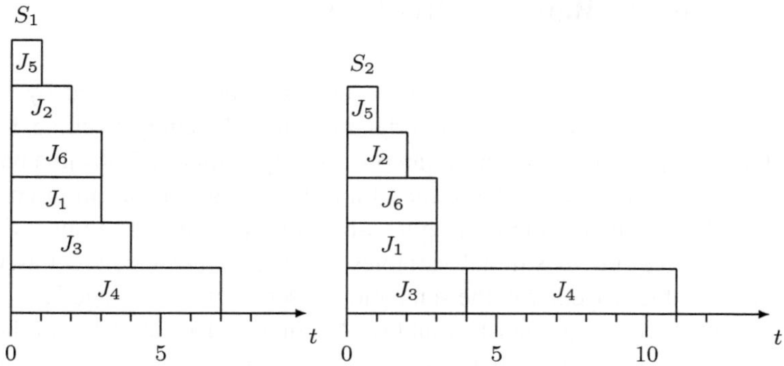


**Fig. 4.2** Two schedules for a parallel batching problem

they are supposed to be included in the processing time. Two schedules $S_1$ and $S_2$ are represented in Fig. 4.2 with only one batch in $S_1$ (containing all the jobs) and two batches in $S_2$. The evaluation of the schedules are the following: $C_{\max}(S_1) = 7$, $C_{\max}(S_2) = 11$, $\sum C_j(S_1) = 42$ (all jobs complete at time 7), $\sum C_j(S_2) = 31$ (all the jobs except $J_4$ complete at time 4, job $J_4$ completes at time 11), $L_{\max}(S_1) = \max(7-9, 7-11, 7-13, 7-14, 7-18, 7-19) = -2$, and $L_{\max}(S_2) = \max(4-9, 4-11, 4-13, 11-14, 4-18, 4-19) = -3$. ◇

Single-agent batch scheduling models have been intensively studied in the last decade. The application domains for these models include (but are not limited to) temperature testing operations in computer chip manufacturing (Uzsoy and Yang 1997), production of metal sheets on a multi-head hole-punching machine (Gavranovic and Finke 2000), machine part manufacturing in containers such as boxes, palettes, or carts (Cheng and Kovalyov 2001), manufacturing of computer parts of different types (Cheng et al. 2004b), scheduling of chemical (photolytical, galvanic) baths (Oulamara et al. 2005), vulcanization operations on press-machines in tire manufacturing (see for instance Oulamara et al. (2009)), etc.

In this chapter, we consider that the jobs belong to two agents and that there is a single batching machine. In the following, remember that we consider the non compatible case, i.e. the jobs of one batch belong to only one agent. Moreover, a constant batch setup time denoted by $s_k$ is associated to each batch of agent $k$, $k \in \{A, B\}$.

In the following sections, polynomial and pseudo-polynomial time dynamic programming algorithms are derived for single machine s-batching and p-batching scheduling problems with various combinations of the objective functions, except the total weighted completion time, because minimizing this function is already strongly NP-hard (Albers and Brucker 1993) in the single-agent case.

## 4.2 Two-Agent s-Batching Problems

In the following, we consider two sets of jobs $\mathcal{J}^A$ and $\mathcal{J}^B$, owned by the two competing agents $A$ and $B$, on a single serial unbounded batching machine. It means that the batching processing machine can process any number of jobs in a batch.

We start this section by the definition of a mixed integer linear program, that is able to model any type of single machine s-batching problem. The interest of this model is that it requires positional variables (or *assignment* variables) as well as precedence variables together in the same model (see Sect. 2.3.3, page 32).

We define binary (assignment) variables $x^A_{j,\ell}$ equal to 1 if job $J^A_j$ is in the batch number $\ell$ of agent $A$, and 0 otherwise, $\forall j$, $1 \leq j \leq n_A$, $\forall \ell$, $1 \leq \ell \leq n_A$ and similarly $x^B_{j,\ell}$ for agent $B$. These two sets of variables allow to assign the jobs to batches and the following constraints ensure that each job is exactly in one batch.

$$\sum_{\ell=1}^{n_k} x^k_{j,\ell} = 1, \forall j, 1 \leq j \leq n_k, \forall k \in \{A, B\} \tag{4.1}$$

The binary variables $z^k_\ell$ allow to know if a batch of agent $k$ is empty or not, with the following constraints.

$$z^k_\ell \geq x^k_{j,\ell}, \quad \forall\, j, 1 \leq j \leq n_k, \forall \ell, 1 \leq \ell \leq n_k, \forall k \in \{A, B\} \tag{4.2}$$

$$z^k_\ell \leq \sum_{j=1}^{n_k} x^k_{j,\ell}, \forall \ell, 1 \leq \ell \leq n_k, \forall k \in \{A, B\} \tag{4.3}$$

We denote by $CB^k_\ell$ the completion time of the batch $\ell$ of agent $k$ (noted $\mathcal{B}^k_\ell$). Then, we define binary (precedence) variables $y_{\ell,\ell'}$ equal to 1 if the batch $\mathcal{B}^A_\ell$ precedes $\mathcal{B}^B_{\ell'}$, and 0 otherwise. These variables allow to define a sequence of batches between agent $A$ and agent $B$ through the following constraints.

$$CB^A_\ell \geq CB^B_{\ell'} + s_A z^A_\ell + \sum_{j=1}^{n_A} p^A_j x^A_{j,\ell} - M y_{\ell,\ell'}, \quad \forall \ell, 1 \leq \ell \leq n_A, \forall \ell', 1 \leq \ell' \leq n_B \tag{4.4}$$

$$CB^B_{\ell'} \geq CB^A_\ell + s_B z^B_{\ell'} + \sum_{j=1}^{n_B} p^B_j x^B_{j,\ell'} - M(1 - y_{\ell,\ell'}), \quad \forall \ell, 1 \leq \ell \leq n_A, \forall \ell', 1 \leq \ell' \leq n_B \tag{4.5}$$

Then, we fix an order between the batches of each agent. We impose that batch $\mathcal{B}^k_\ell$ precedes batch $\mathcal{B}^k_{\ell+1}$, with the following constraints.

$$CB_1^k \geq s_k + \sum_{j=1}^{n_k} p_j^k x_{j,1}^k, \forall k \in \{A, B\} \tag{4.6}$$

$$CB_\ell^k \geq CB_{\ell-1}^k + s_k z_\ell^k + \sum_{j=1}^{n_k} p_j^k x_{j,\ell}^k, \quad \forall \ell, 2 \leq \ell \leq n_k, \forall k \in \{A, B\} \tag{4.7}$$

These definitions can be used to define the value of various criteria. Let $C_j^k$ denote the completion time of the job $J_j^k \in \mathcal{J}^k$. This value is given by the following constraints.

$$C_j^k \geq CB_\ell^k - M(1 - x_{j,\ell}^k), \quad \forall j, 1 \leq j \leq n_k, \forall \ell, 1 \leq \ell \leq n_k, \forall k \in \{A, B\} \tag{4.8}$$

We terminate the definition of this model with the following objective functions.

$$C_{\max}^k = CB_{n_B}^k, \forall k \in \{A, B\} \tag{4.9}$$

$$L_{\max}^k \geq C_j^k - d_j^k, \forall j, 1 \leq j \leq n_k, \forall k \in \{A, B\} \tag{4.10}$$

$$\sum C_j^k = \sum_{j=1}^{n_k} C_j^k, \forall k \in \{A, B\} \tag{4.11}$$

## 4.2.1 Functions $f_{\max}$, $f_{\max}$

### 4.2.1.1 Problem $1|CO, s-batch, f_{\max}^B \leq Q|f_{\max}^A$

In the COMPETING scenario, let consider problem $1|CO, s-batch, f_{\max}^B \leq Q|f_{\max}^A$. We can derive an algorithm that determines whether or not there exists a solution to the feasibility problem $1|CO, s-batch, f_{\max}^A \leq y, f_{\max}^B \leq Q|-$, where $y \in [lb_A, ub_A]$, with $lb_k$ and $ub_k$ for $k \in \{A, B\}$ a lower bound and an upper bound of $f_{\max}^k$, given by:

$$lb_k = \min_{1 \leq j \leq n_k} \left\{ f_j^k(s_1 + p_j^k) \right\} \tag{4.12}$$

$$ub_k = \max_{1 \leq j \leq n_k} \left\{ f_j^k(T) \right\} \tag{4.13}$$

where $T = n_A s_A + n_B s_B + P$ with $P$ the total processing time of jobs.

For each value $y$ and $Q$, one can compute deadlines $\tilde{d}_j^A(y)$ and $\tilde{d}_j^B(Q)$ on the completion times of jobs $J_j^A$ and $J_j^B$, respectively. The idea is that $1|CO, s-batch, f_{\max}^A \leq y, f_{\max}^B \leq Q|-$ has a feasible solution if and only if there is a schedule in which each job completes within its deadline.

We assume that we have an explicit expression for the inverse function $(f_j^k)^{-1}(t), k \in \{A, B\}$. So $\tilde{d}_j^k$ can be computed in constant time such that

$$f_j^A(C_j^A) \leq y \text{ for } C_j^A \leq \tilde{d}_j^A \text{ and } f_j^A(C_j^A) > y \text{ for } C_j^A > \tilde{d}_j^A$$
$$\text{and } f_j^B(C_j^B) \leq Q \text{ for } C_j^B \leq \tilde{d}_j^B \text{ and } f_j^B(C_j^B) > Q \text{ for } C_j^B > \tilde{d}_j^B.$$

Otherwise, the deadlines can be computed in $O(n \log T)$ time. Of course, for a given value of $T$, the deadline of a job can be calculated in $O(\log T)$ time by a binary search in the interval $[0, T]$, because we have:

$$\tilde{d}_j^A(y) = \max\{\tau | f_j^A(\tau) \leq y, s_A + p_j^A \leq \tau \leq T\} \tag{4.14}$$

$$\tilde{d}_j^B(Q) = \max\{\tau | f_j^B(\tau) \leq Q, s_B + p_j^B \leq \tau \leq T\} \tag{4.15}$$

In what follows, we suppose that, given $y$, the jobs are numbered by nondecreasing order of the deadlines, i.e., $\tilde{d}_1^A(y) \leq \cdots \leq \tilde{d}_{n_A}^A(y)$ and $\tilde{d}_1^B(Q) \leq \cdots \leq \tilde{d}_{n_B}^B(Q)$.

The following property (Kovalyov et al. 2012b) can be easily established.

**Lemma 4.1.** *If a feasible schedule exists for $1|CO, s-batch, f_{\max}^A \leq y, f_{\max}^B \leq Q|-$, there is one in which the jobs of each agent are processed in the Earliest Deadline First (EDF) order.*

The idea is that a schedule with values $f_{\max}^A \leq y$ and $f_{\max}^B \leq Q$ exists if and only if, when regarding $\tilde{d}_j^A(y)$ and $\tilde{d}_j^B(Q)$ as due dates, a schedule exists such that the maximum lateness of all the $n$ jobs is non-positive. Hence, we can propose a dynamic programming algorithm to solve the problem of minimizing the maximum lateness of all the $n$ jobs with due dates $\tilde{d}_j^A(y)$ and $\tilde{d}_j^B(Q)$. However, the problem is not precisely the same problem as the $1|s-batch|L_{\max}$, since the jobs of different agents cannot be scheduled in the same batch. Therefore, Webster and Baker's algorithm (Webster and Baker 1995) for $1|s-batch|L_{\max}$ cannot be used to determine an optimal solution. In Kovalyov et al. (2012b), a new dynamic programming algorithm is proposed. In this dynamic programming algorithm, $L(i_A, i_B)$ is defined as the minimum value of maximum lateness when the job subset $\{J_{i_A}^A, J_{i_A+1}^A, \ldots, J_{n_A}^A\} \cup \{J_{i_B}^B, J_{i_B+1}^B, \ldots, J_{n_B}^B\}$ is scheduled from time zero. Following a similar logic to Webster and Baker's algorithm, a single batch is appended to the beginning of a current schedule. An optimal solution value is given by $L(1, 1)$. The recursive dynamic programming algorithm is described in Algorithm 19.

For each $i_A$ and $i_B$, $L(i_A, i_B)$ can be computed in $O(n)$ time. Hence, all values $L(i_A, i_B)$ can be computed in $O(n_A n_B n)$ time. We use binary search to enumerate

**Algorithm 19** for problem $1|CO, s-batch, f_{\max}^B \leq Q|f_{\max}^A$

**for** $j := 1$ **to** $n_A$ **do**
  Calculate $\tilde{d}_j^A(y)$ via (4.14)
**end for**
**for** $j := 1$ **to** $n_B$ **do**
  Calculate $\tilde{d}_j^B(Q)$ via (4.15)
**end for**
$L(n_A+1, n_B+1) := 0$
**for** $i_A := n_A + 1$ **downto** 1 **do**
  **for** $i_B := n_B + 1$ **downto** 1 **do**
    **if** $(i_A, i_B) \neq (n_A+1, n_B+1)$ **then**
      $L(i_A, i_B) :=$

$$\min \begin{cases} \min_{i_A+1 \leq j \leq n_A+1} \left\{ \max \begin{cases} s_A + \sum_{h=i_A}^{j-1} p_h^A - \tilde{d}_{i_A}^A(y), \\ L(j, i_B) + s_A + \sum_{h=i_A}^{j-1} p_h^A \end{cases} \right. \\ \min_{i_B+1 \leq j \leq n_B+1} \left\{ \max \begin{cases} s_B + \sum_{h=i_B}^{j-1} p_h^B - \tilde{d}_{i_B}^B(Q), \\ L(i_A, j) + s_B + \sum_{h=i_B}^{j-1} p_h^B \end{cases} \right. \end{cases}$$

    **end if**
  **end for**
**end for**
**return** the solution that minimizes $L(1, 1)$

the values of $y \in [lb_A, ub_A]$, which requires $O(\log Y_A)$ iterations, where $Y_A = ub_A - lb_A$. In conclusion, the following result holds.

**Theorem 4.1.** *An optimal solution to problem* $1|CO, s-batch, f_{\max}^B \leq Q|f_{\max}^A$ *can be obtained in* $O((n_A n_B n) \log Y_A)$ *time.*

### 4.2.2 *Functions* $C_{\max}$, $C_{\max}$

#### 4.2.2.1 Problem $1|CO, s-batch, C_{\max}^B \leq Q|C_{\max}^A$

The problem considered here is denoted $1|CO, s - batch, C_{\max}^B \leq Q|C_{\max}^A$. The following property was established in Kovalyov et al. (2012b).

**Lemma 4.2.** *If an optimal schedule exists, there exists one in which the jobs of each agent form a single batch.*

*Proof.* Let $LB = s_A + \sum_{j \in \mathcal{J}^A} p_j^A + s_B + \sum_{j \in \mathcal{J}^B} p_j^B = s_A + s_B + \sum_{j \in \mathcal{J}} p_j$, and let $LB' = s_A + \sum_{j \in \mathcal{J}^A} p_j^A$. It is clear that $LB'$ is a lower bound for $C_{\max}^A$ and $LB$ is a lower bound for the global $C_{\max}$. It is possible to build a feasible solution for problem $1|s - batch, C_{\max}^B \leq Q|C_{\max}^A$ by using Algorithm 20.

This algorithm builds a feasible solution, if one exists, with $C_{\max}^A = LB'$ if $Q \geq LB$, otherwise, we have $C_{\max}^A = LB$. So for problem $1|CO, s-batch, C_{\max}^B \leq Q|C_{\max}^A$, an optimal schedule can be obtained in $O(n)$. □

**Algorithm 20** for problem $1|CO, s-batch, C_{\max}^{B} \leq Q|C_{\max}^{A}$

$\sigma := ()$ // initial empty schedule
$P_A := \sum_{j \in \mathcal{J}^A} p_j^A$
$P_B := \sum_{j \in \mathcal{J}^B} p_j^B$
**if** $s_A + s_B + P_A + P_B \leq Q$ **then**
    Schedule jobs of agent $A$ in the first batch
    Schedule jobs of agent $B$ in the second batch
    $\sigma := \mathcal{J}^A|\mathcal{J}^B$ // concatenation of two job sets
**else**
    **if** $s_B + P_B \leq Q$ **then**
        Schedule jobs of agent $B$ in the first batch
        Schedule jobs of agent $A$ in the second batch
        $\sigma := \mathcal{J}^B|\mathcal{J}^A$
    **end if**
**end if**
**if** $\sigma \neq ()$ **then**
    **return** $\sigma$
**else**
    **return** 'There is no solution'
**end if**

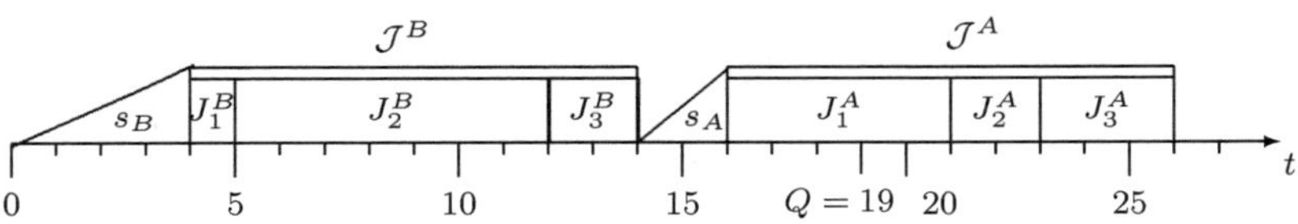


**Fig. 4.3** Solution to the $1|CO, s-batch, C_{\max}^{B} \leq Q|C_{\max}^{A}$ problem

In view of this property, problem $1|CO, s-batch, C_{\max}^{B} \leq Q|C_{\max}^{A}$ is trivial and can be easily solved in polynomial time.

*Example 4.3.* Let consider the following 6-job instance, where jobs $J_1^A$ to $J_3^A$ belong to $\mathcal{J}^A$ and jobs $J_1^B$ to $J_3^B$ belong to $\mathcal{J}^B$:

| $J_j^k$ | $J_1^A$ | $J_2^A$ | $J_3^A$ | $J_1^B$ | $J_2^B$ | $J_3^B$ |
|---|---|---|---|---|---|---|
| $p_j^k$ | 5 | 2 | 3 | 1 | 7 | 2 |

We assume that $s_A = 2$ and $s_B = 4$ and we fix $Q = 19$.

We have $P_A = 10$ and $P_B = 10$. $s_A + s_B + P_A + P_B = 2+4+10+10 = 26 > Q$ and $s_B + P_B = 14 \leq Q$. Therefore, the optimal solution is obtained by sequencing the jobs of $\mathcal{J}^B$ first in one batch and then the jobs of $\mathcal{J}^A$ in another batch. The corresponding schedule is represented in Fig. 4.3. ◇

#### 4.2.2.2 Problem $1|CO, s-batch|\mathcal{P}(C^A_{\max}, C^B_{\max})$

The problem $1|CO, s-batch|\mathcal{P}(C^A_{\max}, C^B_{\max})$ has only two Pareto optimal solutions: one corresponds to the solution where $\mathcal{J}^A$ precedes $\mathcal{J}^B$, and the other corresponds to the solution where $\mathcal{J}^B$ precedes $\mathcal{J}^A$.

### 4.2.3 *Functions* $C_{\max}$, $L_{\max}$

#### 4.2.3.1 Problem $1|CO, s-batch, L^B_{\max} \leq Q|C^A_{\max}$

We consider now the problem $1|CO, s - batch, L^B_{\max} \leq Q|C^A_{\max}$. Without loss of generality, we suppose that the jobs of $\mathcal{J}^B$ are numbered in EDD order, i.e. $d^B_1 \leq d^B_2 \leq \ldots \leq d^B_{n_B}$. Kovalyov et al. (2012b) present the following lemma.

**Lemma 4.3.** *If an optimal schedule for problem* $1|CO, s - batch, L^B_{\max} \leq Q|C^A_{\max}$ *exists, then there is one in which the jobs of* $\mathcal{J}^A$ *form a single batch and the jobs of* $\mathcal{J}^B$ *are processed in EDD order.*

*Proof.* Let us first show that the jobs of $\mathcal{J}^A$ form a single batch. If $\pi^*$ is an optimal schedule for which this does not hold, a new schedule $\pi$ can be built by moving all jobs in $\mathcal{J}^A$ into the last batch of agent $A$. This can only improve the value of $L^B_{\max}$ (since jobs of $\mathcal{J}^B$ are moved backwards) as well as $C^A_{\max}$ (since at least one setup $s_A$ is saved). So there is no interest in scheduling the jobs of agent $A$ in several batches.

Let us now suppose that in such schedule $\pi$ not all the jobs of $\mathcal{J}^B$ are processed in EDD order, i.e., there is a batch $\mathcal{B}^B_\ell$ scheduled before batch $\mathcal{B}^B_t$ with $J^B_i \in \mathcal{B}^B_\ell$ and $J^B_j \in \mathcal{B}^B_t$, and $d^B_j < d^B_i$. Let $\pi'$ be the schedule obtained by moving job $J^B_i$ from $\mathcal{B}^B_\ell$ to $\mathcal{B}^B_t$. Note that $C^A_{\max}(\pi') \leq C^A_{\max}(\pi)$. Moreover, the completion time of batch $\mathcal{B}^B_\ell$ is reduced by $p^B_i$, while the completion time of batch $\mathcal{B}^B_t$ does not increase. Therefore, the lateness of all jobs in $\mathcal{J}^B$ except $J^B_i$ does not increase. On the other hand, since $d^B_j < d^B_i$, the lateness of $J^B_i$ in $\pi'$ does not exceed that of $J^B_j$ in $\pi$, thus $L^B_{\max}(\pi') \leq L^B_{\max}(\pi)$. Continuing this exchange process, we get an optimal schedule with the desired property. □

Let now $\mathcal{B}^A$ be the only batch of agent $A$. According to Lemma 4.3, the optimal schedule is of the form $(\pi_B, \mathcal{B}^A, \pi'_B)$ where $\pi_B$ and $\pi'_B$ are sequences of batches of agent $B$, either of which can be empty. Note that $L^B_{\max} \leq Q$ is equivalent to $C^B_j \leq \tilde{d}^B_j$, $1 \leq j \leq n_B$, where $\tilde{d}^B_j = d^B_j + Q$.

In the single-agent case, given jobs $J_1, \ldots, J_n$ with *deadlines* $\tilde{d}_j$, $1 \leq j \leq n$, the problem of determining a feasible schedule respecting the deadlines can be solved by Algorithm 21 with $t = 0$ as input (Hochbaum and Landy 1994).

According to Algorithm 21, if job $n$ is included in some batch, a feasible schedule is obtained. Otherwise, some job cannot be included in a batch without violating the earliest deadline of this batch, in which case no feasible schedule exists.

**Algorithm 21** for problem $1|s-batch, \tilde{d}_j|-$

Let $t$ be the start time of the schedule // $t$ is given on input of the algorithm
Renumber the jobs so that $\tilde{d}_1 \leq \tilde{d}_2 \leq \cdots \leq \tilde{d}_n$
$i := 1$
$b := 1$
**repeat**
    Denote by $k$ the maximal job index such that $t + s + \sum_{j=i}^{k} p_j \leq \tilde{d}_i$
    **if** there exists a job with index $k$ **then**
        Build a batch $\mathcal{B}_b$ with the jobs $(J_i, \ldots, J_k)$
        $b := b + 1$
        $t := t + s + \sum_{j=i}^{k} p_j$
        $i := k + 1$
    **else**
        **return** 'There is no feasible solution'
    **end if**
**until** (job $n$ is included in some batch) **or** (there is no feasible solution)
**return** all batches

Algorithm 21 requires $O(n \log n)$ time for re-indexing the jobs, and $O(n)$ time for building the batches. Note that this algorithm, for any number of jobs, constructs a feasible schedule with the minimum number of batches, thus, minimizes the makespan.

This algorithm can be applied to solve $1|CO, s-batch, L_{\max}^B \leq Q|C_{\max}^A$. In fact, in view of Lemma 4.3, if we know after which job $J_k^B$ is scheduled the batch $\mathcal{B}^A$ of agent $A$, then we can solve the problem in $O(n_B)$ time by applying Hochbaum and Landy's algorithm twice: first for jobs $J_1^B, \ldots, J_k^B$, starting at time 0, and then for jobs $J_{k+1}^B, \ldots, J_{n_B}^B$ starting at $C_k^B + s_A + P_A$ ($k = 0$ indicates that $\mathcal{B}^A$ precedes all jobs in $\mathcal{J}^B$). In conclusion, the following result holds.

**Theorem 4.2.** *Algorithm 22 solves the $1|CO, s-batch, L_{\max}^B \leq Q|C_{\max}^A$ problem in $O(n_A + n_B^2)$ time.*

Note that $C_{\max}^A$ is nondecreasing with $k$, while $L_{\max}^B$ is nonincreasing with $k$. Therefore, the optimal index $k^*$ can be found by a binary search over the range $0, \ldots, n_B$, and applying Algorithm 21 twice for each value of $k$. The smallest value of $k$ for which the algorithm provides a feasible solution yields the optimal schedule. Therefore, the complexity of steps 15–31 of Algorithm 22 can be improved. In this case, the complexity reduces to $O(n_A + n_B \log n_B)$ time.

*Example 4.4.* Let consider the following 8-job instance with $n_A = n_B = 4$:

| $J_j^k$ | $J_1^A$ | $J_2^A$ | $J_3^A$ | $J_4^A$ | $J_1^B$ | $J_2^B$ | $J_3^B$ | $J_4^B$ |
|---|---|---|---|---|---|---|---|---|
| $p_j^k$ | 3 | 3 | 4 | 2 | 1 | 5 | 1 | 3 |
| $d_j^B$ | | | | | 11 | 15 | 19 | 23 |

**Algorithm 22** for problem $1|CO, s-batch, L^B_{\max} \leq Q|C^A_{\max}$

Renumber the jobs of $\mathcal{J}^B$ in EDD order
$P_A := \sum_{i \in \mathcal{J}^A} p_i^A$
$\mathcal{B}^A := \mathcal{J}^A$
**for** $i = 1$ **to** $n_B$ **do**
  $\tilde{d}_i^B := d_i^B + Q$
**end for**
Apply Algorithm 21 to job set $\mathcal{J}^B$ with $t := s_A + P_A$
Denote by $\pi_B^{\prime(i)}$ the sequence of batches obtained if any
**if** there is no feasible solution **then**
  nofeasible := **true**
**else**
  **return** $(\mathcal{B}^A, \pi_B^{\prime(i)})$ // optimal solution
**end if**
$i := 1$
**while** (nofeasible = **true**) **and** $(i \leq n_B)$ **do**
  Apply Algorithm 21 to job set $\{J_1^B, \ldots, J_i^B\}$ with $t := 0$
  **if** there is feasible solution **then**
    Denote by $\pi_B^{(i)}$ the sequence of batches obtained
  **else**
    $\pi_B^{(i)} := \emptyset$
  **end if**
  Apply Algorithm 21 to job set $\{J_{i+1}^B, \ldots, J_{n_B}^B\}$ with $t := C_i^B(\pi_B^{(i)}) + s_A + P_A$
  **if** there is feasible solution **then**
    Denote by $\pi_B^{\prime(i)}$ the sequence of batches obtained
  **else**
    $\pi_B^{\prime(i)} := \emptyset$
  **end if**
  **if** $(\pi_B^{(i)} \neq \emptyset)$ **and** $(\pi_B^{\prime(i)} \neq \emptyset)$ **then**
    **return** $(\pi_B^{(i)}, \mathcal{B}^A, \pi_B^{\prime(i)})$
  **end if**
**end while**
**return** 'There is no feasible solution'

We assume that $s_A = 3$ and $s_B = 1$ and $Q = 8$. We represent in Fig. 4.4 a sequence $S_1$ where the jobs of agent $A$ are scheduled first, and then the jobs of agent $B$ in EDD order. The makespan for $A$ is $C^A_{\max} = 15$ but the maximum lateness for the jobs of agent $B$ is $L^B_{\max} = \max(15, 11, 7, 3) = 15$, which is not acceptable. In Fig. 4.5, a sequence $S_2$ is presented. A first batch composed by the two first jobs of agent $B$ precedes the jobs of agent $A$, and the remaining jobs of agent $B$ terminate the schedule in a last batch. Here, $C^A_{\max} = 22$ and $L^B_{\max} = \max(-4, -8, 8, 4) = 8$, which is now acceptable. Let consider the following sequence $S_3$: $\mathcal{B}_1 = (J_1^B)$; $\mathcal{B}_2 = (\mathcal{J}^A)$; $\mathcal{B}_3 = (J_2^B)$; $\mathcal{B}_4 = (J_3^B)$; $\mathcal{B}_5 = (J_4^B)$. In $S_3$, a first batch composed by the first job of agent $B$ precedes the jobs of agent $A$, and the three remaining jobs of agent $B$ terminate the schedule in three different batches. In $S_3$, we have $C^A_{\max} = 17$ and $L^B_{\max} = \max(-8, 8, 6, 6) = 8$, which is a Pareto optimal solution. ◇

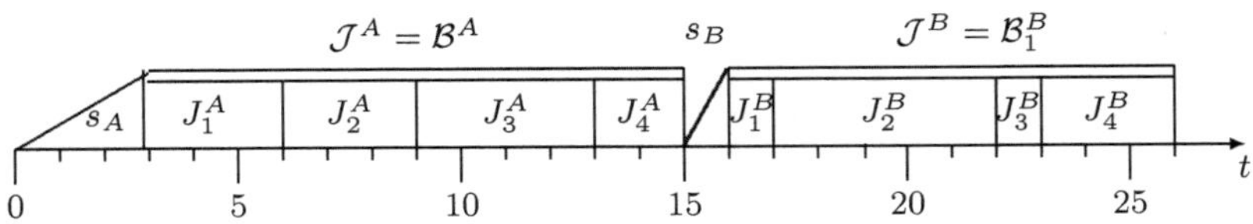


**Fig. 4.4** Not a feasible solution for the $1|CO, s - batch, L^B_{\max} \leq Q|C^A_{\max}$ problem

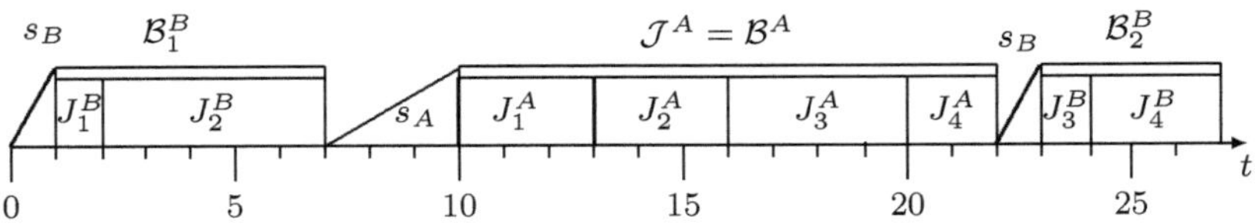


**Fig. 4.5** Feasible solution for the $1|CO, s - batch, L^B_{\max} \leq Q|C^A_{\max}$ problem

#### 4.2.3.2 Problem $1|CO, s - batch, C^A_{\max} \leq Q|L^B_{\max}$

Let us now turn to the symmetric problem $1|CO, s - batch, C^A_{\max} \leq Q|L^B_{\max}$. In this case, Lemma 4.3 still holds. It means that the optimal schedule is of the form $(\pi_B, \mathcal{B}^A, \pi'_B)$ where $\pi_B$ and $\pi'_B$ are sequences of batches of agent $B$, eventually one of them being empty.

Note that for the schedule $(\pi_B, \mathcal{B}^A, \pi'_B)$, the makespan for agent $A$ is completely determined by the number of jobs $k$ preceding $\mathcal{B}^A$ and the number of batches $b$ in the sequence $\pi_B$. It is given by:

$$C^A_{\max}(k, b) = bs_B + \sum_{j=1}^{k} p^B_j + s_A + P_A$$

Hence, given $k$ and $b$, the problem reduces to constructing two schedules:

- $\pi_B = \pi^{(k,b)}$, that minimizes the maximum lateness of jobs $J^B_1, \ldots, J^B_k$ starting at time zero and forming $b$ batches,
- $\pi'_B = \pi^{(k+1)}$, that minimizes the maximum lateness of jobs $J^B_{k+1}, \ldots, J^B_{n_B}$ starting at time $C^A_{\max}(k, b)$ (if $k = n_B$, $\pi'_B$ is empty and in this case we define $L^B_{\max}(\pi^{(n_B+1)}) = -\infty$).

An optimal solution has the form $(\pi^{(k,b)}, \mathcal{B}^A, \pi^{(k+1)})$, and the optimal value of $L^B_{\max}$ is given by:

$$L^B_{\max} = \max_{0 \leq b \leq k \leq n_B} \left\{ \max\{L^B_{\max}(\pi^{(k,b)}), L^B_{\max}(\pi^{(k+1)})\} : C^A_{\max}(k, b) \leq Q \right\}$$

For a given $k$, $0 \leq k \leq n_B$, determining an optimal schedule $\pi^{(k+1)}$ is equivalent to solving the single-agent scheduling problem $1|s - batch|L_{\max}$. In Webster and Baker (1995) it is shown that there exists an optimal schedule for this problem in which jobs are sequenced in EDD order, and a keen backward dynamic programming algorithm with batch insertion is proposed, working as follows.

Given the job set $\{J_1, \ldots, J_n\}$, let $L(i)$ be the minimum value of the maximum lateness for the job subset $\{J_i, \ldots, J_n\}$, when the first batch contains job $i$ and starts after time $s$. We let $L(n+1) = -\infty$, and define the recursion function:

$$L(i) = \min_{i<k\leq n+1} \left\{ \max \left\{ L(k) + s + \sum_{h=i}^{k-1} p_h, s + \sum_{h=i}^{k-1} p_h - d_i \right\} \right\} \tag{4.16}$$

Function (4.16) is computed for $i = n, n-1, \ldots, 1$. The optimal value is given by $L(1)$.

By applying Webster and Baker's algorithm, we derive an optimal schedule $\pi^{(k+1)}$, $k = 0, 1, \ldots, n_B - 1$ in $O(n_B^2)$ time. All the schedules $\pi^{(k,b)}$, $0 \leq b \leq k \leq n_B$, can be found in $O(n_B^3)$ time by a forward dynamic programming algorithm, as follows (Kovalyov et al. 2012a). Let $L(b,k)$ denote the minimum value of the maximum lateness of the job subset $\{J_1^B, \ldots, J_k^B\}$ when these jobs are scheduled in EDD order in $b$ batches from time zero. The following recursion formula holds:

$$L(b,k) = \min_{1\leq i\leq k-1} \left\{ \max \left\{ L(b-1,i), bs_B + \sum_{j=1}^{k} p_j^B - d_{i+1}^B \right\} \right\} \tag{4.17}$$

The recursion function (4.17) is evaluated for $1 \leq b \leq k \leq n_B$. According to (4.17), a single batch is appended at the end of a current schedule. Each value $L(b,k)$ can be calculated in $O(k)$ time. Hence, all the values $L(b,k)$ and corresponding schedules $\pi^{(k,b)}$, $0 \leq b \leq k \leq n_B$, can be found in $O(n_B^3)$ time. The algorithm is initialized with $L(0,0) = -\infty$ and $\pi^{(0,0)} = \emptyset$. In conclusion, the following result holds.

**Theorem 4.3.** *Problem* $1|CO, s-batch, C_{\max}^A \leq Q|L_{\max}^B$ *can be solved in* $O(n_A + n_B^3)$ *time.*

#### 4.2.3.3 Problem $1|CO, s-batch|\mathcal{P}(C_{\max}^A, L_{\max}^B)$

Let us now turn to problem $1|CO, s-batch|\mathcal{P}(C_{\max}^A, L_{\max}^B)$. Each Pareto optimal solution can be found by solving a logarithmic number of instances of the $\varepsilon$-constraint problem. However, in this case, the problem is even easier. In fact, suppose that $F_B$ is the value of the optimal solution of $1|CO, s-batch, C_{\max}^A \leq Q|L_{\max}^B$ for some $Q$. To obtain a Pareto optimal solution, we only need to solve *one* instance of the symmetric problem, i.e., $1|CO, s-batch, L_{\max}^B \leq F_B|C_{\max}^A$. If $F_A$ is the optimal value of such an instance, the pair $(F_A, F_B)$ is Pareto optimal. Similarly, the *next* Pareto optimal solution can be generated by solving $1|CO, s-batch, C_{\max}^A \leq F_A - \varepsilon|L_{\max}^B$ (for sufficiently small $\varepsilon$) and thereafter one instance of the symmetric problem. In this way, the whole Pareto set can be obtained. Hence, the complexity of this task is essentially related to the size of the Pareto set. In this case, the Pareto set has a polynomial number of solutions. This is due to the fact that the structure of any strict Pareto optimal solution is of the form $(\pi^{(k,b)}, \mathcal{B}^A, \pi^{(k+1)})$ where jobs of $\mathcal{J}_A$ are inserted after certain batches of jobs of $\mathcal{J}_B$. The makespan for agent $A$ is completely determined by the number of jobs $k, 0 \leq k \leq n_B$ preceding $\mathcal{B}^A$ and thereafter the number of batches $b, 0 \leq b \leq k \leq n_B$ in the sub-sequence $\pi^{(k,b)}$. Hence, the size of the Pareto set is bounded by $O(n_B)$.

In conclusion, the following result holds:

**Theorem 4.4.** *Problem* $1|CO, s-batch|\mathcal{P}(C^A_{\max}, L^B_{\max})$ *can be solved in* $O(n_A n_B + n_B^4)$.

### 4.2.4 Functions $f_{\max}, \sum C_j$

#### 4.2.4.1 Problem $1|CO, s-batch, f^B_{\max} \leq Q|\sum C^A_j$

Let us now turn to problem $1|CO, s-batch, f^B_{\max} \leq Q|\sum C^A_j$. Dealing with $Q$, we assume that deadlines $\tilde{d}^B_j(Q)$ on the completion times of jobs $J^B_j$ are computed in constant time such that (see Sect. 4.2.1):

$$f^B_j(C^B_j) \leq Q \Leftrightarrow C^B_j \leq (f^B_j)^{-1}(Q)(= \tilde{d}^B_j(Q)) \tag{4.18}$$

Let ED($Q$) be the Earliest Deadline order of jobs with respect to these deadlines. Assume that jobs of agent $A$ are numbered according to the SPT order $p^A_1 \leq \cdots \leq p^A_{n_A}$ and jobs of agent $B$ are numbered according to ED($Q$) order: $\tilde{d}^B_1(Q) \leq \cdots \leq \tilde{d}^B_{n_B}(Q)$.

The following property proposed in Kovalyov et al. (2012b) holds.

**Lemma 4.4.** *There exists an optimal schedule for the problem* $1|CO, s-batch, f^B_{\max} \leq Q|\sum C^A_j$, *if one exists, in which the jobs of agent A are processed in the SPT order and the jobs of agent B are processed in the ED(Q) order, respectively.*

Algorithm 23 (Kovalyov et al. 2012a) is a dynamic programming algorithm that solves this scheduling problem, where a single batch is appended to the end of a current schedule. We denote by $F(b_A, i_A, b_B, i_B)$ the minimum total completion time of jobs of $\mathcal{J}^A$, subject to the condition that the first $i_A$ jobs of agent $A$ are scheduled in $b_A$ batches, the first $i_B$ jobs of agent $B$ are scheduled in $b_B$ batches and the deadlines for the latter jobs are satisfied. $F(b_A, i_A, b_B, i_B)$ is the recursion function. The optimal value corresponds to $\min\{F(b_A, n_A, b_B, n_B) \mid 1 \leq b_A \leq n_A, 1 \leq b_B \leq n_B\}$.

We define $C(b_A, i_A, b_B, i_B)$ the completion time of the last job scheduled:

$$C(b_A, i_A, b_B, i_B) = s_A b_A + s_B b_B + \sum_{i=1}^{i_A} p^A_i + \sum_{i=1}^{i_B} p^B_i \tag{4.19}$$

A decision in the DP algorithm is whether to schedule next a job of agent $A$ or a job of agent $B$.

**Algorithm 23** for problem $1|CO, s-batch, f_{\max}^B \leq Q|\sum C_j^A$

$F(0,0,b_B,i_B) := 0$ for $0 \leq b_B \leq i_B \leq n_B$
$F(b_A,i_A,b_B,i_B) := +\infty$ for $1 \leq b_A \leq i_A \leq n_A$ and $1 \leq i_B \leq b_B \leq n_B$
Calculate $\tilde{d}_j^B(Q)$ such that $f_j^B(C_j) \leq Q$
**for** $b_A := 0$ **to** $n_A$ **do**
  **for** $i_A := b_A$ **to** $n_A$ **do**
    **for** $b_B := 0$ **to** $n_B$ **do**
      **for** $i_B := b_B$ **to** $n_B$ **do**
        **if** $(b_A,i_A,b_B,i_B) \neq (0,0,0,0)$ **then**
          Calculate $C(b_A,i_A,b_B,i_B)$ via 4.19
          $F(b_A,i_A,b_B,i_B) := \min\{F^A(b_A,i_A,b_B,i_B), F^B(b_A,i_A,b_B,i_B)\}$
        **end if**
      **end for**
    **end for**
  **end for**
**end for**

- If a job of agent $A$ is scheduled, there are two cases. If the last batch is a batch of agent $A$, either this job is included in this batch or it starts a new batch; Otherwise, it starts a new batch. In any case, it has no impact on $f_{\max}^B$, the only impact is on $\sum C_j^A$. The new cost for $A$ is the cost of the first $b_A - 1$ batches plus the cost of the last batch. Because we do not know which batch is the last one and how many jobs it contains, the new cost can be expressed as follows:

$$F^A(b_A,i_A,b_B,i_B) = \min_{b_A-1 \leq j \leq i_A-1} \Big\{F(b_A-1,j,b_B,i_B) + (i_A-j)C(b_A,i_A,b_B,i_B)\Big\}$$

- If a job of agent $B$ is scheduled, it has no impact on $\sum C_j^A$ and we have to consider only the limit for $f_{\max}^B$. This sort of decision is only possible if we have $C(b_A,i_A,b_B,i_B) \leq \tilde{d}_{j+1}^B(Q)$. In this case, the cost is unchanged and we have the following expression:

$$F^B(b_A,i_A,b_B,i_B) = \min_{b_B-1 \leq j \leq i_B-1} \Big\{F(b_A,i_A,b_B-1,j)\Big\} + f(b_A,i_A,b_B,i_B)$$

where $f(b_A,i_A,b_B,i_B) = 0$ if $C(b_A,i_A,b_B,i_B) \leq \tilde{d}_{j+1}^B(Q)$ and $+\infty$ otherwise. $F(b_A,i_A,b_B,i_B)$ equals the minimum between $F^A(b_A,i_A,b_B,i_B)$ and $F^B(b_A,i_A,b_B,i_B)$ (see Algorithm 23).

Since each value $F(b_A,i_A,b_B,i_B)$ can be computed in $O(n)$ time, the following result holds.

**Theorem 4.5.** *An optimal solution to problem* $1|CO, s-batch, f_{\max}^B \leq Q|\sum C_i^A$ *can be found in* $O(n n_A^2 n_B^2)$ *time.*

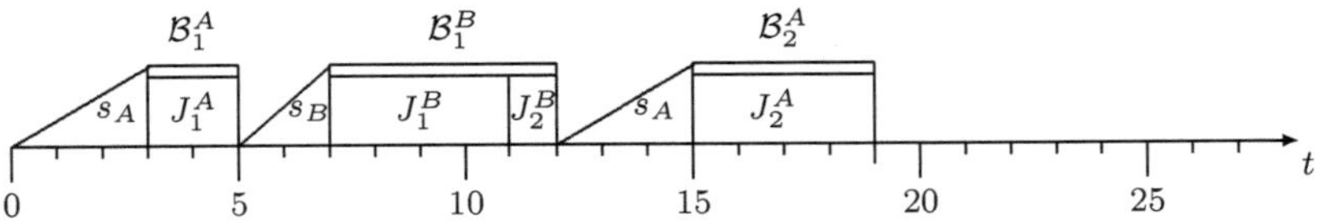


**Fig. 4.6** Solution to the $1|CO, s-batch, f_{\max}^B \leq Q|\sum C_j^A$ problem

*Example 4.5.* Let consider the following 4-job instance, where jobs $J_1^A$ and $J_2^A$ belong to $\mathcal{J}^A$ and jobs $J_1^B$ and $J_2^B$ belong to $\mathcal{J}^B$:

| $J_j^k$ | $J_1^A$ | $J_2^A$ | $J_1^B$ | $J_2^B$ |
|---|---|---|---|---|
| $p_j^k$ | 2 | 4 | 4 | 1 |
| $d_j^B$ | | | 9 | 11 |

We assume that the jobs of $\mathcal{J}^B$ are subject to due dates and that the function $f_j^B(t)$ is defined by:

$$f_j^B(t) = 2t - d_j^B, \forall j \in \mathcal{J}^B$$

It is easy to see that $f_j^B(t) \leq Q \Leftrightarrow 2t - d_j^B \leq Q \Leftrightarrow t \leq (Q + d_j^B)/2$. Therefore, for each job $J_j^B$ we define a deadline $\tilde{d}_j^B(Q) = (Q + d_j^B)/2$. With $Q = 19$, we obtain:

| $J_j^B$ | $J_1^B$ | $J_2^B$ |
|---|---|---|
| $\tilde{d}_j^B$ | 14 | 15 |

We suppose that $s_A = 3$ and $s_B = 2$. The optimal solution is given by the sequence $(\{J_1^A\}, \{J_1^B, J_2^B\}, \{J_1^A\})$ (it is not possible in this example to finish the sequence by a job of agent $B$ for deadline reasons). The sequence is represented in Fig. 4.6. We have $f_{\max}^B = \max(24-9, 24-11) = 15 \leq 19$ and $\sum C_j^A = 5 + 19 = 24$. $\diamond$

#### 4.2.4.2 Problem $1|CO, s-batch, \sum C_j^A \leq Q|f_{\max}^B$

Let us now turn to the symmetric problem, denoted $1|CO, s-batch, \sum C_j^A \leq Q|f_{\max}^B$. We can derive an algorithm that determines whether there exists a solution to the feasibility problem $1|CO, s-batch, \sum C_j^A \leq Q, f_{\max}^B \leq y|-$, where $y \in [lb_B, ub_B]$ with $lb_B$ and $ub_B$ given by Eqs. (4.12) and (4.13).

The idea is that problem $1|CO, s-batch, \sum C_j^A \leq Q, f_{\max}^B \leq y|-$ has a solution if and only if there is a schedule in which $\sum C_j^A \leq Q$ and each job of agent $B$

completes within its deadline $\tilde{d}_j^B(y)$ defined as in (4.18), with $y$ in place of $Q$. As usual, we assume that $\tilde{d}_j^B(y)$ is computed in constant time through an explicit expression for the inverse function $(f_j^B)^{-1}(t)$.

Suppose that jobs of agent $B$ are numbered according to deadlines, $\tilde{d}_1^B(y) \leq \cdots \leq \tilde{d}_{n_B}^B(y)$ and jobs of agent $A$ are numbered in SPT order, $p_1^A \leq \cdots \leq p_{n_A}^A$. Let ED($y$) be the Earliest Deadline order. We have the following property.

**Lemma 4.5.** *If one exists, there exists a feasible solution to problem* $1|CO, s-batch, \sum C_i^A \leq Q, f_{\max}^B \leq y|-$ *in which the jobs of agent B are processed in the ED(y) order and the jobs of agent A are processed in SPT order.*

Hence, a feasible solution can be obtained by dynamic programming Algorithm 23, where we should consider $\tilde{d}_i^B(y)$ instead of $\tilde{d}_i^B(Q)$.

A feasible solution, if it exists, corresponds to the state $(b_A, n_A, b_B, n_B)$ such that $F(b_A, n_A, b_B, n_B) \leq Q$, $1 \leq b_A \leq n_A$ and $1 \leq b_B \leq n_B$. Thus, verifying if $1|CO, s-batch, \sum C_j^A \leq Q, f_{\max}^B \leq y|-$ has a solution can be done in $O(nn_A^2 n_B^2)$ time.

So, an optimal solution value for the problem $1|CO, s-batch, \sum C_i^A \leq Q|f_{\max}^B$ corresponds to $\min\{y \mid F(b_A, n_A, b_B, n_B) \leq Q \text{ with } 1 \leq b_A \leq n_A, 1 \leq b_B \leq n_B\}$. Let $Y_B = ub_B - lb_B$ (where $ub_B$ and $lb_B$ are given by (4.12) and (4.13)). In conclusion, the following result holds.

**Theorem 4.6.** *An optimal solution to problem* $1|CO, s-batch, \sum C_i^A \leq Q|f_{\max}^B$ *can be found in* $O(n_A^2 n_B^2 n \log Y_B)$ *time.*

## 4.2.5 *Functions* $f_{\max}$, $\sum w_j U_j$

### 4.2.5.1 Problem $1|CO, s-batch, f_{\max}^B \leq Q|\sum w_j^A U_j^A$

Let us now turn to problem $1|CO, s-batch, f_{\max}^B \leq Q|\sum w_j^A U_j^A$.

**Proposition 4.1.** *The problem* $1|CO, s-batch, f_{\max}^B \leq Q|\sum w_j^A U_j^A$ *is NP-hard.*

*Proof.* If $Q$ is sufficiently large and if the setup time is equal to 0, there is no need to constitute batches, and the problem is equivalent to the single-agent scheduling problem $1||\sum w_j U_j$, which is NP-hard (Karp 1972). □

Given $Q$, similarly to Sect. 4.2.1, we can associate a *deadline* $\tilde{d}_j^B(Q)$ to each job $J_j^B$ in constant time. Let ED($Q$) be the Earliest Deadline order with respect to deadlines $\tilde{d}_j^B(Q)$. We assume that jobs in $\mathcal{J}^A$ are numbered in EDD order, i.e. $d_1^A \leq \cdots \leq d_{n_A}^A$, and that jobs in $\mathcal{J}^B$ are numbered in ED($Q$) order, i.e., $\tilde{d}_1^B(Q) \leq \cdots \leq \tilde{d}_{n_B}^B(Q)$. One can easily establish the following property.

**Lemma 4.6.** *If an optimal schedule for problem* $1|CO, s-batch, f_{\max}^B \leq Q|\sum w_j^A U_j^A$ *exists, there is one in which the late jobs of agent A form a single* *batch that is processed at the end of the schedule, the early jobs of agent A are processed in EDD order, and the jobs of agent B are processed in ED(Q) order.*

In what follows, for simplicity, we write $\tilde{d}_j^B$ instead of $\tilde{d}_j^B(Q)$.

Lemma 4.6 allows to devise a dynamic programming solution algorithm.

Let $C(i_A, i_B, W_A, k, e)$ be the minimum completion time of the last early job, in a schedule where the first $i_A$ jobs of agent $A$ and the first $i_B$ jobs of agent $B$ are scheduled, the total weight of the late jobs for agent $A$ does not exceed $W_A$, the last scheduled batch is composed of jobs of agent $k$, $k \in \{A, B\}$, and the last batch is $(J_e^k, J_{e+1}^k, \dots, J_{i_k}^k)$. Note that if $k = A$, the last batch must complete within $d_e^A$, and if $k = B$, the last batch must complete within $\tilde{d}_e^B$.

In the recursion, a job $J_{i_k}^k$ is scheduled at the end of the partial schedule. There are five alternatives:

1. The last batch belongs to agent $A$ ($k = A$) and either
   - Job $J_{i_A}^A$ is late,
   - Or job $J_{i_A}^A$ is assigned to the last early batch of agent $A$ (if the batch still completes within $d_e^A$),
   - Or job $J_{i_A}^A$ starts a new early batch (if the new batch completes within $d_{i_A}^A$).
2. The last batch belongs to agent $B$ ($k = B$) and either
   - Job $J_{i_B}^B$ is assigned to the last early batch of agent $B$ (if the batch still completes within $\tilde{d}_e^B$),
   - Or job $J_{i_B}^B$ starts a new early batch (if the new batch completes within $\tilde{d}_{i_B}^B$).

The dynamic program is given in Algorithm 24, where we have the following definitions:

$$\phi(i_A, i_B, W_A, A, e) = \begin{cases} 0 & \text{if } C(i_A - 1, i_B, W_A, A, e) + p_{i_A}^A \le d_e^A \\ +\infty & \text{otherwise} \end{cases}$$

$$\phi(i_A, i_B, W_A, B, e) = \begin{cases} 0 & \text{if } C(i_A, i_B - 1, W_A, B, e) + p_{i_B}^B \le \tilde{d}_e^B \\ +\infty & \text{otherwise} \end{cases}$$

$$\psi^1(i_A, i_B, W_A, \ell, h) = \begin{cases} 0 & \text{if } C(i_A - 1, i_B, W_A, \ell, h) + s_A + p_{i_A}^A \le d_{i_A}^A \\ +\infty & \text{otherwise} \end{cases}$$

$$\psi^2(i_A, i_B, W_A, \ell, h) = \begin{cases} 0 & \text{if } C(i_A, i_B - 1, W_A, \ell, h) + s_B + p_{i_B}^B \le \tilde{d}_{i_B}^B \\ +\infty & \text{otherwise} \end{cases}$$

The optimal value of $W_A^*$ is given by:

$$W_A^* = \min\{W_A \mid C(n_A, n_B, W_A, k, e) < +\infty, W_A = 0, 1, \dots, \hat{W}_A, \\ k \in \{A, B\},\ e = 1, \dots, n_k\}$$

where $\hat{W}_A$ is the total weight of all jobs in $\mathcal{J}^A$.

**Algorithm 24** for problem $1|CO, s-batch, f_{\max}^{B} \leq Q|\sum w_j^A U_j^A$

$\hat{W}_A := \sum_{j=1}^{n_A} w_j^A$
**for** $k := A$ **to** $B$ **do**
  **for** $e := 1$ **to** $n_k$ **do**
    $C(0,0,0,k,e) := 0$
  **end for**
**end for**
**for** $k := A$ **to** $B$ **do**
  **for** $e := 1$ **to** $n_k$ **do**
    **if** $(i_A, i_B, W_A, k, e) \neq (0,0,0,k,e)$ **then**
      $C(i_A, i_B, W_A, k, e) := \infty$
    **end if**
  **end for**
**end for**
**for** $i_A := 1$ **to** $n_A$ **do**
  **for** $i_B := 1$ **to** $n_B$ **do**
    **for** $W_A := 0$ **to** $\hat{W}_A$ **do**
      **for** $k := A$ **to** $B$ **do**
        **for** $e := 1$ **to** $i_k$ **do**
          **if** $(k = A)$ **and** $(e < i_A)$ **then**
            $C(i_A, i_B, W_A, A, e) :=$

$$\min \begin{cases} C(i_A - 1, i_B, W_A - w_{i_A}^A, A, e), \\ C(i_A - 1, i_B, W_A, A, e) + p_{i_A}^A + \phi(i_A, i_B, W_A, A, e) \end{cases}$$

          **end if**
          **if** $(k = B)$ **and** $(e < i_B)$ **then**
            $C(i_A, i_B, W_A, B, e) := C(i_A, i_B - 1, W_A, B, e) + p_{i_B}^B + \phi(i_A, i_B, W_A, B, e)$
          **end if**
          **if** $(k = A)$ **and** $(e = i_A)$ **then**
            $C(i_A, i_B, W_A, A, e) :=$
            $\min \Big\{ C(i_A - 1, i_B, W_A, \ell, h) + s_A + p_{i_A}^A + \psi^1(i_A, i_B, W_A, \ell, h) : 1 \leq h \leq A - 1 \text{ if } \ell = A \text{ and } 1 \leq h \leq i_B \text{ if } \ell = B \Big\}$
          **end if**
          **if** $(k = B)$ **and** $(e = i_B)$ **then**
            $C(i_A, i_B, W_A, B, e) :=$
            $\min \Big\{ C(i_A, i_B - 1, W_A, \ell, h) + s_B + p_{i_B}^B + \psi^2(i_A, i_B, W_A, \ell, h) : 1 \leq h \leq i_A \text{ if } \ell = A \text{ and } 1 \leq h \leq B - 1 \text{ if } \ell = B \Big\}$
          **end if**
        **end for**
      **end for**
    **end for**
  **end for**
**end for**
**return** $W_A^*$

Let us consider the complexity of Algorithm 24. There are $O(n_A n_B n \hat{W}_A)$ entries for $C(n_A, n_B, W_A, k, e)$. Each of them can be computed in $O(n)$, so that we have the following result.

**Theorem 4.7.** *Algorithm 24 solves problem* $1|CO, s - batch, f_{\max}^B \leq Q|\sum w_j^A U_j^A$ *in* $O(n_A n_B n^2 \hat{W}_A)$ *time.*

For the unweighted case, because $\hat{W}_A = n_A$, the algorithm runs in polynomial time.

**Corollary 4.1.** *Algorithm 24 solves* $1|CO, s - batch, f_{\max}^B \leq Q|\sum U_j^A$ *in time* $O(n_A^2 n_B n^2)$.

#### 4.2.5.2 Problem $1|CO, s - batch, \sum w_j^A U_j^A \leq Q|f_{\max}^B$

Let us now turn to the symmetric problem $1|CO, s - batch, \sum w_j^A U_j^A \leq Q|f_{\max}^B$. The resolution of this problem will use Algorithm 24 iteratively.

Let consider a given value of $y \in [lb_B, ub_B]$, $lb_B$ and $ub_B$ given by Eqs. (4.12) and (4.13). It is possible to solve problem $1|CO, s - batch, f_{\max}^B \leq y|\sum w_j^A U_j^A$ by Algorithm 24. If the value of $W_A^*$ is less than or equal to $Q$, $y$ can be decreased, otherwise, $y$ has to be increased. Fixing the optimal value of $y$ can be done by a binary search.

Therefore, an optimal schedule for $1|CO, s - batch, \sum w_j^A U_j^A \leq Q|f_{\max}^B$ can be obtained in $O((n_A n_B n) Q \log Y_B)$ with $Y_B = ub_B - lb_B$.

**Corollary 4.2.** *Algorithm 24 used iteratively as described above can solve problem* $1|CO, s - batch, \sum U_j^A \leq Q|f_{\max}^B$ *in* $O(n_A^2 n_B n \log Y_B)$, *i.e. in polynomial time, because* $Q \leq n_A$.

#### 4.2.5.3 Problem $1|CO, s - batch|\mathcal{P}(f_{\max}^A, \sum U_j^B)$

Let us now consider problem $1|CO, s - batch|\mathcal{P}(f_{\max}^A, \sum U_j^B)$. Each Pareto optimal solution can be found by solving a logarithmic number of instances of the $\varepsilon$-constraint problem. However, in this case, the problem is even easier. Let consider that $F_{Q=n_B}^{A*}$ denotes the value of the optimal solution for agent $A$ to problem $1|CO, s - batch, \sum U_j^B \leq Q|f_{\max}^A$ with $Q = n_B$. To obtain a first Pareto optimal solution, we only need to solve *one* instance of the symmetric problem, i.e., $1|CO, s - batch, f_{\max}^A \leq Q|\sum U_j^B$ with $Q = F_{Q=n_B}^{A*}$. If $U_Q^{B*}$ denotes the optimal value of this problem, the pair $(F_{Q=n_B}^A, U_Q^{B*})$ is a Pareto optimal solution.

The *next* Pareto optimal solution can be generated by solving problem $1|CO, s - batch, \sum U_j^B \leq Q|f_{\max}^A$ problem with $Q = n_B - 1$. We obtain an optimal solution with value $F_{Q=n_B-1}^{A*}$ and the symmetric problem is solved, and so on. By doing this, the whole Pareto set can be obtained. Hence, the complexity of this algorithm is essentially related to the size of the Pareto set. In this case, the Pareto set has a polynomial number of solutions, which is bounded by $n_B$. Hence, the size of the Pareto set is bounded by $O(n_B)$.

In conclusion, the following result holds.

**Theorem 4.8.** *Problem* $1|CO, s-batch|\mathcal{P}(f^A_{\max}, \sum U^B_j)$ *can be solved in* $O(n_A^2 n_B n^2)$ *time.*

## 4.2.6 Functions $C_{\max}$, $\sum C_j$

### 4.2.6.1 Problem $1|CO, s-batch, \sum C^B_j \leq Q|C^A_{\max}$

Let us now turn to problem $1|CO, s-batch, \sum C^B_j \leq Q|C^A_{\max}$. Assume that the jobs of agent $B$ are numbered in SPT order $p^B_1 \leq \cdots \leq p^B_{n_B}$. We have the following property (Kovalyov et al. 2012b).

**Lemma 4.7.** *If an optimal schedule for problem* $1|CO, s-batch, \sum C^B_j \leq Q|C^A_{\max}$ *exists, there is one in which the jobs of agent A form a single batch and the jobs of agent B are processed in SPT order.*

By the same reasoning as presented in Sect. 4.2.3.1, and according to Lemma 4.7, an optimal schedule is of the form $(\pi_B, \mathcal{B}^A, \pi'_B)$ where $\pi_B$ and $\pi'_B$ (possibly empty) contain only batches of jobs of agent $B$, and $\mathcal{B}^A$ is the only batch of agent $A$ jobs.

We remark that for each solution of the form $(\pi_B, \mathcal{B}^A, \pi'_B)$, the makespan $C^A_{\max}$ only depends on the number of jobs $k$ and the number of batches $b$ in the partial schedule $\pi_B$. Hence, as in Sect. 4.2.3.2, given $k$ and $b$, the problem reduces to constructing two schedules:

- $\pi_B = \pi^{(k,b)}$, that minimizes the total completion time of the job set $\{J^B_1, \ldots, J^B_k\}$ starting at time zero and forming $b$ batches,
- $\pi'_B = \pi^{(k+1)}$, that minimizes the total completion time of jobs at the end of the schedule $\{J^B_{k+1}, \ldots, J^B_{n_B}\}$, assuming that they start at time zero.

Hence, the optimal schedule corresponds to the minimum value of:

$$C^A_{\max}(k,b) = b.s_B + \sum_{j=1}^{k} p^B_j + s_A + P_A \tag{4.20}$$

over $(b,k)$ such that $0 \leq b \leq k \leq n_B$ and such that:

$$\sum_{j=1}^{k} C^B_j(\pi^{(k,b)}) + (n_B - k)C^A_{\max}(k,b) + \sum_{j=k+1}^{n_B} C^B_j(\pi^{(k+1)}) \leq Q \tag{4.21}$$

**Algorithm 25** for problem $1|CO, s-batch, \sum C_i^B \le Q|C_{\max}^A$

Renumber jobs of agent $B$ in SPT order
$F(0,0) := 0$
$F(1,k) = k(s_B + \sum_{i=1}^k p_i^B)$ // initial value
**for** $b := 2$ **to** $n_B$ **do**
  **for** $k := b$ **to** $n_B$ **do**
    $F(b,k) := \min_{1\le j\le k-1} \left\{F(b-1,j) + (k-j)\left(bs_B + \sum_{i=1}^k p_i^B\right)\right\}$
  **end for**
**end for**
**return** $C_{\max}^A(k,b)$ defined in (4.20) and satisfying (4.21)

The whole set of schedules $\pi^{(k+1)}$, $0 \le k \le n_B - 1$, can be found in $O(n_B^2)$ time by a backward dynamic programming algorithm with batch insertion proposed by Coffman et al. (1990). Such an algorithm solves the single-agent problem $1|s-batch|\sum C_j$ to optimality and works as follows.

Given the job set $\{J_1, \dots, J_n\}$, let $F(i)$ be the minimum value of the total completion time restricted to the job set $\{J_i, J_{i+1}, \dots, J_n\}$, where the schedule starts at time zero with a setup time $s$. The recursion function for $i = n, n-1, \dots, 1$ is:

$$F(i) = \min_{i+1\le h\le n+1} \left\{F(h) + (n-i+1)\left(s + \sum_{j=i}^{h-1} p_j\right)\right\} \quad (4.22)$$

For each value of $h$, formula (4.22) considers that a batch $(J_i, \dots, J_{h-1})$ is appended at the beginning of the partial schedule containing jobs $(J_h, \dots, J_n)$. Such first batch completes at time $s + \sum_{j=i}^{h-1} p_j$ and, therefore, its contribution to the total completion time is $(h-i)\left(s + \sum_{j=i}^{h-1} p_j\right)$. Due to the insertion of this batch, the processing of the subsequent batches (containing jobs $J_h, \dots, J_n$) is delayed by time $s + \sum_{j=i}^{h-1} p_j$, so the contribution of subsequent batches becomes $F(h) + (n-h+1)\left(s + \sum_{j=i}^{h-1} p_j\right)$. Adding up the two contributions, we get the expression (4.22), which is initialized with $F(n+1) = 0$.

For what concerns schedules $\pi^{(k,b)}$, $0 \le b \le k \le n_B$, these can all be found by the dynamic programming Algorithm 25 (Kovalyov et al. 2012a), where a single batch is appended at the end of a current schedule and $F(b,k)$ is the minimum total completion time of jobs $\{J_1^B, \dots, J_k^B\}$ in $b$ batches from time zero.

For given $k$ and $b$, the value $F(b,k)$ is computed in $O(k)$ time. Hence, all the values $F(b,k)$ and corresponding schedules $\pi^{(k,b)}$, $0 \le b \le k \le n_B$, can be found in $O(n_B^3)$ time. In conclusion, considering that $P_A$ can be computed in $O(n_A)$, the following theorem holds.

**Theorem 4.9.** *The problem* $1|CO, s-batch, \sum C_i^B \le Q|C_{\max}^A$ *can be solved in* $O(n_B^3 + n_A)$ *time.*

Note that (4.22) and Algorithm 25 can also be used to solve the symmetric problem $1|CO, s-batch, C_{\max}^A \leq Q|\sum C_j^B$. In fact, one only needs to select, among the $O(n_B^2)$ pairs $(k, b)$, the one such that

$$C_{\max}^A(\pi^{(k,b)}) = bs_B + \sum_{j=1}^{k} p_j^B + s_A + P_A \leq Q$$

and that minimizes

$$\sum_{j=1}^{k} C_j^B(\pi^{(k,b)}) + (n_B - k)\left(bs_B + \sum_{j=1}^{k} p_j^B + s_A + P_A\right) + \sum_{j=k+1}^{n_B} C_j^B(\pi^{(k+1)}).$$

#### 4.2.6.2 Problem $1|CO, s-batch|\mathcal{P}(C_{\max}^A, \sum C_j^B)$

Let us now consider problem $1|CO, s-batch|\mathcal{P}(C_{\max}^A, \sum C_j^B)$. Each Pareto optimal solution can be found by solving a logarithmic number of instances of the $\varepsilon$-constraint problem. However, suppose that $F_Q^B$ is the value of the optimal solution of problem $1|CO, s-batch, C_{\max}^A \leq Q|\sum C_j^B$. Let $Q = T = n_A s_A + n_B s_B + \sum_{i \in \mathcal{J}^A} p_i^A + \sum_{i \in \mathcal{J}^B} p_i^B$. To obtain a Pareto optimal solution, we only need to solve *one* instance of the symmetric problem, i.e., problem $1|CO, s-batch, \sum C_j^B \leq F_Q^B|C_{\max}^A$. If $F^A$ is the optimal value of the problem, the pair $(F^A, F_Q^B)$ is Pareto optimal. Similarly, the *next* Pareto optimal solution can be generated by solving $1|CO, s-batch, C_{\max}^A \leq F^A - p_k^B|\sum C_i^B$ where $p_k^B$ is the processing time of the job of agent $B$ scheduled just before the first job of agent $A$ in the previous Pareto solution, and thereafter one instance of the symmetric problem. In this way, the whole Pareto set can be obtained. Note that the scheduling of jobs of agent $B$ which are processed after $\mathcal{J}^A$ is given by solving problem $1|CO, s-batch|\sum C_j$ by using the algorithm of Coffman et al. (1990).

Hence, the complexity of this enumeration is essentially related to the size of the Pareto set. In this case, the Pareto set has a polynomial number of solutions. This is due to the fact that the structure of any strict Pareto optimal solution is of the form $(\pi^{(k,b)}, \mathcal{B}^A, \pi^{(k+1)})$ where jobs of $\mathcal{J}^A$ are inserted after certain batches of jobs of $\mathcal{J}^B$. The makespan for agent $A$ is completely determined by the number of jobs $k, 0 \leq k \leq n_B$ preceding $\mathcal{B}^A$ and the number of batches $b, 0 \leq b \leq k \leq n_B$ in the sub-sequence $\pi^{(k,b)}$. Hence, the size of the Pareto set is bounded by $O(n_B)$.

In conclusion, the following result holds.

**Theorem 4.10.** *Problem* $1|CO, s-batch|\mathcal{P}(C_{\max}^A, \sum C_j^B)$ *can be solved in* $O(n_B^4 + n_A n_B)$.

### 4.2.7 Functions $\sum C_j$, $\sum C_j$

#### 4.2.7.1 Problem $1|CO, s-batch, \sum C_j^B \leq Q|\sum C_j^A$

Let us now turn to problem $1|CO, s-batch, \sum C_j^B \leq Q|\sum C_j^A$. Its NP-hardness follows from the complexity of problem $1|CO, \sum C_j^B \leq Q|\sum C_j^A$ (see Theorem 3.20, page 110), since the former problem reduces to the latter letting $s_A = s_B = 0$.

By a simple pairwise argument, one can establish the following lemma.

**Lemma 4.8.** *There exists an optimal schedule for $1|CO, s-batch, \sum C_j^B \leq Q|\sum C_j^A$ problem, if one exists, in which the jobs of each agent are processed in SPT order.*

Based on Lemma 4.8, a pseudo-polynomial time dynamic programming algorithm can be derived. Assume that the jobs are numbered in SPT order, i.e., $p_1^A \leq \cdots \leq p_{n_A}^A$ and $p_1^B \leq \cdots \leq p_{n_B}^B$.

Let $F(i_A, i_B, q)$ be the value of the optimal solution of the problem restricted to the job set $\{J_{i_A}^A, J_{i_A+1}^A, \ldots, J_{n_A}^A\} \cup \{J_{i_B}^B, J_{i_B+1}^B, \ldots, J_{n_B}^B\}$ starting at time 0, provided that the total completion time for agent $B$ is smaller than or equal to $q$. In the functional equation, the contribution of a single batch appended at the beginning of the schedule is taken into account.

We denote by $F^A(i_A, i_B, q)$ the total completion time of agent $A$ if the decision is to schedule job $J_{i_A}^A$ just before the solution obtained with $F(i_A+1, i_B, q)$. This job can constitute a new batch, either only with this job or with other jobs already scheduled. Therefore, we will consider these possibilities in the recursive relation. Similarly, we denote by $F^B(i_A, i_B, q)$ the total completion time of agent $A$ if the decision is to schedule job $J_{i_B}^B$ before the solution obtained with $F(i_A+1, i_B, q)$. We have:

$$F^A(i_A, i_B, q) = \min_{j=i_A+1}^{n_A+1} \left\{F\left(j, i_B, q - n_B^{(i_B)} P_A^{(i_A, j-1)}\right) + n_A^{(i_A)} P_A^{(i_A, j-1)}\right\}$$

with $P_k^{(i,j)} = s_k + \sum_{h=i}^{j} p_h^k$ for $1 \leq i \leq j \leq n_k$, $\forall k \in \{A, B\}$ and $n_k^{(i_k)} = n_k - i_k + 1$ the number of jobs of agent $k$ already scheduled.

$$F^B(i_A, i_B, q) = \min_{j=i_B+1}^{n_B+1} \left\{F\left(i_A, j, q - n_B^{(i_B)} P_B^{(i_B, j-1)}\right) + n_A^{(i_A)} P_B^{(i_B, j-1)}\right\}$$

Notice that $F^A(i_A, i_B, q)$ and $F^B(i_A, i_B, q)$ are set to $+\infty$ if $q > Q$.

The optimal solution $\sigma^*$ is given by

$$\min\left\{F(1, 1, q) : q \in [s_B + \sum_{j=1}^{n_B} p_j^B, Q]\right\}$$

**Algorithm 26** for problem $1|CO, s - batch, \sum C_j^B \leq Q|\sum C_j^A$

**for** $k := A$ **to** $B$ **do**
  **for** $i := 1$ **to** $n_k$ **do**
    **for** $j := i$ **to** $n_k$ **do**
      Compute $P_A^{(i,j)}$
      Compute $P_B^{(i,j)}$
    **end for**
  **end for**
**end for**
$F(n_A + 1, n_B + 1, 0) := 0$
**for** $i_A := 1$ **to** $n_A$ **do**
  **for** $i_B := 1$ **to** $n_B$ **do**
    **for** $q := 1$ **to** $Q$ **do**
      **if** $(i_A, i_B, t) \neq (n_A + 1, n_B + 1, 0)$ **then**
        $F(i_A, i_B, t) := +\infty$
      **end if**
    **end for**
  **end for**
**end for**
**for** $i_A := n_A$ **downto** 1 **do**
  **for** $i_B := n_B$ **downto** 1 **do**
    **for** $q = 0$ **to** $Q$ **do**
      **if** $(i_A, i_B) \neq (n_A, n_B)$ **then**
        $F(i_A, i_B, q) := \min\left\{F^A(i_A, i_B, q), F^B(i_A, i_B, q)\right\}$
      **end if**
    **end for**
  **end for**
**end for**
**return** $\sigma^*$

The corresponding dynamic programming algorithm is presented in details in Algorithm 26.

For each choice of the values $i_A$ and $i_B$, $F(i_A, i_B, t)$ is computed in $O(n)$ time. Hence, the necessary time to compute all values $F(i_A, i_B, t)$ is no more than $O(n_A n_B n Q)$ time. In conclusion, the following result holds.

**Theorem 4.11.** *An optimal solution to problem* $1|CO, s - batch, \sum C_j^B \leq Q|\sum C_j^A$ *can be found in* $O(n_A n_B n Q)$ *time.*

#### 4.2.7.2 Problem $1|CO, s - batch|\mathcal{P}(\sum C_j^A, \sum C_j^B)$

We now consider the problem $1|CO, s - batch|\mathcal{P}(\sum C_j^A, \sum C_j^B)$. Even in the COMPETING scenario of the single machine problem without batches, denoted $1|CO|\mathcal{P}(\sum C_j^A, \sum C_j^B)$, the size of the Pareto set may not be polynomial (see Sect. 3.9.2). Hence, the size of the Pareto set with batches is also exponential.

### 4.2.8 Functions $\sum w_j U_j$, $\sum w_j U_j$

#### 4.2.8.1 Problem $1|CO, s-batch, \sum w_j^B U_j^B \leq Q|\sum w_j^A U_j^A$

Let us now turn to problem $1|CO, s-batch, \sum w_j^B U_j^B \leq Q|\sum w_j^A U_j^A$.

**Proposition 4.2.** *The problem* $1|CO, s-batch, \sum w_j^B U_j^B \leq Q|\sum w_j^A U_j^A$ *is NP-hard.*

*Proof.* The result follows from the NP-hardness of the single-agent problem $1||\sum w_j U_j$ (Karp 1972). □

Before introducing a pseudo-polynomial dynamic programming algorithm to solve problem $1|CO, s-batch, \sum w_j^B U_j^B \leq Q|\sum w_j^A U_j^A$, we give some properties to characterize the optimal solutions of this problem.

The first property is that we can put all late jobs of each agent into one batch scheduled after all "early" batches. Hence, an optimal schedule is of the form $(E^{(k_A,k_B)}, T^{(n_A-k_A,n_B-k_B)})$ where $E^{(k_A,k_B)}$ is the subsequence of $k_A$ jobs of agent $A$ and $k_B$ jobs of agent $B$ that are early and are scheduled first in $b$ batches, and $T^{(n_A-k_A,n_B-k_B)}$ is the subsequence of $n_A - k_A$ jobs of agent $A$ forming at most one batch and $n_B - k_B$ jobs of agent $B$ forming at most one batch, and are scheduled at the end of the sequence.

For the second property, we have.

**Lemma 4.9.** *If an optimal schedule for problem* $1|CO, s-batch, \sum w_j^B U_j^B \leq Q|\sum w_j^A U_j^A$ *exists, there is one in which the early jobs of each agent are processed in EDD order.*

*Proof.* Consider an optimal schedule for which the property does not hold, i.e., batch $\mathcal{B}_\ell^k$ of agent $k$ ($k$ is either $A$ or $B$), is scheduled before batch $\mathcal{B}_t^k$ with $J_i^k \in \mathcal{B}_\ell^k$ and $J_j^k \in \mathcal{B}_t^k$, $d_j^k < d_i^k$ and both batches are early. Thus, if we move job $J_i^k$ from $\mathcal{B}_\ell^k$ to $\mathcal{B}_t^k$, the completion time of batch $\mathcal{B}_\ell^k$ (as well as the completion time of all batches between $\mathcal{B}_\ell^k$ and $\mathcal{B}_t^k$) is reduced by $p_i^k$, without increasing the completion time of batch $\mathcal{B}_t^k$, and hence $J_i^k$ remains early. Continuing this exchange reasoning, we obtain an optimal schedule with the desired property. □

According to previous properties, we assume that the jobs of each agent are numbered in EDD order, i.e., $d_1^A \leq \cdots \leq d_{n_A}^A$ and $d_1^B \leq \cdots \leq d_{n_B}^B$.

A dynamic programming algorithm can be proposed, similar to the algorithm for the single-agent problem given in Brucker and Kovalyov (1996), and following a similar reasoning that led to Algorithm 24.

Let $C(i_A, i_B, W_A, W_B, k, e)$ be the minimum completion time of the last early job, in a schedule with the first $i_A$ jobs of agent $A$ and the first $i_B$ jobs of agent $B$, in which the total weights of late jobs do not exceed $W_A$ and $W_B$ for the two agents, respectively, the last scheduled batch is of agent $k$, $k \in \{A, B\}$, and the last batch is $(J_e^k, J_{e+1}^k, \ldots, J_{i_k}^k)$. Note that the last batch must complete within $d_e^k$.

In the recursion, a job $J_{i_k}^k$ is added to the end of a partial schedule. There are three alternatives:

1. Job $J_{i_k}^k$ is late,
2. Job $J_{i_k}^k$ is assigned to the last early batch of agent $k$ (if the batch still completes within $d_e^k$),
3. Job $J_{i_k}^k$ starts a new early batch (if the new batch completes within $d_{i_k}^k$).

The dynamic program is given in Algorithm 27, where we have:

$$\phi(i_A, i_B, W_A, W_B, A, e) = \begin{cases} 0 & \text{if } C(i_A - 1, i_B, W_A, W_B, A, e) + p_{i_A}^A \le d_e^A \\ +\infty & \text{otherwise} \end{cases}$$

$$\phi(i_A, i_B, W_A, W_B, B, e) = \begin{cases} 0 & \text{if } C(i_A, i_B - 1, W_A, W_B, B, e) + p_{i_B}^B \le d_e^B \\ +\infty & \text{otherwise} \end{cases}$$

$$\psi^1(i_A, i_B, W_A, W_B, \ell, h) = \begin{cases} 0 & \text{if } C(i_A - 1, i_B, W_A, W_B, \ell, h) + s_A + p_{i_A}^A \le d_{i_A}^A \\ +\infty & \text{otherwise} \end{cases}$$

$$\psi^2(i_A, i_B, W_A, W_B, \ell, h) = \begin{cases} 0 & \text{if } C(i_A, i_B - 1, W_A, W_B, \ell, h) + s_B + p_{i_B}^B \le d_{i_B}^B \\ +\infty & \text{otherwise} \end{cases}$$

The optimal value $W_A^*$ is given by:

$$W_A^* = \min\{W_A \mid C(n_A, n_B, W_A, W_B, k, e) < +\infty, W_A = 0, 1, \ldots, \hat{W}_A, \\ W_B = 0, 1, \ldots, Q,\ k \in \{A, B\},\ e = 1, \ldots, n_k\},$$

where $\hat{W}_A$ is the sum of all weights of agent $A$. In conclusion, one has the following theorem.

**Theorem 4.12.** *An optimal schedule for* $1|CO, s{-}batch, \sum w_j^B U_j^B \le Q| \sum w_j^A U_j^A$ *can be found in time in* $O((n_A^2 n_B + n_A n_B^2)\hat{W}_A Q)$.

Note that this implies that the unweighted problem $1|CO, s - batch, \sum U_j^B \le Q| \sum U_j^A$ can be solved in polynomial time, since $\hat{W}_A = n_A$ and $Q \le n_B$.

**Corollary 4.3.** *This dynamic programming algorithm solves the scheduling problem* $1|CO, s - batch, \sum U_j^B \le Q| \sum U_j^A$ *in* $O(n_A^3 n_B^2 + n_A^2 n_B^3)$ *time.*

**Algorithm 27** for problem $1|CO, s-batch, \sum w_j^B U_j^B \leq Q|\sum w_j^A U_j^A$

$\hat{W}_A := \sum_{j=1}^{n_A} w_j^A$
$C(0,0,0,0,k,e) := 0$
**for** $k := A$ **to** $B$ **do**
  **for** $e := 1$ **to** $n_k$ **do**
    **if** $(i_A, i_B, W_A, W_B, k, e) \neq (0,0,0,0,k,e)$ **then**
      $C(i_A, i_B, W_A, W_B, k, e) := +\infty$
    **end if**
  **end for**
**end for**
**for** $i_A := 1$ **to** $n_A$ **do**
  **for** $i_B := 1$ **to** $n_B$ **do**
    **for** $W_A := 0$ **to** $\hat{W}_A$ **do**
      **for** $W_B := 0$ **to** $Q$ **do**
        **for** $k \in \{A, B\}$ and $e = 1, \ldots, i_k$ **do**
          **if** $(k = A)$ **and** $(e < i_A)$ **then**
            $v_1 := C(i_A - 1, i_B, W_A - w_{i_A}^A, W_B, A, e)$
            $v_2 := C(i_A - 1, i_B, W_A, W_B, A, e) + p_{i_A}^A + \phi(i_A, i_B, W_A, W_B, A, e)$
            $C(i_A, i_B, W_A, W_B, A, e) := \min\{v_1; v_2\}$
          **end if**
          **if** $(k = B)$ **and** $(e < i_B)$ **then**
            $v_1 := C(i_A, i_B - 1, W_A, W_B - w_{i_B}^B, B, e)$
            $v_2 := C(i_A, i_B - 1, W_A, W_B, B, e) + p_{i_B}^B + \phi(i_A, i_B, W_A, W_B, B, e)$
            $C(i_A, i_B, W_A, W_B, B, e) := \min\{v_1; v_2\}$
          **end if**
          **if** $(k = A)$ **and** $(e = i_A)$ **then**
            $v_1 := \min_{1 \leq h \leq i_A - 1} \{C(i_A - 1, i_B, W_A, W_B, A, h) + s_A + p_{i_A}^A + \psi^1(i_A, i_B, W_A, W_B, A, h)\}$
            $v_2 := \min_{1 \leq h \leq i_B} \{C(i_A - 1, i_B, W_A, W_B, B, h) + s_A + p_{i_A}^A + \psi^1(i_A, i_B, W_A, W_B, B, h)\}$
            $C(i_A, i_B, W_A, W_B, A, e) := \min\{v_1; v_2\}$
          **end if**
          **if** $(k = B)$ **and** $(e = i_B)$ **then**
            $v_1 := \min_{1 \leq h \leq i_A} \{C(i_A, i_B - 1, W_A, W_B, A, h) + s_B + p_{i_B}^B + \psi^2(i_A, i_B, W_A, W_B, A, h)\}$
            $v_2 := \min_{1 \leq h \leq i_B - 1} \{C(i_A, i_B - 1, W_A, W_B, B, h) + s_B + p_{i_B}^B + \psi^2(i_A, i_B, W_A, W_B, B, h)\}$
            $C(i_A, i_B, W_A, W_B, B, e) := \min\{v_1; v_2\}$
          **end if**
        **end for**
      **end for**
    **end for**
  **end for**
**end for**
**return** $W_A^*$

#### 4.2.8.2 Problem $1|CO, s-batch|\mathcal{P}(\sum U_j^A, \sum U_j^B)$

We next address problem $1|CO, s - batch|\mathcal{P}(\sum U_j^A, \sum U_j^B)$. Without loss of generality, let assume that $n_A \leq n_B$. In order to compute the Pareto set for problem $1|s - batch|\mathcal{P}(\sum U_j^A, \sum U_j^B)$, one can solve at most $n_A + 1$ problems of type $1|s - batch, \sum U_j^A \leq Q|\sum U_j^B$ for $Q = n_A, n_A - 1, \ldots, 0$. In conclusion, the following result holds:

**Theorem 4.13.** *Problem $1|CO, s - batch|\mathcal{P}(\sum U_j^A, \sum U_j^B)$ can be solved in $O(n_A^4 n_B^2 + n_A^3 n_B^3)$ time.*

## 4.3 Two-Agent P-Batching Problems

In this section, we consider two sets of jobs $\mathcal{J}^A$ and $\mathcal{J}^B$ owned by two competing agents $A$ and $B$, on an unbounded single parallel batching machine on which the jobs can be processed in batches. All jobs in the same batch start and finish their processing at the same time. The processing time of each batch is equal to the longest processing time of the jobs in the batch.

As in the previous section, the jobs should be scheduled on the parallel-batching machine under the restriction that jobs of different agents cannot be processed in a common batch. In the following, we only address the COMPETING scenario, and results for various combinations of regular scheduling criteria are presented.

### *4.3.1 Preliminary Results*

We start by establishing a simple but important property. If there are two jobs belonging to the same agent $J_i^k$ and $J_j^k$ such that $p_i^k \leq p_j^k$ and $d_i^k \geq d_j^k$, then $J_i^k$ can always be assigned to the same batch as job $J_j^k$. As its contribution to the objective function value is dominated by $J_j^k$, we can delete $J_i^k$ from $\mathcal{J}^k$ without affecting the solution, and we can discard $J_i^k$ from further consideration. Therefore, whenever the job due dates are relevant, one can assume without loss of generality that SPT and EDD orders coincide, i.e., $p_1^k \leq p_2^k \leq \ldots \leq p_{n_k}^k$ and $d_1^k \leq d_2^k \leq \ldots \leq d_{n_k}^k$, $\forall k \in \{A, B\}$.

For the single-agent batching scheduling problem with any regular objective function $f$, denoted $1|p - batch|f$, Brucker et al. (1998) show that there exists an optimal schedule which is an *SPT-batch* schedule, i.e., a schedule where each batch is formed by jobs which are consecutive in the SPT ordering of all jobs. This result is generalized by Li and Yuan (2012) to the two-agent case.

*Property 4.1.* For any pair $f^A, f^B$ of regular objective functions, there exists an optimal schedule for problem $1|p - batch, f^B \leq Q|f^A$ such that the jobs of each batch are consecutive in the SPT ordering of the jobs of the respective agent.

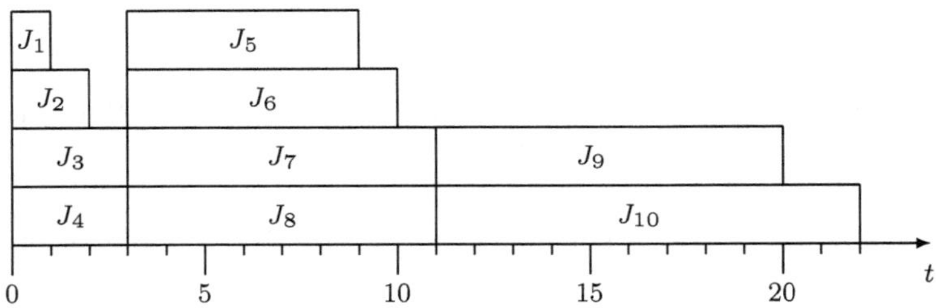


**Fig. 4.7** Illustration of an SPT-batch schedule

As usual, when $f^k$ is a max-type function which is bounded, we associate with each job $J_j^k$ a deadline $\tilde{d}_j^k(Q)$ as described in Sect. 4.2.1. A schedule is feasible if and only if all the deadlines are respected.

In view of these results, we assume in the following that the jobs of each agent are numberer according to SPT order. Moreover, note that the batch set-up time $s$ can be added to each processing time, and hence it can be disregarded. In the following we therefore assume that set-up times are equal to zero.

*Example 4.6.* Let consider the following 10-job instance with only one agent (jobs are numbered in SPT order).

| $J_j$ | $J_1$ | $J_2$ | $J_3$ | $J_4$ | $J_5$ | $J_6$ | $J_7$ | $J_8$ | $J_9$ | $J_{10}$ |
|---|---|---|---|---|---|---|---|---|---|---|
| $p_j^k$ | 1 | 2 | 3 | 3 | 6 | 7 | 8 | 8 | 9 | 11 |

We represent in Fig. 4.7 an SPT-batch schedule with three batches. ◇

## 4.3.2 *Functions* $f_{\max}$, $f_{\max}$

### 4.3.2.1 Problem $1|CO, p-batch, f_{\max}^B \leq Q|f_{\max}^A$

Let us consider problem $1|CO, p-batch, f_{\max}^B \leq Q|f_{\max}^A$. The problem is solved by applying a binary search to the feasibility problem $1|CO, p-batch, f_{\max}^B \leq Q, f_{\max}^A \leq y|-$, with $y \in [lb_A, ub_A]$, $lb_A$ and $ub_A$ given by Eqs. (4.12) and (4.13).

For each value $y$ and $Q$, one can compute deadlines $\tilde{d}_i^A(y)$ and $\tilde{d}_i^B(Q)$ for the completion times of jobs of $\mathcal{J}^A$ and $\mathcal{J}^B$, respectively. The idea is that problem $1|CO, p-batch, f_{\max}^B \leq Q, f_{\max}^A \leq y|-$ has solution if and only if there is a schedule in which each job completes within its deadline. The $\tilde{d}_j^k$ are computed in constant time, because we assume that we have an explicit expression for the inverse function $(f_j^k)^{-1}(t)$, $\forall J_j^k, k \in \{A, B\}$.

Recall that all the jobs of agent $A$ are numbered so that $p_1^A \leq p_2^A \leq \cdots \leq p_{n_A}^A$ and $d_1^A \leq d_2^A \leq \cdots \leq d_{n_A}^A$. Li and Yuan (2012) propose a forward dynamic

**Algorithm 28** for problem $1|CO, p-batch, f^A_{\max} \le y, f^B_{\max} \le Q|-$

$C_y(0,0) := 0$
**for** $i_A := 1$ **to** $n_A$ **do**
  **for** $i_B := 1$ **to** $n_B$ **do**
    Compute $\sigma_1(i_A, i_B)$
    Compute $\sigma_2(i_A, i_B)$
    **if** $(\sigma_1(i_A, i_B) = \emptyset)$ **and** $(\sigma_2(i_A, i_B) = \emptyset)$ **then**
      $C_y(i_A, i_B) := +\infty$
    **else**
      $v_1^A := \min_{\ell_A \in \sigma_1(i_A, i_B)}\{C_y(\ell_A, i_B) + p^A_{i_A}\}$
      $v_1^B := \min_{\ell_B \in \sigma_2(i_A, i_B)}\{C_y(i_A, \ell_B) + p^B_{i_B}\}$
      $C_y(i_A, i_B) := \min\{v_1^A, v_1^B\}$
    **end if**
  **end for**
**end for**
**if** $C_y(n_A, n_B) \neq +\infty$ **then**
  **return** 'Schedule is feasible'
**else**
  **return** 'Schedule is not feasible'
**end if**

programming algorithm to solve problem $1|CO, p\text{-}batch, f^B_{\max} \le Q, f^A_{\max} \le y|-$ in polynomial time, described in Algorithm 28.

For a given $y$, $C_y(i_A, i_B)$ denotes the minimum makespan for SPT-batch schedules containing jobs $\{J_1^A, \ldots, J^A_{i_A}\} \cup \{J_1^B, \ldots, J^B_{i_B}\}$, respecting $f^A_{\max} \le y$ and $f^B_{\max} \le Q$ for the first $i_A$ and $i_B$ jobs of both agents. We set $C_y(i_A, i_B) = +\infty$ if there is no feasible schedule for jobs $\{J_1^A, \ldots, J^A_{i_A}\} \cup \{J_1^B, \ldots, J^B_{i_B}\}$, i.e. no feasible schedule for these jobs respects their deadline $\tilde{d}^A_j(y)$ and $\tilde{d}^B_j(Q)$.

In Algorithm 28, we denote by $\sigma_1(i_A, i_B)$ the set of indices of jobs of agent $A$, starting from $\ell_A$, that can be scheduled in the same batch as $J^A_{i_A}$ and such that the deadline of job $J^A_{\ell_A+1}$ is respected. Suppose that the last current batch belongs to agent $A$, and call $J^A_{\ell_A+1}$ the first job of $A$ in the last current batch. In this case, $\sigma_1(i_A, i_B)$ is the set of candidate values for index $\ell_A$. Note that since the last batch spans from $J^A_{\ell_A+1}$ to $J^A_{i_A}$, its length is given by $p^A_{i_A}$ and it has to complete within $d^A_{\ell_1+A}(y)$. Hence, one has:

$$\sigma_1(i_A, i_B) = \left\{0 \le \ell_A \le i_A - 1 : C_y(\ell_A, i_B) + p^A_{i_A} \le \tilde{d}^A_{\ell_A+1}(y)\right\}$$

Similarly, if the last batch belongs to $B$, and contains jobs $(J^B_{\ell_B+1}, \ldots, J^B_{i_B})$, the set $\sigma_2(i_A, i_B)$ of candidate values for index $\ell_B$ must ensure that the last batch can feasibly complete within its deadlines, hence:

$$\sigma_2(i_A, i_B) = \left\{0 \le \ell_B \le i_B - 1 : C_y(i_A, \ell_B) + p^B_{i_B} \le \tilde{d}^B_{\ell_B+1}(Q)\right\}$$

Note that the recursion described in Algorithm 28 can be stopped, and one can deduce that there is no feasible solution, if $C_y(i_A, i_B) = +\infty$ has been obtained

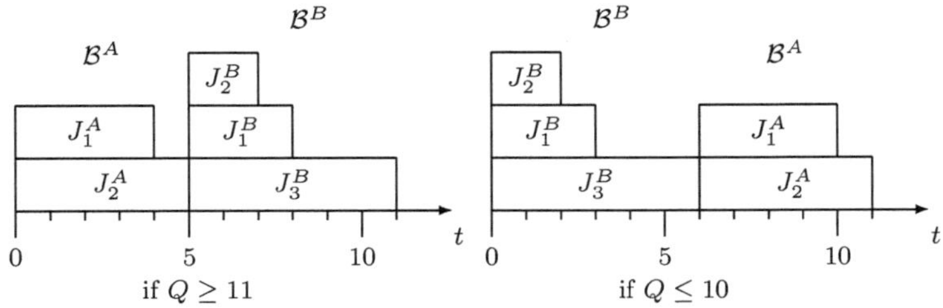


**Fig. 4.8** Two solutions for the $1|CO, p-batch, C_{\max}^B \leq Q|C_{\max}^A$ problem

for some $(i_A, i_B)$. For a given $y$, this dynamic programming algorithm requires $O(nn_An_B)$ time to compute $C_y(n_A, n_B)$.

Let $Y_A = ub_A - lb_A$. To solve the two-agent batching problem, we only need to determine $\min\{y : C_y(n_A, n_B) < +\infty\}$, which can be done by using binary search on $Y_A$. For each value of $y$, we first compute the deadline $\tilde{d}_j^A(y)$ for jobs of agent $A$, then we call the dynamic programming algorithm to determine $C_y(n_A, n_B)$. In conclusion one has the following result.

**Theorem 4.14.** *Problem* $1|CO, p-batch, f_{\max}^B \leq Q|f_{\max}^A$ *can be solved in* $O(nn_An_B \log Y_A)$ *time.*

### 4.3.3 *Functions* $C_{\max}$, $C_{\max}$

#### 4.3.3.1 Problem $1|CO, p-batch, C_{\max}^B \leq Q|C_{\max}^A$

Let us now turn to problem $1|CO, p-batch, C_{\max}^B \leq Q|C_{\max}^A$. As for the serial batch problem $1|CO, s-batch, C_{\max}^B \leq Q|C_{\max}^A$, presented in Sect. 4.2.2.1, the following property holds.

*Property 4.2.* In the problem $1|CO, p-batch, C_{\max}^B \leq Q|C_{\max}^A$, if an optimal schedule exists, there is one in which all jobs of agent $A$ are scheduled in a single batch and all jobs of agent $B$ are scheduled in a single batch.

*Example 4.7.* Let consider the following 5-job instance with $n_A = 2$ and $n_B = 3$:

| $J_j^k$ | $J_1^A$ | $J_2^A$ | $J_1^B$ | $J_2^B$ | $J_3^B$ |
|---|---|---|---|---|---|
| $p_j^k$ | 4 | 5 | 3 | 2 | 6 |

If $Q \leq 10$, it is not possible to schedule the batch $\mathcal{B}^B$ of $\mathcal{J}^B$ last, therefore the solution is $(\mathcal{B}^B, \mathcal{B}^A)$. If $Q \geq 11$, the solution is $(\mathcal{B}^A, \mathcal{B}^B)$. Figure 4.8 gives these two solutions. ◇

**Algorithm 29** for problem $1|CO, p-batch, C^B_{\max} \leq Q|C^A_{\max}$

**if** $\max_{1\leq j\leq n_A}\{p^A_j\} + \max_{1\leq j\leq n_B}\{p^B_j\} \leq Q$ **then**
    Schedule jobs of agent $A$ in the first batch
    Schedule jobs of agent $B$ in the second batch
    $\sigma := \mathcal{J}^A|\mathcal{J}^B$ // concatenation of two job sets
**else**
    **if** $\max_{1\leq j\leq n_B}\{p^B_j\} \leq Q$ **then**
        Schedule jobs of agent $B$ in the first batch
        Schedule jobs of agent $A$ in the second batch
        $\sigma := \mathcal{J}^B|\mathcal{J}^A$
    **end if**
**end if**
**if** $\sigma \neq ()$ **then**
    **return** $\sigma$
**else**
    **return** 'There is no feasible solution'
**end if**

In conclusion one has the following result.

**Theorem 4.15.** *By using Algorithm 29, problem* $1|CO, p-batch, C^B_{\max} \leq Q|f^A_{\max}$ *can be solved in* $O(n)$ *time.*

## 4.3.4 Functions $C_{\max}$, $L_{\max}$

### 4.3.4.1 Problem $1|CO, p-batch, L^B_{\max} \leq Q|C^A_{\max}$

Let us now consider the problem $1|CO, p-batch, L^B_{\max} \leq Q|C^A_{\max}$. It is easy to see that the following lemma holds.

**Lemma 4.10.** *There exists an optimal schedule for the problem* $1|CO, p-batch, L^B_{\max} \leq Q|C^A_{\max}$, *if one exists, in which the jobs of agent A form a single batch and the jobs of agent B are processed in SPT-batch sequence.*

*Proof.* This results from Property 4.1 where $SPT$-batch sequence is dominant and it is easy to show that all jobs of agent $A$ are scheduled in a single batch. □

Let $\mathcal{B}^A$ be the only batch of agent $A$. According to Lemma 4.10, the optimal schedule is of the form $(\pi_B, \mathcal{B}^A, \pi'_B)$ where $\pi_B$ and $\pi'_B$ are sequences of batches of agent $B$, one of them being possibly empty. It means that $\pi_B$ is the partial schedule of the first $j$ jobs of agent $B$ and the $n_B - j$ remaining jobs define the partial schedule $\pi'_B$.

Note that $L^B_{\max} \leq Q$ is equivalent to $C^B_j \leq \tilde{d}^B_j$, $j = 1, \ldots, n_B$, where $\tilde{d}^B_j = d^B_j + Q$. Note that in view of Property 4.1, we can assume $d^B_1 \leq d^B_2 \leq \cdots \leq d^B_{n_B}$.

The overall idea for solving problem $1|CO, p-batch, L^B_{\max} \leq Q|C^A_{\max}$ is the following:

Step 1. To determine the optimal sub-sequence $\pi_B$, we solve the single-agent, bicriteria p-batch problem $1|p-batch|\mathcal{P}(C_{\max}, L_{\max})$ on the first $j$ jobs of agent $B$. This step is done by using the algorithm of He et al. (2007).

Step 2. To determine the optimal sub-sequence $\pi'_B$, we solve the single-agent, monocriterion p-batch problem $1|p-batch|L_{\max}$ only on the remaining jobs of agent $B$. This step is done by using the algorithm of Brucker et al. (1998).

### Step 1: Computing $\pi_B$ by Solving $1|BI, p-batch|\mathcal{P}(L^B_{\max}, C^A_{\max})$

In view of the structure $(\pi_B, \mathcal{B}^A, \pi'_B)$ of an optimal schedule, in order to compute $\pi_B$, we observe that the starting time of $\pi'_B$ is equal to the completion time of $\pi_B$ plus $\max_{1\leq i\leq n_A}\{p^A_i\}$. Hence, we have to consider all the compromise solutions with criteria $L^B_{\max}$ and $C^B_{\max}$ for the first $j$ jobs of $\mathcal{J}^B$. Therefore, one must solve $n_B+1$ bicriteria problems $1|BI, p-batch|\mathcal{P}(L_{\max}, C_{\max})$, for the first $j$ jobs of $\mathcal{J}^B$, $0 \leq j \leq n_B$. It is shown in He et al. (2007) that the number of Pareto optimal points for $1|BI, p-batch|\mathcal{P}(C_{\max}, L_{\max})$ is bounded by $O(n^2)$, therefore the procedure can run in $O(n^3_B)$ time. Before describing the method, we show the following proposition.

*Property 4.3.* There exists an optimal solution $\bar{\sigma} = (\bar{\pi}_B, \mathcal{B}^A, \bar{\pi}'_B)$ of problem $1|CO, p-batch, L^B_{\max} \leq Q|C^A_{\max}$, such that $\bar{\pi}_B$ is a Pareto optimal solution of problem $1|BI, p-batch|\mathcal{P}(L_{\max}, C_{\max})$ restricted to the jobs in $\bar{\pi}_B$.

*Proof.* Let $\sigma^* = (\pi_B{}^*, \mathcal{B}^A, \pi'_B{}^*)$ be an optimal solution of problem $1|CO, p-batch, L^B_{\max} \leq Q|C^A_{\max}$. If $\pi_B{}^*$ is not Pareto optimal for problem $1|BI, p-batch|\mathcal{P}(C_{\max}, L_{\max})$, there exists a Pareto optimal schedule $\pi$ of the first $j$ jobs of agent $B$ that dominates it, i.e., such that $C_{\max}(\pi) \leq C^B_{\max}(\pi_B{}^*)$ and $L^B_{\max}(\pi) \leq L^B_{\max}(\pi_B{}^*)$. Let $\bar{\sigma} = (\pi, \mathcal{B}^A, \pi'_B{}^*)$ be the schedule obtained from $\sigma^*$ by replacing the partial schedule $\pi_B{}^*$ with $\pi$. Clearly, $C^A_{\max}(\bar{\sigma}) = C^B_{\max}(\pi) + p^A_{\max} \leq C^B_{\max}(\sigma^*) + p^A_{\max} = C^A_{\max}(\sigma^*)$, and since $\sigma^*$ is optimal, $C^A_{\max}(\bar{\sigma}) = C^A_{\max}(\sigma^*)$. Now $L^B_{\max}(\bar{\sigma}) = \max\left\{L^B_{\max}(\pi), L_{\max}(\pi'_B{}^*)\right\}$. Since $L^B_{\max}(\sigma^*) = \max\left\{L^B_{\max}(\pi_B{}^*), L_{\max}(\pi'_B{}^*)\right\}$ and $L^B_{\max}(\pi) \leq L^B_{\max}(\pi_B{}^*)$, then $L^B_{\max}(\bar{\sigma}) \leq L^B_{\max}(\sigma^*) \leq Q$. Hence, $\bar{\sigma}$ is feasible and optimal for $1|CO, p-batch, L^B_{\max} \leq Q|C^A_{\max}$. □

### Step 2: Computing $\pi'_B$ by Solving $1|p-batch|L_{\max}$

First of all, we recall the dynamic programming algorithm presented in Brucker et al. (1998) for the single-agent parallel batching problem $1|p-batch|L_{\max}$. Solving this problem with the remaining jobs of $\mathcal{J}^B$ will easily allow to check if the condition $L^B_{\max} \leq Q$ holds.

Let $L(i)$ be the minimum value of the maximum lateness for SPT-batch schedules containing jobs $J_i, J_{i+1}, \ldots, J_n$, if the processing starts at time zero. Let

$\mathcal{B} = \{J_i, \ldots, J_{j-1}\}$ (with processing time $p_{j-1}$) be the first batch. Its lateness is given by $p_{j-1} - d_i$. The insertion of such batch delays by $p_{j-1}$ all subsequent batches, so that their overall maximum lateness is therefore $L(j) + p_{j-1}$. In conclusion, we get the following recursion function.

$$L(i) = \min_{i+1 \leq j \leq n+1} \{\max\{L(j) + p_{j-1}, p_{j-1} - d_i\}\} \tag{4.23}$$

for $i = n, n-1, \ldots, 1$. The initial value is $L(n+1) = -\infty$ and the optimal value is given by $L(1)$. It can be computed in $O(n^2)$ time.

Hence, for a given $j$, the second partial schedule $\pi'_B$ for an optimal solution can be obtained by solving the $1|p{-}batch|L_{\max}$ problem, by applying this DP algorithm to the jobs $(j, \ldots, n_B)$ if the first batch starts at the completion time of job $J_j^B$ plus $p_{\max}^A$. This step is done in $O(n_B^2)$ time.

Resolution Method for Finding $\sigma^*$

For each $0 \leq j \leq n_B$, let $\mathcal{Y}^j$ be the set of Pareto optimal solutions of the problem $1|BI, p - batch|\mathcal{P}(C_{\max}, L_{\max})$ applied to the jobs $J_1^B, \ldots, J_j^B$ obtained by the procedure described at step 1, and denote by $(\pi_B)^{i,j}$ each element of $\mathcal{Y}^j$. For each $0 \leq j \leq n_B$, we denote as $(\pi'_B)^j$ the optimal schedule for $1|p{-}batch|L_{\max}$ obtained by the procedure described at step 2.

For a given $j \in \{0, 1, \ldots, n_B\}$, and for each $(\pi_B)^{i,j} \in \mathcal{Y}^j$, we define a global solution $\sigma^{i,j} = ((\pi_B)^{i,j}, \mathcal{B}^A, (\pi'_B)^j)$,

The optimal solution to problem $1|CO, p - batch, L_{\max}^B \leq Q|C_{\max}^A$ is a sequence $\sigma^{i,j}$ such that $L_{\max}^B(\sigma^{i,j}) \leq Q$ and $C_{\max}^A(\sigma^{i,j})$ is minimum.

Now, we can derive a polynomial time algorithm to solve problem $1|CO, p - batch, L_{\max}^B \leq Q|C_{\max}^A$, which is based on the algorithm in Qi et al. (2013) (see Algorithm 30).

Step 1 in Algorithm 30 requires time $n_B \log n_B$. Step 2 requires time $n_A$. Determining all $(\pi'_B)^j$ (steps 3–5) can be done in $O(n_B^3)$ time. For each $j$, He's algorithm allows to compute the set $\mathcal{Y}^j$ in time $O(n_B^3)$. Since this has to be run for $j = 0, \ldots, n_B$ times, steps 6–8 in Algorithm 30 require time $O(n_B^4)$. Since $|\mathcal{Y}^j| = O(n^2)$, there are $O(n_B^3)$ global solution, from which at step 9 the best is selected. In conclusion, one has the following result.

**Theorem 4.16.** *Algorithm 30 solves problem* $1|CO, p - batch, L_{\max}^B \leq Q|C_{\max}^A$ *in* $O(n_A + n_B^4)$ *time.*

#### 4.3.4.2 Problem $1|CO, p - batch, C_{\max}^B \leq Q|L_{\max}^A$

Let us turn now to the symmetric problem $1|CO, p - batch, C_{\max}^B \leq Q|L_{\max}^A$. From Property 4.3, the structure of an optimal solution is $(\pi_B, \mathcal{B}^A, \pi'_B)$, where

**Algorithm 30** for problem $1|CO, p-batch, L^B_{\max} \leq Q|C^A_{\max}$

1: Arrange the jobs of $\mathcal{J}^B$ in SPT order
2: $p^A_{\max} := \max_{i \in \mathcal{J}^A}(p^A_i)$
3: **for** $j := 0$ **to** $n_B$ **do**
4: Solve problem $1|p-batch|L^B_{\max}$ by Brucker's algorithm (4.23) to determine $(\pi'_B)^j$ and corresponding to it $L^B_{\max}(\pi'_B)^j$
5: **end for**
6: **for** $j := 0$ **to** $n_B$ **do**
7: Solve problem $1|p-batch|(C_{\max}, L_{\max})$ by He's algorithm to calculate $\mathcal{Y}^j$
8: **end for**
9: Determine the set of non dominated solutions and keep the solution $(\sigma^{i,j})^*$ with minimum $C^A_{\max}(\sigma^{i,j})$ and satisfying $L^B_{\max}(\sigma^{i,j}) \leq Q$
10: **return** $(\sigma^{i,j})^*$

schedule $\pi'_B$ starts at time $C^B_j + p^A_{\max}$. Hence, an optimal schedule can be found by Algorithm 30 where in step 9 we select the solution that minimizes $L^A_{\max}$ where $C^B_{\max} \leq Q$.

In conclusion, one has the following result.

**Theorem 4.17.** *Problem* $1|CO, p{-}batch, C^B_{\max} \leq Q|L^A_{\max}$ *can be solved in* $O(n_A + n_B^4)$.

### 4.3.5 Functions $f_{\max}, \sum f_j$

#### 4.3.5.1 Problem $1|CO, p-batch, f^B_{\max} \leq Q|\sum f^A_j$

Let us consider the problem $1|CO, p-batch, f^B_{\max} \leq Q|\sum f^A_j$ when agent $A$ wants to minimize a general sum-type function. Note that this scheduling problem is in general NP-hard, e.g. when $\sum f^A_j = \sum w^A_j U^A_j$ (see Brucker et al. 1998). We next present a pseudo-polynomial time dynamic programming algorithm proposed by Li and Yuan (2012) that solves this problem. As usual, for the jobs of agent B, we define deadlines $\tilde{d}^B_j = (f^B_j)^{-1}(Q)$.

Let $F(i_A, i_B, t)$ be the minimum objective value for SPT-batch schedules where the jobs $\{J^A_1, \ldots, J^A_{i_A}\} \cup \{J^B_1, \ldots, J^B_{i_B}\}$ are scheduled, subject to the constraint that the last batch completes at time $t$ and no job of agent $B$ is tardy.

As a consequence of Property 4.1, when considering $F(i_A, i_B, t)$, there are two possible decisions concerning the last batch of the partial schedule:

1. The last batch belongs to agent $A$, and is denoted by $J^A_{\ell_A+1}, \ldots, J^A_{i_A}$ with $\ell_A < i_A$,
2. The last batch belongs to agent $B$, and is denoted by $J^B_{\ell_B+1}, \ldots, J^B_{i_B}$ with $\ell_B < i_B$.

**Algorithm 31** for problem $1|CO, p-batch, f_{\max}^B \leq Q|\sum f_j^A$

1: $F(0,0,0) := 0$
2: **for** $t \neq 0$ **do**
3: $\quad F(0,0,t) := +\infty$
4: **end for**
5: **for** $i_A := 1$ **to** $n_A$ **do**
6: $\quad$ **for** $i_2 := 1$ **to** $n_B$ **do**
7: $\quad\quad$ **for** $t := 0$ to $P$ **do**
8: $\quad\quad\quad v_1^A := \min_{0 \leq l_A \leq i_A - 1} \left\{ F(l_A, i_B, t - p_{i_A}^A) + \sum_{i=l_A+1}^{i_A} f_i^A(t) \right\}$
9: $\quad\quad\quad v_1^B := \min_{l_B \in \sigma(i_A, i_B, t)} \{F(i_A, l_B, t - p_{i_B}^B)\}$
10: $\quad\quad\quad F(i_A, i_B, t) := \min \{v_1^A, v_1^B\}$
11: $\quad\quad$ **end for**
12: $\quad$ **end for**
13: **end for**
14: **return** the schedule corresponding to $F(n_A, n_B, t)$

Therefore, it is possible to derive a dynamic programming algorithm (Algorithm 31) where $\sigma(i_A, i_B, t)$ denotes the set of candidate values for index $\ell_B$. Since the deadline of job $J_{\ell_B+1}^B$ must be respected, one has:

$$\sigma(i_A, i_B, t) = \{0 \leq \ell_B \leq i_B - 1 : t \leq \tilde{d}_{\ell_B+1}^B\}$$

Since the last batch belongs to either agent $A$ or agent $B$, the optimal objective value is equal to $\min\{F(n_A, n_B, t) : p_{n_A}^A + p_{n_B}^B \leq t \leq P\}$.

For each value of $i_A$ and for each $t$, all sums $\sum_{i=\ell_A+1}^{i_A} f_i^A(t)$ can be evaluated in $O(n_A)$. Since $i_A$ ranges from 1 to $n_A$ and $t$ from $p_{i_A}^A$ to $P = \sum_{i=1}^{i_A} p_i^A + \sum_{i=1}^{n_B} p_i^B$, all sums appearing in step 6 can be computed in a preprocessing step in $O(n_A^2 P)$ time, and each application of the recursive formula requires $O(n_A + n_B)$ time. Since $i_A$, $i_B$ and $P$ assume $n_A$, $n_B$ and $P$ values respectively, in conclusion one has the following result.

**Theorem 4.18.** *Problem* $1|CO, p - batch, f_{\max}^B \leq Q|\sum f_j^A$ *can be solved in* $O(n n_A n_B P)$ *time.*

## 4.3.6 Functions $\sum f_j$, $\sum f_j$

### 4.3.6.1 Problem $1|CO, p-batch, \sum f_j^B \leq Q|\sum f_j^A$

Let us now turn to problem $1|CO, p-batch, \sum f_j^B \leq Q|\sum f_j^A$. For such NP-hard scheduling problem, we report a pseudo-polynomial-time dynamic programming algorithm by Li and Yuan (2012).

**Algorithm 32** for problem $1|CO, p-batch, \sum f_j^B \leq Q|\sum f_j^A$

**for** $q \geq 0$ **do**
    $F(0,0,0,q) := 0$
**end for**
**for** $q < 0$ **do**
    $F(i_A, i_B, t, q) := +\infty$
**end for**
**for** $(i_A, i_B, t) \neq (0,0,0)$ **do**
    **if** $q < 0$ **then**
        $F(i_A, i_B, t, q) := +\infty$
    **end if**
**end for**
**for** $i_A := 1$ **to** $n_A$ **do**
    **for** $i_B := 1$ **to** $n_B$ **do**
        **for** $t := 0$ **to** $P$ **do**
            **for** $q := 0$ **to** $Q$ **do**
                $F(i_A, i_B, t, q) := \min\{F(i_A, i_B, t, q)^A, F(i_A, i_B, t, q)^B\}$
            **end for**
        **end for**
    **end for**
**end for**
**return** the schedule corresponding to $\min\{F(n_A, n_B, t, Q) : p_{n_A}^A + p_{n_B}^B \leq t \leq P\}$

Let $F(i_A, i_B, t, q)$ denote the minimum objective value for partial SPT-batch schedules of jobs $\{J_1^A, \ldots, J_{i_A}^A\} \cup \{J_1^B, \ldots, J_{i_B}^B\}$, subject to the constraint that the last batch completes at time $t$ and the objective value of agent $B$ is at most $q$. According to Property 4.1, there exists a schedule corresponding to $F(i_A, i_B, t, q)$ in which the last batch contains jobs $J_{\ell_A+1}^A, \ldots, J_{i_A}^A$ with $\ell_A < i_A$ or $J_{\ell_B+1}^B, \ldots, J_{i_B}^B$ with $\ell_B < i_B$.

We denote by:

$$F(i_A, i_B, t, q)^A = \min_{0 \leq \ell_A \leq i_A - 1} \{F(\ell_A, i_B, t - p_{i_A}^A, q) + \sum_{j=\ell_A+1}^{i_A} f_j^A(t)\}$$

$$F(i_A, i_B, t, q)^B = \min_{0 \leq \ell_B \leq i_B - 1} \{F(i_A, \ell_B, t - p_{i_B}^B, q - \sum_{j=\ell_B+1}^{i_B} f_j^B(t))\}$$

A dynamic programming algorithm can be derived (see Algorithm 32).
The optimal solution $\sigma^*$ has an objective value which corresponds to

$$\min\{F(n_A, n_B, t, Q) : p_{n_A}^A + p_{n_B}^B \leq t \leq P\}$$

The partial sums $\sum_{i=1}^{i_A} f_i^A(t)$ for $i_A = 1, \ldots, n_A$, $t = p_{i_A}^A, \ldots, \sum_{i=1}^{i_A} p_i^A + \sum_{i=1}^{n_B} p_i^B$, can be evaluated in a preprocessing step in $O(n^2 P)$ time and it is the

**Table 4.1** Polynomial solvable serial batching problems

| Problem | Complexity | Section | Page |
|---|---|---|---|
| $1\|CO, s-batch, f^B_{\max} \le Q\|f^A_{\max}$ | $O(n_A n_B n \log Y_A)$ | 4.2.1.1 | 151 |
| $1\|CO, s-batch, C^B_{\max} \le Q\|C^A_{\max}$ | $O(n)$ | 4.2.2.1 | 153 |
| $1\|CO, s-batch, L^B_{\max} \le Q\|C^A_{\max}$ | $O(n_A + n_B^2)$ | 4.2.3.1 | 155 |
| $1\|CO, s-batch, C^A_{\max} \le Q\|L^B_{\max}$ | $O(n_A + n_B^3)$ | 4.2.3.2 | 158 |
| $1\|CO, s-batch, f^B_{\max} \le Q\|\sum C^A_j$ | $O(n n_A^2 n_B^2)$ | 4.2.4.1 | 160 |
| $1\|CO, s-batch, \sum C^A_j \le Q\|f^B_{\max}$ | $O(n_A^2 n_B^2 n \log Y_B)$ | 4.2.4.2 | 162 |
| $1\|CO, s-batch, f^B_{\max} \le Q\|\sum U^A_j$ | $O(n_A^2 n_B^2 n^2)$ | 4.2.5.1 | 163 |
| $1\|CO, s-batch, \sum w^A_j U^A_j \le Q\|f^B_{\max}$ | $O(n_A^2 n_B n \log Y_B)$ | 4.2.5.2 | 166 |
| $1\|CO, s-batch, \sum C^B_j \le Q\|C^A_{\max}$ | $O(n_A + n_B^3)$ | 4.2.6.1 | 167 |
| $1\|CO, s-batch, \sum U^B_j \le Q\|\sum U^A_j$ | $O(n_A^3 n_B^2 + n_A^2 n_B^3)$ | 4.2.8.1 | 172 |

**Table 4.2** Enumeration of the Pareto set serial batching problems

| Problem | Size | Section | Page |
|---|---|---|---|
| $1\|CO, s-batch\|\mathcal{P}(C^A_{\max}, C^B_{\max})$ | 2 | 4.2.2.2 | 155 |
| $1\|CO, s-batch\|\mathcal{P}(C^A_{\max}, L^B_{\max})$ | $O(n_B)$ | 4.2.3.3 | 159 |
| $1\|CO, s-batch\|\mathcal{P}(f^A_{\max}, \sum U^B_j)$ | $O(n_B)$ | 4.2.5.3 | 166 |
| $1\|CO, s-batch\|\mathcal{P}(C^A_{\max}, \sum C^B_j)$ | $O(n_B)$ | 4.2.6.2 | 169 |
| $1\|CO, s-batch\|\mathcal{P}(\sum C^A_j, \sum C^B_j)$ | Exponential | 4.2.7.2 | 171 |
| $1\|CO, s-batch\|\mathcal{P}(\sum U^A_j, \sum U^B_j)$ | $n_A + 1$ | 4.2.8.2 | 175 |

same for the partial sums $\sum_{i=1}^{i_B} f_i^B(t)$ for $i_B = 1, \ldots, n_B, t = p^B_{i_B}, \ldots, \sum_{i=1}^{n_A} p^A_i + \sum_{i=1}^{i_B} p^B_i$. Each application of the recursive formula requires $O(n_A + n_B) = O(n)$ time. In conclusion, one has the following result.

**Theorem 4.19.** *Problem $1|CO, p-batch, \sum f^B_j \le Q|\sum f^A_j$ can be solved in $O(n n_A n_B P Q)$ time.*

## 4.4 Tables

Further, most of the suggested algorithms can be modified to handle bounded batch sizes and any number of agents. Tables 4.1, 4.2 and 4.3 present computational complexity results for two-agent single machine s-batching problems. Tables 4.4 and 4.5 present computational complexity results for two-agent single machine

**Table 4.3** $NP$-hard serial batching problems

| Problem | Complexity | Section | Page |
|---|---|---|---|
| $1\|CO, s-batch, f^B_{\max} \leq Q\|\sum w^A_j U^A_j$ | $O(n_A n_B n^2 W_A)$ | 4.2.5.1 | 163 |
| $1\|CO, s-batch, \sum C^B_j \leq Q\|\sum C^A_j$ | $O(n_A n_B n Q)$ | 4.2.7.1 | 170 |
| $1\|CO, s-batch, \sum w^B_j U^B_j \leq Q\|\sum w^A_j U^A_j$ | $O(n_A^2 n_B + n_A n_B^2 \hat{W}_A Q)$ | 4.2.8.1 | 172 |

**Table 4.4** Polynomial solvable parallel batching problems

| Problem | Complexity | Section | Page |
|---|---|---|---|
| $1\|CO$, p-batch, $f^B_{\max} \leq Q\|f^A_{\max}$ | $O(n n_A n_B \log(Y_A))$ | 4.3.2.1 | 176 |
| $1\|CO$, p-batch, $C^B_{\max} \leq Q\|C^A_{\max}$ | $O(n)$ | 4.3.3.1 | 178 |
| $1\|CO$, p-batch, $L^B_{\max} \leq Q\|C^A_{\max}$ | $O(n_A + n_B^4)$ | 4.3.4.1 | 179 |
| $1\|CO$, p-batch, $C^B_{\max} \leq Q\|L^A_{\max}$ | $O(n_A + n_B^4)$ | 4.3.4.2 | 181 |

**Table 4.5** $NP$-hard parallel batching problems

| Problem | Complexity | Section | Page |
|---|---|---|---|
| $1\|CO, p-batch, f^B_{\max} \leq Q\|\sum f^A_j$ | $O(n n_A n_B P)$ | 4.3.5.1 | 182 |
| $1\|CO$, p-batch, $\sum f^B_j \leq Q\|\sum f^A_j$ | $O(n n_A n_B P Q)$ | 4.3.6.1 | 183 |

p-batching problems. Several problems are NP-hard because the classical single machine problems (i.e. without batching and only one criterion) are NP-hard. In Tables 4.1 and 4.3, $T = n_A s_A + n_B s_B + P$, $P$ is the total processing time of all jobs, and $W^k = \sum_{j=1}^{n_k} w^k_j, k \in \{A, B\}$.

## 4.5 Bibliographic Remarks

In this section, we give some remarks and the main references related to scheduling on batching machines. As in the scheduling literature, intensive research has been done involving a single batching machine *without job compatibilities*, where jobs have families and only the jobs of the same family can be assigned to the same batch. Also, problems with *job compatibilities* have been studied for various objective functions and additional constraints. We refer the reader mainly to the following review papers and books that cover many parts of research done on single objective batching scheduling problems: Brucker et al. (1998), Potts and Kovalyov (2000), Potts et al. (2001) and Brucker (2007).

### 4.5.1 Serial Batching Problems

In this chapter, we focused only on unbounded batching machine without job family compatibilities in the COMPETING scenario. It is also interesting to study the same problems with other hypotheses, such as bounded batching machines, job compatibilities, different scenarios, etc. Li and Yuan (2012) study two-agent problems on a serial batching machine where jobs of both agents can be assigned to the same batch. This difference makes the results of their paper inapplicable to the problems studied in this chapter and vice versa. All the proposed algorithms are based on dynamic programming. Mor and Mosheiov (2011) and Feng et al. (2011) consider the model presented in this chapter (see Sect. 4.2). Mor and Mosheiov (2011) assume that jobs have unit processing times, the objective functions are $\sum C_j^A$ and $\sum C_j^B$, and the constraint that batches of the second agent are processed continuously. They suggest an $O(n^{3/2})$ time algorithm. Feng et al. (2011) assume that setup times are identical ($s_A = s_B = s$) and the objective functions are $C_{\max}^A$ and $L_{\max}^B$. They present an $O(n_A + n_B^4)$ algorithm for finding the set of Pareto solutions.

### 4.5.2 Parallel Batching Problems

We focus in this chapter on parallel batching problems in the COMPETING scenario, with unbounded batching machine and without job family compatibilities. Some other models can be found in the literature. Tan et al. (2011) consider non-identical job sizes and objective functions $C_{\max}^A$ and $C_{\max}^B$. Since the problem is NP-hard in the strong sense, the authors develop an ant colony algorithm to find the set of Pareto solutions. The specificities of the model in Sabouni and Jolai (2010) are the job compatibilities, which restrict jobs of different agents to be placed in the same batch. The authors consider the objective functions $C_{\max}^A$ and $L_{\max}^B$. In Li and Yuan (2012) various combinations of regular objective functions are considered. Concerning approximation schemes, we refer to Nong et al. (2008) where the authors study scheduling family jobs with release dates on a bounded batching machine to minimize the makespan (for only one agent). A polynomial-time approximation scheme for the identical job length model and an approximation algorithm with a worst-case ratio for the non-identical job length model are given.

# Chapter 5
# Parallel Machine Scheduling Problems

This chapter presents some results on scheduling jobs on parallel machines with the COMPETITIVE and the INTERFERING scenario. First, we study the case where job preemption is allowed, i.e. when the processing of a job can be interrupted and resumed later, eventually on another machine. Next, we study the case without job preemption.

The chapter is composed of five sections. In Sect. 5.1, we consider parallel machine scheduling problems without job preemption. In Sects. 5.2 and 5.3, we consider preemptable parallel machine scheduling problems with arbitrary and equal job processing times, respectively. We end the chapter with Sects. 5.4 and 5.5 including, respectively, complexity tables and bibliographic remarks.

## 5.1 Preemptive Jobs

In this section, we assume that preemption is allowed, i.e., a job processing can be interrupted and resumed later, possibly on another machine. Scheduling jobs on parallel machines when preemption is allowed has attracted researchers' attention for a long time (Brucker 2007; Pinedo 2008). Mc Naughton studied preemptive independent job scheduling problems with various objective functions (Mc Naughton 1959). In particular, the author proposes a polynomial time algorithm for solving problem $Pm|pmtn|C_{\max}$. Mc Naughton's algorithm can be described as follows: select the jobs one by one in any order and fill up the machines $M_1, M_2, \ldots, M_m$ within the time interval $[0, LB]$, where $LB$ is a lower bound for the makespan. We have:

$$LB = \max\left\{\frac{1}{m}\sum_{j=1}^{n} p_j; \max_{j=1}^{n} p_j\right\}$$

A. Agnetis et al., *Multiagent Scheduling*, DOI 10.1007/978-3-642-41880-8_5, 

For a given machine $M_i$ that performs job $J_j$, if time *LB* is reached before the end of $J_j$, this job is preempted and its remaining processing time is performed at time 0 on the next machine $M_{i+1}$.

Most of the classical multicriteria parallel machine scheduling problems deal with two criteria (see T'Kindt and Billaut 2006). For example, in Mohri et al. (1999), the authors study the $Pm|BI, pmtn, C_{\max} \leq Q|L_{\max}$ problem for $m = 2$ or $m = 3$ machines. In the following, we focus on the COMPETING and INTERFERING scenarios.

## 5.1.1 Functions $f_{\max}$, $f_{\max}$

### 5.1.1.1 Problem $Rm|IN, pmtn, C^B_{\max} \leq Q|C^A_{\max}$

We start by considering the case of unrelated machines in the INTERFERING scenario (in which we recall that $\mathcal{J} = \mathcal{J}^A \supseteq \mathcal{J}^B$).

In this section, a set $\mathcal{M}$ of $m$ unrelated parallel machines is shared between two agents in order to schedule their sets of jobs, when they both want to minimize the makespan.

While we illustrate how to solve problem $Rm|IN, pmtn, C^B_{\max} \leq Q|C^A_{\max}$, the whole procedure, with minor adjustments, can be applied to problem $Rm|IN, pmtn, f^B_{\max} \leq Q|f^A_{\max}$ in which all jobs in $J_j \in \mathcal{J}^A$ hold the same linear, monotonically nondecreasing function of the jobs completion times $f^A_j(C_j) = f^A C_j$ and similarly $f^B_j(C_j) = f^B C_j$ for $J_j \in \mathcal{J}^B$.

Following the two-phase exact approach proposed for solving the classical problem $Rm|pmtn|L_{\max}$, we can show that problem $Rm|IN, pmtn, C^B_{\max} \leq Q|C^A_{\max}$ is polynomially solvable (Sadi et al. 2013). In the first phase, a linear program is proposed, which takes into account all the constraints of the feasible problem and gives the optimal function value $C^{A^*}_{\max}$ along with the processing time fraction of each job to be carried out on each machine. Therefore, this linear program returns the proportion of each job to execute on each machine. In the second phase, the problem is to find a feasible solution to the preemptive open shop problem denoted by $Om|pmtn, \tilde{d}_j|-$. In the second phase, the schedule of jobs to be executed on each machine is computed by solving a matching problem, which determines a feasible schedule of job fractions, respecting the optimal function value obtained at phase 1.

### 5.1.1.2 Phase 1: Assignment of Preempted Jobs to Machines

For the proposed linear program, let $x_{j,i}$ ($\forall i$, $1 \leq i \leq m$ and $\forall j$, $1 \leq j \leq n_A$) be the decision variables that represent the fraction of processing time of job $J_j$ executed on machine $M_i$, $x_{j,i} \in [0, 1]$. Here, $C^A_{\max}$ is a continuous variable. The proposed linear program is the following.

$$(P1)\ \text{Minimize}\ C^A_{\max} \tag{5.1}$$

$$\text{subject to}\ \sum_{i=1}^{m} x_{j,i} = 1,\ J^A_j \in \mathcal{J}^A \tag{5.2}$$

$$C^A_{\max} - \sum_{j=1}^{n_A} p_{j,i} x_{j,i} \geq 0,\ M_i \in \mathcal{M} \tag{5.3}$$

$$C^A_{max} - \sum_{i=1}^{m} p_{j,i} x_{j,i} \geq 0,\ J^A_j \in \mathcal{J}^A \tag{5.4}$$

$$Q - \sum_{j=1}^{n_B} p_{j,i} x_{j,i} \geq 0,\ M_i \in \mathcal{M} \tag{5.5}$$

$$Q - \sum_{i=1}^{m} p_{j,i} x_{j,i} \geq 0,\ J^B_j \in \mathcal{J}^B \tag{5.6}$$

$$\text{variables}\ C^A_{max} \geq 0 \tag{5.7}$$

$$x_{j,i} \in [0,1],\ J^A_j \in \mathcal{J}^A,\ M_i \in \mathcal{M} \tag{5.8}$$

Constraints (5.2) impose that every job $J^A_j$ is completely assigned to the machines. Constraints (5.3) impose that the total processing time of the jobs assigned to machine $M_i$ is less than or equal to $C^A_{\max}$. Constraints (5.4) require that the total processing time of each job, performed on several machines, is less than or equal to $C^A_{\max}$. Constraints (5.5) and (5.6) guarantee the respect of the $\varepsilon$−constraints. Constraints (5.5) require that the sum of job processing times related to agent B and assigned to machine $M_i$ is less than or equal to $Q$. Constraints (5.6) guarantee that the total processing time of job $J^B_j \in \mathcal{J}^B$ is less than or equal to $Q$.

It is clear that if problem $(P1)$ has no feasible solution, then the main problem has no feasible solution either. Otherwise, for each feasible schedule verifying (5.2)–(5.7), a feasible schedule can be identified, where there is no job overlapping, no machine overbooking and the total processing amount of each job over all machines does not exceed $Q$. The value of the optimal solution of problem $(P1)$ is denoted by $C^{A*}_{\max}$.

#### 5.1.1.3 Phase 2: Construction of a Feasible Solution

From $(P1)$, the ratio $x_{j,i}$ of job $J_j$ which must be performed on a machine $M_i$ is known. The problem of phase 2 is equivalent to a preemptive open-shop scheduling problem with deadlines, denoted by $Om|pmtn, \tilde{d}^A_j, \tilde{d}^B_j|-$. Here, $\tilde{d}^A_j = \tilde{d}^A = C^{A*}_{\max}$ for all $J_j \in \mathcal{J}^A$. Since $\mathcal{J}^B \subseteq \mathcal{J}^A$, the makespan for $\mathcal{J}^B$ cannot exceed that of $\mathcal{J}^A$, and therefore we set $\tilde{d}^B_j = \tilde{d}^B = \min\{Q, C^{A*}_{\max}\}$ for all $J_j \in \mathcal{J}^B$. Later on, the quantities $x_{j,i}$ constitute "tasks" $o_{j,i}$ of job $J_j$ of duration $p_{j,i}x_{j,i}$, to be performed on machine $M_i$.

A feasible preemptive schedule for the open shop problem with deadlines can be obtained in polynomial time by using the algorithm proposed by Cho and Sahni (1981).

Suppose first that $\tilde{d}^B < \tilde{d}^A$. In this case, we distinguish the intervals $[0, \tilde{d}^B[$ and $[\tilde{d}^B, \tilde{d}^A]$, of length $I_1 = \tilde{d}^B$ and $I_2 = \tilde{d}^A - \tilde{d}^B$ respectively.

The quantity of processing time of the task $o_{j,i}$ that can be scheduled during the $k$-th interval (of length $I_k$) is denoted by $q_{j,i,k}$, $k = 1, 2$. Let consider now the following system of linear constraints.

$$(P2) \text{ Minimise } - \tag{5.9}$$

$$\text{subject to} \sum_{j=1}^{n} q_{j,i,k} \leq I_k, \; k = 1, 2, \; M_i \in \mathcal{M} \tag{5.10}$$

$$\sum_{i=1}^{m} q_{j,i,k} \leq I_k, \; k = 1, 2, \; J_j \in J^A \tag{5.11}$$

$$q_{j,i,1} + q_{j,i,2} = p_{j,i}x_{j,i}, \; M_i \in \mathcal{M}, \; J_j \in J^A \tag{5.12}$$

$$q_{j,i,2} = 0, \; M_i \in \mathcal{M}, \; J_j \in J^B \tag{5.13}$$

$$\text{variables } q_{j,i,k} \geq 0, \; M_i \in \mathcal{M}, \; J_j \in J^A, \; k = 1, 2 \tag{5.14}$$

Constraints (5.10) ensure that the amount of processing time assigned to each machine and during each time interval cannot exceed the interval length. Constraints (5.11) avoid any overlapping of tasks on the machines. Constraints (5.12) guarantee the assignment of the total tasks of jobs to the machines. Constraints (5.13) guarantee the assignment of tasks in their interval.

Suppose now that $\tilde{d}^B = \tilde{d}^A$. In this case, the same approach applies, with just a *single* time interval $[0, \tilde{d}^A]$, so that we can simply let the amount of job $J_j$ on machine $M_i$ equal to $q_{j,i,1} = p_{j,i}x_{j,i}$ for all $j \in \mathcal{J}^A$, $M_i \in \mathcal{M}$.

At this point, for each interval $k$ the amount of processing of job $J_j$ on machine $M_i$ during interval $k$ is given, for all $i, j, k$. The last step is therefore to plan the detailed sequence of tasks on each machine so that different jobs do not overlap. To accomplish this, we apply an approach in (Brucker 2007, see Algorithm 33) to one interval at a time, i.e., we associate a bipartite graph $G_k = (\mathcal{J}, \mathcal{M}, E, \phi_k)$ with each interval $k$, where $\mathcal{J}$ is the set of job nodes, $\mathcal{M}$ is the set of machine nodes and $E$ is the set of edges $(J_j, M_i)$ for $j \in \mathcal{J}$, $i \in \mathcal{M}$ and $\phi_k(j,i) = q_{j,i,k}$ ($j = 1, \ldots, n$, $i = 1, \ldots, m$, $k \in \{1, 2\}$) the weight of arc $(J_j, M_i)$ (Fig. 5.1).

Using Algorithm 33, at each iteration, the procedure finds a maximum cardinality matching $\rho$ and schedules $\delta$ time units of $|\rho|$ different jobs on the machines specified by $\rho$, where $\delta = \min_{(J_j, M_i) \in \rho} q_{j,i,k}$. This technique avoids an overlapping of tasks in the final schedule.

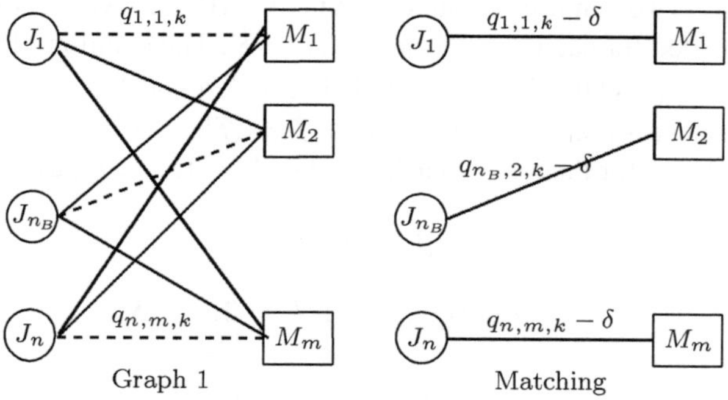


**Fig. 5.1** Graph $G_k$ at step 1 and at step 2

**Algorithm 33** Matching procedure for a feasible solution

Let $G_k = (\mathcal{N}, \mathcal{M}, E, \phi_k)$ be a bipartite graph // $G_k$ is given on input
Initial schedule $\sigma = ()$ // initial empty schedule
**while** $E \neq \emptyset$ **do**
    Seek for the maximum matching $\rho$ in $G_k$ // See Fig. 5.1, Graph 1
    $\delta = \min_{(J_j, M_i) \in \rho} \phi_k(j, i)$
    **for** each $(J_j, M_i) \in \rho$ **do**
        Schedule $\delta$ processing time units of $J_j$ at the end of machine $M_i$
        Update $\sigma$
        $\phi_k(j, i) := \phi_k(j, i) - \delta$ // See Fig. 5.1, Matching
        **if** $\phi_k(j, i) = 0$ **then**
            Eliminate $(J_j, M_i)$
        **end if**
    **end for**
**end while**
**return** $\sigma$

At each iteration of the matching procedure for interval $k$, at least one arc $(J_j, M_i)$ of the maximum matching is such that $\delta = \phi_k(j, i)$. Hence for interval $k$, there are at most $n \times m$ iterations. Therefore, the procedure runs in $O(nm)$. The matching can be calculated in $O(nm\sqrt{n+m})$ by using the algorithm described in Hopcroft and Karp (1973). Thus, the step 2 runs in $O(n^2m^2\sqrt{n+m})$ time.

**Theorem 5.1.** *An optimal solution to problem $Rm|IN, pmtn, C^B_{\max} \leq Q|C^A_{\max}$ can be obtained in polynomial time.*

#### 5.1.1.4 Problem $Rm|IN, pmtn, C^k_{\max} \leq Q_k, k = 2, \ldots, K|C^1_{\max}$

The procedure described for the two-agent case can be generalized to the case of $K$ agents, i.e. to problem $Rm|IN, pmtn, C^k_{\max} \leq Q_k, k = 2, \ldots, K|C^1_{\max}$. For what concerns phase 1, we can use the same formulation (P1), in which constraints (5.5) and (5.6) are added for each agent $k$, $k = 2, \ldots, K$. The solution of (P1) returns a minimum value $C^{1^*}_{\max}$ and values $x^*_{j,i}$ for all $1 \le j \le n$ and $1 \le i \le m$.

For what concerns phase 2, recalling that $\mathcal{J} = \mathcal{J}^1 \supseteq \mathcal{J}^2 \supseteq \ldots \supseteq \mathcal{J}^K$, we can define the deadlines for the jobs of each agent $k$ ($k = 1, \ldots, K$) as follows:

$$\tilde{d}^1 = C^{1^*}_{\max}$$

$$\tilde{d}^k = \min\{Q_k, \tilde{d}^{k-1}\} \;\; k = 2, \ldots, K$$

Letting $I_k = \tilde{d}^k - \tilde{d}^{k-1}$, we can now write model (P2) as:

$$(P2') \text{ Minimise} - \tag{5.15}$$

$$\text{subject to} \sum_{j=1}^{n} q_{j,i,k} \le I_k,\; k = 1, \ldots, K, M_i \in \mathcal{M} \tag{5.16}$$

$$\sum_{i=1}^{m} q_{j,i,k} \le I_k,\; k = 1, \ldots, K, J_j \in \mathcal{J}^1 \tag{5.17}$$

$$\sum_{k=1}^{K} q_{j,i,k} = p_{j,i} x_{j,i},\; M_i \in \mathcal{M},\; J_j \in \mathcal{J}^1 \tag{5.18}$$

$$q_{j,i,k} = 0,\; i \in \mathcal{M},\; k = 1, \ldots, K,\; J_j \in \mathcal{J}^{K-k+2} \tag{5.19}$$

$$\text{variables } q_{j,i,k} \ge 0,\; M_i \in \mathcal{M},\; J_j \in \mathcal{J}^1,\; k = 1, \ldots, K \tag{5.20}$$

Since some interval may be actually void (if $\tilde{d}^k = \tilde{d}^{k-1}$ for some $k$), one is left with running the matching procedure for $H \le K$ nonempty intervals. At each iteration of the matching procedure for interval $h$, $1 \le h \le H$, at least one arc $(J_j, M_i)$ of the maximum matching is such that $\delta = \phi_h(j, i)$. For interval $h$, there are at most $n \times m$ iterations, and so the procedure runs in $O(nmK)$. Thus, step 2 runs in $O(n^2 m^2 K \sqrt{n+m})$ time. Therefore, the problem can be solved in polynomial time.

### 5.1.2 Functions $f_{\max}$, $\sum C_j$

#### 5.1.2.1 Problem $P2|CO, pmtn, f^B_{\max} \le Q|\sum C^A_j$

For the preemptive scheduling problem in the COMPETING scenario, one can notice that while problem $P2|CO, pmtn, f^B_{\max} \le Q|\sum C^A_j$ is polynomial and quite simple to solve, the problem $P3|CO, pmtn, f^B_{\max} \le Q|\sum C^A_j$ is open. Wan et al. (2010)

**Algorithm 34** for problem $P2|CO, pmtn, f^B_{max} \leq Q|\sum C^A_j$

1: Renumber the jobs in $\mathcal{J}^A$ in SPT order
2: **for** $j \in \mathcal{J}^B$ **do**
3: Compute deadlines $\tilde{d}^B_j$ such that $f^B_{max} \leq Q$
4: **end for**
5: Schedule jobs in $\mathcal{J}^B$ backwards so that each job completes as close to its deadline as possible.
6: Schedule jobs in $\mathcal{J}^A$ as early as possible alternatively on the two machines via the preemptive SPT rule (if necessary, reschedule jobs in $\mathcal{J}^B$ on the other machine).
7: **return** the global schedule.

consider two identical machines that are shared by two competing agents. The objective of the second agent is to schedule its jobs so that function $f^B_{max}$ is less than a given value $Q$ and the objective of the first agent is to minimize the total completion time of jobs. They propose a polynomial time algorithm described in Algorithm 34.

The first step of the algorithm is to sort the jobs of agent $B$ in EDD order and to schedule them backward, starting by the job with maximum deadline, so that they complete as close to their deadlines as possible. This schedule leaves some empty places for the jobs of agent $A$ on both machines. The jobs of $\mathcal{J}^A$ are considered in SPT order and scheduled in these intervals. To give more details on step 6 of Algorithm 34, dealing with the scheduling of jobs in $\mathcal{J}^A$, let $J^A_j$ be the currently scheduled job on machine $M_e$. If it can be completely scheduled on $M_e$, no action is required and we can pass to the next job $J^A_{j+1}$. Otherwise, a job of $J^B$, say, $J^B_h$, is encountered at time $t$, before the end of $J^A_j$. Let $x$ denote the length of the unscheduled portion of $J^A_j$. Consider the following two cases:

1. If the other machine $M_{e'}$ is idle at $t$, we continue processing $J^A_j$ on $M_{e'}$, possibly until completion.
2. If the other machine $M_{e'}$ is busy at $t$, a portion of length $x$ of $J^B_h$ is moved to an earlier idle time on $M_{e'}$ to make room for $J^A_j$.

These two conditions are used until no further move is possible, or $J^A_j$ is completed. If none of these two conditions hold, $J^A_j$ is preempted and resumed at the first available time. In any case, $J^A_j$ completes as soon as possible. In Wan et al. (2010) it is shown that the following complexity result holds.

**Theorem 5.2.** *Problem $P2|CO, pmtn, f^B_{max} \leq Q|\sum C^A_j$ can be solved in $O(n_A \log n_A + n_B \log n_B)$ time by Algorithm 34.*

About the running time of Algorithm 34, Wan et al. (2010) suppose implicitly that the functions $f^B_j$ are known and the deadlines $\tilde{d}^B_j$ for each job $J^B_j$ are computed in constant time, i.e. deadline $\tilde{d}^B_j$ corresponds to the latest completion time $C^B_j$ for which $f^B_j(C^B_j) = Q$ and the inverse function $(f^B_j)^{-1}$ is known. It is possible to extend this result to the case in which the $f^B_j$ are non-decreasing functions and the

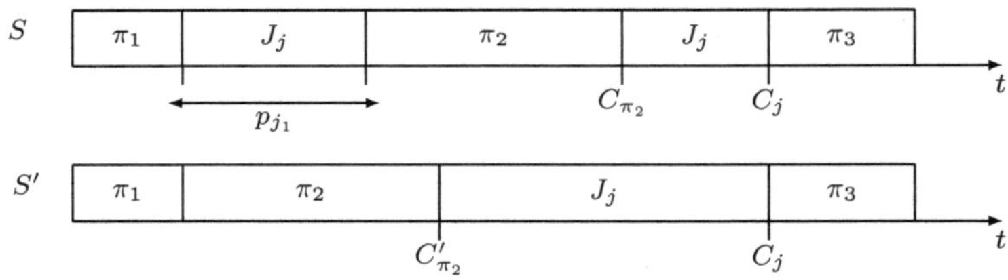


**Fig. 5.2** Sequences $S$ and $S'$

inverse function is not known. For each job $J_j^B$, the deadline $\tilde{d}_j^B(Q)$ is computed as follows.

$$\tilde{d}_j^B(Q) = \max\{\tau : f_j^B(\tau) \leq Q, 0 \leq \tau \leq T\}$$

where $T$ is the sum of the completion times of all jobs. Therefore, the deadlines can be computed in $O(n_B \log T)$ time by a binary search in $[0, T]$.

### 5.1.3 *Functions* $\sum f_j, \sum f_j$

#### 5.1.3.1 Problem $Pm|IN, pmtn, \sum C_j^B \leq Q|\sum C_j^A$

To prove that this problem is NP-hard, we will first show that problem $1|IN, pmtn, \sum C_j^B \leq Q|\sum C_j^A$ is NP-hard.

**Proposition 5.1.** *Problem* $1|IN, pmtn, \sum C_j^B \leq Q|\sum C_j^A$ *is NP-hard.*

*Proof.* Let $S$ be a feasible schedule for the $1|IN, pmtn, \sum C_j^B \leq Q|\sum C_j^A$ problem, where a job $J_j$ is preempted. We have $\sum C_j^B(S) \leq Q$. We assume that $S = \pi_1/J_j/\pi_2/J_j/\pi_3$ with $\pi_1$, $\pi_2$ and $\pi_3$ three sub-sequences of jobs (the notation $a/b$ stands for the concatenation of $a$ and $b$). We denote by $p_{j_1}$ the duration of job $J_j$ before $\pi_2$. Let $S'$ be the same sequence where $J_j$ is not preempted (i.e., shifted to the right). We have $S' = \pi_1/\pi_2/J_j/\pi_3$ (see Fig. 5.2).

Shifting $J_j$ to the right does not modify its completion time and allows the jobs of $\pi_2$ to complete $p_{i_1}$ time units earlier: $C'_{\pi_2} = C_{\pi_2} - p_{j_1}$. If $J_j \in \mathcal{J}^B$, then $\sum C_j^B(S) \leq Q$. Because the completion of $J_j$ does not change and because the completion times for the jobs of $\bar{\mathcal{J}}^A$ in $\pi_2$ (if any) only decrease (the completion times of other jobs is unchanged) and we have $\sum C_j^B(S') \leq Q$. The same reasoning applies if $J_i \in \bar{\mathcal{J}}^A$. In that case, we can state:

$$\sum C_j^B(S') \leq \sum C_j^B(S) \leq Q$$

$$\sum C_j^A(S') = \sum C_j^A(S) - p_{j_1}|\pi_2| < \sum C_j^A(S)$$

Therefore, $S'$ dominates $S$ and there is no need to preempt a job to minimize the sum of completion times. Thus, there is no preemption in any optimal solution.

Because the nonpreemptive problem $1|IN, \sum C_j^B \leq Q|\sum C_j^A$ is NP-hard (Sect. 3.9.1, Theorem 3.21), the proof follows. □

The same reasoning shows that problem $Pm|CO, pmtn, \sum f_j^B \leq Q|\sum f_j^A$ (and hence $Pm|ND, pmtn, \sum f_j^B \leq Q|\sum f_j^A$) is NP-hard. In conclusion, the following theorem holds:

**Proposition 5.2.** *Problem* $1|\beta_{sc}, pmtn, \sum C_j^B \leq Q|\sum C_j^A$ *is NP-hard, with* $\beta_{sc} \in \{CO, IN, ND\}$.

Clearly, this result implies that also $Pm|\beta_{sc}, pmtn, \sum f_j^B \leq Q|\sum f_j^A$ is NP-hard, where $f_j^k$ is a monotonically non decreasing function of the completion time $C_j$, with $\beta_{sc} \in \{CO, IN, ND\}$.

## 5.2 Non-preemptive Jobs with Arbitrary Processing Times

### 5.2.1 Preliminary Results

Recall that if the decision problem $\pi$ reduces to $\pi'$, we use the notation $\pi \propto \pi'$ (see Sect. 2.2.1, page 25). In the following, $\Gamma$, $\Gamma_1$ and $\Gamma_2$ are sets of regular criteria, namely $\Gamma_1 = \{C_{max}, L_{max}, \sum U_i, \sum T_i, \sum w_i T_i, \sum w_i U_i\}$, $\Gamma_2 = \{\sum C_i, \sum w_i C_i\}$, and $\Gamma = \Gamma_1 \cup \Gamma_2$. Let $\beta_{sc} \in \{ND, IN, CO\}$.

**Proposition 5.3.** *The following reductions from the classical scheduling problem hold.*

1. $Pm||C_{max} \propto Pm|\beta, f^B \leq Q|C_{max}^A$, $\forall f^B \in \Gamma$.
2. $Pm|\beta_{sc}, f^B \leq Q|C_{max}^A \propto Pm|\beta_{sc}, f^B \leq Q|f^A$, $\forall f^A \in \Gamma_1$, $\forall f^B \in \Gamma$.

*Proof.* These claims are direct consequences of the complexity of problem $Pm||C_{max}$, with a sufficiently large value of $Q$. □

**Proposition 5.4.** *Problems* $Pm|\beta_{sc}, f^B \leq Q|f^A$ *are NP-hard,* $\forall f^A \in \Gamma$ *and* $\forall f^B \in \Gamma$.

*Proof.* We consider the decision version of the problems. We first show that $Pm|\beta_{sc}, f^A \leq Q_A, f^B \leq Q_B|-$, $\forall f^A \in \Gamma_1$, $\forall f^B \in \Gamma$, is NP-complete. Then, we show that $Pm|\beta_{sc}, f^A \leq Q_A, f^B \leq Q_B|-$, $\forall f^A \in \Gamma_2$, $\forall f^B \in \Gamma$, is NP-complete.

The first claim is given by step 2 of Proposition 5.3.

We know that problem $Pm|\beta_{sc}, C_{max}^B \leq Q_B|-$ is NP-complete. Hence problem $Pm|\beta_{sc}, C_{max}^B \leq Q_B, f^A \leq Q_A|-$ is NP-complete as well, $\forall f^A \in \Gamma$. This is also true for $f^A = \sum C_i^A$. And because it is true for $C_{max}^B$, it is also true for any $f^B \in \Gamma_1$. Thus, problem $Pm|\beta, f^B \leq Q_B, \sum C_j^A \leq Q_A|-$ is NP-complete, $\forall f^B \in \Gamma_1$.

We know that problem $Pm|\beta_{sc}, \sum C_j^B \leq Q_B, \sum C_j^A \leq Q_A|-$ is NP-complete (Proposition 5.2). So problem $Pm|\beta_{sc}, f^B \leq Q_B, \sum C_j^A \leq Q_A|-$ is NP-complete $\forall f^B \in \Gamma$. This is also true for $\sum w_j C_j^A$, i.e. for problems $Pm|\beta_{sc}, f^B \leq Q_B$, $f^A \leq Q_A|-$, $\forall f^B \in \Gamma$ and $\forall f^A \in \Gamma_2$. □

In the following, we show that some NP-hard problems with non-preemptive INTERFERING jobs can be solved in pseudo-polynomial time by dynamic programming algorithms.

## 5.2.2 *Functions* $C_{\max}$, $C_{\max}$

### 5.2.2.1 Problem $Pm|IN, C_{max}^B \leq Q|C_{max}^A$

In this section, we discuss a problem with identical parallel machines and makespan as objective functions in the INTERFERING scenario. We present the results in the two-agent case and give ideas for a generalization to the case of $K$ agents when possible.

The scheduling problem $Pm|IN, C_{max}^B \leq Q, C_{max}^A \leq UB|-$ is equivalent to the single-agent problem $Pm|\tilde{d}_i|C_{max}$ where $\tilde{d}_j^B = Q, \forall J_j^B \in \mathcal{J}^B$. Remember that the jobs of $\mathcal{J}^B$ are numbered from 1 to $n_B$ and the jobs of $\bar{\mathcal{J}}^A$ (i.e. jobs in $\mathcal{J}^A$ and not in $\mathcal{J}^B$) from 1 to $n_A - n_B$.

We define the following recursive function (Blazewicz et al. 2007) as follows: $F_{j_1,j_2}(t_1,\dots,t_m)$ is equal to *true* if the jobs $J_1^B,\dots,J_{j_B}^B$ of $\mathcal{J}^B$ and $J_1^A,\dots,J_{j_A}^A$ of $\bar{\mathcal{J}}^A$ can be scheduled on $M_1,\dots,M_m$ so that each machine $M_i$ is busy in the interval $[0, t_i]$, and $F_{j_A,j_B}(t_1,\dots,t_m)$ is equal to *false* otherwise.

We define

$$F_{0,0}(0,\dots,0) = \text{true}$$
$$F_{0,0}(t_1,\dots,t_m) = \text{false}, \ \forall(t_1,\dots,t_m) \neq (0,\dots,0).$$

The recursive relation is given by:

$$F_{j_A,j_B}(t_1,\dots,t_m) = \bigvee_{i=1}^{m} F_{j_A-1,j_B}(t_1,\dots,t_i - p_{j_A},\dots,t_m)$$
$$\vee \bigvee_{i=1}^{m} \left(F_{j_A,j_B-1}(t_1,\dots,t_i - p_{j_B},\dots,t_m) \wedge (t_i \leq Q)\right)$$

$$\text{for } j_A = 1\dots n_A - n_B,\ j_B = 1\dots n_B,\ t_i \in [0, ub]$$

with $ub = P$, the sum of all processing times. Then, the optimal makespan value is given by

$$C_{max}^{A*} = \min_{t_1,t_2,\ldots,t_m} \{\max\{t_1, t_2, \ldots, t_m\} : F_{n_A - n_B, n_B}(t_1, \ldots, t_m) = true\}$$

In conclusion, the following result holds.

**Theorem 5.3.** *An optimal solution for problem $Pm|IN, C_{max}^B \leq Q|C_{max}^A$ can be obtained in $O(n^2 ub^m)$ time.*

#### 5.2.2.2 Problem $Pm|IN, C_{max}^2 \leq Q_2, \ldots, C_{max}^K \leq Q_K|C_{max}^1$

Note that this result can be generalized to the case of $K$ agents. An optimal schedule for $Pm|IN, C_{max}^2 \leq Q_2, \ldots, C_{max}^K \leq Q_K|C_{max}^1$ can be obtained in $O(n^K ub^m)$.

#### 5.2.2.3 Problem $P2|CO, C_{max}^B \leq Q|C_{max}^A$

Let us turn to the COMPETING scenario. By following a similar idea to the INTERFERING scenario, we can derive another dynamic programming algorithm. We define function $F_{j_A,j_B}(t_1, t_2, t_1^A, t_2^A) = true$ if the jobs $J_1^A, \ldots, J_{j_A}^A$ of $\mathcal{J}^A$ and the jobs $J_1^B, \ldots, J_{j_B}^B$ of $\mathcal{J}^B$ can be scheduled on $M_1$ and $M_2$ so that each machine $M_i$ is busy in the interval $[0, t_i]$, with $t_i^A$ the completion time on machine $M_i$ of the last job of agent $A$. This function is equal to *false* otherwise.

We define

$$F_{0,0}(0,0,0,0) = \text{true and}$$
$$F_{0,0}(t_1, t_2, t_1^A, t_2^A) = \text{false } \forall (t_1, t_2, t_1^A, t_2^A) \neq (0,0,0,0).$$

The recursive relation is given by:

$$\begin{aligned} F_{j_A,j_B}(t_1, t_2, t_1^A, t_2^A) = {} & F_{j_A-1,j_B}(t_1 - p_{j_A}, t_2, t_1^A - p_{j_A}, t_2^A) \wedge (t_1 = t_1^A) \\ & \vee F_{j_A-1,j_B}(t_1, t_2 - p_{j_A}, t_1^A, t_2^A - p_{j_A}) \wedge (t_2 = t_2^A) \\ & \vee F_{j_A,j_B-1}(t_1 - p_{j_B}, t_2, t_1^A, t_2^A) \wedge (t_1 \leq Q) \\ & \vee F_{j_A,j_B-1}(t_1, t_2 - p_{j_B}, t_1^A, t_2^A) \wedge (t_2 \leq Q) \end{aligned}$$

where $j_1 = 1 \ldots n_A$, $j_2 = 1 \ldots n_B$, $t_i \in [0, ub]$, $t_i^A \in [0, ub]$. Then, the optimal makespan value is given by

$$C_{max}^{A*} = \min_{t_1,t_2,t_1^A,t_2^A} \{\max(t_1^A, t_2^A) : F_{n_A,n_B}(t_1, t_2, t_1^A, t_2^A) = true\}$$

Therefore, we have the following result.

**Theorem 5.4.** *An optimal solution to problem $P2|CO, C^B_{max} \leq Q|C^A_{max}$ can be obtained in $O(n_A n_B ub^4)$ time.*

Notice that this DP algorithm can be extended to the $m$-machine case.

### 5.2.3 Functions $C_{\max}$, $\sum C_j$

#### 5.2.3.1 Problem $Pm|IN, \sum C^B_j \leq Q|C^A_{\max}$

In this section, we consider the INTERFERING scenario. The objective of agent $A$ is and the objective of agent $B$ is total completion time. We consider the $\varepsilon$-constraint approach where $\sum C^B_j$ has to be less than or equal to $Q$. We will see that problem $Pm|IN, \sum C^B_j \leq Q|C^A_{\max}$ can be solved in pseudo-polynomial time by a dynamic programming algorithm. The algorithm exploits the following property:

**Lemma 5.1.** *There is an optimal solution to $Pm|IN, \sum C^B_j \leq Q|C^A_{\max}$ in which, for each machine $M_i$, the jobs of $J^B$ allocated to $M_i$ are scheduled in SPT order and precede all jobs of $\bar{\mathcal{J}}^A$ allocated to $M_i$.*

In view of this result, we suppose that the jobs in $J^B$ are numbered in SPT order. Let $F_{j_A,j_B}(t_1,\ldots,t_{m-1},q)$ be the recursive function defined by:

$F_{j_A,j_B}(t_1,\ldots,t_{m-1},q) =$

*true* if jobs 1 to $j_A$ of $\bar{\mathcal{J}}^A$ and 1 to $j_B$ of $\mathcal{J}^B$ can be scheduled on $M_1,\ldots,M_m$ so that each machine $M_i$ is busy in the interval $[0,t_i]$ and the sum of completion times of jobs of $\mathcal{J}^B$ is equal to $q$, with $q$ the total completion time of jobs in $\mathcal{J}^B$, $0 \leq q \leq Q$.

*false* otherwise.

We define

$$F_{0,0}(0,\ldots,0) = true$$

$$F_{0,0}(t_1,\ldots,t_m,q) = false, \forall (t_1,\ldots,t_m) \neq (0,\ldots,0), 0 \leq q \leq Q$$

The recursive relation is the following.

$$F_{j_A,j_B}(t_1,\ldots,t_m,q) = \bigvee_{i=1}^{m} F_{j_A-1,j_B}(t_1,\ldots,t_i - p_{j_A},\ldots,t_m,q)$$

$$\vee \bigvee_{i=1}^{m} \left(F_{j_A,j_B-1}(t_1,\ldots,t_i - p_{j_B},\ldots,t_m,q-t_i) \wedge (q \leq Q)\right)$$

where $j_A = 1\ldots n_A - n_B$, $j_B = 1\ldots n_B$, $t_i \in [0,ub]$, $q \in [0,Q]$.

This dynamic programming algorithm determines the assignment of jobs to machines, which is sufficient to deduce an optimal schedule. The optimal makespan value is given by

$$C_{max}^{A*} = \min_{t_1,t_2,\dots,t_m} \left\{ \max\{t_1, t_2, \dots, t_m\} : F_{n_A-n_B,n_B}(t_1, \dots, t_m, q) = true \right\}$$

In conclusion, for a given upper bound $Q$ on the total completion time of jobs of agent $B$, we have the following result.

**Theorem 5.5.** *An optimal solution to problem $Pm|IN, \sum C_j^B \leq Q|C_{\max}^A$ can be obtained in $O(n^2 ub^m Q)$ time.*

#### 5.2.3.2 Problem $Pm|IN, C_{\max}^B \leq Q|\sum C_j^A$

Let us turn now to the symmetric case, i.e. agent $A$ wants to minimize $\sum C_j^A$, and the makespan of the jobs in $\mathcal{J}^B$ should be less than or equal to a given value $Q$. We next show that $Pm|IN, C_{\max}^B \leq Q|\sum C_j^A$ can be solved in pseudo-polynomial time by a dynamic programming algorithm. The algorithm exploits the following property:

**Lemma 5.2.** *In any optimal solution to $Pm|IN, C_{\max}^B \leq Q|\sum C_j^A$, for each machine $M_i$, all the jobs scheduled up to the last job of $J^B$ are in SPT order, and all the remaining jobs (all belonging to $\bar{J}^A$) are also scheduled in SPT order.*

In view of this result, we suppose in the following that both the jobs of $\mathcal{J}^B$ and the jobs of $\mathcal{J}^A$ are numbered in SPT order. Then, we let $F_{j_A,j_B}(t_1, \dots, t_m)$ denote the total completion time of the jobs of $\mathcal{J}^A$ when the first $j_A$ jobs of $\bar{\mathcal{J}}^A$ and the first $j_B$ jobs of $\mathcal{J}^B$ are scheduled on the $m$ machines, and the makespan of the $m$ machines is $t_1, t_2, \dots, t_m$ respectively.

We define

$$F_{0,0}(0, \dots, 0) = 0$$

$$F_{0,0}(t_1, \dots, t_m) = +\infty, \forall (t_1, \dots, t_m) \neq (0, \dots, 0)$$

$$F_{j_A,j_B}(t_1, \dots, t_m) = +\infty, \text{ if } t_i \notin [0, ub].$$

$$F_{j_A,j_B}(t_1, \dots, t_m) =$$

$$\min_{i=1,\dots,m} \begin{cases} F_{j_A-1,j_B}(t_1, \dots, t_i - p_{j_1}, \dots, t_m) + t_i \\ F_{j_A,j_B-1}(t_1, \dots, t_i - p_{j_2}, \dots, t_m) + t_i, \text{ if } t_i \leq Q \\ F_{j_A,j_B-1}(t_1, \dots, t_i - p_{j_2}, \dots, t_m) + \infty, \text{ if } t_i > Q \end{cases}$$

where $j_A = 1 \dots n_A - n_B$, $j_B = 1 \dots n_B$, $t_i \in [0, ub]$, $q \in [0, Q]$.

The optimal total completion time is given by:

$$\sum_{J_j \in J^A} C_j = \min_{(t_1,\dots,t_m)} \{F_{n_A - n_B, n_B}(t_1, \dots, t_m)\}$$

In conclusion, we have the following result, in which as usual $ub$ is an upper bound on a machine makespan (e.g., the total processing time of the jobs).

**Theorem 5.6.** *An optimal solution to problem $Pm|IN, C_{\max}^B \le Q|\sum C_j^A$ can be obtained in $O(n_A n_B ub^m)$ time.*

#### 5.2.3.3 Problem $Pm|CO, C_{max}^B \le Q|\sum C_j^A$

Let us consider now the COMPETING scenario. This problem is binary NP-hard (see Proposition 5.2.1). In Zhao and Lu (2013) it is shown that this problem is NP-hard even when $m = 2$ and $n_B = 2$.

In what follows, we refer to Balasubramanian et al. (2009), in which the problem $Pm|CO, C_{max}^B \le Q|\sum C_j^A$ is addressed.

On each machine, it is easy to show that the schedule has a specific structure (as in the single-machine case, see Sect. 3.2.1):

**Lemma 5.3.** *In any optimal solution to $Pm|CO, C_{max}^B \le Q|\sum C_j^A$, for each machine $M_i \in \mathcal{M}$, it holds:*

- *The schedule on $M_i$ consists of three consecutive blocks: first some jobs of $\mathcal{J}^A$ are scheduled, then a block of jobs of $\mathcal{J}^B$, followed by the remaining jobs of $\mathcal{J}^A$.*
- *All jobs of $J^A$ on $M_i$ are scheduled in SPT order.*

Therefore, we assume that the jobs of agent $A$ are numbered in SPT order. However, as underlined in Balasubramanian et al. (2009), the starting times of the jobs in $J^A$ on the $m$ machines may *not* follow the SPT ordering. Consider in fact the following counterexample.

*Example 5.1.* Let $m = 2$ machines. We consider that $n_A = 3$, $n_B = 2$ and we have the following processing times:

| $J_j^k$ | $J_1^A$ | $J_2^A$ | $J_3^A$ | $J_1^B$ | $J_2^B$ |
|---|---|---|---|---|---|
| $p_j^k$ | 1 | 1 | 2 | 8 | 8 |

If the makespan of agent $B$ has to be less than or equal to $Q = 10$, then in any optimal schedule, the jobs of $\mathcal{J}^B$ complete at time 10. Jobs $J_1^A$ and $J_2^A$ are scheduled on the first machine, followed by job $J_1^B$ and job $J_3^A$ is scheduled on $M_2$, followed by job $J_2^B$. The total completion time of the jobs of agent $A$ is equal to $\sum C_j^A = 5$.

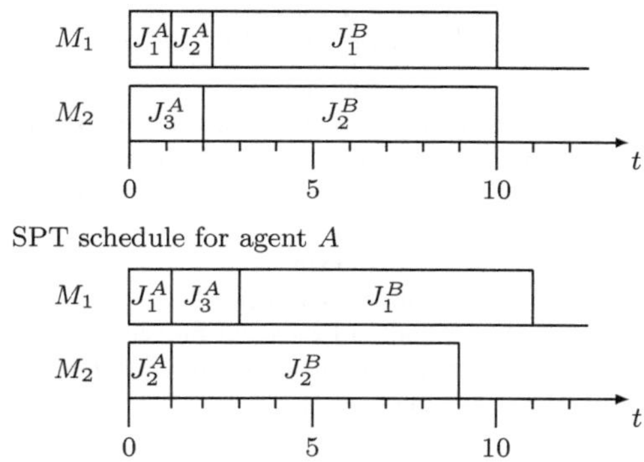


**Fig. 5.3** Example for problem $Pm|CO, C^B_{max} \le Q|\sum C^A_j$

**Algorithm 35** for problem $Pm|CO, C^B_{\max} \le Q|\sum C^A_j$

$\sigma^* := ()$ // initial empty schedule
$\sum C^A_j(\sigma^*) := +\infty$
**for** $j := 1$ **to** $n_A$ **do**
  Construct a partial SPT schedule for the $j$ first jobs of agent $A$
  Calculate $(t_1, t_2, \ldots, t_m)$ // $t_i$ is the maximal job completion time on $M_i$
  Apply Algorithm 36 to schedule the jobs of agent $B$ on the $m$ machines that are available at time $(t_1, t_2, \ldots, t_m)$
  $(t'_1, t'_2, \ldots, t'_m) :=$ updated vector of machine completion times
  Schedule the $n_A - j$ remaining jobs in SPT order on the $m$ machines that are available at time $(t'_1, t'_2, \ldots, t'_m)$
  Calculate the makespan $C^B_{\max}$
  **for** $i := 1$ **to** $m$ **do**
    **if** there is a machine $M_i$ where jobs of agent $B$ complete before $C^B_{\max}$ **then**
      Shift to the left the first jobs of block $\pi_3(i)$ (jobs in $\pi_2(i)$ are right shifted) so that the jobs in $\pi_2(i)$ do not complete after $C^B_{\max}$ // jobs in $\pi_2(i)$ are right shifted
    **end if**
  **end for**
  Denote by $\sigma_j$ the schedule obtained
  **if** $(C^B_{\max}(\sigma_j) \le Q)$ **and** $(\sum C^A_j(\sigma_j) < \sum C^A_j(\sigma^*))$ **then**
    $\sigma^* := \sigma_j$
  **end if**
**end for**
**return** $\sigma^*$

Note that for this example, the schedule of jobs of agent $A$ in SPT order gives the same value for $\sum C^A_j$, but $C^B_{\max} = 11$ (see Fig. 5.3). This solution is thus dominated. ◇

Based on the results of Conway et al. (1967) to solve the $Pm||\sum C_j$ problems optimally (jobs are scheduled in SPT order) and the heuristic of Graham (1966) for the $Pm||C_{\max}$ problem (jobs are scheduled in Longest Processing Time (LPT) order), Balasubramanian et al. (2009) propose a heuristic (Algorithm 35) to generate a set of near non-dominated points where the SPT and LPT heuristics are used iteratively.

**Algorithm 36** for problem $Pm|unavail|C_{\max}$ (MLPT heuristic)

Create the $m^0$ dummy jobs
Add the dummy jobs to the other ones to obtain $\mathcal{J}$
Arrange all the jobs of $\mathcal{J}$ in LPT order
Assume now that all the machines are ready at time zero
**while** $\mathcal{J} \neq \emptyset$ **do**
  $J_{[1]} :=$ the first job in $\mathcal{J}$
  **if** $J_{[1]}$ is a dummy job **then**
    **if** the smallest loaded machine has already received one dummy job **then**
      Among all the machines which have only received real jobs, select the machine with the smallest job $J_f$
      Replace $J_f$ by $J_{[1]}$
      $\mathcal{J} := \mathcal{J} \setminus \{J_{[1]}\}$
      $\mathcal{J} := \mathcal{J} \cup \{J_f\}$
      $J_{[1]} := J_f$
    **else**
      Assign job $J_{[1]}$ to the smallest loaded machine
      $\mathcal{J} := \mathcal{J} \setminus \{J_{[1]}\}$
    **end if**
  **else**
    Assign job $J_{[1]}$ to the smallest loaded machine
    $\mathcal{J} := \mathcal{J} \setminus \{J_{[1]}\}$
  **end if**
**end while**
Shift all the dummy jobs to the head of their assigned machine
**return** final schedule

Following Lemma 5.2, on each machine $M_i$, the jobs of the two agents are split in three blocks: a block $\pi_1(i)$ of $j_A$ jobs of agent $A$, followed by a block $\pi_2(i)$ of $j_B$ jobs of agent $B$, followed by a block $\pi_3(i)$ of the remaining jobs of agent $A$ assigned to $M_i$. Any of these blocks may be empty.

In Algorithm 35, the schedule of the jobs of agent $B$ is done by the algorithm of Lee (1991), denoted MLPT. This algorithm solves the $Pm||C_{\max}$ problem when some machines are not available at time zero ($Pm|unavail|C_{\max}$ problem). The author provide a "modified LPT" (MLPT) algorithm where the makespan obtained by MLPT is bounded by $\frac{4}{3}C^*_{\max}$ ($C^*_{\max}$ being the optimal makespan).

Let $a_i$ denote the earliest time that machine $M_i$ can start to process the jobs. Let $m^0$ be the number of machines with $a_i > 0$. In MLPT algorithm, Lee (1991) considers $a_i$ as the processing time of a dummy job $J_i$. We merge the dummy jobs with the jobs to schedule and this gives the set $\mathcal{J}$ with $n + m^0$ jobs.

To optimally solve the problem $Pm|CO, C^B_{\max} \leq Q|\sum C^A_j$, a mixed integer programming model is proposed in Balasubramanian et al. (2009).

In the proposed time-indexed formulation, the decision variables are $x_{j,t} = 1$ if job $J_j$ starts at time $t$, and 0 otherwise. Let $P = \sum_{j=1}^{n_A} p^A_j + \sum_{j=1}^{n_B} p^B_j$ be the maximum possible start time of a job. The time indexed formulation for problem $Pm|CO, C^B_{\max} \leq Q|\sum C^A_j$ is the following.

$$\text{Minimize} \sum_{j \in \mathcal{J}^A} \sum_{t=0}^{P} x_{j,t}(t + p_j) \tag{5.21}$$

$$\text{subject to} \sum_{t=0}^{Q-p_j} x_{j,t} = 1, \ \forall j \in \mathcal{J}^B \tag{5.22}$$

$$\sum_{t=0}^{P} x_{j,t} = 1, \ \forall j \in \mathcal{J}^A \tag{5.23}$$

$$\sum_{j \in \mathcal{J}} \sum_{s=\max(0,t-p_j+1)}^{t} x_{j,s} \le m, \ \forall t \in P \tag{5.24}$$

$$\text{variables } x_{j,t} \in \{0,1\}, \ \forall j \in \mathcal{J}, \forall t \in P \tag{5.25}$$

In this model, the objective function gives the total completion time of only job of agent $A$. The set of constraints (5.22) ensures that each job of agent $B$ is scheduled exactly once and that no job in $\mathcal{J}^A$ completes after $Q$. The set of constraints (5.23) ensures that each job of agent $A$ is scheduled exactly once. The set of constraints (5.24) ensures that at each time $t$, no more than $m$ jobs have been started and are not yet completed. The set of constraints (5.25) are integrality constraints on the decision variables.

## 5.2.4 Functions $\sum C_j$, $\sum C_j$

### 5.2.4.1 Problem $Pm|IN, \sum C_j^B \le Q|\sum C_j^A$

In the INTERFERING scenario, we consider the case where the total completion time is the objective function of both agents $A$ and $B$. The problem $Pm|IN, \sum C_j^B \le Q|\sum C_j^A$ can be solved in pseudo-polynomial time by a dynamic programming algorithm as follows. In what follows, we suppose that the jobs in $J^A$ are numbered in SPT order.

In a partial schedule, in addition to the total completion time of jobs in $\mathcal{J}^B$, denoted by $q$, we must save the information related to the completion time of the last job on each machine, denoted by $t_i$, $i = 1, \dots, m$. In the following recursive function, we let $F_{j_A,j_B}(t_1, \dots, t_m, q)$ be the total completion time of the jobs of agent $A$ when the first $j_A$ jobs of $\bar{\mathcal{J}}^A$ and the first $j_B$ jobs of $\mathcal{J}^B$ are scheduled on $m$ identical parallel machines, and machine $M_i$ completes at time $t_i$, $i = 1, \dots, m$, with $q \le Q$.

$$F_{0,0}(0, \dots, 0) = 0$$

$$F_{0,0}(t_1, \dots, t_m, q) = +\infty, \ \forall (t_1, \dots, t_m, q) \ne (0, \dots, 0)$$

$$F_{j_A,j_B}(t_1, \dots, t_m, q) = +\infty, \ \text{if } t_i \notin [0, ub] \text{ or } q < 0.$$

$$F_{j_A,j_B}(t_1,\ldots,t_m,q) =$$

$$\min_{i=1,\ldots,m} \begin{cases} F_{j_A-1,j_B}(t_1,\ldots,t_i - p^A_{j_A},\ldots,t_m,q) + t_i \\ F_{j_A,j_B-1}(t_1,\ldots,t_i - p_{j_B},\ldots,t_m,q - t_i) + t_i, \text{ if } q \le Q \\ F_{j_A,j_B-1}(t_1,\ldots,t_i - p_{j_B},\ldots,t_m,q - t_i) + \infty, \text{ if } q > Q \end{cases}$$

$$\forall j_1 \in \{1,\ldots,n-n_B\}, \forall j_2 \in \{1,\ldots,n_B\}, \forall t_i \in [0,ub], \forall q \in [0,Q]$$

The optimal solution is obtained by $\min\{F_{n_A-n_B,n_B}(t_1,\ldots,t_m,q) : t_i \in [0,ub], \forall q \in [0,Q]\}$. In conclusion, we have the following result.

**Theorem 5.7.** *An optimal solution to problem $Pm|IN,\sum C^B_j \le Q|\sum C^A_j$ can be obtained in $O(n^2 ub^m Q)$ time.*

#### 5.2.4.2 Problem $Pm|IN|\mathcal{P}(\sum C^A_j, \sum C^B_j)$

Concerning problem $Pm|IN|\mathcal{P}(\sum C^A_j, \sum C^B_j)$, we recall that in the INTERFERING scenario, even for the single machine problem $1|IN|\mathcal{P}(\sum C^A_j, \sum C^B_j)$, the size of the Pareto set may not be polynomial (see Sect. 3.9.2). Therefore, the size of the Pareto set is exponential in the parallel machine context.

## 5.3 Non-preemptive Jobs with Identical Processing Times

In this section we consider that *all* jobs have the same processing time, whatever the agent, i.e., $p^k_j = p$, $\forall k$, $\forall J^k_j \in \mathcal{J}^k$. However, it is possible to associate a specific due date and a specific weight to each job. We consider uniform parallel machines, i.e., the processing time of a job only depends on the performing machine. More precisely, as explained in Sect. 1.2.2, a coefficient of speed $v_i$ is associated to machine $M_i$ and the processing time of a job $J_j$ is equal to $p_{j,i} = p_j/v_i$. In our case, $p_{j,i} = p/v_i$, $\forall j \in \mathcal{J}$.

### 5.3.1 *Functions $f_{\max}$, $f_{\max}$*

#### 5.3.1.1 Problem $Qm|CO, p_j = p, f^B_{\max} \le Q|f^A_{\max}$

We consider in this section the case in which each agent wants to minimize a general regular max-type cost function $f^k_{\max}$, i.e., we consider the $\varepsilon$-constraint problem $Qm|CO, p_j = p, f^B_{\max} \le Q|f^A_{\max}$.

Since we are dealing with equal-size jobs, the completion time of the job scheduled in position $\ell$ on machine $M_i$ is equal to $C_{[\ell],i} = \ell p/v_i$, where $v_i$ is

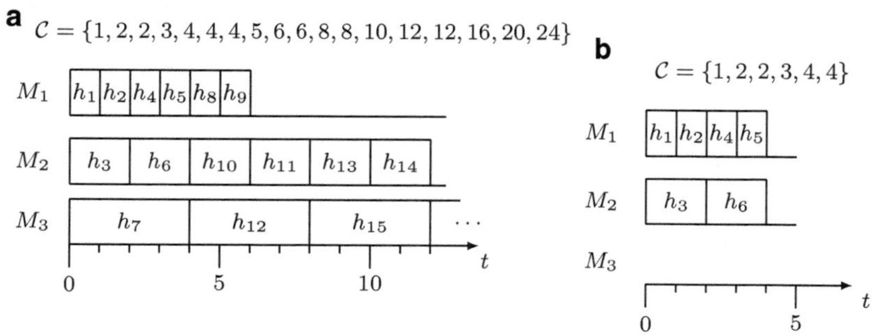


**Fig. 5.4** Relation between vector $\mathcal{C}$ and time intervals

the processing speed of machine $M_i$ and we introduce the set of completion times of jobs on machine $M_i$, denoted by $\mathcal{C}_i = \{C_{[\ell],i} : 1 \leq \ell \leq n\}$. In particular, we let $\mathcal{C}$ denote the set of the $n_A + n_B$ smallest possible completion times, some completion times being possibly present more than once in $\mathcal{C}$. We assume that the elements of $\mathcal{C}$ are sorted in non decreasing order and $\mathcal{C}_{[k]}$ refers to the $k$th completion time in $\mathcal{C}$.

*Example 5.2.* Let consider an instance with $m = 3$ machines, $p = 1$ and $n_A = 3$ jobs and $n_B = 3$ jobs. Speeds of the machines are the following.

| $M_i$ | $M_1$ | $M_2$ | $M_3$ |
|---|---|---|---|
| $v_i$ | 1 | 1/2 | 1/4 |

We have $\mathcal{C}_1 = \{1, 2, 3, 4, 5, 6\}$ on machine $M_1$, $\mathcal{C}_2 = \{2, 4, 6, 8, 10, 12\}$ on machine $M_2$ and $\mathcal{C}_3 = \{4, 8, 12, 16, 20, 24\}$ on machine $M_3$. Therefore, $\bigcup_{i=1}^{m} \mathcal{C}_i = \{1, 2, 2, 3, 4, 4, 4, 5, 6, 6, 8, 8, 10, 12, 12, 16, 20, 24\}$. We only keep the 6 smallest values and we have $\mathcal{C} = \{1, 2, 2, 3, 4, 4\}$. To each completion time of $\mathcal{C}$ corresponds a time interval $h_t$, as represented in Fig. 5.4 (in part (a) the first 16 intervals are represented and in part (b) only the $n = 6$ sufficient intervals). ◇

A deadline $\tilde{d}_j^B$ can be associated to each job of $\mathcal{J}^B$ so that $f_j^B(C_j^B) \leq Q$ if $C_j^B \leq \tilde{d}_j^B$ ($(f_j^B)^{-1}$ is supposed to be computable in constant time). The method which is used to solve this problem is inspired by the backward Lawler's algorithm (Lawler 1973) for the single objective scheduling problem $1|prec|f_{\max}$. The algorithm presented in Algorithm 37 can be implemented in $O(n^2)$.

#### 5.3.1.2 Problem $Qm|CO, p_j = p|\mathcal{P}(f_{\max}^A, f_{\max}^B)$

The calculation of the set of Pareto optimal solutions for the problem of scheduling independent equal sized jobs of two COMPETING agents $A$ and $B$ on $m$ uniform parallel machines is analyzed in Elvikis et al. (2011).

**Algorithm 37** for problem $Qm|CO, p_j = p, f^B_{\max} \le Q|f^A_{\max}$

Build $\mathcal{C}$<br>
$t := \mathcal{C}_{[n]}$<br>
$\mathcal{S}^A := \mathcal{J}^A$<br>
$\mathcal{S}^B := \{J^B_j \in \mathcal{J}^B : \tilde{d}^B_j \le t\}$<br>
$k := n$<br>
**while** $\mathcal{S}^A \cup \mathcal{S}^B \ne \emptyset$ **do**<br>
    **if** $\mathcal{S}^B \ne \emptyset$ **then**<br>
        **for** $J^B_j \in \mathcal{S}^B$ **do**<br>
            **if** $J^B_j$ has minimum $f^B_j(t)$ **then**<br>
                $\sigma(k) := J^B_j$<br>
            **end if**<br>
        **end for**<br>
    **else**<br>
        **for** $J^A_j \in \mathcal{S}^A$ **do**<br>
            **if** $J^A_j$ has minimum $f^A_j(t)$ **then**<br>
                $\sigma(k) := J^A_j$<br>
            **end if**<br>
        **end for**<br>
    **end if**<br>
    $k := k - 1$<br>
    $t := \mathcal{C}_{[k]}$<br>
    Update $\mathcal{S}^A$<br>
    Update $\mathcal{S}^B$<br>
**end while**<br>
**return** $\sigma$

Starting with $Q = \max_{J^B_j \in J^B}\{f^B_j(\mathcal{C}_{[n]})\}$, Algorithm 37 proposed for problem $Qm|CO, p_j = p, f^B_{\max} \le Q|f^A_{\max}$ is used and it can be shown that it returns a Pareto solution, let $(f^A_0, f^B_0)$ denote its value to the two agents. Then, $Q$ is updated as $f^B_0 - 1$, and another Pareto solution can be computed via Algorithm 37. It is possible to show (Elvikis et al. 2011) that the whole Pareto set can be enumerated very efficiently, exploiting the relationship between consecutive Pareto optimal schedules. In Elvikis et al. (2011), the authors use properties and propose a coding which runs in $O(n_A^2 + n_B^2 + n_A n_B \log n_B)$ time with $O(n n_B)$ memory.

## 5.3.2 *Functions* $f_{\max}$, $C_{\max}$

### 5.3.2.1 Problem $Qm|CO, p_j = p, C^B_{\max} \le Q|f^A_{\max}$

Recalling the definition of set $\mathcal{C}$ given in Sect. 5.3.1, let $k$ be the index of the completion time in $\mathcal{C}$ such that $\mathcal{C}_{[k]} \le Q$ and $\mathcal{C}_{[k+1]} > Q$. It is easy to show that there is an optimal solution to $Qm|CO, p_j = p, C^B_{\max} \le Q|f^A_{\max}$ in which the completion times between $\mathcal{C}_{[k-n_B+1]}$ and $\mathcal{C}_{[k]}$ are assigned to the jobs of $\mathcal{J}^B$.

The remaining completion times are assigned to the jobs of $\mathcal{J}^A$ with an algorithm similar to Algorithm 37.

#### 5.3.2.2 Problem $Qm|CO, p_j = p|\mathcal{P}(f^A_{\max}, C^B_{\max})$

In any feasible solution to this problem, the value of $C^B_{\max}$ is at least $\mathcal{C}_{[n_B]}$, which occurs when the jobs of $\mathcal{J}^B$ have the $n_B$ smallest completion times in $\mathcal{C}$. Hence, throughout the set of all Pareto optimal solutions, $C^B_{\max}$ has values $\mathcal{C}_{[n_B]}$, $\mathcal{C}_{[n_B+1]}$, $\ldots$, $\mathcal{C}_{[n_A+n_B]}$. Hence, there are $O(n_A)$ Pareto optimal solutions and each of them can be found applying the algorithm proposed for problem $Qm|CO, p_j = p, C^B_{\max} \leq Q|f^A_{\max}$ with $Q = \mathcal{C}_{[k]}, k = n_B, \ldots, n_A + n_B$.

### 5.3.3 *Functions $C_{\max}$, $C_{\max}$*

#### 5.3.3.1 Problem $Qm|CO, p_j = p|\mathcal{P}(C^A_{\max}, C^B_{\max})$

The problem $Qm|CO, p_j = p|\mathcal{P}(C^A_{\max}, C^B_{\max})$ is indeed trivial. In fact, it is obvious that the $Qm|CO, p_j = p|\mathcal{P}(C^A_{\max}, C^B_{\max})$ problem admits only two Pareto solutions in the criteria space: $(C^A_{\max} = \mathcal{C}_{[n_A]}, C^B_{\max} = \mathcal{C}_{[n]})$ and $(C^A_{\max} = \mathcal{C}_{[n]}, C^B_{\max} = \mathcal{C}_{[n_B]})$, which completely define the assignment of jobs to completion times.

### 5.3.4 *Functions $L_{\max}$, $C_{\max}$*

#### 5.3.4.1 Problem $Qm|CO, p_j = p|\mathcal{P}(L^A_{\max}, C^B_{\max})$

Following the same approach as presented in Sect. 5.3.2.2, we can show that the scheduling problem $Qm|CO, p_j = p|\mathcal{P}(L^A_{\max}, C^B_{\max})$ can be solved very efficiently. We first recall a result from single-agent scheduling.

**Lemma 5.4.** *Given an instance of problem $Qm|p_j = p|L_{\max}$, there exists an optimal solution in which jobs are assigned in EDD order to the completion times.*

Lemma 5.4 trivially extends to the two-agent problem $Qm|CO, p_j = p, C^B_{\max} \leq Q|L^A_{\max}$, in which jobs in $J^A$ are EDD ordered. We can then use the same approach introduced for $Qm|CO, p_j = p, C^B_{\max} \leq Q|f^A_{\max}$ (Sect. 5.3.2.1). Hence, letting $k$ be such that $\mathcal{C}_{[k]} \leq Q$ and $\mathcal{C}_{[k+1]} > Q$, it is easy to show that there is an optimal solution to $Qm|CO, p_j = p, C^B_{\max} \leq Q|L^A_{\max}$ in which all jobs in $J^B$ are scheduled to complete at $\mathcal{C}_{[k-n_B+1]}, \ldots, \mathcal{C}_{[k]}$. The remaining completion times are assigned to the jobs of $\mathcal{J}^A$ in EDD order. In conclusion, there are at most $n_A + 1$ possible Pareto solutions, that can all be enumerated in $O(n \log n)$.

## 5.3.5 Functions $\sum f_j, C_{\max}$

### 5.3.5.1 Problem $Qm|CO, p_j = p|\mathcal{P}(\sum f_j^A, C_{\max}^B)$

Because the objective functions are regular and following the same approach as in Sect. 5.3.1 for problem $Qm|CO, p_j = p|\mathcal{P}(f_{\max}^A, f_{\max}^B)$, the determination of the Pareto set is obtained by solving iteratively the $\varepsilon$-constraint version of the problem. For the latter problem with $C_{\max}^B \leq Q$, minimizing the objective function of agent $A$ is equivalent to finding an optimal assignment of the jobs of agent $A$ to the completion times $\{\mathcal{C}_{[1]}, \ldots, \mathcal{C}_{[k-n_B]}\} \cup \{\mathcal{C}_{[k+1]}, \ldots, \mathcal{C}_{[n]}\}$ of $\mathcal{C}$ where $k$ verifies $\mathcal{C}_{[k]} \leq Q$ and $\mathcal{C}_{[k+1]} > Q$. This is an assignment problem that can be solved in $O(n_A^3)$ (see Dessouky et al. (1990)).

As there are at most $(n_A + 1)$ possible completion times for the last job of the block of jobs in $\mathcal{J}^B$, one can deduce that there are at most $(n_A + 1)$ Pareto optimal schedules.

In some special cases for function $\sum f_j^A$, the problem $Qm|CO, p_j = p|\mathcal{P}(\sum f_j^A, C_{\max}^B)$ can be solved even more efficiently:

- If $\sum f_j^A = \sum w_j^A C_j^A$, the jobs of $\mathcal{J}^A$ are assigned to the completion times $\{\mathcal{C}_{[1]}, \ldots, \mathcal{C}_{[k-n_B]}\} \cup \{\mathcal{C}_{[k+1]}, \ldots, \mathcal{C}_{[n]}\}$ of $\mathcal{C}$ in WSPT order, i.e., by non increasing order of $w_j^A$, since processing times are identical.
- If $\sum f_j^A = \sum w_j^A T_j^A$ with $T_j^A = \max(0, C_j^A - d_j^A)$ and the additional assumption that the weights $w_j^A$ and due dates $d_j^A$ are agreeable (i.e., $d_j^A \leq d_{j'}^A \Rightarrow w_j^A \geq w_{j'}^A$), the jobs of $\mathcal{J}^A$ are assigned to the completion times $\{\mathcal{C}_{[1]}, \ldots, \mathcal{C}_{[k-n_B]}\} \cup \{\mathcal{C}_{[k+1]}, \ldots, \mathcal{C}_{[n]}\}$ of $\mathcal{C}$ in EDD order.

In both such special cases, $Qm|CO, p_j = p|\mathcal{P}(\sum f_j^A, C_{\max}^B)$ can be solved in $O(n \log n)$.

## 5.3.6 Functions $\sum U_j, C_{\max}$

### 5.3.6.1 Problem $Qm|CO, p_j = p|\mathcal{P}(\sum U_j^A, C_{\max}^B)$

For this problem, again the jobs of $J^B$ are scheduled to complete at $n_B$ consecutive completion times in $\mathcal{C}$. As a consequence, there are at most $n_A + 1$ Pareto optimal solutions. It is clear that in a Pareto solution, the jobs before the block of $\mathcal{J}^B$ are early jobs (since otherwise, by shifting the jobs to the end, the makespan for $\mathcal{J}^B$ can be reduced without changing the number of tardy jobs). Furthermore, we can limit to considering schedules in which the early jobs are scheduled in EDD order.

The first Pareto solution is obtained by first assigning the jobs of $\mathcal{J}^B$ to the last completion times in $\mathcal{C}$. We sort the jobs of $\mathcal{J}^A$ in EDD order and we start assigning them in this order to the first $n_A$ completion times. When a job of $\mathcal{J}^A$ is late if

**Algorithm 38** for problem $Qm|CO, p_j = p|\mathcal{P}(\sum U_j^A, C_{\max}^B)$

```
Build C
Arrange the jobs of J^A in EDD order
t := n
R := ∅ // the initial set of Pareto solutions
while t ≥ n_B do
    Assign the jobs of J^B to the completion times at position t − n_B + 1 to t in C
    r := 1
    j := 1
    while (j ≤ n_A) and (r ≤ t − n_B) do
        if C_[r] ≤ d_j^A then
            r := r + 1
            Assign J_j^A to the completion time at position r in C
        else
            Move J_j^A to the end of the schedule
        end if
        j := j + 1
    end while
    Shift block J^B to the left if necessary to obtain solution σ
    R := R ∪ {σ}
    t := t − 1
end while
Remove the weak Pareto solutions from R
return R
```

assigned to a completion time $\mathcal{C}_{[r]}$, it is moved to the end of the schedule and the jobs of $J^B$ are left shifted accordingly. Then, the next jobs in $\mathcal{J}^A$ are tried out to complete at $\mathcal{C}_{[r]}$, until the first job which is early when assigned to $\mathcal{C}_{[r]}$ is found. Then, we continue considering $\mathcal{C}_{[r+1]}$ and so on, until all jobs of $J^A$ are assigned a completion time.

The next Pareto solution is found by left-shifting each job of $\mathcal{J}^B$ to the previous position in $\mathcal{C}$ with respect to the previous Pareto optimal solution. As before, the new tardy jobs of $\mathcal{J}^A$ are moved to the end of the schedule and the process iterates. This algorithm is described in Algorithm 38.

*Example 5.3.* Let us illustrate this algorithm with the following instance. Let $n_A = 6$, $n_B = 5$, and $p = 1$. The due dates of jobs of $\mathcal{J}^A$ are the following.

| $J_j^A$ | $J_1^A$ | $J_2^A$ | $J_3^A$ | $J_4^A$ | $J_5^A$ | $J_6^A$ |
|---|---|---|---|---|---|---|
| $d_j^A$ | 1 | 1 | 3 | 5 | 6 | 7 |

We assume that there are $m = 3$ machines with speeds 1, 1/2 and 1/4 as in Example 5.2. The vector of completion times $\mathcal{C}$ is equal to $\mathcal{C} = \{1, 2, 2, 3, 4, 4, 4, 5, 6, 6, 7\}$.

First, the jobs of $\mathcal{J}^B$ are assigned to the completion times $\{4, 5, 6, 6, 7\}$. In this case, job $J_1^A$ can complete at time 1 and is assigned to the first completion time of $\mathcal{C}$.

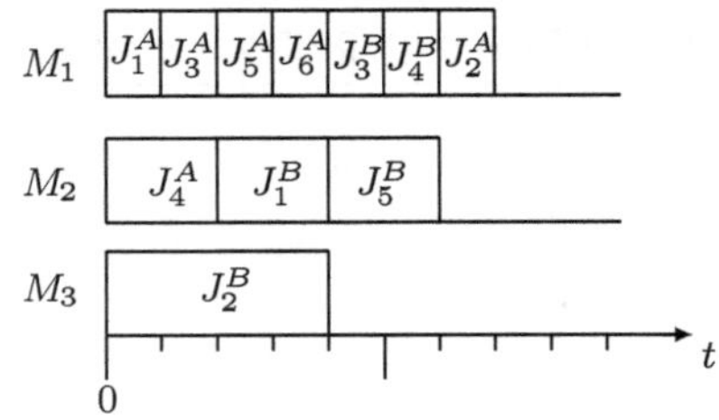


**Fig. 5.5** Pareto solution with $(\sum U_j^A, C_{\max}^B) = (1, 6)$

Job $J_2^A$ cannot complete at time 2, thus this job is put at the end of the schedule. Then, job $J_3^A$ can complete at time 2, job $J_4^A$ can complete at time 2, job $J_5^A$ can complete at time 3, and job $J_6^A$ can complete at time 4. There is one tardy job, so $\sum U_j^A = 1$. Because one job of $\mathcal{J}^A$ is late, it is possible to shift the block $\mathcal{J}^B$ to the right by one position. Finally, the assignment to the completion times of $\mathcal{C}$ is given by $(J_1^A, J_3^A, J_4^A, J_5^A, J_6^A, J_1^B, J_2^B, J_3^B, J_4^B, J_5^B, J_2^A)$. The makespan of $\mathcal{J}^B$ is equal to 6 and the schedule is represented in Fig. 5.5.

For the second Pareto solution, the jobs of $\mathcal{J}^B$ are assigned to the completion times $\{4, 4, 4, 5, 6\}$. Nothing changes for jobs $J_1^A$ to $J_5^A$, assigned to the same positions. Job $J_6^A$ is scheduled in position 11 and is not late. The solution is again a vector $(\sum U_j^A, C_{\max}^B) = (1, 6)$. ◇

## 5.4 Tables

In Table 5.1, we summarize the results in the preemptive case. In Tables 5.2 and 5.3, we summarize the results in the non-preemptive case with the epsilon-constraint approach and the Pareto front enumeration, respectively. In Table 5.4, we summarize the results in the non-preemptive case with equal-length jobs. The running times of the different algorithms are given in the tables.

## 5.5 Bibliographic Remarks

In this section, we give some remarks on main references related to multiagent parallel machine scheduling problems. We give some references to the reader who wants to enter more into the details on these problems.

### *5.5.1 Preemptive Jobs*

Note that there are few results dealing with parallel machines multiagent scheduling problems when preemption of jobs is allowed. The first study on monocriterion

**Table 5.1** Preemptive case

| Problem | Complexity | Section | Page |
|---|---|---|---|
| $Rm\|IN,pmtn,\ f^B_{\max} \leq Q\|f^A_{\max}$ | $O(n^2m^2\sqrt{n+m})$ | 5.1.1.1 | 190 |
| $Rm\|IN,pmtn,\ f^k_{\max} \leq Q_k, k=2,\ldots,K\|f^1_{\max}$ | $O(n^2m^2K\sqrt{n+m})$ | 5.1.1.4 | 193 |
| $P2\|CO,pmtn,\ f^B_{\max} \leq Q\|\sum C^A_j$ | $O(n_A \log n_A + n_B \log n_B)$ | 5.1.2.1 | 194 |
| $Pm\|IN,pmtn,\ \sum C^B_j \leq Q\|\sum C^A_j$ | NP-hard | 5.1.3.1 | 196 |
| $Pm\|IN,pmtn,\ \sum f^B_j \leq Q\|\sum f^A_j$ | NP-hard | 5.1.3.1 | 196 |

**Table 5.2** Non-preemptive jobs – Epsilon-constraint approach

| Problem | Complexity | Section | Page |
|---|---|---|---|
| $Pm\|IN, C^B_{\max} \leq Q\|C^A_{max}$ | $O(n^2UB^m)$ | 5.2.2.1 | 198 |
| $Pm\|IN, C^2_{\max} \leq Q_2,\ldots,C^K_{max} \leq Q_K\|C^1_{max}$ | $O(n^KUB^m)$ | 5.2.2.2 | 199 |
| $P2\|CO, C^B_{\max} \leq Q\|C^A_{max}$ | $O(n_An_BUB^4)$ | 5.2.2.3 | 199 |
| $Pm\|IN, \sum C^B_j \leq Q\|C^A_{\max}$ | $O(n^2UB^mQ)$ | 5.2.3.1 | 200 |
| $Pm\|IN, C^B_{\max} \leq Q\|\sum C^A_j$ | $O(n^2UB^m)$ | 5.2.3.2 | 201 |
| $Pm\|CO, C^B_{\max} \leq Q\|\sum C^A_j$ | NP-hard | 5.2.3.3 | 202 |
| $Pm\|IN, \sum C^B_j \leq Q\|\sum C^A_j$ | $O(n^2UB^mQ)$ | 5.2.4.1 | 205 |

**Table 5.3** Non-preemptive jobs – Pareto front enumeration

| Problem | Size | Section | Page |
|---|---|---|---|
| $Pm\|IN\|\mathcal{P}(\sum C^A_j, \sum C^B_j)$ | Nonpolynomial | 5.2.4.2 | 206 |

**Table 5.4** Non-preemptive case with equal-length jobs

| Problem | Complexity/size | Section | Page |
|---|---|---|---|
| $Qm\|CO, p_j = p, f^B_{\max} \leq Q\|f^A_{\max}$ | $O(n^2)$ | 5.3.1.1 | 206 |
| $Qm\|CO, p_j = p\|\mathcal{P}(f^A_{\max}, f^B_{\max})$ | $O(n^3)$ | 5.3.1.2 | 207 |
| $Qm\|CO, p_j = p, C^B_{\max} \leq Q\|f^A_{\max}$ | $O(n^2)$ | 5.3.2.1 | 208 |
| $Qm\|CO, p_j = p\|\mathcal{P}(f^A_{\max}, C^B_{\max})$ | | 5.3.2.2 | 209 |
| $Qm\|CO, p_j = p\|\mathcal{P}(C^A_{\max}, C^B_{\max})$ | $O(n^2_A)$ | 5.3.3.1 | 209 |
| $Qm\|CO, p_j = p\|\mathcal{P}(L^A_{\max}, C^B_{\max})$ | | 5.3.4.1 | 209 |
| $Qm\|CO, p_j = p\|\mathcal{P}(\sum f^A_j, C^B_{\max})$ | $(n_A + 1)$ | 5.3.5.1 | 210 |
| $Qm\|CO, p_j = p\|\mathcal{P}(\sum U^A_j, C^B_{\max})$ | | 5.3.6.1 | 210 |

scheduling problems on parallel machines is due to McNaughton 1959, where the objective function to minimize is the makespan. Then, one of more interesting results is to solve the classical feasibility scheduling problem denoted by $Rm|pmtn, \tilde{d}_j|-$ (Brucker 2007). The idea for solving this problem can be generalized for solving problem $Rm|IN, pmtn, f^k_{\max} \leq Q_k, k = 2, \ldots K|f^1_{\max}$, where all the agents have the same objective function (see Sect. 5.1). The complexity of the proposed algorithm can be improved by following the approach proposed in Sedeño-Noda et al. (2006) for solving the preemptive open shop problem with time-windows, based on network flow approaches to check feasibility and a max-flow parametrical algorithm to minimize the makespan. Other objective functions are considered in Mohri et al. (1999), dealing with the $P3|MU, pmtn, C_{\max} \leq Q|L_{\max}$ problem. The authors propose a polynomial time algorithm to enumerate the whole Pareto set based on the $\varepsilon$-constraint approach. Minimizing both the total completion time of jobs and the makespan criteria in multicriteria scenario has been studied in Leung and Young (1989), where the linear combination is considered and a polynomial time algorithm is proposed. These results can be extends to the NONDISJOINT scenario.

### 5.5.2 Non-preemptive Jobs with Arbitrary Processing Times

In this case, without simplifying hypotheses, any problem is NP-hard. Therefore, the challenge is to propose pseudo-polynomial time algorithms, most often based on dynamic programming. The next step is then to propose (Fully) Polynomial Approximation Schemes, as in Kellerer and Strusevich (2010) or in Zhao and Lu (2013). In the latter, the authors consider identical parallel machines in the COMPETING scenario with the $\varepsilon$-constraint approach, where the objective of agent $B$ is $C^B_{\max} \leq Q$ and the objective of agent $A$, to minimize is either $C^A_{\max}$ or $\sum C^A_j$. In Wan et al. (2010), the authors consider identical parallel machines when processing times are controllable (see Sect. 6.4) and propose approximation schemes and algorithms with performance guarantee. The minimization of the total completion time with deadlines and additional constraints can also catch our attention. For example, in Su (2009), the identical parallel machine scheduling problem with job deadlines and machine eligibility constraints is considered. The objective is to minimize the total completion time, and every job can be processed only on a specified subset of machines. This problem is NP-hard. These methods and results can be adapted in the INTERFERING scenario to solve a problem with two agents $A$ and $B$, where agent $B$ aims to minimize a regular objective function $f^B_{\max}$ and the objective function of the agent $A$ to minimize is the total completion time.

### 5.5.3 Non-preemptive Jobs with Identical Processing Times

The scheduling problem with uniform parallel machines and identical jobs was studied in the seminal work of Dessouky et al. (1990). The authors introduce the vector of earliest possible completion times $C$ and propose a resolution method that can be used for general regular functions and its improvement in case of classical scheduling objective functions. In the BICRITERIA scenario, Tuzikov et al. (1998) consider general objective functions $f^A_{\max}$, $\sum f^A_j$ and $f^B_{\max}$ with the $\varepsilon$-constraint approach. Based on the Lawler's backward algorithm (Lawler 1973) for the $1|prec|f_{\max}$ problem, polynomial time algorithms are proposed for obtaining the set of Pareto solutions. The problem in the multiagent context has been addressed in Elvikis et al. (2011) and T'kindt (2012). The authors propose a polynomial time generic algorithm with a better time complexity.

# Chapter 6
# Scheduling Problems with Variable Job Processing Times

In this chapter, we consider agent scheduling problems in which job processing times are *variable*. This means that the processing times, contrary to other chapters of the book, are *not fixed* and may change depending on such parameters as job starting times, job positions in schedule or the amount of resources allocated to jobs. Though problems of this type appear in many applications and non-fixed job processing times are studied in scheduling theory from over a few decades, agent scheduling problems with variable job processing times only recently started to be a new subject of research.

The chapter is composed of six sections. In Sect. 6.1, we give a short introduction to scheduling problems with variable job processing times. The main part of the chapter is composed of Sects. 6.2–6.4, in which we review agent scheduling problems with time-dependent, position-dependent and controllable job processing times, respectively. In Sect. 6.5, we present tables summarizing the time complexity statuses of considered earlier scheduling problems. We end the chapter by Sect. 6.6 with bibliographic remarks.

## 6.1 Introduction

In this section, we recall some definitions and results applied in the chapter. First, we introduce the reader to the phenomenon of job processing times variability and propose a classification of main forms of the variability. Next, we describe some extensions of the three-field notation that we use in the book. Further, we present basic results concerning scheduling problems with variable processing times. We complete the section by several examples of single- and two-agent scheduling problems with variable job processing times.

A. Agnetis et al., *Multiagent Scheduling*, DOI 10.1007/978-3-642-41880-8_6, 

### 6.1.1 Main Forms of Variable Job Processing Times

One of the basic assumptions of scheduling theory is that the processing times of the jobs are *fixed*, known in advance and described by *numbers*. However, this is very restrictive, since it does not allow one to consider many practical problems in which jobs have *variable* processing times. For example, jobs may deteriorate – and deterioration increases the time needed for their processing, job processing times may change in view of learning or ageing effects, or they may depend on the amount of a resource allocated to the jobs etc.

The variability of job processing times may be modeled in various ways. In this chapter, we consider the following forms of variable job processing times described by *functions* or *intervals*:

- *Time-dependent job processing times* – the processing time of a job is a function of the job starting time;
- *Position-dependent job processing times* – the processing time of a job is a function of the position of the job in schedule;
- *Controllable job processing times* – the processing time of a job is varying in some interval between a certain minimum and maximum value.

Now, we briefly describe the mentioned above forms of variable job processing times, limiting the presentation only to these job processing time forms that appear in agent scheduling literature.

#### 6.1.1.1 Time-Dependent Job Processing Times

This is the most popular form of variable job processing times. In this case, the processing times of jobs are functions of the job starting times. Scheduling problems with job processing times of this type are considered in that branch of scheduling theory known as *time-dependent scheduling* (Gawiejnowicz 2008).

Time-dependent processing times appear in many important problems in which any delay in processing causes an increase (a decrease) of the processing times of executed jobs. Examples are the problems of scheduling maintenance procedures, planning the sequences of derusting operations, modeling the issues related to fire fighting, financial problems such as the repayment of multiple loans, military problems such as recognizing aerial threats etc.

There are two main research directions in time-dependent scheduling, each having its own specificity and possible application areas. Though, under some assumptions, the results from both these directions are mutually related, at present they are developing rather separately.

The first direction concerns scheduling problems in which job processing times are *non-decreasing* (or *increasing*) functions of the job starting times. This means that job processing times *deteriorate* in time, i.e. a job that is started later has not lower (not larger) processing time than the same job started earlier. Jobs that have time-dependent deteriorating processing times are called *deteriorating jobs*. Most of the literature on time-dependent scheduling concerns scheduling deteriorating jobs.

The simplest form of job deterioration is *proportional deterioration*. In this case, we assume that job processing time $p_j$ is in the form of

$$p_j = b_j t, \tag{6.1}$$

where $b_j > 0$ for $1 \leq j \leq n$ and $t$ denotes the starting time of job $J_j$. Coefficient $b_j$ is called the *deterioration rate* of job $J_j$, $1 \leq j \leq n$. Moreover, in order to avoid the trivial case when all processing times of jobs executed on a machine are equal to zero, we assume that the first scheduled job starts at time $t_0 > 0$ from which the machine is available for processing.

A more general form of job deterioration is *proportional-linear deterioration*. In this case, job processing time $p_j$ is in the form of

$$p_j = b_j(a + bt), \tag{6.2}$$

where $t_0 = 0$, $b_j > 0$ for $1 \leq j \leq n$, $a \geq 0$ and $b \geq 0$.

The next form of job deterioration is *linear deterioration*. In this case, job processing time $p_j$ is a linear function of the job starting time,

$$p_j = a_j + b_j t, \tag{6.3}$$

where $t_0 = 0$, $a_j > 0$ and $b_j > 0$ for $1 \leq j \leq n$. Coefficient $a_j$ is called the *basic processing time* of job $J_j$, $1 \leq j \leq n$.

Throughout the chapter we write that deteriorating jobs have *proportional*, *proportional-linear* or *linear processing times*, if the processing times are in the form of (6.1), (6.2) or (6.3), respectively.

Notice that some relations hold among the above mentioned forms of job deterioration. Proportional job deterioration (6.1) is a special case of proportional-linear deterioration (6.2) that, in turn, is a special case of linear deterioration (6.3). Hence, any time-dependent scheduling problem with linear (proportional-linear) job processing times includes as a special case the problem with proportional-linear (proportional) job processing times.

The second direction in time-dependent scheduling concerns the study of such problems in which job processing times are *non-increasing* (or *decreasing*) functions of the job starting times. This, in turn, means that job processing times *shorten* in time, i.e. the processing time of a job becomes shorter if it is started later. Jobs with time-dependent processing times of this type are called *shortening jobs*. Scheduling problems with shortening jobs are relatively less explored than those with deteriorating jobs.

The simplest form of job processing time shortening is *proportional-linear shortening* in which job processing time $p_j$ is in the form of

$$p_j = b_j(a - bt), \tag{6.4}$$

where *shortening rates* $b_j$ are rational, satisfy the condition

$$0 < b_j b < 1 \tag{6.5}$$

and the condition

$$b\left(\sum_{i=1}^{n} b_i - b_j\right) < 1 \tag{6.6}$$

holds for $1 \leq j \leq n$. Conditions (6.5) and (6.6) assure that job processing times (6.4) are positive in any non-idle schedule.

A special case of proportional-linear shortening is the case when $a = 1$, i.e. when job processing time $p_j$ is in the form of

$$p_j = b_j(1 - bt), \tag{6.7}$$

where $b_j > 0$ for $1 \leq j \leq n$ and $b > 0$. In this case, condition (6.6) takes the form of

$$b\left(\sum_{j=1}^{n} b_j - b_{\min}\right) < 1,$$

where $b_{\min} := \min_{1 \leq j \leq n}\{b_j\}$.

The next type of job shortening is *linear shortening*, in which job processing times are decreasing linear functions of the job starting times. In this case, processing time $p_j$ is in the form of

$$p_j = a_j - b_j t, \tag{6.8}$$

where *shortening rates* $b_j$ are rational and conditions

$$0 < b_j < 1 \tag{6.9}$$

and

$$b_j\left(\sum_{i=1}^{n} a_i - a_j\right) < a_j \tag{6.10}$$

hold for $1 \leq j \leq n$. Notice that conditions (6.9) and (6.10) are generalizations of conditions (6.5) and (6.6), respectively.

Throughout the chapter we write that shortening jobs have *proportional-linear* or *linear processing times*, if the processing times are in the form of (6.4) or (6.8), respectively.

#### 6.1.1.2 Position-Dependent Job Processing Times

This is the second popular form of variable job processing times. In this case, job processing times are functions of the job positions in schedule. Scheduling problems of this type are considered in the second active research area in scheduling theory called *position-dependent scheduling*.

Position-dependent job processing times occur in manufacturing systems, in which the assembly time of a product is a function of skills of the worker who is involved in the process of making the product. Because the skills have an impact on the process, the assembly time is a function of the worker's experience. Moreover, since the latter can be expressed by the number of products made by the worker earlier, this time is a function of the product position in a schedule.

Similarly, as in the case of time-dependent job processing times, there are two main research directions in position-dependent scheduling. The first is the most popular and, in a sense, it is similar to the one with shortening jobs: the processing time of a job is a non-increasing (a decreasing) function of the job position in a schedule. Since the aim of this form of job processing time is to model so-called *learning effect*, problems of this kind are called *scheduling problems with learning effect*.

The simplest form of learning effect is *log-linear learning effect* in which the processing time $p_{j,r}$ of job $J_j$ $(1 \leq j \leq n)$ scheduled in position $r$ is in the form of

$$p_{j,r} = p_j r^{\alpha}. \tag{6.11}$$

Here $p_j$ is the *basic processing time* of job $J_j$, $\alpha < 0$ is the *learning index*, and $r$ denotes the position of $J_j$ in the schedule, $1 \leq r \leq n$.

Another form of learning effect is *linear learning effect* that, in a sense, is similar to linear shortening. In this case,

$$p_{j,r} = p_j - \beta_j r, \tag{6.12}$$

where $p_j$ is the basic processing time of job $J_j$ and $\beta_j$ is the *learning factor* $(0 < \beta_j < \frac{p_j}{n}$ for $1 \leq j \leq n)$.

Throughout the chapter we write that position-dependent jobs have *log-linear* or *linear position-dependent processing times with learning effect*, if the processing times are in the form of (6.11) or (6.12), respectively.

A separate class of scheduling problems with learning effect takes into account the impact of previously scheduled jobs. This form of learning effect is called *past-sequence-dependent learning effect*. For example, job processing times with past-sequence-dependent learning effect may be in the form of

$$p_{j,r} = p_j \max\left\{\left(1 + \sum_{k=1}^{r-1} p_{[k]}\right)^{\alpha}, \beta\right\}, \tag{6.13}$$

$$p_{j,r} = p_j \left(1 + \sum_{k=1}^{r-1} p_{[k]}\right)^{\alpha}, \tag{6.14}$$

or

$$p_{j,r} = p_j \left(\frac{1 + \sum_{k=1}^{r-1} p_{[k]}}{1 + \sum_{k=1}^{r-1} p_k}\right)^{\alpha}, \tag{6.15}$$

where $p_j$, $p_{[k]}$, $\alpha < 0$ and $0 < \beta < 1$ denote the basic processing time of job $J_j$, the processing time of the job in position $k$, the *learning index* and the *truncation parameter*, respectively.

Throughout the chapter we write that position-dependent jobs have *past-sequence-dependent processing times with learning effect*, if the processing times are in the form of (6.13), (6.14) or (6.15).

The second form of position-dependent variable job processing times has a similar nature to that one of deteriorating jobs, since the processing time of a job is a non-decreasing (or an increasing) function of the job position in a schedule. Since this form of position-dependent job processing times is related to so-called *ageing effect*, problems of this kind are called *scheduling problems with ageing effect*.

The simplest form of ageing effect is *log-linear ageing effect* that has the same form as log-linear learning effect but with positive exponent. In this case, job processing time $p_{j,r}$ is in the form of

$$p_{j,r} = p_j r^{\beta}, \tag{6.16}$$

where $p_j$ is the basic processing time of job $J_j$ and the *ageing index* $\beta > 0$.

A similar change of the sign of a parameter that has an impact on job processing time may concern also other forms of learning effect. For example, position-dependent job processing times with ageing effect may be in the form of

$$p_{j,r} = p_j + \beta_j r, \tag{6.17}$$

$$p_{j,r} = p_j \left(1 + \sum_{k=1}^{r-1} p_{[k]}\right)^{\beta}, \tag{6.18}$$

or

$$p_{j,r} = p_j \left(\frac{1 + \sum_{k=1}^{r-1} p_{[k]}}{1 + \sum_{k=1}^{r-1} p_k}\right)^{\beta}, \tag{6.19}$$

where $p_j$ is the basic processing time of job $J_j$ and $\beta > 0$.

Notice that ageing effects of the forms (6.16), (6.17), (6.18) and (6.19) are counterparts of learning effects of the forms (6.11), (6.12), (6.14) and (6.15), respectively.

Throughout the chapter we write that position-dependent jobs have *log-linear* or *linear position-dependent processing times with ageing effect*, if the processing times are in the form of (6.16) or (6.17), respectively. Similarly, we write that position-dependent jobs have *past-sequence-dependent processing times with ageing effect*, if the processing times are in the form of (6.18) or (6.19), respectively.

#### 6.1.1.3 Controllable Job Processing Times

This is the third popular form of variable job processing times. In this case, job processing times are described by *intervals*, i.e., the processing time of a job varies between a minimum and a maximal value that are specific for each job. Moreover, the processing time of a job is expressed by a non-increasing function of the amount of a *resource* allocated to a given job. This resource may be continuous or discrete and, in most cases, it is non-renewable and its availability is limited by an upper bound. Scheduling problems of this type are considered in the third active research area in scheduling theory called *resource-dependent scheduling*.

Controllable job processing times appear in some industrial applications such as the problem of organizing the production at a blacksmith's division in a steel mill. In this case, the job processing times vary within certain limits and they require resources such as gas or power. Allotted resources may change job processing times but since the former are scarce, a *cost* has to be paid for each unit of resource employed.

There are two main forms of controllable job processing times. The first form of controllable job processing times, called *convex*, assumes that the processing time $p_j$ of job $J_j$ is a convex function of the resource amount $u_j$ allocated to $J_j$. Since no agent scheduling problems with convex controllable job processing times were considered so far, we do not discuss this form here.

The second form of controllable job processing times is called *linear*. In this case, the processing time $p_j$ of job $J_j$ is a linear function of the amount $u_j$ of a resource allocated to the job, i.e.

$$p_j = \overline{p}_j - \nu_j u_j, \tag{6.20}$$

where $0 \leq u_j \leq \overline{u}_j \leq \frac{p_j}{\nu_j}$. The values $\overline{p}_j$, $\overline{u}_j$ and $\nu_j > 0$ are called the *non-compressed* (*maximal*) *processing time*, the upper bound on the amount of allocated resource and the *compression rate* of job $J_j$, $1 \leq j \leq n$.

There is another possible form of linear controllable job processing times. In this form, we let the actual processing time $p_j \in [\underline{p}_j, \overline{p}_j]$, where $\underline{p}_j \leq \overline{p}_j$ for $1 \leq j \leq n$. The maximal processing time can be *compressed* (decreased) at the cost $c_j x_j$, where

$$x_j = \overline{p}_j - p_j \tag{6.21}$$

is the *amount of compression of job* $J_j$ and $c_j$ is the *compression cost per unit time*. This implies that the processing time $p_j$ of controllable job $J_j$ is in the form of

$$p_j = \overline{p}_j - x_j, \tag{6.22}$$

where $\overline{p}_j$ and $x_j$ are defined as in (6.20) and (6.21), respectively. In this form, the cost of compression is usually measured by the total compression *cost function* $\sum_j c_j x_j$.

Throughout the chapter we write that jobs have *controllable linear processing times*, if the processing times are in the form of (6.20) or (6.22).

Notice that any solution to a scheduling problem with controllable job processing times has two components. Namely, if job processing times are in the form of (6.20), a solution to the problem is specified by (i) a vector of resource amounts allocated to each job and (ii) a schedule. Similarly, if job processing times are in the form of (6.22), the solution is specified by (i) a vector of job processing times compressions and (ii) a schedule.

Moreover, in scheduling problems with controllable job processing times, two criteria are used to measure the quality of a schedule, namely a scheduling criterion and a cost function measuring the cost of job compression in the evaluated schedule.

The forms of variable job processing times that we consider in the chapter are summarized in Table 6.1.

## 6.1.2 Notation for Variable Job Scheduling Problems

In the section, we introduce several extensions to the three-field notation defined earlier to address agent scheduling problems with variable job processing times.

### 6.1.2.1 Notation for Single-Agent Time-Dependent Job Scheduling Problems

To denote scheduling problems with time-dependent job processing times, in the second field of problem notation we give the form of the functions that describe the processing times.

*Example 6.1.* (a) Symbol $1|p_j = b_j t|\sum C_j$ denotes the single-agent, single-machine time-dependent scheduling problem with proportional processing times of jobs and the objective of minimizing total completion time, $\sum C_j$.

(b) Symbol $1|p_j = a_j + b_j t|C_{\max}$ denotes the single-agent, single-machine time-dependent scheduling problem with linear processing times of jobs and the objective of minimizing the maximum completion time, $C_{\max}$. ◇

**Table 6.1** Summary of main forms of variable job processing times

| Job processing time name | Job processing time form |
|---|---|
| Time-dependent job processing times | |
| Proportional deterioration | $b_j t$ |
| Proportional-linear deterioration | $b_j(a + bt)$ |
| Linear deterioration | $a_j + b_j t$ |
| Proportional-linear shortening | $b_j(a - bt)$ |
| Linear shortening | $a_j - b_j t$ |
| Position-dependent job processing times | |
| Log-linear learning effect | $p_j r^{\alpha}$ |
| Linear learning effect | $p_j - \beta_j r$ |
| Past-sequence-dependent learning effect | $p_j \max\left\{\left(1 + \sum_{k=1}^{r-1} p_{[k]}\right)^{\alpha}, \beta\right\}$ |
| Past-sequence-dependent learning effect | $p_j \left(1 + \sum_{k=1}^{r-1} p_{[k]}\right)^{\beta}$ |
| Past-sequence-dependent learning effect | $p_j \left(\frac{1+\sum_{k=1}^{r-1} p_{[k]}}{1+\sum_{k=1}^{r-1} p_k}\right)^{\alpha}$ |
| Log-linear ageing effect | $r_j r^{\beta}$ |
| Linear ageing effect | $p_j + \beta_j r$ |
| Past-sequence-dependent ageing effect | $p_j \left(1 + \sum_{k=1}^{r-1} p_{[k]}\right)^{\beta}$ |
| Past-sequence-dependent ageing effect | $p_j \left(\frac{1+\sum_{k=1}^{r-1} p_{[k]}}{1+\sum_{k=1}^{r-1} p_k}\right)^{\beta}$ |
| Controllable job processing time | |
| Linear compression | $\overline{p}_j - v_j u_j$ |
| Linear compression | $\overline{p}_j - x_j$ |

If necessary, in the second field of the notation we specify other requirements concerning a given time-dependent scheduling problem.

*Example 6.2.* (a) Symbol $1|p_j = b_j t, s_j = b'_j t, GT|f_{\max}$ denotes the single-agent, single-machine time-dependent batch scheduling problem with proportional job processing times, proportional setup times and the objective of minimizing the maximum cost, $f_{\max}$. Symbol '$GT$' stands for *group technology*, and it means that jobs are partitioned into groups, and jobs in the same group must be processed consecutively, without idle times. A setup time is required when switching between jobs of different groups.

(b) Symbol $1|p_j = a_j + b_j t|\sum w_j C_j + L_{\max}$ denotes the single-agent, single-machine time-dependent scheduling problem with linear processing times and the objective of minimizing the sum of the total weighted completion time and the maximum lateness, $\sum w_j C_j + L_{\max}$. ◇

#### 6.1.2.2 Notation for Single-Agent Position-Dependent Job Scheduling Problems

We denote in a similar way scheduling problems with position-dependent job processing times.

*Example 6.3.* Symbol $1|p_{j,r} = p_j\left(1+\sum_{k=1}^{r-1} p_{[k]}\right)|\sum C_j$ denotes the single-agent, single-machine scheduling problem with past-sequence-dependent ageing effect with $\beta = 1$ and the objective of minimizing the $\sum C_j$. ◇

For clarity, we use different symbols for different forms of position-dependent job processing times. For example, in order to distinguish between different forms of learning and ageing effects, we denote negative and positive exponents appearing in these forms as $\alpha$ and $\beta$, respectively. Thus, in the second field of the three-field notation we do not further specify assumptions on the parameters, which are given in the description of the considered problem.

*Example 6.4.* (a) Symbol $1|p_{j,r} = p_j r^{\beta}|\sum C_j$ denotes the single-agent, single-machine scheduling problem with log-linear ageing effect and the objective of minimizing the $\sum C_j$. Since the positive exponent $\beta$ is specific for the ageing effect, we do not specify in the second field that $\beta > 0$.

(b) Symbol $1|p_{j,r} = p_j r^{\alpha}|C_{\max}$ denotes the single-agent, single-machine scheduling problem with log-linear learning effect and the objective of minimizing the $C_{\max}$. Similarly to the previous case, we omit the assumption $\alpha < 0$, since the negative exponent $\alpha$ is specific for this form of learning effect.

(c) Symbol $1|p_{j,r} = p_j - \beta r|f_{\max}$ denotes the single-agent, single-machine scheduling problem with linear learning effect and the objective of minimizing the $f_{\max}$. Since the coefficient $\beta$ in the form of learning effect is positive, we do not specify in the second field that $0 < \beta < \frac{p_j}{n}$ for $1 \le j \le n$.

(d) Symbol $1|p_{j,r} = p_j\left(1+\sum_{k=1}^{r-1} p_{[k]}\right)^{\beta}|\sum U_j$ denotes the single-agent, single-machine scheduling problem with the past-sequence-dependent ageing effect and the objective of minimizing the $\sum U_j$. As in Examples 6.4 (a), (c), we do not specify in the second field the assumption $\beta > 0$. ◇

#### 6.1.2.3 Notation for Single-Agent Controllable Job Scheduling Problems

We denote scheduling problems with controllable job processing times using similar rules as in the previous two cases.

*Example 6.5.* (a) Symbol $1|p_j = \overline{p}_j - x_j|f_{\max}$ denotes the single-agent, single-machine scheduling problem with linear controllable job processing times and the objective of minimizing the $f_{\max}$.

(b) Symbol $1|p_j = \overline{p}_j - x_j|\sum C_j + \sum c_j x_j$ denotes the single-agent, single-machine scheduling problem with linear controllable job processing times and the objective of minimizing the sum of the total completion time and the total compression cost, $\sum_j C_j + \sum_j c_j x_j$. ◇

#### 6.1.2.4 Notation for Two-Agent Variable Job Scheduling Problems

We extend the notation introduced earlier in the book to denote two-agent scheduling problems with variable job processing times.

For brevity, if jobs of both agents are of the same form and share the same additional requirements, we use the same notation as for single-agent problems. Otherwise, we describe the job characteristics separately.

*Example 6.6.* (a) Symbol $1|p_j = b_j t|\sum w_j^A C_j^A + L_{\max}^B$ denotes the single-machine, two-agent scheduling problem in which *both* agents have proportional time-dependent job processing times and the objective is to minimize the *sum* of the total weighted completion time of jobs of agent $A$ and the maximum lateness of jobs of agent $B$, $\sum w_j^A C_j^A + L_{\max}^A$.

(b) Symbol $1|p_j^A = b_j^A t, p_j^B = a_j^B + b_j^B t|\sum w_j^A C_j^A + L_{\max}^B$ denotes the same problem as the one described in Example 6.6 (a), with the difference that now deteriorating jobs of agent $B$ have linear processing times.

(c) Symbol $1|p_{j,r}^A = p_j^A r^\alpha, p_{j,r}^B = p_j^B r^\beta, \sum U_j^B = 0|\sum T_j^A$ denotes the single-machine, two-agent scheduling problem in which position-dependent jobs of agent $A$ have log-linear job processing times with learning effect, position-dependent jobs of agent $B$ have log-linear job processing times with ageing effect, and the objective of agent $A$ is to minimize the total tardiness, provided that the no job of agent $B$ is tardy ($\varepsilon$-constrained approach). ◇

We use symbol '$\circ$' in the second field of the notation to denote standard circumstances, i.e., if the processing times of jobs are fixed, the jobs are non-preemptable, there are no ready times, deadlines and there are no precedence constraints among the jobs.

*Example 6.7.* Symbol $1|p_j^A = \overline{p}_j^A - x_j^A, r_j^A, d_j^A, pmtn^A, \circ^B|\sum c_j^A x_j^A, f_{\max}^B$ denotes the two-agent single-machine scheduling problems in which the objective of agent $A$ is to minimize the total compression cost, $\sum c_j^A x_j^A$, while the objective of agent $B$ is to minimize the maximum cost, $f_{\max}^B$. Jobs of agent $A$ can be preempted, have linear controllable processing times and possess ready times and deadlines, while jobs of agent $B$ cannot be preempted, have fixed processing times, and possess neither ready times nor deadlines. ◇

### 6.1.3 *Basic Results on Variable Job Scheduling*

In this section, we recall several basic results on scheduling jobs with variable processing times. Since our aim is to compare the difficulty of single- and two-agent scheduling problems of this type, the results can be viewed as special cases of two-agent problems considered in the subsequent sections.

#### 6.1.3.1 Single-Agent Time-Dependent Job Scheduling Problems

The first part of basic results from this group concerns time-dependent proportional job processing times (6.1).

**Theorem 6.1.** (*a*) *Problem* $1|p_j = b_j t|C_{\max}$ *is solvable in* $O(n)$ *time and*

$$C_{\max}(\sigma) = t_0 \prod_{j=1}^{n} \left(1 + b_{[j]}\right) \tag{6.23}$$

*does not depend on schedule* $\sigma$ *for the problem.*

(*b*) *Problem* $1|p_j = b_j t|L_{\max}$ *is solvable in* $O(n \log n)$ *time by scheduling jobs in non-decreasing order of due dates.*

(*c*) *Problem* $1|p_j = b_j t|f_{\max}$ *is solvable in* $O(n^2)$ *time by scheduling jobs using modified algorithm by Lawler (1973).*

(*d*) *Problem* $1|p_j = b_j t|\sum C_j$ *is solvable in* $O(n \log n)$ *time by scheduling jobs in non-decreasing order of deterioration rates and*

$$\sum C_j(\sigma) = t_0 \sum_{j=1}^{n} \prod_{k=1}^{j} \left(1 + b_{[k]}\right). \tag{6.24}$$

(*e*) *Problem* $1|p_j = b_j t|\sum w_j C_j$ *is solvable in* $O(n \log n)$ *time by scheduling jobs in non-decreasing order of* $\frac{b_j}{w_j(1+b_j)}$ *ratios.*

(*f*) *Problem* $1|p_j = b_j t|\sum U_j$ *is solvable in* $O(n \log n)$ *time by scheduling jobs using modified algorithm by Moore (1968).*

Formulae (6.23) and (6.24) can be proved by induction with respect to the number of jobs. Theorem 6.1 (*b*), (*e*) can be proved by a pairwise job interchange argument (Mosheiov 1994) or by using properties of so-called *isomorphic scheduling problems* (Gawiejnowicz and Kononov 2012). The time complexity of problem $1|p_j = b_j t|\sum T_j$ is unknown.

Scheduling problems with time-dependent proportional-linear job processing times (6.2) are not more difficult than those with time-dependent proportional job processing times.

**Theorem 6.2.** (*a*) *Problem* $1|p_j = b_j(a + bt)|C_{\max}$ *is solvable in* $O(n)$ *time and*

$$C_{\max}(\sigma) = \left(t_0 + \frac{a}{b}\right) \prod_{j=1}^{n} \left(1 + b_{[j]} b\right) - \frac{a}{b} \tag{6.25}$$

*does not depend on schedule* $\sigma$ *for the problem.*

(*b*) *Problem* $1|p_j = b_j(a + bt)|L_{\max}$ *is solvable in* $O(n \log n)$ *time by scheduling jobs in non-decreasing order of due dates.*

(*c*) *Problem* $1|p_j = b_j(a+bt)|f_{\max}$ *is solvable in* $O(n^2)$ *time by scheduling jobs using modified algorithm by Lawler (1973).*
(*d*) *Problem* $1|p_j = b_j(a+bt)|\sum C_j$ *is solvable in* $O(n \log n)$ *time by scheduling jobs in non-decreasing order of* $\frac{b_j}{1+b_j b}$ *ratios and*

$$\sum C_j(\sigma) = \left(t_0 + \frac{a}{b}\right) \sum_{j=1}^{n} \prod_{k=1}^{j} \left(1 + b_{[k]}b\right) - \frac{na}{b}. \tag{6.26}$$

(*e*) *Problem* $1|p_j = b_j(a+bt)|\sum w_j C_j$ *is solvable in* $O(n \log n)$ *time by scheduling jobs in non-decreasing order of* $\frac{b_j}{w_j(1+b_j b)}$ *ratios.*
(*f*) *Problem* $1|p_j = b_j(a+bt)|\sum U_j$ *is solvable in* $O(n \log n)$ *time by scheduling jobs using modified algorithm by Moore (1968).*
(*g*) *If* $a = 0$ *and* $b = 1$, *then problem* $1|p_j = b_j(a+bt)|\sum T_j$ *is NP-hard.*

Formulae (6.25) and (6.26) can be proved by induction with respect to the number of jobs. Theorem 6.2 (*b*), (*e*) can be proved by a pairwise job interchange argument (Kononov 1998) or by using properties of mentioned earlier isomorphic scheduling problems (Gawiejnowicz and Kononov 2012). Theorem 6.2 (*d*) follows from Theorem 6.2 (*e*) with $w_j = 1$ for $1 \le j \le n$. Theorem 6.2 (*g*) follows from a result by Du and Leung (1990). The time complexity of problem $1|p_j = b_j(a+bt)|\sum T_j$ is unknown if $a = 0$ and $b = 1$.

Similar results to those of Theorem 6.2 can be obtained also for linear-proportional shortening job processing times (6.4). For example, replacing in (6.25) coefficients $a$ and $b$ by $-b$ and 1, respectively, we obtain the formula

$$C_{\max}(\sigma) = \left(t_0 - \frac{1}{b}\right) \prod_{k=1}^{n} \left(1 - b_{[k]}b\right) + \frac{1}{b} \tag{6.27}$$

for the maximum completion time in problem $1|p_j = b_j(1-bt)|C_{\max}$. This type of mutual relations between a scheduling problem with deteriorating jobs and the corresponding problem with shortening jobs is studied in Gawiejnowicz et al. (2009a), where one can find a transformation between instances of these two classes of time-dependent scheduling problems.

Unlike scheduling problems with time-dependent proportional or time-dependent proportional-linear job processing times, most scheduling problems with time-dependent linear processing times (6.3) are difficult. Only the case of the $C_{\max}$ criterion is easy, while other criteria either lead to NP-hard problems or their time complexity is unknown.

**Theorem 6.3.** (*a*) *Problem* $1|p_j = a_j + b_j t|C_{\max}$ *is solvable in* $O(n \log n)$ *time by scheduling jobs in non-increasing order of ratios* $\frac{b_j}{a_j}$ *and*

$$C_{\max}(\sigma) = \sum_{i=1}^{n} a_{[i]} \prod_{k=i+1}^{n} (1 + b_{[k]}) + t_0 \prod_{i=1}^{n} (1 + b_{[i]}). \qquad (6.28)$$

(*b*1) *Problem* $1|p_j = a_j + b_j t|L_{\max}$ *is NP-hard, even if only one* $a_k \neq 0$ *for some* $1 \leq k \leq n$*, and due dates of all jobs with* $a_j = 0$ *are equal.*
(*b*2) *Problem* $1|p_j = a_j + b_j t|L_{\max}$ *is NP-hard, even if there are only two distinct due dates.*

(*c*) *Problem* $1|p_j = a_j + b_j t|f_{\max}$ *is NP-hard.*
(*d*) *Problem* $1|p_j = a_j + b_j t|\sum w_j C_j$ *is NP-hard.*
(*e*) *Problem* $1|p_j = a_j + b_j t|\sum U_j$ *is NP-hard.*
(*f*) *Problem* $1|p_j = a_j + b_j t|\sum T_j$ *is NP-hard.*

Formula (6.28) can be proved by induction with respect to the number of jobs. Theorem 6.3 ($b1$) can be proved using described below reduction from the following decision problem called SUBSET PRODUCT (Johnson 1982).

> SUBSET PRODUCT
> Instance: A finite set $Y = \{y_1, y_2, \ldots, y_p\}$ of integers and an integer $H$
> Question: Is there a subset $Y' \subseteq Y$ such that
> $$\prod_{y_j \in Y'} y_j = H?$$

The reduction from the SUBSET PRODUCT to the decision version of problem $1|p_j = a_j + b_j t|L_{\max}$ is as follows. We are given $n = p + 1$ jobs to be scheduled on a single machine from time $t_0 = 1$, where $a_0 = 1$, $b_0 = 0$, $d_0 = H + 1$ and $a_j = 0$, $b_j = y_j - 1$, $d_j = \frac{\bar{Y}(H+1)}{H}$ for $1 \leq j \leq p$, with $\bar{Y} = \prod_{j=1}^{p} y_j$. The threshold $G = 0$. To prove Theorem 6.3 ($b1$) it is sufficient to show that the SUBSET PRODUCT problem has a solution if and only if for the above instance of problem $1|p_j = a_j + b_j t|L_{\max}$ there exists a schedule with the maximum lateness not greater than $G$ (Kononov 1997).

Theorem 6.3 ($b2$) can be proved in a similar way using a more complicated reduction from the PARTITION PROBLEM (Bachman and Janiak 2000). Theorem 6.3 ($c$), ($e$) and ($f$) follow from Theorem 6.3 ($b$). The time complexity of problem $1|p_j = a_j + b_j t|\sum C_j$ is unknown, even if $a_j = 1$ for $1 \leq j \leq n$.

Some of the problems mentioned in Theorems 6.1–6.3 are closely related. For example, there exists a mutual relation between problems $1|p_j = a_j + b_j t|C_{\max}$ and $1|p_j = b_j t|\sum C_j$, since by assuming in formula (6.28) that $t_0 = 0$ and $a_{[i]} = 1$ for $1 \leq i \leq n$, we obtain formula (6.24) with $t_0 = 1$. Conversely, by assuming in formula (6.24) that $t_0 = 1$, we obtain formula (6.28) with $t_0 = 0$ and $a_{[i]} = 1$

for $1 \leq i \leq n$. Similar mutual relations between other pairs of time-dependent scheduling problems with deteriorating jobs and consequences of such relations are discussed in Gawiejnowicz et al. (2009b), where one can find a transformation between such pairs of problems.

#### 6.1.3.2 Single-Agent Position-Dependent Job Scheduling Problems

The first group of results in this area concerns position-dependent log-linear job processing times (6.11).

**Theorem 6.4.** (*a*) *Problem* $1|p_{j,r} = p_j r^\alpha|C_{\max}$ *is solvable in* $O(n \log n)$ *time by scheduling jobs in non-decreasing order of* $p_j$ *values and*

$$C_{\max}(\sigma) = t_0 + \sum_{j=1}^{n} \left(p_{[j]} j^\alpha\right). \tag{6.29}$$

(*b*) *If basic job processing times and due dates are* agreeable, *i.e.* $p_i \leq p_j$ *implies* $d_i \geq d_j$ *for* $1 \leq i \neq j \leq n$, *then problem* $1|p_{j,r} = p_j r^\alpha|L_{\max}$ *is solvable in* $O(n \log n)$ *time by scheduling jobs in non-decreasing order of due dates.*

(*c*) *Problem* $1|p_{j,r} = p_j r^\alpha|\sum C_j$ *is solvable in* $O(n \log n)$ *time by scheduling jobs in non-decreasing order of* $p_j$ *values and*

$$\sum_{j=1}^{n} C_j(\sigma) = nt_0 + \sum_{j=1}^{n} (n - j + 1) p_{[j]} j^\alpha. \tag{6.30}$$

(*d*1) *If all basic job processing times are equal, i.e.,* $p_j = p$ *for* $1 \leq j \leq n$, *then problem* $1|p_{j,r} = p_j r^\alpha|\sum w_j C_j$ *is solvable in* $O(n \log n)$ *time by scheduling jobs in non-decreasing order of* $w_j$ *values.*

(*d*2) *If job weights satisfy the equality* $w_j = w p_j$ *for* $1 \leq j \leq n$, *then problem* $1|p_{j,r} = p_j r^\alpha|\sum w_j C_j$ *is solvable in* $O(n \log n)$ *time by scheduling jobs in non-decreasing order of* $p_j$ *values.*

(*d*3) *If basic job processing times and job weights are agreeable, i.e.* $p_i \leq p_j$ *implies* $w_i \geq w_j$ *for* $1 \leq i \neq j \leq n$, *then problem* $1|p_{j,r} = p_j r^\alpha|\sum w_j C_j$ *is solvable in* $O(n \log n)$ *time by scheduling jobs in non-decreasing order of* $\frac{p_j}{w_j}$ *ratios.*

(*e*) *Problem* $1|p_j = p_j r^\alpha|\sum T_j$ *is NP-hard.*

Formulae (6.29) and (6.30) can be proved by induction with respect to the number of jobs. Theorem 6.4 (*e*) follows from the NP-hardness of problem $1||T_{\max}$ (Du and Leung 1990), which is a special case of problem $1|p_j = p_j r^\alpha|\sum T_j$ when $\alpha = 0$. In general, when $\alpha \neq 0$, the time complexity of problem $1|p_{j,r} = p_j r^\alpha|\sum T_j$ is unknown. Similarly, the time complexity of problems $1|p_{j,r} = p_j r^\alpha|L_{\max}$, $1|p_{j,r} =$

$p_j r^{\alpha}|f_{\max}$, $1|p_{j,r} = p_j r^{\alpha}|\sum w_j C_j$ and $1|p_{j,r} = p_j r^{\alpha}|\sum U_j$ without additional assumptions on $\alpha$ is unknown.

Similar results to those of Theorem 6.4 hold also for log-linear ageing effect (6.16), since it differs from log-linear learning effect only by the replacement of the negative exponent $\alpha$ by the positive exponent $\beta$.

The next group of results on position-dependent job processing times concerns linear processing times (6.12) with $\beta_j = \beta$ for $1 \le j \le n$.

**Theorem 6.5.** *(a) Problem $1|p_{j,r} = p_j - \beta r|C_{\max}$ is solvable in $O(n)$ time and*

$$C_{\max}(\sigma) = t_0 + \sum_{j=1}^{n} p_{[j]} - \frac{n(n+1)}{2}\beta \tag{6.31}$$

*does not depend on schedule $\sigma$.*

*(b) Problem $1|p_{j,r} = p_j - \beta r|\sum C_j$ is solvable in $O(n \log n)$ time by scheduling jobs in non-decreasing order of $p_j$ values and*

$$\sum_{j=1}^{n} C_j(\sigma) = nt_0 + \sum_{j=1}^{n}(n-j+1)p_{[j]} - \frac{n(n+1)(n+2)}{6}\beta. \tag{6.32}$$

Formulae (6.31) and (6.32) can be proved by induction with respect to the number of jobs. Counterparts of Theorem 6.5 $(a)$, (b) for job processing times in the form of $p_{j,r} = p_j - \beta_j r$, where $1 \le j \le n$, are given in Bachman and Janiak (2004).

Similar results to those of Theorem 6.5 hold also for the linear ageing effect (6.17), since it differs from the linear learning effect only by the sign before the ageing factor $\beta$.

The last group of results on position-dependent job processing times concerns past-sequence-dependent processing times (6.14).

**Theorem 6.6.** *(a) Problem $1|p_{j,r} = p_j \left(1 + \sum_{k=1}^{r-1} p_{[k]}\right)^{\alpha}|C_{\max}$ is solvable in $O(n \log n)$ time by scheduling jobs in non-decreasing order of $p_j$ values.*

*(b) Problem $1|p_{j,r} = p_j \left(1 + \sum_{k=1}^{r-1} p_{[k]}\right)^{\alpha}|\sum C_j$ is solvable in $O(n \log n)$ time by scheduling jobs in non-decreasing order of $p_j$ values.*

*(c) If basic job processing times and job weights are agreeable as in Theorem 6.4 $(d3)$, then problem $1|p_{j,r} = p_j \left(1 + \sum_{k=1}^{r-1} p_{[k]}\right)^{\alpha}|\sum w_j C_j$ is solvable in $O(n \log n)$ time by scheduling jobs in non-decreasing order of ratios $\frac{p_j}{w_j}$.*

The time complexity of problem $1|p_{j,r} = p_j \left(1 + \sum_{k=1}^{r-1} p_{[k]}\right)^{\alpha}|\sum w_j C_j$ without additional assumptions is unknown. The same concerns the problems $1|p_{j,r} = p_j \left(1 + \sum_{k=1}^{r-1} p_{[k]}\right)^{\alpha}|L_{\max}$ and $1|p_{j,r} = p_j \left(1 + \sum_{k=1}^{r-1} p_{[k]}\right)^{\alpha}|\sum U_j$.

Similar results to those of Theorem 6.6 hold also for position-dependent job processing times in the form of (6.18).

#### 6.1.3.3 Single-Agent Controllable Job Scheduling Problems

In the section, we recall basic results concerning the single-agent single-machine controllable job scheduling problem $1|p_j = \overline{p}_j - x_j|\sum w_j C_j + \sum c_j x_j$.

For the first time the above problem was formulated and studied by Vickson (1980a,b). Recalling that $x_j$ denotes the shortening of job $J_j$, one has the following two properties.

*Property 6.1.* For problem $1|p_j = \overline{p}_j - x_j|\sum w_j C_j + \sum c_j x_j$, there exists an optimal schedule such that for all $1 \leq j \leq n$ either $x_j = 0$ or $x_j = \overline{p}_j$.

*Property 6.2.* In optimal schedule for problem $1|p_j = \overline{p}_j - x_j|\sum w_j C_j + \sum c_j x_j$, jobs are arranged in non-decreasing order of ratios $\frac{p_j}{w_j}$.

The complexity of the problem has been established by Wan et al. (2001).

**Theorem 6.7.** *Problem* $1|p_j = \overline{p}_j - x_j|\sum w_j C_j + \sum c_j x_j$ *is NP-hard.*

The proof of Theorem 6.7 is based on a complex reduction from EVEN-ODD PARTITION problem (Garey and Johnson 1979); we refer the reader to Wan et al. (2001) for details of that proof.

### 6.1.4 *Examples of Variable Job Scheduling Problems*

In this section, we present few examples of scheduling problems with variable job processing times introduced in Sect. 6.1.1, in order to give the reader a deeper insight into the specificity of the problems. Since in all these examples job processing times are described by monotonically increasing or decreasing functions, throughout this section we consider only non-idle sequences.

#### 6.1.4.1 Examples of Time-Dependent Job Scheduling Problems

We first consider two single-agent time-dependent scheduling problems with proportional job processing times (6.1).

*Example 6.8.* The simplest scheduling problems with proportional job processing times (6.1) are problems $1|p_j = b_j t|C_{\max}$ and $1|p_j = b_j t|\sum C_j$.

Consider the following instance of the problem with $n = 3$ jobs and $t_0 = 1$:

| $j$ | 1 | 2 | 3 |
|---|---|---|---|
| $b_j$ | 5 | 2 | 1 |

There exist $3! = 6$ job sequences for this instance, but job processing times are different in different sequences. For example, in sequence $(J_2, J_1, J_3)$ we have $p_2 = 2 \times S_2 = 2 \times 1 = 2$ and $C_2 = 3$, $p_1 = 5 \times S_1 = 5 \times 3 = 15$ and $C_1 = 18$, and $p_3 = 1 \times S_3 = 18$ and $C_3 = 36$, while in sequence $(J_3, J_2, J_1)$ we have $p_3 = 1 \times S_1 = 1 \times 1 = 1$ and $C_1 = 2$, $p_2 = 2 \times S_2 = 2 \times 2 = 4$ and $C_2 = 6$, and $p_1 = 5 \times S_1 = 30$ and $C_1 = 36$.

The list of all sequences for the instance, with corresponding values of job processing times, job completion times, the $C_{\max}$ and $\sum C_j$, are given in the following table.

| Sequence $\sigma$ | $p_{[1]}$ | $C_{[1]}$ | $p_{[2]}$ | $C_{[2]}$ | $p_{[3]}$ | $C_{[3]}$ | $C_{\max}(\sigma)$ | $\sum C_j(\sigma)$ |
|---|---|---|---|---|---|---|---|---|
| $(J_1, J_2, J_3)$ | 5 | 6 | 12 | 18 | 18 | 36 | 36 | 50 |
| $(J_1, J_3, J_2)$ | 5 | 6 | 6 | 12 | 24 | 36 | 36 | 54 |
| $(J_2, J_1, J_3)$ | 2 | 3 | 15 | 18 | 18 | 36 | 36 | 56 |
| $(J_2, J_3, J_1)$ | 2 | 3 | 3 | 6 | 30 | 36 | 36 | 45 |
| $(J_3, J_1, J_2)$ | 1 | 2 | 10 | 12 | 24 | 36 | 36 | 48 |
| $(J_3, J_2, J_1)$ | 1 | 2 | 4 | 6 | 30 | 36 | 36 | 44 |

Notice that the job processing times $p_{[k]}$, where $k = 1, 2, 3$, are different for different sequences $\sigma$. However, as stated by Theorem 6.1 $(a)$ and $(d)$, the maximum completion time $C_{\max}(\sigma)$ is the same for all $\sigma$, while the total completion time $\sum C_j(\sigma)$ depends on $\sigma$. The optimal sequence for the $\sum C_j$ criterion, according to Theorem 6.1 $(d)$, is the sequence $\sigma^\star = (J_3, J_2, J_1)$ with $\sum C_j(\sigma^\star) = 44$. ◇

*Example 6.9.* Another polynomially solvable time-dependent scheduling problem with proportional job processing times (6.1) is problem $1|p_j = b_j t|L_{\max}$.

Consider the following instance of the problem with $n = 3$ jobs and $t_0 = 1$:

| $j$ | 1 | 2 | 3 |
|---|---|---|---|
| $b_j$ | 1 | 3 | 2 |
| $d_j$ | 12 | 4 | 24 |

All possible sequences for the instance, with corresponding values of job processing times, job completion times, job latenesses and the $L_{\max}$, are given in the table below.

| Sequence $\sigma$ | $p_{[1]}$ | $C_{[1]}$ | $L_{[1]}$ | $p_{[2]}$ | $C_{[2]}$ | $L_{[2]}$ | $p_{[3]}$ | $C_{[3]}$ | $L_{[3]}$ | $L_{\max}(\sigma)$ |
|---|---|---|---|---|---|---|---|---|---|---|
| $(J_1, J_2, J_3)$ | 1 | 2 | −10 | 6 | 8 | 4 | 16 | 24 | 0 | 4 |
| $(J_1, J_3, J_2)$ | 1 | 2 | −10 | 4 | 6 | −18 | 18 | 24 | 20 | 20 |
| $(J_2, J_1, J_3)$ | 3 | 4 | 0 | 4 | 8 | −4 | 16 | 24 | 0 | 0 |
| $(J_2, J_3, J_1)$ | 3 | 4 | 0 | 8 | 12 | −12 | 12 | 24 | 12 | 12 |
| $(J_3, J_1, J_2)$ | 2 | 3 | −21 | 3 | 6 | −6 | 18 | 24 | 20 | 20 |
| $(J_3, J_2, J_1)$ | 2 | 3 | −21 | 9 | 12 | 8 | 12 | 24 | 12 | 12 |

The optimal sequence for this instance, according to Theorem 6.1 $(b)$, is $\sigma^\star = (J_2, J_1, J_3)$, with $L_{\max}(\sigma^\star) = 0$. ◇

The next example in the section concerns a single-machine time-dependent scheduling problem with linear job processing times (6.3).

*Example 6.10.* Problem $1|p_j = a_j + b_j t|C_{\max}$ is the only known non-trivial single-agent time-dependent scheduling problem with linear job processing times (6.3) that is solvable in polynomial time.

Consider the following instance of the problem with $n = 3$ jobs and $t_0 = 0$:

| $j$ | 1 | 2 | 3 |
|---|---|---|---|
| $a_j$ | 1 | 2 | 3 |
| $b_j$ | 3 | 1 | 2 |

All possible sequences for the instance, with corresponding values of job processing times, job completion times and the $C_{\max}$, are given in table below.

| Sequence $\sigma$ | $p_{[1]}$ | $C_{[1]}$ | $p_{[2]}$ | $C_{[2]}$ | $p_{[3]}$ | $C_{[3]}$ | $C_{\max}(\sigma)$ |
|---|---|---|---|---|---|---|---|
| $(J_1, J_2, J_3)$ | 1 | 1 | 3 | 4 | 11 | 15 | 15 |
| $(J_1, J_3, J_2)$ | 1 | 1 | 5 | 6 | 8 | 14 | 14 |
| $(J_2, J_1, J_3)$ | 2 | 2 | 7 | 9 | 21 | 30 | 30 |
| $(J_2, J_3, J_1)$ | 2 | 2 | 7 | 9 | 28 | 37 | 37 |
| $(J_3, J_1, J_2)$ | 3 | 3 | 10 | 13 | 15 | 28 | 28 |
| $(J_3, J_2, J_1)$ | 3 | 3 | 5 | 8 | 25 | 33 | 33 |

The optimal sequence for the instance, according to Theorem 6.3 $(a)$, is sequence $\sigma^\star = (J_1, J_3, J_2)$ with $C_{\max}(\sigma^\star) = 14$. ◇

#### 6.1.4.2 Examples of Position-Dependent Job Scheduling Problems

The next example illustrates the computation of position-dependent job processing times with log-linear learning effect (6.11) or ageing effect (6.16).

*Example 6.11.* Position-dependent log-linear job processing times with learning effect (6.11), where $p_{j,r} = p_j r^{\alpha}$ ($\alpha < 0$), and position-dependent log-linear job processing times with ageing effect (6.16), where $p_{j,r} = p_j r^{\beta}$ ($\beta > 0$), are ones of the simplest forms of position-dependent job processing times.

In the first case, we have the following table of job processing times $p_{j,r}$, in which the job processing time in position $j, r$ ($1 \leq j, r \leq n$) is equal to the basic job processing time $p_j$ divided by $r^{|\alpha|}$:

| $r$ | $p_{1,r}$ | $p_{2,r}$ | $p_{3,r}$ | $\ldots$ | $p_{n,r}$ |
|---|---|---|---|---|---|
| 1 | $p_1$ | $p_2$ | $p_3$ | $\ldots$ | $p_n$ |
| 2 | $\frac{p_1}{2^{\lvert\alpha\rvert}}$ | $\frac{p_2}{2^{\lvert\alpha\rvert}}$ | $\frac{p_3}{2^{\lvert\alpha\rvert}}$ | $\ldots$ | $\frac{p_n}{2^{\lvert\alpha\rvert}}$ |
| 3 | $\frac{p_1}{3^{\lvert\alpha\rvert}}$ | $\frac{p_2}{3^{\lvert\alpha\rvert}}$ | $\frac{p_3}{3^{\lvert\alpha\rvert}}$ | $\ldots$ | $\frac{p_n}{3^{\lvert\alpha\rvert}}$ |
| $\ldots$ | $\ldots$ | $\ldots$ | $\ldots$ | $\ldots$ | $\ldots$ |
| $n$ | $\frac{p_1}{n^{\lvert\alpha\rvert}}$ | $\frac{p_2}{n^{\lvert\alpha\rvert}}$ | $\frac{p_3}{n^{\lvert\alpha\rvert}}$ | $\ldots$ | $\frac{p_n}{n^{\lvert\alpha\rvert}}$ |

In the second case, the job processing time in position $j, r$ ($1 \leq j, r \leq n$) is equal to the basic processing time $p_j$ multiplied by $r^{\beta}$:

| $r$ | $p_{1,r}$ | $p_{2,r}$ | $p_{3,r}$ | $\ldots$ | $p_{n,r}$ |
|---|---|---|---|---|---|
| 1 | $p_1$ | $p_2$ | $p_3$ | $\ldots$ | $p_n$ |
| 2 | $p_1 2^{\beta}$ | $p_2 2^{\beta}$ | $p_3 2^{\beta}$ | $\ldots$ | $p_n 2^{\beta}$ |
| 3 | $p_1 3^{\beta}$ | $p_2 3^{\beta}$ | $p_3 3^{\beta}$ | $\ldots$ | $p_n 3^{\beta}$ |
| $\ldots$ | $\ldots$ | $\ldots$ | $\ldots$ | $\ldots$ | $\ldots$ |
| $n$ | $p_1 n^{\beta}$ | $p_2 n^{\beta}$ | $p_3 n^{\beta}$ | $\ldots$ | $p_n n^{\beta}$ |

$\diamond$

Similar tables can be obtained for other forms of position-dependent job processing times. For example, in the case of position-dependent job processing times (6.12) and (6.17), in the above two tables, for any $1 \leq r \leq n$, one should just replace division by $r^{|\alpha|}$ with subtraction of $r\beta$, and multiplication by $r^{\beta}$ with addition of $r\beta$, respectively.

#### 6.1.4.3 Examples of Controllable Job Scheduling Problems

The example below illustrates the computation of controllable job processing times in the form of (6.22).

*Example 6.12.* Consider the following instance of the controllable job scheduling problem $1|p_j = \overline{p}_j - x_j|\sum C_j + \sum c_j x_j$ with $n = 3$ jobs and $t_0 = 0$:

| $j$ | 1 | 2 | 3 |
|---|---|---|---|
| $\overline{p}_j$ | 2 | 1 | 3 |
| $c_j$ | 1 | 3 | 2 |

Consider first the case when all jobs have been crashed by 50 %, i.e. when $x_1 = 1$, $x_2 = \frac{1}{2}$ and $x_3 = \frac{3}{2}$. Then, job processing times, job completion times and the values of the $\sum C_j + \sum c_j x_j$ criterion for all possible sequences are as follows:

| Sequence $\sigma$ | $p_{[1]}$ | $C_{[1]}$ | $p_{[2]}$ | $C_{[2]}$ | $p_{[3]}$ | $C_{[3]}$ | $\sum C_j(\sigma) + \sum c_j x_j(\sigma)$ |
|---|---|---|---|---|---|---|---|
| $(J_1, J_2, J_3)$ | 1 | 1 | $\frac{1}{2}$ | $\frac{3}{2}$ | $\frac{3}{2}$ | 3 | 11 |
| $(J_1, J_3, J_2)$ | 1 | 1 | $\frac{3}{2}$ | $\frac{5}{2}$ | $\frac{1}{2}$ | 3 | 12 |
| $(J_2, J_1, J_3)$ | $\frac{1}{2}$ | $\frac{1}{2}$ | 1 | $\frac{3}{2}$ | $\frac{3}{2}$ | 3 | $\frac{21}{2}$ |
| $(J_2, J_3, J_1)$ | $\frac{1}{2}$ | $\frac{1}{2}$ | $\frac{3}{2}$ | 2 | 1 | 3 | 11 |
| $(J_3, J_1, J_2)$ | $\frac{3}{2}$ | $\frac{3}{2}$ | 1 | $\frac{5}{2}$ | $\frac{1}{2}$ | 3 | $\frac{25}{2}$ |
| $(J_3, J_2, J_1)$ | $\frac{3}{2}$ | $\frac{3}{2}$ | $\frac{1}{2}$ | 2 | 1 | 3 | 12 |

Notice that if jobs are not compressed at all, i.e. when $x_1 = x_2 = x_3 = 0$, sequence $(J_2, J_1, J_3)$ yields the minimum total completion time (equal to 10).

If all jobs are crashed by 50 %, i.e., when $x_1 = 1$, $x_2 = \frac{1}{2}$ and $x_3 = \frac{3}{2}$, the minimum value of the objective $\sum C_j(\sigma) + \sum c_j x_j(\sigma)$ is attained with two sequences, $(J_1, J_2, J_3)$ and $(J_2, J_3, J_1)$.

If all jobs have been crashed by 75 %, i.e., when $x_1 = \frac{3}{2}$, $x_2 = \frac{3}{4}$ and $x_3 = \frac{9}{4}$, the values of job processing times, job completion times and the $\sum C_j + \sum c_j x_j$ criterion for all possible sequences for the instance are as follows:

| Sequence $\sigma$ | $p_{[1]}$ | $C_{[1]}$ | $p_{[2]}$ | $C_{[2]}$ | $p_{[3]}$ | $C_{[3]}$ | $\sum C_j(\sigma) + \sum c_j x_j$ |
|---|---|---|---|---|---|---|---|
| $(J_1, J_2, J_3)$ | $\frac{1}{2}$ | $\frac{1}{2}$ | $\frac{1}{4}$ | $\frac{3}{4}$ | $\frac{3}{4}$ | $\frac{3}{2}$ | 11 |
| $(J_1, J_3, J_2)$ | $\frac{1}{2}$ | $\frac{1}{2}$ | $\frac{3}{4}$ | $\frac{5}{4}$ | $\frac{1}{4}$ | $\frac{3}{2}$ | $\frac{23}{2}$ |
| $(J_2, J_1, J_3)$ | $\frac{1}{4}$ | $\frac{1}{4}$ | $\frac{1}{2}$ | $\frac{3}{4}$ | $\frac{3}{4}$ | $\frac{3}{2}$ | $\frac{43}{4}$ |
| $(J_2, J_3, J_1)$ | $\frac{1}{4}$ | $\frac{1}{4}$ | $\frac{3}{4}$ | 1 | $\frac{1}{2}$ | $\frac{3}{2}$ | 11 |
| $(J_3, J_1, J_2)$ | $\frac{3}{4}$ | $\frac{3}{4}$ | $\frac{1}{2}$ | $\frac{5}{4}$ | $\frac{1}{4}$ | $\frac{3}{2}$ | $\frac{47}{4}$ |
| $(J_3, J_2, J_1)$ | $\frac{3}{4}$ | $\frac{3}{4}$ | $\frac{1}{4}$ | 1 | $\frac{1}{2}$ | $\frac{3}{2}$ | $\frac{23}{2}$ |

As one can observe, the minimum value of the $\sum C_j(\sigma) + \sum c_j x_j$ criterion is equal to $\frac{43}{4}$, attained for sequence $(J_2, J_1, J_3)$. ◇

#### 6.1.4.4 Example of a Two-Agent Variable Job Scheduling Problem

We complete this section with an example of a two-agent single-machine scheduling problem with variable job processing times.

*Example 6.13.* Consider the $\varepsilon$-constraint approach to the two-agent single-machine scheduling problem with time-dependent proportional job processing times, i.e., problem $1|p_j = b_j t, C^B_{\max} \leq Q|L^A_{\max}$. The aim is to find a schedule such that the schedule minimizes the maximum lateness $L^A_{\max}$ for agent $A$, provided that the maximum completion time $C^B_{\max}$ for agent $B$ does not exceed a given upper bound $Q \geq 0$.

Let us consider the following instance of the problem: $t_0 = 1, n_A = 2, n_B = 1$, $p^A_1 = t$, $d^A_1 = 6$, $p^A_2 = 2t$, $d^A_2 = 12$, $p^B_1 = 3t$.

All possible sequences for this instance, along with job completion times and the values of $L^A_{\max}$ and $C^B_{\max}$, are given in table below.

| Sequence $\sigma$ | $p_{[1]}$ | $C_{[1]}$ | $p_{[2]}$ | $C_{[2]}$ | $p_{[3]}$ | $C_{[3]}$ | $L^A_{\max}(\sigma)$ | $C^B_{\max}(\sigma)$ |
|---|---|---|---|---|---|---|---|---|
| $(J^A_1, J^A_2, J^B_1)$ | 1 | 2 | 4 | 6 | 18 | 24 | 12 | 6 |
| $(J^A_1, J^B_1, J^A_2)$ | 1 | 2 | 6 | 8 | 16 | 24 | −4 | 24 |
| $(J^A_2, J^A_1, J^B_1)$ | 2 | 3 | 3 | 6 | 18 | 24 | 12 | 3 |
| $(J^A_2, J^B_1, J^A_1)$ | 2 | 3 | 9 | 12 | 12 | 24 | 18 | 3 |
| $(J^B_1, J^A_1, J^A_2)$ | 3 | 4 | 4 | 8 | 16 | 24 | 2 | 24 |
| $(J^B_1, J^A_2, J^A_1)$ | 3 | 4 | 8 | 12 | 12 | 24 | 18 | 12 |

Notice that in all schedules corresponding to sequences from the table we have $C_{[3]} = 24$, since by Theorem 6.1 $(a)$ the value of $C_{\max}$ does not depend on schedule of time-dependent proportional jobs.

Notice also that different values of $Q$ may or may not be restrictive. For example, if $Q < 3$ then no schedule is feasible; if $3 \leq Q \leq 6$ then three schedules are feasible and two of them, $(J^A_1, J^A_2, J^B_1)$ and $(J^A_2, J^A_1, J^B_1)$, are optimal; if $Q \geq 24$ then all schedules are feasible but only one, $(J^A_1, J^B_1, J^A_2)$, is optimal. ◇

This example ends the introductory part of the chapter. In the next three sections we give a systematic presentation of agent scheduling problems with variable job processing times defined in Sect. 6.1.1.

Coherently with the notation in the rest of the book, we denote start time and completion time of job $J_i$ in a schedule $\sigma$ by $S_i(\sigma)$ and $C_i(\sigma)$, respectively.

Moreover, given two jobs $J_i$ and $J_j$, we will often denote by $\sigma$ and $\sigma'$ two schedules such that job $J_i$ immediately precedes job $J_j$ in $\sigma$, $J_j$ immediately precedes job $J_i$ in $\sigma'$ and the rest of the schedule is the same in $\sigma$ and $\sigma'$, i.e.

$$\sigma : \ldots, J_i, J_j, \ldots$$

$$\sigma' : \ldots, J_j, J_i, \ldots$$

Finally, by $x_{(i)}$ we denote the $i$th element of a non-decreasingly sorted sequence $x_1, x_2, \ldots, x_k$, i.e., $x_{(1)} \leq x_{(2)} \leq \ldots x_{(i)} \leq \cdots \leq x_{(k)}$.

## 6.2 Two-Agent Time-Dependent Job Scheduling Problems

In this section, we give a detailed presentation of the two-agent scheduling problems with variable job processing times described in Sect. 6.1.1.

### 6.2.1 *Proportional Deteriorating Job Processing Times*

In the section, we consider two-agent time-dependent scheduling problems with proportional deteriorating job processing times (6.1).

#### 6.2.1.1 $1|CO, p_j = b_j t, C^B_{\max} \leq Q|L^A_{\max}$

In problem $1|CO, p_j = b_j t,\ C^B_{\max} \leq Q|L^A_{\max}$ one has to find a schedule such that the maximum lateness $L^A_{\max}$ for jobs of agent $A$ is minimal, provided that the maximum completion time $C^B_{\max}$ for jobs of agent $B$ does not exceed a given upper bound $Q \geq 0$. The problem has been considered in Liu and Tang (2008), and it is a time-dependent counterpart of the two-agent scheduling problem with fixed job processing times, $1|CO, C^B_{\max} \leq Q|L^A_{\max}$. Time-dependent proportional job processing times are in the form of (6.1).

An optimal algorithm for the problem is based on the following properties.

*Property 6.3.* An optimal schedule for problem $1|CO, p_j = b_j t, C^B_{\max} \leq Q|L^A_{\max}$ is a non-idle schedule.

The property holds, since both criteria $L^A_{\max}$ and $C^B_{\max}$ are regular.

*Property 6.4.* Given an instance of $1|CO, p_j = b_j t, C^B_{\max} \leq Q|L^A_{\max}$, the maximum completion time for agent $B$ is given by formula (6.23) and the value does not depend on schedule.

The property follows from Theorem 6.1 $(a)$.

*Property 6.5.* For problem $1|CO, p_j = b_j t, C^B_{\max} \leq Q|L^A_{\max}$, there exists an optimal schedule in which the jobs of agent $A$ are scheduled in non-decreasing order of due dates.

The property follows from Theorem 6.1 $(b)$.

*Property 6.6.* For problem $1|CO, p_j = b_j t, C^B_{\max} \leq Q|L^A_{\max}$, there exists an optimal schedule in which jobs of agent $B$ are scheduled consecutively in a single block.

The property can be proved by a pairwise job interchange argument. In view of this property, we can replace all jobs of $\mathcal{J}^B$ by a single artificial job $J_B$.

The main idea of an optimal algorithm for problem $1|CO, p_j = b_j t,\ C^B_{\max} \leq Q|L^A_{\max}$, based on Properties 6.3–6.6, is as follows. We arrange the jobs of $\mathcal{J}^A$ in

**Algorithm 39** for problem $1|CO, p_j = b_j t, C^B_{\max} \leq Q|L^A_{\max}$

1: $u := t_0 \prod_j (1 + b^A_{[j]}) \prod_j (1 + b^B_{[j]})$<br>
2: Arrange all jobs of agent $A$ in non-decreasing order of due dates $d^A_i$<br>
3: Create artificial job $J_B$ composed of all jobs of agent $B$<br>
4: **for** $i := n_A + 1$ **downto** 1 **do**<br>
5:     Create schedule $\sigma$ of all jobs of agent $A$ in which job $J_B$ is in position $i$<br>
6:     **if** $C_{J_B}(\sigma) \leq Q$ **then**<br>
7:         **return** $\sigma$<br>
8:     **end if**<br>
9: **end for**<br>
10: **return** 'Input instance is not feasible'

non-decreasing order of their due dates and create the artificial job $J_B$. Next, at each iteration, we schedule the job $J_B$ in a given position, starting from position $n_A + 1$, and check whether the completion time of job $J_B$ does not exceed the upper bound $Q$. If so, we return the schedule; otherwise, we decrease the position of $J_B$ by one and pass to the next iteration.

The pseudocode of the algorithm is presented above (see Algorithm 39).

**Theorem 6.8.** *Algorithm 39 generates an optimal schedule for problem $1|CO, p_j = b_j t, C^B_{\max} \leq Q|L^A_{\max}$ in $O(n_A \log n_A + n_A n_B)$ time.*

*Proof.* The correctness of Algorithm 39 follows from Properties 6.3–6.6. Lines 1, 2 and 3 need $O(n_A + n_B)$, $O(n_A \log n_A)$ and $O(n_B)$ time, respectively. Loop **for** in lines 4–9 is performed $O(n_A)$ times, and the creation of schedule $\sigma$ in line 5 needs $O(n_A + n_B)$ time, while checking the condition in sentence **if** in line 6 can be done in a constant time if we remember the results of the previous iteration. Therefore, the overall running time of Algorithm 39 is equal to $n_A + n_B + n_A \log n_A + n_A n_B = O(n_A \log n_A + n_A n_B)$. □

#### 6.2.1.2 $1|CO, p_j = b_j t, f^B_{\max} \leq Q|\sum C^A_j$

We next address problem $1|CO, p_j = b_j t, f^B_{\max} \leq Q|\sum C^A_j$. This problem has been considered by Liu and Tang (2008) and it is a time-dependent counterpart of the two-agent scheduling problem with fixed job processing times, $1|CO, f^B_{\max} \leq Q|\sum C^A_j$. Time-dependent proportional job processing times are in the form of (6.1).

Hereafter we assume that the cost functions $f^B_i$ of jobs of $\mathcal{J}^B$ are regular, and their values can be computed in a constant time.

An optimal algorithm for problem $1|CO, p_j = b_j t, f^B_{\max} \leq Q|\sum C^A_j$ is based on Properties 6.3–6.4, which still hold for the problem, and the following two new properties. Let $u$ be defined as in Algorithm 39.

*Property 6.7.* If, in a feasible instance of problem $1|CO, p_j = b_j t, f^B_{\max} \leq Q|\sum C^A_j$, there is a job $J^B_k \in \mathcal{J}^B$ such that $f^B_k(u) \leq Q$, then there exists an optimal schedule for the instance in which job $J^B_k$ is scheduled in the last position, and there is no optimal schedule in which a job of $\mathcal{J}^A$ is scheduled in the last position.

The property can be proved by contradiction.

*Property 6.8.* If, in a feasible instance of problem $1|CO, p_j = b_j t, f^B_{\max} \leq Q|\sum C^A_j$, for all jobs $J^B_k \in \mathcal{J}^B$ it holds $f^B_k(u) > Q$, then in any optimal schedule the job $J^A_l \in \mathcal{J}^A$ having largest deterioration rate is scheduled in the last position.

The property can be proved by a pairwise job interchange argument.

Properties 6.7–6.8 imply that in any optimal schedule for problem $1|CO, p_j = b_j t, f^B_{\max} \leq Q|\sum C^A_j$, jobs of $\mathcal{J}^A$ are arranged in non-decreasing order of their deterioration rates. Similarly as in Chap. 3, given a value of $Q$, for each job $J^B_j$ one can define a *'deadline'* $D^B_i$ such that $f^B_i(C^B_i) \leq Q$ if $C^B_i \leq D^B_i$ and $f^B_i(C^B_i) > Q$ otherwise. Each $D^B_i$ can be computed in constant time if the inverse functions $f^{B^{-1}}_i$ are available, otherwise it requires $O(\log n_B)$ time.

The main idea of the algorithm for problem $1|CO, p_j = b_j t, f^B_{\max} \leq Q|\sum C^A_j$ is as follows. At each iteration, we select an unscheduled job to be scheduled in the last position. If it is possible, we select a job of agent $B$, otherwise we select a job of agent $A$ having largest deterioration rate. If all jobs of agent $A$ have already been scheduled, and no job of agent $B$ can be feasibly scheduled in the current last position, the instance is infeasible.

The pseudocode of the algorithm is presented below (see Algorithm 40).

**Theorem 6.9.** *Algorithm 40 generates an optimal schedule for problem* $1|CO, p_j = b_j t, f^B_{\max} \leq Q|\sum C^A_j$ *in* $O(n_A \log n_A + n_B \log n_B)$ *time.*

*Proof.* The correctness of Algorithm 40 follows from Properties 6.3–6.4 and 6.7–6.8. Line 1 and 2 both need $O(n_A + n_B)$ time. Line 3 and 4 need $O(n_A \log n_A)$ and $O(n_B \log n_B)$ time, respectively. Loop **while** in lines 6–19 is performed $n_A + n_B$ times, and each its iteration needs a constant time, since there is selected only a single job. Hence, the overall running time of Algorithm 40 is $O(n_A \log n_A + n_A \log n_A)$. □

#### 6.2.1.3 $1|CO, p_j = b_j t, \sum U^B_j = 0|\sum T^A_j$

We next consider the problem of minimizing the total tardiness $\sum T^A_j$ of jobs of agent $A$, given that no job of agent $B$ is tardy. Time-dependent proportional job processing times are in the form of (6.1).

For this problem, Gawiejnowicz et al. (2011) proposed a branch-and-bound algorithm based on Properties 6.9–6.12 given below.

**Algorithm 40** for problem $1|CO, p_j = b_j t, f^B_{\max} \leq Q|\sum C^A_j$

$J := \mathcal{J}^A \cup \mathcal{J}^B$
$u := t_0 \prod_j (1 + b^A_{[j]}) \prod_j (1 + b^B_{[j]})$
Arrange all agent $A$ jobs in non-decreasing order of deterioration rates $b^A_i$
Arrange all agent $B$ jobs in non-decreasing order of 'deadlines' $D^A_i$
$\sigma := \emptyset$
**while** there exist in $J$ unscheduled jobs **do**
  **if** there exists job $J^B_k \in \mathcal{J}^B$ such that $f^B_k(u) \leq Q$ **then**
    $J_{sel} := J^B_k$
  **else**
    **if** all agent $B$ jobs have been scheduled **then**
      **return** 'Input instance is infeasible'
    **else**
      $J_{sel} :=$ agent $A$ job with the largest deterioration rate
    **end if**
  **end if**
  Schedule job $J_{sel}$ in the last position in $\sigma$
  $J := J \setminus \{J_{sel}\}$
  $u := \frac{u}{1+b_{sel}}$
**end while**
**return** $\sigma$

Property 6.9 gives conditions under which a schedule $\sigma$ dominates $\sigma'$, i.e. when $\sum_j T^A_j(\sigma) \leq \sum_j T^A_j(\sigma')$.

*Property 6.9.* Let $B_i := 1 + b_i$, $B_j := 1 + b_j$ and $B_{ij} = B_{ji} := (1 + b_i)(1 + b_j)$. Schedule $\sigma$ dominates schedule $\sigma'$ if *any* of the following holds:

(*a*) $J_i \in \mathcal{J}^A$ and $J_j \in \mathcal{J}^A$ are such that $B_{ij}t < d_j$;
(*b*) $J_i \in \mathcal{J}^A$ and $J_j \in \mathcal{J}^A$ are such that $B_i t \geq d_i$, $B_j t \geq d_j$ and $b_i < b_j$;
(*c*) $J_i \in \mathcal{J}^B$ and $J_j \in \mathcal{J}^A$ are such that $B_{ij}t \geq d_j$;
(*d*) $J_i \in \mathcal{J}^B$ and $J_j \in \mathcal{J}^A$ are such that $B_i t \geq d_i$ and $B_{ji}t \geq d_i$ or
(*e*) $J_i \in \mathcal{J}^B$ and $J_j \in \mathcal{J}^B$ are such that $B_i t \geq d_i$, $B_{ij}t \geq d_j$.

Property 6.9 can be proved by a pairwise job interchange argument.

The next two results, Property 6.10 and 6.11, allow to determine a sequence of unscheduled jobs and the feasibility of a given schedule, and are used to speed up the search of the tree of all possible schedules. Proofs of these properties follow from definitions of schedule dominance and feasibility.

Let $\pi$ denote a sequence of unscheduled jobs. Also, let $(\pi, [k+1], \ldots, [n])$ be the schedule in which the order of the last $n-k$ jobs has been determined backwards and $(\pi^{\nearrow}, [k+1], \ldots, [n])$ be the schedule in which unscheduled jobs are arranged in non-decreasing order of due dates.

*Property 6.10.* If in sequence $\pi^{\nearrow}$ there are no tardy jobs, then schedule $(\pi^{\nearrow}, [k+1], \ldots, [n])$ dominates any schedule in the form of $(\pi, [k+1], \ldots, [n])$.

**Algorithm 41** for problem $1|CO, p_j = b_j t, \sum U_j^B = 0|\sum T_j^A$

1: Create base population $P_0$
2: Evaluate $P_0$
3: **while** does not hold stop condition **do**
4: Create temporary population $T_i$ by using a preselection operator to $P_i$
5: Create offspring population $O_i$ by using crossing and mutation operators to $T_i$
6: Evaluate $O_i$
7: Create a new population $P_{i+1}$ by using a postselection operator to $P_i$ and $O_i$
8: **end while**
9: **return** the best solution in $P_i$

*Property 6.11.* If agent $B$ job $J_{[i]}$ is such that $t_0 \prod_{j \in \pi}(1 + b_j) \prod_{j=k+1}^{i}(1 + b_{[j]}) \geq d_{[i]}$ for $k + 1 \leq i \leq n$, then $(\pi, [k + 1], \ldots, [n])$ is not a feasible schedule.

The next result, Property 6.12, gives a lower bound on the total tardiness for jobs in $\mathcal{J}^A$. Let $\sigma = (\pi, [k+1], \ldots, [n])$ denote a schedule in which the order of the last $n - k$ jobs has been determined backwards, and assume that among the unscheduled jobs there are $k_A$ jobs from $\mathcal{J}^A$ and $k_B$ jobs from $\mathcal{J}^B$, where $k_A + k_A = k$.

*Property 6.12.* Given $\sigma = (\pi, [k + 1], \ldots, [n])$, then

$$\sum T_j^A(\pi) \geq \sum_{i=1}^{k_A} \max\left\{C_{(i)}^A(\pi) - d_{(i)}^A, 0\right\}$$

and

$$\sum T_j^A(\sigma) \geq \sum_{i=1}^{k_A} \max\left\{C_{(i)}^A(\sigma) - d_{(i)}^A, 0\right\} + \sum_{k_A+1 \leq i \leq k, J_{[i]} \in \mathcal{J}^A} T_{[i]}^A(\sigma).$$

*Proof.* Since $C_{[j]}(\sigma) = t_0 \prod_{i=1}^{j}(1 + b_{[i]}) \geq t_0 \prod_{i=1}^{j}(1 + b_{(i)})$ for $1 \leq j \leq k$, $t_0 \prod_{i=1}^{j}(1 + b_{(i)})$ is a lower bound on the completion time of job $J_{[j]}$ in $\sigma$. Moreover, since the jobs of agent $B$ cannot be tardy, we should complete the jobs in $\mathcal{J}^B$ as late as possible but before their due dates. We can do this by checking whether the completion time of a given job does not exceed its deadline and if so, putting the job in a right place in a schedule. Repeating this procedure a number of times, we obtain the given two bounds. □

For this problem, the same authors proposed a genetic algorithm, using the *TEAC* library developed by Gawiejnowicz et al. (2006). In this algorithm, implemented in C#, the operator of mutation was called with probability 0.02, the operator of crossing was called with probability 0.80, the size of the offspring population was equal to 50 individuals, and tournament preselection (with tournament size equal to 5) and random postselection have been used. The stop condition was passing 100 generations. The pseudocode of the algorithm is given above (see Alg. 41).

#### 6.2.1.4 $1|CO, p_j = b_j t, s_j = b'_j t, GT, f^B_{\max} \le Q|\sum C^A_j$

This batch scheduling problem, considered by Liu et al. (2010a), is an immediate extension of the problem presented in Sect. 6.2.1.2.

Compared to the latter case, where all jobs belong to the same group, now jobs are divided into a number of distinct groups, each group corresponds to a batch, and a sequence-dependent setup time is needed between jobs from different groups. Both time-dependent proportional job processing times and setup times are in the form of (6.1). The aim is to find a schedule of batches and to schedule jobs in each batch.

Problem $1|CO, p_j = b_j t, s_j = b'_j t, GT, f^B_{\max} \le Q|\sum C^A_j$ is not more difficult than problem $1|CO, p_j = b_j t, f^B_{\max} \le Q|\sum C^A_j$, since it can still be solved in $O(n_A \log n_A + n_B \log n_B)$ time by modifying the algorithm for the latter problem presented in Sect. 6.2.1.2.

### 6.2.2 *Proportional-Linear Deteriorating Job Processing Times*

In the section, we consider two-agent time-dependent scheduling problems with proportional-linear deteriorating job processing times (6.2).

#### 6.2.2.1 $1|CO, p_j = b_j(a + bt), C^B_{\max} \le Q|L^A_{\max}$ and $1|CO, p_j = b_j(a + bt), f^B_{\max} \le Q|\sum C^A_j$

Both the problems, $1|CO, p_j = b_j(a + bt), C^B_{\max} \le Q|L^A_{\max}$ and $1|CO, p_j = b_j(a + bt), f^B_{\max} \le Q|\sum C^A_j$, considered by Liu et al. (2011), are straightforward extensions of problems presented in Sects. 6.2.1.1 and 6.2.1.2, respectively. Time-dependent proportional-linear job processing times are in the form of (6.2).

The replacement of proportional job processing times (6.1) by proportional-linear job processing times (6.2) does not increase the time complexity of these problems. Moreover, algorithms for these two problems are based on the same properties and have almost the same form as their counterparts for proportional job processing times. As implied by Theorems 6.1 ($a$) and 6.2 ($a$), the only minor differences concern formulae for computing the values of $u$ and $C_{\max}$.

#### 6.2.2.2 $1|CO, p_j = b_j(a + bt), s_j = b'_j(a' + b't), GT, f^B_{\max} \le Q|\sum C^A_j$

This problem, considered by Liu et al. (2010a), is a similar extension of problem $1|CO, p_j = b_j t, f^B_{\max} \le Q|\sum C^A_j$ as the one presented in Sect. 6.2.1.4. Time-dependent proportional-linear job processing times and setup times are in the form of (6.2).

The new problem, $1|CO, p_j = b_j(a + bt), s_j = b'_j(a' + b't), GT, f^B_{\max} \leq Q|\sum C^A_j$, can be solved in $O(n_A \log n_A + n_B \log n_B)$ time using a modified version of the algorithm for problem $1|CO, p_j = b_j t, s_j = b'_j t, f^B_{\max} \leq Q|\sum C^A_j$ discussed in Sect. 6.2.1.4.

### 6.2.3 Linear Deteriorating Job Processing Times

In the section, we consider two-agent time-dependent scheduling problems with linear deteriorating job processing times (6.3).

#### 6.2.3.1 $1|CO, p_j = a_j + bt, \sum U^B_j = 0|\sum w^A_j C^A_j$

In problem $1|CO, p_j = a_j + bt, \sum U^B_j = 0|\sum w^A_j C^A_j$, similarly to Sect. 6.2.1.3, the jobs of $\mathcal{J}^B$ are constrained to be performed within their due dates, but now agent $A$ wants to minimize the total weighted completion time. This problem has been considered by Lee et al. (2010). Time-dependent linear job processing times are in the form of (6.3) with a common deterioration rate, $b_j = b$ for all jobs. Notice that the strong NP-hardness of this problem is implied by that of problem $1|CO, \sum U^B_j = 0|\sum w^A_j C^A_j$ considered in Chap. 3.

In Lee et al. (2010), the authors proposed for this problem a branch-and-bound algorithm based on the following result.

*Property 6.13.* Let $P_i := a_i + bt$, $P_j := a_j + bt$ and $P_{ij} := a_i(1+b) + (1+b)^2 t$. Schedule $\sigma$ dominates schedule $\sigma'$ if *any* of the following holds:

(*a*) $J_i \in \mathcal{J}^A$ and $J_j \in \mathcal{J}^A$ are such that $w_j P_i < w_i P_j$ and $a_i \leq a_j$;
(*b*) $J_i \in \mathcal{J}^A$ and $J_j \in \mathcal{J}^B$ are such that $P_{ij} + a_j < d_j$ and $a_i < a_j$;
(*c*) $J_i \in \mathcal{J}^A$ and $J_j \in \mathcal{J}^A$ are such that $(1 + b)t + a_i \leq d_i$, $P_{ij} + a_j \leq d_j$ and $a_i < a_j$.

Property 6.13 can be proved by a pairwise job interchange argument.

Note that, given a schedule $\sigma$, its feasibility can be checked by verifying whether there exists a job $J^B_j$ such that $S^B_j(\sigma)(1 + b) + a^B_j > d^B_j$. If such a job exists, then $\sigma$ is not feasible.

As a lower bound of the total weighted completion time of a schedule $\sigma$ in which the order of the first $k$ jobs have been determined and in the set of unscheduled jobs there are $k_A$ jobs of agent $A$ and $k_B$ jobs of agent $B$, $k_A + k_B = n - k$, Lee et al. (2010) apply the value

$$\sum_{1 \leq i \leq k, J_{[i]} \in \mathcal{J}^A} w_{[i]} C_{[i]}(\sigma) + LB_{US}, \tag{6.33}$$

where $LB_{US}$ is calculated as follows (see Algorithm 42).

**Algorithm 42** for calculation lower bound $LB_{US}$ for problem $1|CO, p_j = a_j + bt, \sum U_j^B = 0|\sum w_j^A C_j^A$

**for** $j := 1$ **to** $n - k$ **do**
  $\hat{C}_{[k+j]} := C_{[k]}(1+b)^j + \sum_{i=1}^{j} a_{(k+i)}(1+b)^{j-i}$
**end for**
Arrange all jobs of agent $A$ in non-decreasing order of weights $w_i^A$
Arrange all jobs of agent $B$ in non-decreasing order of due dates $d_i^B$
$ic := 0$
$ia := n_A$
$ib := n_B$
**while** $ic \geq n - k$ **do**
  $LB_{US} := \sum_{j=1}^{n_A} w_{(n_A-j+1)}^A C_{(j)}^A$
  **if** $\hat{C}_{[n-k]} \leq d_{(ib)}^B$ **then**
    $C_{(ib)}^B := \hat{C}_{[n-ic]}$
    $ib := ib - 1$
  **else**
    $C_{(ia)}^A := \hat{C}_{[n-k]}$
    $ia := ia - 1$
  **end if**
  $ic := ic + 1$
**end while**
**return** $LB_{US}$

The authors also use three $O(n^2)$ heuristics that construct initial suboptimal schedules for the considered exact algorithm.

#### 6.2.3.2 $1|CO, p_j = a_j + bt, L_{\max}^B \leq Q|\sum w_j^A U_j^A$

This problem has been considered by Wu et al. (2013b). Jobs have time-dependent linear processing times of the same form as those in Sect. 6.2.3.1.

Similarly as for the problems considered in Sect. 6.2.3.1, also for problem $1|CO, p_j = a_j + bt, L_{\max}^B \leq Q|\sum w_j^A U_j^A$ a branch-and-bound algorithm has been proposed, based on the following result.

*Property 6.14.* Let $P_i := a_i + (1+b)t$, $P_j := a_j + (1+b)t$, $P_{ij} := a_j + a_i(1+b) + (1+b)^2 t$ and $P_{ji} := a_i + a_j(1+b) + (1+b)^2 t$. Schedule $\sigma$ dominates schedule $\sigma'$ if *any* of the following holds:

($a$) $J_i \in \mathcal{J}^A$ and $J_j \in \mathcal{J}^A$ are such that $P_{ji} > d_i \geq P_i$, $a_i \leq a_j$ and $P_{ij} \leq d_j$;
($b$) $J_i \in \mathcal{J}^A$ and $J_j \in \mathcal{J}^B$ are such that $P_j > d_j$, $P_{ji} > d_i \geq P_i$ and $a_i \leq a_j$;
($c$) $J_i \in \mathcal{J}^A$ and $J_j \in \mathcal{J}^A$ are such that $P_{ij} > d_j \geq P_j$, $P_{ji} > d_i \geq P_i$, $w_i > w_j$ and $a_i < a_j$;
($d$) $J_i \in \mathcal{J}^A$ and $J_j \in \mathcal{J}^A$ are such that $P_j > d_j$, $P_i < d_i$ and $a_i < a_j$;
($e$) $J_i \in \mathcal{J}^A$ and $J_j \in \mathcal{J}^A$ are such that $P_{ij} \leq d_j$, $P_{ji} \leq d_i$ and $a_i < a_j$;
($f$) $J_i \in \mathcal{J}^B$ and $J_j \in \mathcal{J}^B$ are such that $P_i - d_i \leq Q < P_{ji} - d_i$ and $P_{ij} - d_j \leq Q$;

(g) $J_i \in \mathcal{J}^B$ and $J_j \in \mathcal{J}^B$ are such that $P_{ji} - d_i \le Q$, $P_{ij} - d_j \le Q$ and $a_i < a_j$;
(h) $J_i \in \mathcal{J}^A$ and $J_j \in \mathcal{J}^B$ are such that $P_{ji} > d_i$ and $P_{ij} - d_j \le Q$.

Property 6.14 can be proved by a pairwise job interchange argument.

As in the previous section, the feasibility of a schedule $\sigma$ can be checked by verifying whether there exists a job $J_j^B$ such that $S_j^B(\sigma)(1+b) + a_j - d_j^B > Q$. If such a job exists, schedule $\sigma$ is not feasible.

As a lower bound of the total weighted number of tardy jobs of a schedule $\sigma$ in which $k$ jobs have been fixed, Wu et al. (2013b) apply the value

$$\sum_{1 \le i \le k, J_i \in \mathcal{J}^A} w_{[i]} U_{[i]}(\sigma) + LB_{US},$$

where $LB_{US}$ is computed by an algorithm (see Wu et al. 2013b, Sect. 3.2) similar to Algorithm 42.

For the considered problem, the authors propose also a tabu search algorithm; we refer the reader to Wu et al. (2013b, Sect. 4) for details.

### 6.2.4 Proportional-Linear Shortening Job Processing Times

In the section, we consider two-agent time-dependent scheduling problems with proportional-linear shortening job processing times (6.4).

#### 6.2.4.1 $1|CO, p_j = b_j(1 - bt)|f_{\max}^A, f_{\max}^B$

This problem, considered by Yin et al. (2012b), is a time-dependent counterpart of problem $1|CO, f_{\max}^B \le Q|f_{\max}^A$ considered in Chap. 3. We deal here with shortening jobs and job processing times in the form of (6.7).

The introduction of variable job processing times does not make problem $1|CO, p_j = b_j(1-bt), f_{\max}^B \le Q|f_{\max}^A$ more difficult than $1|CO, f_{\max}^B \le Q|f_{\max}^A$, since the former problem still can be solved in $O(n_A^2 + n_B \log n_B)$ time by slightly modified algorithm for the latter problem.

The modified algorithm uses formula (6.27) for computing job completion times, a counterpart of Property 6.3 for shortening job processing times and the following result that gives similar properties to those concerning problem $1||f_{\max}^A, f_{\max}^B$.

*Property 6.15.* (a) If, in a given schedule, the last job is completed at time $t$ and if there is a job $J_j^B$ such that $f_{\max}^B(\max\{0, d_j^B - (t + b_j^B(1-bt))\}) \le Q$, then there exists an optimal schedule in which a job $J_j \in \mathcal{J}^2$ completes at time $t$ and there exists no optimal schedule in which a job $J_i \in \mathcal{J}^A$ completes at time $t$.

$(b)$ If, in a given schedule, the last job completes at time $t$, and for any job $J_j^B$ one has $f_j^B(\max\{0, d_j^B - (t + b_j^B(1 - bt))\}) > Q$, then there exists an optimal schedule in which the job $J_i^A$ with the minimum cost is scheduled at time $t$.

$(c)$ In an optimal schedule, jobs in $\mathcal{J}^B$ are scheduled in non-decreasing order of 'deadlines' $D_j^B$ defined as in Sect. 6.2.1.2.

Using Property 6.15, similar to what presented in Chap. 3, one can find a Pareto optimal schedule in $O(n_A^2 + n_B^2)$ time.

## 6.3 Two-Agent Position-Dependent Job Scheduling Problems

In this section, we consider several two-agent scheduling problems with position-dependent job processing times.

### 6.3.1 *Log-Linear Position-Dependent Job Processing Times with Learning Effect*

In this section, we consider two-agent scheduling problems with position-dependent log-linear job processing times (6.11).

#### 6.3.1.1 $1|CO, p_{j,r} = p_j r^\alpha, \sum U_j^B \leq Q|\sum T_j^A$

The problem, considered by Wu et al. (2011), is a position-dependent counterpart of problem $1|CO, p_j = b_j t, \sum U_j^B = 0|\sum T_j^A$ from Sect. 6.2.1.3. Log-linear job processing times with learning effect are in the form of (6.11). The aim is to find a schedule such that the total tardiness $\sum T_j^A$ for agent $A$ is minimal, provided that no job of agent $B$ is tardy.

In Wu et al. (2011), the authors propose a branch-and-bound algorithm based on the following counterpart of Property 6.9.

*Property 6.16.* Let $P_i = p_i r^\alpha$, $P_j := p_j r^\alpha$, $P_{ij} := p_i r^\alpha + p_j (r+1)^\alpha$, $P_{ji} := p_j r^\alpha + p_i (r+1)^\alpha$ and $R := r^\alpha - (r+1)^\alpha$, where $1 \leq r \leq n$. Schedule $\sigma$ dominates schedule $\sigma'$ if *any* of the following holds:

$(a)$ $J_i \in \mathcal{J}^A$ and $J_j \in \mathcal{J}^A$ are such that $p_i < p_j$, $S_i(\sigma) + P_i \geq d_i$ and $S_i(\sigma) + P_j \geq d_j$;

$(b)$ $J_i \in \mathcal{J}^A$ and $J_j \in \mathcal{J}^A$ are such that $p_i \leq p_j$, $S_i(\sigma) + P_j \leq d_j \leq S_i(\sigma) + P_{ij}$, $S_i(\sigma) + P_i \geq d_i$ and $p_i \frac{2r^\alpha - (r+1)^\alpha}{R} + \frac{S_i(\sigma) - d_j}{R} < p_j$;

$(c)$ $J_i \in \mathcal{J}^A$ and $J_j \in \mathcal{J}^A$ are such that $p_i < p_j$ and $S_i(\sigma) + P_{ij} \leq d_j$;

(*d*) $J_i \in \mathcal{J}^A$ and $J_j \in \mathcal{J}^A$ are such that $p_i \leq p_j$, $S_i(\sigma) + P_i \leq d_i \leq S_i(\sigma) + P_{ji}$, $S_i(\sigma) + P_{ij} \geq d_j$ and $p_i + \frac{d_i - d_j}{R} < p_j$;
(*e*) $J_i \in \mathcal{J}^A$ and $J_j \in \mathcal{J}^A$ are such that $S_i(\sigma) + P_j \geq d_j$, $S_i(\sigma) + P_{ji} \leq d_i$ and $p_i \frac{r^\alpha}{R} < p_j$;
(*f*) $J_i \in \mathcal{J}^A$ and $J_j \in \mathcal{J}^A$ are such that $p_i < p_j$ and $S_i(\sigma) + P_{ij} \leq d_j$;
(*g*) $J_i \in \mathcal{J}^A$ and $J_j \in \mathcal{J}^B$ are such that $S_i(\sigma) + \min\{P_{ij}, P_j\} \geq d_j$, $S_i(\sigma) + P_i \leq d_i$ and $p_i \frac{r^\alpha}{R} < p_j$;
(*h*) $J_i \in \mathcal{J}^B$ and $J_j \in \mathcal{J}^A$ are such that $p_i < p_j$, $S_i(\sigma) + P_{ij} \leq d_j$ and $S_i(\sigma) + P_i \leq d_i$;
(*i*) $J_i \in \mathcal{J}^B$ and $J_j \in \mathcal{J}^B$ are such that $p_i < p_j$, $S_i(\sigma) + P_i \leq d_i$, and $S_i(\sigma) + P_{ij} \leq d_j$.

Wu et al. (2011) check the feasibility of a schedule $\sigma$ verifying whether there exists a job $J_k$ such that $S_k(\sigma) + p_{\min}(k+1) > d^B_{\min}$, where $p_{\min}$ is the minimal basic processing time among unscheduled jobs and $d^B_{\min}$ is the smallest due date among jobs of $\mathcal{J}^B$. If such a job exists, schedule $\sigma$ is not feasible.

As a lower bound of the total tardiness of a schedule $\sigma$ in which $k$ jobs have been fixed, the authors apply the value

$$\sum_{1 \leq i \leq k, J_i \in \mathcal{J}^A} T_{[i]}(\sigma) + LB_{US},$$

where $LB_{US}$ is computed by an algorithm (see Wu et al. 2013b, Algorithm 1) similar to Algorithm 42. In order to construct initial suboptimal schedules for the considered exact algorithm, they use two $O(n^2)$ heuristics.

#### 6.3.1.2 $1|CO, p_{j,r} = p_j r^\alpha, C^B_{\max} \leq Q|\sum w^A_j C^A_j$

This problem has been considered by Li and Hsu (2012). Position-dependent log-linear job processing times with learning effect are in the form of (6.11). For this problem, Li and Hsu (2012) proposed a branch-and-bound algorithm based on the following result.

*Property 6.17.* Let $P_i := p_i r^\alpha$, $P_j := p_j(r+1)^\alpha$ and $P_{ij} := p_i r^\alpha + p_j(r+1)^\alpha$. Schedule $\sigma$ dominates schedule $\sigma'$ if *any* of the following holds:

(*a*) $J_i \in \mathcal{J}^A$ and $J_j \in \mathcal{J}^A$ are such that $\frac{p_j}{p_i} \geq \frac{w_j}{w_i} > 1$ and $S_i(\sigma) + P_{ij} \leq Q$;
(*b*) $J_i \in \mathcal{J}^B$ and $J_j \in \mathcal{J}^B$ are such that $\frac{p_j}{p_i} \geq \frac{w_j}{w_i} > 1$;
(*c*) $J_i \in \mathcal{J}^A$ and $J_j \in \mathcal{J}^B$ are such that $\frac{p_j}{p_i} \geq \frac{w_j}{w_i} > 1$ and $S_i(\sigma) + P_i \leq Q$;
(*d*) $J_i \in \mathcal{J}^B$ and $J_j \in \mathcal{J}^A$ are such that $\frac{p_j}{p_i} \geq \frac{w_j}{w_i} > 1$ and $S_i(\sigma) + P_{ij} < Q$.

The authors check the feasibility of a schedule $\sigma$ by verifying whether there exists a job $J^A_k$ such that $S^A_k(\sigma) > Q$ or $S^A_k(\sigma) + p_{\min}(k+1)^\alpha > Q$, where $p_{\min}$ is the minimal basic processing time among unscheduled jobs. If such a job exists, schedule $\sigma$ is not feasible.

As a lower bound on the total weighted completion time of schedule $\sigma$ in which only the first $k$ jobs are fixed, Li and Hsu (2012) apply the value

$$\sum_{i=1}^{n} w_{[i]} C_{[i]}(\sigma) + \sum_{j=1}^{n-k} w^A_{(k+j)} C^A_{(k+j)}.$$

The authors also proposed for problem $1|CO, p_{j,r} = p_j r^{\alpha}, C^B_{\max} \leq Q|\sum w^A_j C^A_j$ a genetic algorithm. In the algorithm, population size was equal to 40, the probability of cross-over was equal to 1, the probability of mutation was equal to 0.1, selection was made by choosing the best solution from the previous population and the stop condition was passing $2n$ generations; we refer the reader to Li and Hsu (2012, Sect. 4) for details.

## 6.3.2 *Log-Linear Position-Dependent Job Processing Times with Learning and Ageing Effects*

In this section, we consider a two-agent scheduling problem with position-dependent log-linear job processing times (6.11) and (6.16).

### 6.3.2.1 $1|CO, p^A_{j,r} = p^A_j r^{\alpha}, p^B_{j,r} = p^B_j r^{\beta}, L^B_{\max} \leq 0|\sum w^A_j C^A_j$

In this problem, considered by Cheng et al. (2011b), learning and ageing effects (6.11) and (6.16) are combined, i.e. job processing times of agent $A$ are in the form of (6.11), while those of agent $B$ are in the form of (6.16). For this problem, Cheng et al. (2011b) proposed a branch-and-bound algorithm exploiting the following result.

*Property 6.18.* Let $P^2_i := p^2_i r^{\beta}$, $P^2_j := p^2_j (r+1)^{\beta}$, $P^2_{ij} := p^2_i r^{\beta} + p^2_j (r+1)^{\beta}$ and $R := r^{\alpha} - (r+1)^{\alpha}$, where $1 \leq r \leq n$. Schedule $\sigma$ dominates schedule $\sigma'$ if *any* of the following holds:

(*a*) $J_i \in \mathcal{J}^A$ and $J_j \in \mathcal{J}^A$ are such that $\frac{p^1_j}{p^1_i} \geq \frac{w^1_j}{w^1_i} > 1$;

(*b*) $J_i \in \mathcal{J}^B$ and $J_j \in \mathcal{J}^B$ are such that $p^2_i > p^2_j$, $S_i(\sigma) + P^2_i < d^2_i$ and $S_i(\sigma) + P^2_{ij} < d^2_j$;

(*c*) $J_i \in \mathcal{J}^B$ and $J_j \in \mathcal{J}^A$ are such that $S_i(\sigma) + P^2_i < d^2_i$ and $p^2_i < \frac{p^1_j R}{r^{\beta}}$.

The authors show that the feasibility of a schedule $\sigma$ can be checked by verifying whether there exists a job $J^B_j$ such that $S^B_j(\sigma) > d^B_j$ or $S^B_j(\sigma) + p^B_j (k+1)^{\beta} > d^B_j$. If such a job exists, schedule $\sigma$ is not feasible.

As a lower bound of the total weighted completion time of a schedule $\sigma$ with the first $k$ jobs fixed, Cheng et al. (2011b) apply the bound (6.33).

The authors also proposed for the problem a simulated annealing algorithm; we refer the reader to Cheng et al. (2011b, Sect. 4) for details.

### 6.3.3 *Linear Position-Dependent Job Processing Times with Learning and Ageing Effects*

In this section, we consider two-agent scheduling problems with position-dependent linear job processing times with learning effect (6.12) and ageing effect (6.17).

#### 6.3.3.1 $1|CO, p_{j,r} = p_j - \beta r, f^B_{\max} \leq Q|\sum C^A_j$ and $1|CO, p_{j,r} = p_j + \beta r, f^B_{\max} \leq Q|\sum C^A_j$

These problems, considered by Liu et al. (2010b), are position-dependent counterparts of time-dependent scheduling problems studied in Sects. 6.2.1.2, 6.2.1.4, 6.2.2.1 and 6.2.2.2. In both these problems one should find a schedule such that the total completion time $\sum C^A_j$ for agent $A$ jobs is minimal, provided that the maximum cost $f^B_{\max}$ for agent $B$ jobs does not exceed a given upper bound $Q \geq 0$. Position-dependent job processing times are in the form of either (6.12) or (6.17) with $\beta_j = \beta$ for $1 \leq j \leq n$.

For these problems, based on counterparts of Properties 6.3, 6.7, 6.8 and Theorem 6.5 $(a)$, the authors propose algorithms of complexity $O(n_A \log n_A + n_B \log n_B)$ which are obtained by simple modifications of Algorithm 40.

### 6.3.4 *Past-Sequence-Dependent Job Processing Times with Ageing Effect*

In this section, we consider two-agent scheduling problems with past-sequence-dependent job processing times in the form of (6.18) or (6.19).

#### 6.3.4.1 $1|CO, p_{j,r} = p_j\left(1 + \sum_{k=1}^{r-1} p_{[k]}\right), C^B_{\max} \leq Q|\sum C^A_j$ and $1|CO, p_{j,r} = p_j\left(1 + \frac{\sum_{k=1}^{r-1} p_{[k]}}{\sum_{k=1}^{r-1} p_k}\right), C^B_{\max} \leq Q|\sum C^A_j$

These problems, considered by Liu et al. (2013), are past-sequence-dependent counterparts of time-dependent scheduling problems studied in Sects. 6.2.1.2, 6.2.1.4, 6.2.2.1 and 6.2.2.2. Past-sequence-dependent job processing times with ageing effect are in the form of (6.18) or (6.19) with $\beta = 1$. The aim is to find a schedule such that the total completion time $\sum C_j^A$ for agent $A$ is minimal, provided that the maximum completion time $C_{\max}^B$ for agent $B$ does not exceed a given upper bound $Q \geq 0$.

For these problems, based on counterparts of Properties 6.3, 6.7, 6.8 and Theorem 6.5 $(a)$, Liu et al. (2013) proposed algorithms of complexity $O(n_A \log n_A + n_B \log n_B)$ which are immediate modifications of Algorithm 40.

#### 6.3.4.2 $1|CO, p_{j,r} = p_j \left(1 + \sum_{k=1}^{r-1} p_{[k]}\right), f_{\max}^B \leq Q | \sum C_j^A$ and $1|CO, p_{j,r} = p_j \left(1 + \frac{\sum_{k=1}^{r-1} p_{[k]}}{\sum_{k=1}^{r-1} p_k}\right), f_{\max}^B \leq Q | \sum C_j^A$

These problems have been considered by Liu et al. (2013) and generalize the problems analyzed in Sect. 6.3.4.1. Here the objective of agent $B$ is to minimize the maximum cost, $f_{\max}^B$. Both these problems can be solved by the same algorithms as their simpler variants with the $C_{\max}^B$ objective.

#### 6.3.4.3 $1|CO, p_{j,r} = p_j \max\left\{(1 + \sum_{k=1}^{r-1} p_{[k]})^\alpha, \beta\right\}, \sum U_j^B \leq Q | \sum w_j^A C_j^A$

This problem, considered by Cheng et al. (2011a), is the past-sequence-dependent counterpart of problem $1|CO, p_j = a_j + bt, \sum U_j^B \leq Q | \sum w_j^A C_j^A$ presented in Sect. 6.2.3.1. Past-sequence-based job processing times with learning effect are in the form of (6.13).

The authors proposed for the problem a branch-and-bound algorithm based on the following result.

*Property 6.19.* Let $P_i := p_i \max\{P^\alpha, \beta\}$, $P_j := p_j \max\{P^\alpha, \beta\}$ and $P_{ji} := p_j \max\{(P + p_i)^\alpha, \beta\}$, where $P := 1 + \sum_{k=1}^{r-1} p_{[k]}$ and $1 \leq r \leq n$. Schedule $\sigma$ dominates schedule $\sigma'$ if *any* of the following holds:

$(a)$ $J_i \in \mathcal{J}^A$ and $J_j \in \mathcal{J}^A$ are such that $\frac{p_j}{p_i} > 1 \geq \frac{w_j}{w_i}$;
$(b)$ $J_i \in \mathcal{J}^B$ and $J_j \in \mathcal{J}^B$ are such that $p_i < p_j$, $S_i(\sigma) + P_i + P_{ji} < d_j$ and $S_i(\sigma) + P_i < d_i$;
$(c)$ $J_i \in \mathcal{J}^A$ and $J_j \in \mathcal{J}^B$ are such that $p_i < p_j$ and $S_i(\sigma) + P_i + P_{ij} < d_j$;
$(d)$ $J_i \in \mathcal{J}^B$ and $J_j \in \mathcal{J}^A$ are such that $P_i < P_j - P_{ji}$ and $S_i(\sigma) + P_i < d_i$.

Cheng et al. (2011a) check the feasibility of a schedule $\sigma$ verifying whether there exists a job $J_j^B$ such that $S_j^B(\sigma) > d_j^B$ or $S_j^B(\sigma) + P_j > d_j^B$. If such a job exists, schedule $\sigma$ is not feasible; otherwise, it is feasible.

As a lower bound on the total weighted completion time of a schedule $\sigma$ with the first $k$ jobs fixed, the bound (6.33) is applied.

The authors also proposed for the problem a simulated annealing algorithm; we refer the reader to Cheng et al. (2011a, Sect. 3.3) for details.

#### 6.3.4.4 $1|CO, p^A_{j,r} = p^A_j(1 + \sum_{k=1}^{r-1} p_{[k]})^\alpha$, $p^B_{j,r} = p^B_j(1 + \sum_{k=1}^{r-1} p_{[k]})^\beta, L^B_{\max} \le Q|\sum w^A_j C^A_j$

This problem, considered by Wu et al. (2012), is the past-sequence-dependent counterpart of problem $1|CO, p^A_{j,r} = p^A_j r^\alpha, p^B_{j,r} = p^B_j r^\beta, L^B_{\max} \le 0|\sum w^A_j C^A_j$ discussed in Sect. 6.3.2.1. The main difference between these two problems is the replacement in the latter problem the log-linear job processing times (6.11) and (6.16) by past-sequence-dependent job processing times (6.14) and (6.18), respectively.

This replacement does not make problem $1|CO, p^A_{j,r} = p^A_j(1 + \sum_{k=1}^{r-1} p_{[k]})^\alpha$, $p^B_{j,r} = p^B_j(1 + \sum_{k=1}^{r-1} p_{[k]})^\beta, L^B_{\max} \le Q|\sum w^A_j C^A_j$ more difficult compared to its counterpart from Sect. 6.3.2.1, since properties of the former problem have almost the same form as those of the latter one.

For the considered problem, the authors proposed a branch-and-bound algorithm and an ant colony algorithm; we refer the reader to Wu et al. (2012, pp. 1987–1990) for details.

## 6.4 Two-Agent Controllable Job Scheduling Problems

In this section, we present several two-agent scheduling problems with controllable job processing times considered by Wan et al. (2010).

### 6.4.1 *Linear Controllable Job Processing Times with the Total Compression Cost Criterion*

In the section, we consider two-agent controllable job scheduling problems with the total compression cost criterion $\sum c^A_j x^A_j$ for agent $A$, provided that the objective of agent $B$ must not exceed a given upper bound $Q \ge 0$. Moreover, in all the problems only the jobs of agent $A$ have variable processing times of the form (6.22), while jobs of agent $B$ have processing times described by numbers.

#### 6.4.1.1 $1|CO, p^A_j = \overline{p}^A_j - x^A_j, r^A_j, d^A_j, pmtn^A, \circ^B, f^B_{\max} \le Q|\sum c^A_j x^A_j$

Despite the simplifying assumption that only one agent has jobs with variable processing times, only some of the problems of this type can be solved in a

**Algorithm 43** for problem $1|CO, p_j^A = \overline{p}_j^A - x_j^A, r_j^A, d_j^A, pmtn^A, pmtn^B, f_{\max}^B \leq Q|\sum c_j^A x_j^A$

**for** each job $j$ of agent $B$ **do**
    Compute 'deadline' $D_j^B$
    $r_j^B := 0$
    $c_j^B := +\infty$
**end for**
Starting from time $\max_{1 \leq j \leq n_B}\{D_j^B\}$ schedule all agent $B$ jobs backwards in such a way that each of them is as close its deadline as possible
Apply the algorithm by Leung et al. (1994) to generate a schedule $\sigma$ for jobs of both agents
**return** $\sigma$

polynomial time. We start with one of the problems that was shown computationally difficult in Wan et al. (2010).

**Theorem 6.10.** *Problem* $1|CO, p_j^A = \overline{p}_j^A - x_j^A, r_j^A, d_j^A, pmtn^A, \circ^B, f_{\max}^B \leq Q|\sum c_j^A x_j^A$ *is strongly NP-hard.*

*Proof.* The reduction from the 3-PARTITION problem with $3q$ elements and the maximum value $E$ is as follows. We let $n_A = q - 1$ and $n_B = 3q$. Jobs in $\mathcal{J}^A$ have unit processing times and cannot be compressed, i.e., $\underline{p}_j^A = \overline{p}_j^A = 1$. Moreover, job $J_j$ of agent $A$ has release date $r_j^A = j * E + (j - 1)$ and deadline $d_j^A = j * E + j$, where $1 \leq j \leq q - 1$. The criterion of agent $A$ is the total compression cost $\sum_j c_j^A x_j^A$ and the threshold for the cost equals 0.

Jobs of agent $B$ have processing times equal to $a_j$ and can be compressed. The criterion of agent $B$ is $f_{\max}^B = C_{\max}^B$.

The further proof follows by showing that the 3-PARTITION problem has a solution if and only if there exists such a schedule for problem $1|CO, p_j^A = \overline{p}_j^A - x_j^A, r_j^A, d_j^A, pmtn^A, \circ^B, f_{\max}^B \leq Q|\sum c_j^A x_j^A$ that the total cost $\sum_j c_j^A x_j^A = 0$. □

#### 6.4.1.2 $1|CO, p_j^A = \overline{p}_j^A - x_j^A, r_j^A, d_j^A, pmtn^A, pmtn^B, f_{\max}^B \leq Q|\sum c_j^A x_j^A$

This problem is almost the same as the one considered in the previous section, except that now also the jobs of agent $B$ can be preempted. This change makes this new problem polynomially solvable (see Algorithm 43).

Algorithm 43 is based on an algorithm due to Leung et al. (1994) which solves problem $1|CO, p_j = \overline{p}_j - x_j, r_j, d_j, pmtn|\sum c_j x_j$ in $O(n \log n + kn)$ time, where $k$ is the number of *distinct* values of compression costs $c_j$, $1 \leq j \leq n$.

**Theorem 6.11.** *Algorithm 43 generates an optimal schedule for problem* $1|CO, p_j^A = \overline{p}_j^A - x_j^A, r_j^A, d_j^A, pmtn^A, pmtn^B, f_{\max}^B \leq Q|\sum c_j^A x_j^A$ *in* $O(n \log n +$

*$(k+1)n)$ time, where $k$ is the number of distinct values of compression costs $c_j$ of agent $A$.*

The correctness of Algorithm 43 and its running time follow from the correctness and the running time of algorithm by Leung et al. (1994).

Modified versions of Algorithm 43 can be used to solve another two problems, $1|CO, p_j^A = \overline{p}_j^A - x_j^A, r_j^A, d_j^A, pmtn^A, r_j^B, pmtn^B, f_{\max}^B \leq Q|\sum c_j^A x_j^A$ and $1|CO, p_j^A = \overline{p}_j^A - x_j^A, r_j^A, d_j^A, pmtn^A, r_j^B, d_j^B, pmtn^B, f_{\max}^B \leq Q|\sum c_j^A x_j^A$, in which also agent $B$ jobs have ready times or ready times and due dates. In the first case, it is sufficient to use in Step 3 of Algorithm 43 non-zero agent $B$ due dates. In the second case, one need to apply the following result in which 'deadlines' $D_j^B$, defined as in Sect. 6.2.1.2, allow to schedule jobs as late as possible.

*Property 6.20.* For problem $1|CO, p_j^A = \overline{p}_j^A - x_j^A, d_j^A, pmtn^A, pmtn^B, f_{\max}^B|\sum c_j^A x_j^A$ there exists an optimal schedule in which agent $B$ jobs are scheduled as late as possible.

The modified algorithm uses algorithm by Leung et al. (1994) for all jobs of both agents and next, if necessary, applying Property 6.20 it combines pieces of agent $B$ jobs together and moves them towards their 'deadlines'.

## 6.4.2 Linear Controllable Job Processing Times with Other Criteria Than the Total Compression Cost

In this section, we present some two-agent controllable job scheduling problems studied by Wan et al. (2010) which concern other criteria than the total compression cost $\sum c_j^A x_j^A$ discussed in Sect. 6.4.1.

### 6.4.2.1 $1|CO, p_j^A = \overline{p}_j^A - x_j^A, d_j^A, pmtn^A, \circ^B, f_{\max}^B \leq Q|\sum C_j^A + \sum c_j^A x_j^A$ and $1|CO, p_j^A = \overline{p}_j^1 - x_j^A, r_j^A, pmtn^A, \circ^B, f_{\max}^B \leq Q|\sum c_j^A x_j^A + T_{\max}^A$

Wan et al. (2010) claim without proof that by similar reductions from the 3-PARTITION problem as in Sect. 6.4.1.1 one can prove that problems

- $1|CO, p_j^A = \overline{p}_j^A - x_j^A, d_j^A, pmtn^A, \circ^B, f_{\max}^B \leq Q|\sum C_j^A + \sum c_j^A x_j^A$ and
- $1|CO, p_j^A = \overline{p}_j^1 - x_j^A, r_j^A, pmtn^A, \circ^B, f_{\max}^B \leq Q|\sum c_j^A x_j^A + T_{\max}^A$

are strongly NP-hard as well.

#### 6.4.2.2 $1|CO, p_j^A = \overline{p}_j^A - x_j^A, pmtn^A, \circ^B, f_{\max}^B \le Q|\sum C_j^A + \sum c_j^A x_j^A$

This problem has been mentioned at the end of the previous section. In the case when basic job processing times and compression costs of agent $A$ are agreeable, i.e. if $p_i^A \le p_j^A$ implies $c_i^A \le c_j^A$ for arbitrary jobs $J_i$ and $J_j$ of agent $A$, Wan et al. (2010, Sect. 4) proposed to solve this problem by the following algorithm of complexity $O(n_B(n_A + n_B)n_A^2 \log n_A)$.

First, for job $J_j^B$ there is computed 'deadline' $D_j^B$. After that, starting from time $\max_{1 \le j \le n_B}\{D_j^B\}$, a schedule $\sigma$ is built by scheduling all jobs in $\mathcal{J}^B$ backwards, so that each of them is as close to its 'deadline' as possible. Next, the jobs in $\mathcal{J}^A$ are scheduled by the preemptive SPT rule, skipping time slots occupied in $\sigma$ by jobs of $\mathcal{J}^B$. Finally, the jobs of $\mathcal{J}^A$ are accordingly compressed and scheduled again using the preemptive SPT rule.

Similar approaches allow to solve further two-agent scheduling problems with controllable job processing times in the form of (6.22), as reported in Wan et al. (2010, Sects. 4 and 5).

This section ends our presentation of agent scheduling problems with different forms of variable job processing times.

## 6.5 Tables

In the section, we present tables that summarize the time complexity statuses of the scheduling problems considered earlier in the chapter. In all the tables symbols $n$, $n_A$ and $n_B$ denote the total number of jobs of both agents, the number of jobs of agent $A$ and the number of jobs of agent $B$, respectively.

In Table 6.2 we summarize the time complexity statuses of single-agent scheduling problems with time-dependent job processing times considered in Sect. 6.1.3.1.

In Table 6.3 we summarize the time complexity statuses of single-agent scheduling problems with position-dependent job processing times considered in Sect. 6.1.3.2.

In Table 6.4 we summarize the time complexity statuses of two-agent scheduling problems with time-dependent job processing times considered in Sect. 6.1.

In Table 6.5 we summarize the time complexity statuses of single-machine two-agent scheduling problems with position-dependent job processing times considered in Sect. 6.2.

In Table 6.6 we summarize the time complexity statuses of single-machine two-agent scheduling problems with controllable job processing times considered in Sect. 6.3.

**Table 6.2** Time complexity of single-agent time-dependent scheduling problems

| Problem | Time complexity | Reference | Page |
|---|---|---|---|
| $1\|p_j = b_j t\|C_{\max}$ | $O(n)$ | Theorem 6.1 $(a)$ | 228 |
| $1\|p_j = b_j t\|L_{\max}$ | $O(n \log n)$ | Theorem 6.1 $(b)$ | 228 |
| $1\|p_j = b_j t\|f_{\max}$ | $O(n^2)$ | Theorem 6.1 $(c)$ | 228 |
| $1\|p_j = b_j t\|\sum C_j$ | $O(n \log n)$ | Theorem 6.1 $(d)$ | 228 |
| $1\|p_j = b_j t\|\sum w_j C_j$ | $O(n \log n)$ | Theorem 6.1 $(e)$ | 228 |
| $1\|p_j = b_j t\|\sum U_j$ | $O(n \log n)$ | Theorem 6.1 $(f)$ | 228 |
| $1\|p_j = b_j t\|\sum T_j$ | Open | Section 6.1.3.1 | 228 |
| $1\|p_j = b_j(a+bt)\|C_{\max}$ | $O(n)$ | Theorem 6.2 $(a)$ | 228 |
| $1\|p_j = b_j(a+bt)\|L_{\max}$ | $O(n \log n)$ | Theorem 6.2 $(b)$ | 228 |
| $1\|p_j = b_j(a+bt)\|f_{\max}$ | $O(n^2)$ | Theorem 6.2 $(c)$ | 228 |
| $1\|p_j = b_j(a+bt)\|\sum C_j$ | $O(n \log n)$ | Theorem 6.2 $(d)$ | 228 |
| $1\|p_j = b_j(a+bt)\|\sum w_j C_j$ | $O(n \log n)$ | Theorem 6.2 $(e)$ | 228 |
| $1\|p_j = b_j(a+bt)\|\sum U_j$ | $O(n \log n)$ | Theorem 6.2 $(f)$ | 228 |
| $1\|p_j = b_j(a+bt)\|\sum T_j$ | NP-hard[a] | Theorem 6.2 $(g)$ | 228 |
| $1\|p_j = a_j + b_j t\|C_{\max}$ | $O(n \log n)$ | Theorem 6.3 $(a)$ | 229 |
| $1\|p_j = a_j + b_j t\|L_{\max}$ | NP-hard | Theorem 6.3 $(b1)$ and $(b2)$ | 229 |
| $1\|p_j = a_j + b_j t\|f_{\max}$ | NP-hard | Theorem 6.3 $(c)$ | 229 |
| $1\|p_j = a_j + b_j t\|\sum C_j$ | Open[b] | Section 6.1.3.1 | 228 |
| $1\|p_j = a_j + b_j t\|\sum w_j C_j$ | NP-hard | Theorem 6.3 $(d)$ | 229 |
| $1\|p_j = a_j + b_j t\|\sum U_j$ | NP-hard | Theorem 6.3 $(e)$ | 229 |
| $1\|p_j = a_j + b_j t\|\sum T_j$ | NP-hard | Theorem 6.3 $(f)$ | 229 |

[a] If $a = 1$ and $b = 0$, otherwise the problem is open

[b] Even if $a_j = 1$ for $1 \leq j \leq n$

**Table 6.3** Time complexity of single-agent position-dependent scheduling problems

| Problem | Time complexity | Reference | Page |
|---|---|---|---|
| $1\|p_{j,r} = p_j r^\alpha\|C_{\max}$ | $O(n \log n)$ | Theorem 6.4 $(a)$ | 231 |
| $1\|p_{j,r} = p_j r^\alpha\|L_{\max}$ | $O(n \log n)$[a] | Theorem 6.4 $(b)$ | 231 |
| $1\|p_{j,r} = p_j r^\alpha\|f_{\max}$ | Open | Section 6.1.3.2 | 231 |
| $1\|p_{j,r} = p_j r^\alpha\|\sum C_j$ | $O(n \log n)$ | Theorem 6.4 $(c)$ | 231 |
| $1\|p_{j,r} = p_j r^\alpha\|\sum w_j C_j$ | $O(n \log n)$[a] | Theorem 6.4 $(d1)$, $(d2)$ and $(d3)$ | 231 |
| $1\|p_{j,r} = p_j r^\alpha\|\sum U_j$ | Open | Section 6.1.3.2 | 231 |
| $1\|p_{j,r} = p_j r^\alpha\|\sum T_j$ | NP-hard[b] | Theorem 6.4 $(e)$ | 231 |
| $1\|p_{j,r} = p_j - \beta r\|C_{\max}$ | $O(n)$ | Theorem 6.5 $(a)$ | 232 |
| $1\|p_{j,r} = p_j - \beta r\|\sum C_j$ | $O(n \log n)$ | Theorem 6.5 $(b)$ | 232 |
| $1\|p_{j,r} = p_j \left(1 + \sum_{k=1}^{r-1} p_{[k]}\right)^\alpha \|C_{\max}$ | $O(n \log n)$ | Theorem 6.6$(a)$ | 232 |
| $1\|p_{j,r} = p_j \left(1 + \sum_{k=1}^{r-1} p_{[k]}\right)^\alpha \|L_{\max}$ | Open | Section 6.1.3.2 | 231 |
| $1\|p_{j,r} = p_j \left(1 + \sum_{k=1}^{r-1} p_{[k]}\right)^\alpha \|\sum C_j$ | $O(n \log n)$ | Theorem 6.6 $(b)$ | 232 |
| $1\|p_{j,r} = p_j \left(1 + \sum_{k=1}^{r-1} p_{[k]}\right)^\alpha \|\sum w_j C_j$ | $O(n \log n)$[a] | Theorem 6.6 $(c)$ | 232 |
| $1\|p_{j,r} = p_j \left(1 + \sum_{k=1}^{r-1} p_{[k]}\right)^\alpha \|\sum U_j$ | Open | Section 6.1.3.2 | 231 |

[a] Under additional assumptions on $p_j$, $w_j$ or $d_j$; otherwise, the problem is open

[b] If $\alpha = 0$, otherwise the problem is open

**Table 6.4** Time complexity of two-agent time-dependent scheduling problems

| Problem | Time complexity | Reference | Page |
|---|---|---|---|
| $1\|CO, p_j = b_j t, C^B_{\max} \le Q\|L^A_{\max}$ | $O(n_A \log n_A + n_A n_B)$ | Theorem 6.8 | 240 |
| $1\|CO, p_j = b_j t, f^B_{\max} \le Q\|\sum C^A_j$ | $O(n_A \log n_A + n_B \log n_B)$ | Theorem 6.9 | 241 |
| $1\|CO, p_j = b_j t, \sum U^B_j = 0\|\sum T^A_j$ | Open | Section 6.2.1.3 | 241 |
| $1\|CO, p_j = b_j t, s_j = b'_j t,$ | | | |
| $GT, f^B_{\max} \le Q\|\sum C^A_j$ | $O(n_A \log n_A + n_B \log n_B)$ | Section 6.2.1.4 | 244 |
| $1\|CO, p_j = b_j(a + bt), C^B_{\max} \le Q\|L^A_{\max}$ | $O(n_A \log n_A + n_A n_B)$ | Section 6.2.2.1 | 244 |
| $1\|CO, p_j = b_j(a + bt), f^B_{\max} \le Q\|\sum C^A_j$ | $O(n_A \log n_A + n_B \log n_B)$ | Section 6.2.2.1 | 244 |
| $1\|CO, p_j = b_j(a + bt), s_j = b'_j(a' + b't),$ | | | |
| $GT, f^B_{\max} \le Q\|\sum C^A_j$ | $O(n_A \log n_A + n_B \log n_B)$ | Section 6.2.2.2 | 244 |
| $1\|CO, p_j = a_j + bt, \sum U^B_j = 0\|\sum w^A_j C^A_j$ | Strongly NP-hard | Section 6.2.3.1 | 245 |
| $1\|CO, p_j = a_j + bt, L^B_{\max} \le Q\|\sum w^A_j U^A_j$ | Strongly NP-hard | Section 6.2.3.2 | 246 |
| $1\|CO, p_j = b_j(1 - bt)\|f^A_{\max}, f^B_{\max}$ | $O(n^2_A + n_B \log n_B)$ | Section 6.2.4.1 | 247 |

## 6.6 Bibliographic Remarks

In this section, we give some remarks on main references related to scheduling problems with variable job processing times. In view of space limitations, we refer the reader mainly to review papers and books that cover major parts of research done on a particular type of variable job processing times.

### *6.6.1 Time-Dependent Job Scheduling Problems*

The first review on time-dependent scheduling, Gawiejnowicz (1996), covers references on single-machine problems published up to 1995. This review discusses time-dependent scheduling in the context of so-called *discrete-continuous scheduling* in which, apart processors that are *discrete resources*, jobs for completion need also *continuous resources* such as energy or power.

The next time-dependent scheduling review, Alidaee and Womer (1999), covers literature up to 1998. This review also discusses mainly single-machine time-dependent scheduling problems, since to that time only a few authors have considered parallel-machine problems with time-dependent job processing times (Chen 1996, 1997; Kononov 1997).

The last review on time-dependent scheduling so far, Cheng et al. (2004a), discusses references published up to 2003 and includes some new topics at that time such as flow shop scheduling with time-dependent job processing times (Kononov and Gawiejnowicz 2001; Mosheiov 2002).

The most recent discussion of time-dependent scheduling is presented in the book by Gawiejnowicz (2008). This book reviews literature up to 2008, including also non-English references, and discusses in detail single-, parallel- and dedicated-machine time-dependent scheduling problems. In particular, in Chap. 6 of the book are presented proofs of results given in Sect. 6.2.

**Table 6.5** Time complexity of two-agent position-dependent scheduling problems

| Problem | Time complexity | Reference | Page |
|---|---|---|---|
| $1\|CO, p_{j,r} = p_j r^{\alpha}, \sum U_j^B \leq Q\|\sum T_j^A$ | Open | Section 6.3.1.1 | 248 |
| $1\|CO, p_{j,r} = p_j r^{\alpha}, C_{\max}^B \leq Q\|\sum w_j^A C_j^A$ | Open | Section 6.3.1.2 | 249 |
| $1\|CO, p_{j,r}^A = p_j^A r^{\alpha}, p_{j,r}^B = p_j^B r^{\beta}, L_{\max}^B \leq 0\|\sum w_j^A C_j^A$ | Open | Section 6.3.2.1 | 250 |
| $1\|CO, p_{j,r} = p_j - \beta r, f_{\max}^B \leq Q\|\sum C_j^A$ | $O(n_A \log n_A + n_B \log n_B)$ | Section 6.3.3.1 | 251 |
| $1\|CO, p_{j,r} = p_j + \beta r, f_{\max}^B \leq Q\|\sum C_j^A$ | $O(n_A \log n_A + n_B \log n_B)$ | Section 6.3.3.1 | 251 |
| $1\|CO, p_{j,r} = p_j \left(1 + \sum_{k=1}^{r-1} p_{[k]}\right), C_{\max}^B \leq Q\|\sum C_j^A$ | $O(n_A \log n_A + n_B \log n_B)$ | Section 6.3.4.1 | 251 |
| $1\|CO, p_{j,r} = p_j \left(1 + \frac{\sum_{k=1}^{r-1} p_{[k]}}{\sum_{k=1}^{r-1} p_k}\right), C_{\max}^B \leq Q\|\sum C_j^A$ | $O(n_A \log n_A + n_B \log n_B)$ | Section 6.3.4.1 | 251 |
| $1\|CO, p_{j,r} = p_j \left(1 + \sum_{k=1}^{r-1} p_{[k]}\right), f_{\max}^B \leq Q\|\sum C_j^A$ | $O(n_A \log n_A + n_B \log n_B)$ | Section 6.3.4.2 | 252 |
| $1\|CO, p_{j,r} = p_j \left(1 + \frac{\sum_{k=1}^{r-1} p_{[k]}}{\sum_{k=1}^{r-1} p_k}\right), f_{\max}^B \leq Q\|\sum C_j^A$ | $O(n_A \log n_A + n_B \log n_B)$ | Section 6.3.4.2 | 252 |
| $1\|CO, p_{j,r} = p_j \max\left\{(1 + \sum_{k=1}^{r-1} p_{[k]})^{\alpha}, \beta\right\}, \sum U_j^B \leq Q\|\sum w_j^A C_j^A$ | Strongly NP-hard | Section 6.3.4.3 | 252 |
| $1\|CO, p_{j,r}^A = p_j^A(1+\sum_{k=1}^{r-1} p_{[k]})^{\alpha}, p_{j,r}^B = p_j^B(1+\sum_{k=1}^{r-1} p_{[k]})^{\beta}, L_{\max}^B \leq Q\|\sum w_j^A C_j^A$ | Open | Section 6.3.4.4 | 253 |

## 6.6.2 Position-Dependent Job Scheduling Problems

The first position-dependent scheduling review, Bachman and Janiak (2004), covers literature up to 2001 and presents several complexity results on scheduling with position-dependent log-linear and linear job processing times.

The most recent review on position-dependent scheduling, Biskup (2008), discusses references published up to 2007 and covers single- and multiple-machine scheduling problems, in identical parallel and dedicated parallel environments, with many forms of position-dependent job processing times.

**Table 6.6** Time complexity of two-agent scheduling problems with controllable jobs

| Problem | Time complexity | Reference | Page |
|---|---|---|---|
| $1\|CO, p_j^A = \overline{p}_j^A - x_j^A, r_j^A, d_j^A, pmtn^A, \circ^B, f_{\max}^B \leq Q\|\sum c_j^A x_j^A$ | Strongly NP-hard | Theorem 6.10 | 254 |
| $1\|CO, p_j^A = \overline{p}_j^A - x_j^A, d_j^A, pmtn^A, \circ^B, f_{\max}^B \leq Q\|\sum C_j^A + \sum c_j^A x_j^A$ | Strongly NP-hard | Section 6.4.1.1 | 253 |
| $1\|CO, p_j^A = \overline{p}_j^A - x_j^A, r_j^A, pmtn^A, \circ^B, f_{\max}^B \leq Q\|\sum c_j^A x_j^A + T_{\max}^A$ | Strongly NP-hard | Section 6.4.1.1 | 253 |
| $1\|CO, p_j^A = \overline{p}_j^A - x_j^A, r_j^A, d_j^A, pmtn^A, pmtn^B, f_{\max}^B \leq Q\|\sum c_j^A x_j^A$ | $O(n \log n + (k+1)n)$[a] | Theorem 6.11 | 254 |
| $1\|CO, p_j^A = \overline{p}_j^A - x_j^A, pmtn^A, \circ^B, f_{\max}^B \leq Q\|\sum C_j^A + \sum c_j^A x_j^A$ | $O(n_B n n_A^2 \log n_A)$ | Section 6.4.2.2 | 256 |

[a] $k$ denotes the number of distinct values of compression costs

Review by Anzanello and Fogliatto (2011) includes a detailed analysis of curve shapes describing different forms of learning effect. A critical discussion of existing literature on scheduling problems with position-dependent job processing times and a proposal of a unifying view on some of the problems one can find in Rustogi and Strusevich (2012).

In the first two of these reviews are described proofs or given references to results mentioned in Sect. 6.3.

### *6.6.3 Controllable Job Scheduling Problems*

The first survey on scheduling problems with controllable job processing times, Nowicki and Zdrzalka (1990), concerns mainly to single-machine problems, though it also addresses flow shop and parallel-machine problems, and covers references up to 1988.

The most recent review on the subject, Shabtay and Steiner (2007), following the classification scheme introduced in Nowicki and Zdrzalka (1990), presents a detailed discussion of single-, parallel- and dedicated-machine scheduling problems, and covers literature of the subject up to 2006.

Some controllable job scheduling problems are also discussed in reviews by Chen et al. (1998) and Hoogeveen (2005).

In all these reviews are described proofs or are given references to results mentioned in Sect. 6.4.

# References


Agnetis, A., Mirchandani, P., Pacciarelli, D., & Pacifici, A. (2004). Scheduling problems with two competing agents. *Operations Research, 52*, 229–242.

Agnetis, A., Pacciarelli, D., & Pacifici, A. (2007). Multi-agent single machine scheduling. *Annals of Operations Research, 150*, 3–15.

Agnetis, A., de Pascale, G., & Pranzo, M. (2009a). Computing the nash solution for scheduling bargaining problems. *International Journal of Operational Research, 1*, 54–69.

Agnetis, A., Pacciarelli, D., & de Pascale, G. (2009b). A Lagrangian approach to single-machine scheduling problems with two competing agents. *Journal of Scheduling, 12*, 401–415.

Agnetis, A., Nicosia, G., Pacifici, A., & Pferschy, U. (2013). Two agents competing for a shared machine. *Lecture Notes in Computer Science, 8176 LNAI*, 1–14.

Aho, A. V., Hopcroft, J. E., & Ullman, J. D. (1974). *The design and analysis of computer algorithms*. Reading: Addison-Wesley.

Albers, S., & Brucker, P. (1993). The complexity of one-machine batching problems. *Discrete Applied Mathematics, 47*, 87–107.

Alidaee, B., & Womer, N. K. (1999). Scheduling with time dependent processing times: Review and extensions. *Journal of the Operatational Research Society, 50*, 711–720.

Angel, E., Bampis, E., & Gourvès, L. (2005). Approximation results for a bicriteria job scheduling problem on a single machine without preemption. *Information Processing Letters, 94*, 19–27.

Anzanello, M. J., & Fogliatto, F. S. (2011). Learning curve models and applications: Literature review and research directions. *International Journal of Industrial Ergonomics, 41*, 573–583.

Arbib, C., Flammini, M., & Marinelli, F. (2003). Minimum flow time graph ordering. *Lecture Notes on Computer Science, 2880*, 23–33.

Bachman, A., & Janiak, A. (2000). Minimizing maximum lateness under linear deterioration. *European Journal of Operational Research, 126*, 557–566.

Bachman, A., & Janiak, A. (2004). Scheduling jobs with position-dependent processing times. *Journal of the Operational Research Society, 55*, 257–264.

Baker, K., & Smith, J. C. (2003). A multiple criterion model for machine scheduling. *Journal of Scheduling, 6*, 7–16.

Balasubramanian, H., Fowler, J., Keha, A., & Pfund, M. (2009). Scheduling interfering job sets on parallel machines. *European Journal of Operational Research, 199*, 55–67.

Bellman, R. (1957). *Dynamic programming*. Princeton: Princeton University Press.

Bellman, R., & Dreyfus, S. E. (1962). *Applied dynamic programming*. Princeton: Princeton University Press.

Biskup, D. (2008). A state-of-the-art review on scheduling with learning effects. *European Journal of Operational Research, 188*, 315–329.

Blazewicz, J., Ecker, K. H., Pesch, E., Schmidt, G., & Weglarz, J. (2007). *Handbook on scheduling: From theory to applications*. Berlin/Heidelberg: Springer.


A. Agnetis et al., *Multiagent Scheduling*, DOI 10.1007/978-3-642-41880-8,

Bowman, E. H. (1959). The schedule sequencing problem. *Operations Research, 7*, 621–624.

Brewer, P. J., & Plott, C. R. (1996). A binary conflict ascending price (bicap) mechanism for the decentralized allocation of the right to use railroad tracks. *International Journal of Industrial Organization, 14*(6), 857–886.

Brucker, P. (2007). *Scheduling algorithms* (5th ed.). Berlin: Springer.

Brucker, P., & Kovalyov, M. Y. (1996). Single machine batch scheduling to minimize the weighted number of late jobs. *Mathematical Methods of Operations Research, 43*, 1–8.

Brucker, P., Gladky, A., Hoogeveen, H., Kovalyov, M. Y., Potts, C. N., Tautenhahn, T., & van de Velde, S. L. (1998). Scheduling a batching machine. *Journal of Scheduling, 1*(1), 31–54.

Bruno, J., Coffman, E. G., & Sethi, R. (1974). Scheduling indepedant tasks to reduce mean finishing time. *Communications of the ACM, 17*, 382–387.

Chen, Z.-L. (1996). Parallel machine scheduling with time dependent processing times. *Discrete Applied Mathematics, 70*, 81–93.

Chen, Z.-L. (1997). Erratum to parallel machine scheduling with time dependent processing times. *Discrete Applied Mathematics, 75*, 103.

Chen, B., Potts, C. N., & Woeginger, G. J. (1998). A review of machine scheduling: Complexity and approximability. In D. Z. Du & P. M. Pardalos (Eds.), *Handbook of combinatorial optimization* (pp. 21–169). Dordrecht: Kluwer Academic Publishers.

Cheng, T. C. E., & Kovalyov, M. Y. (2001). Single machine batch scheduling with sequential job processing. *IIE Transactions, 33*, 413–420.

Cheng, T. C. E., Ding, Q., & Lin, B. (2004a). A concise survey of scheduling with time-dependent processing times. *European Journal of Operational Research, 152*, 1–13.

Cheng, T. C. E., Kovalyov, M. Y., & Chakhlevich, K. N. (2004b). Batching in a two-stage flowshop with dedicated machines in the second stage. *IIE Transactions, 36*, 87–93.

Cheng, T. C. E., Ng, C., & Yuan, J. J. (2006). Multi-agent scheduling on a single machine to minimize total weighted number of tardy jobs. *Theoretical Computer Science, 362*, 273–281.

Cheng, T. C. E., Ng, C., & Yuan, J. J. (2008). Multi-agent scheduling on a single machine with max-form criteria. *European Journal of Operational Research, 188*, 603–609.

Cheng, T. C. E., Cheng, S. R., Wu, W., Hsu, P. H., & Wu, C. C. (2011a). A two-agent single-machine scheduling problem with truncated sum-of-processing-times-based learning considerations. *Computers and Industrial Engineering, 60*, 534–541.

Cheng, T. C. E., Wu, W., Cheng, S. R., & Wu, C. C. (2011b). Two-agent scheduling with position-based deteriorating jobs and learning effects. *Applied Mathematics and Computation, 217*, 8804–8824.

Cheng, T. C. E., Chung, Y.-H., Liao, S., & Lee, W.-C. (2013). Two-agent singe-machine scheduling with release times to minimize the total weighted completion time. *Computers and Operations Research, 40*, 353–361.

Cho, Y., & Sahni, S. (1981). Preemptive scheduling of independent jobs with release and due times on open, flow and job shops. *Operations Research, 29*, 511–522.

Choi, B., Leung, J.-T., & Pinedo, M. (2009). A note on the complexity of a two-agent, linear combination problem. Technical report, Stern School of Business at New York University, IOMS Department.

Coffman, E. G., Yannakakis, J. M., Magazine, M. J., & Santos, C. A. (1990). Batch sizing and job sequencing on a single machine. *Annals of Operations Research, 26*, 135–147.

Conway, R., Maxwell, W., & Miller, L. (1967). *Theory of scheduling*. Reading: Addison-Wesley

Cook, S. A. (1971). The complexity of theorem proving procedures. In *Third annual ACM symposium on theory of computing (STOC '71)*, Shaker Heights (pp. 151–158). New York: ACM

Cormen, T. H., Leiserson, C. E., & Rivest, R. L. (1994). *Introduction to algorithms*. Cambridge: MIT.

Dessouky, M. I., Lageweg, B. J., Lenstra, J. K., & van de Velde, S. L. (1990). Scheduling identical jobs on uniform parallel machines. *Statistica Neerlandica, 44*, 115–123.

Dileepan, P., & Sen, T. (1988). Bicriterion static scheduling research for a single machine. *Omega. The International Journal of Management Science, 16*, 53–59.

Ding, G., & Sun, S. (2010). Single-machine scheduling problems with two agents competing for makespan. *Lecture Notes in Computer Science, 6328*, 244–255.

Du, J., & Leung, J. (1990). Minimizing total tardiness on one machine is NP-hard. *Mathematics of operations research, 15*, 483–495.

Ehrgott, M., Shao, L., & Schobel, A. (2011). An approximation algorithm for convex multi-objective programming problems. *Journal of Global Optimization, 50*, 397–416.

Elvikis, D., Hamacher, H. W., & T'Kindt, V. (2011). Scheduling two agents on uniform parallel machines with makespan and cost functions. *Journal of Scheduling, 14*, 471–481.

Fan, B., Cheng, T., Li, S., & Feng, Q. (2013). Bounded parallel-batching scheduling with two competing agents. *Journal of Scheduling, 16*, 261–271.

Feng, Q., Yu, Z., & Shang, W. (2011). Pareto optimization of serial-batching scheduling problems on two agents. In *2011 international conference on advanced mechatronic systems (ICAMechS)* (pp. 165–168). ISBN 978-1-4577-1698-0.

Garey, M. R., & Johnson, D. S. (1979). *Computers and intractability: A guide to the theory of $\mathcal{NP}$-completeness*. New York: W.H. Freeman and Company.

Garey, M. R., Johnson, D. S., & Sethi, R. (1976). The complexity of flowshop and jobshop scheduling. *Mathematics of operations research, 1*(2), 117–129.

Gavranovic, H., & Finke, G. (2000). Graph partitioning and set covering for optimal design of production system in the metal industry. In *The second conference on management and control of production and logistics – MCPL'00*, Grenoble.

Gawiejnowicz, S. (1996). Brief survey of continuous models of scheduling. *Foundations of Computing and Decision Sciences, 21*, 81–100.

Gawiejnowicz, S. (2008). *Time-dependent scheduling: EATCS monographs in theoretical computer science*. Berlin/New York: Springer.

Gawiejnowicz, S., & Kononov, A. (2012, in press). Isomorphic scheduling problems. *Annals of Operations Research*. doi:10.1007/s10479-012-1222-2.

Gawiejnowicz, S., Onak, T., & Suwalski, C. (2006). A new library for evolutionary algorithms. *Lecture Notes in Computer Science, 3911*, 414–421.

Gawiejnowicz, S., Kurc, W., & Pankowska, L. (2009a). Conjugate problems in time-dependent scheduling. *Journal of Scheduling, 12*, 543–553.

Gawiejnowicz, S., Kurc, W., & Pankowska, L. (2009b). Equivalent time-dependent scheduling problems. *European Journal of Operational Research, 196*, 919–929.

Gawiejnowicz, S., Lee, W. C., Lin, C. L., & Wu, C. C. (2011). Single-machine scheduling of proportionally deteriorating jobs by two agents. *Journal of the Operational Research Society, 62*, 1983–1991.

Geoffrion, A. M. (1968). Proper efficiency and the theory of vector maximization. *Journal of Mathematical Analysis and Applications, 22*, 618–630.

Geoffrion, A. M. (1974). Lagrangian relaxation for integer programming. *Mathematical Programming Study, 2*, 82–114.

Graham, R. L. (1966). Bounds for certain multiprocessor anomalies. *Bell System Technical Journals, 17*, 1563–1581.

Graham, R. L., Lawler, E. L., Lenstra, J. K., & Rinnooy Kan, A. H. G. (1979). Optimization and approximation in deterministic sequencing and scheduling: A survey. *Annals of Discrete Mathematics, 5*, 287–326.

He, C., Lin, Y., & Yuan, J. (2007). Bicriteria scheduling on a batching machine to minimize maximum lateness and makespan. *Theoretical Computer Science, 381*, 234–240.

Hochbaum, D. (1998). *Approximation algorithms for NP-hard problems*. Boston: PWS Publishing.

Hochbaum, D. S., & Landy, D. (1994). Scheduling with batching: Minimizing the weighted number of tardy jobs. *Operations Research Letters, 16*, 79–86.

Hoogeveen, J. A. (1996). Single-machine scheduling to minimize a function of two or three maximum cost criteria. *Journal of Algorithms, 21*, 415–433.

Hoogeveen, H. (2005). Multicriteria scheduling. *European Journal of Operational Research, 167*, 592–623.

Hoogeveen, J. A., & van de Velde, S. L. (1995). Minimizing total completion time and maximum cost simultaneously is solvable in polynomial time. *Operations Research Letters, 17*, 205–208.

Hopcroft, J. E., & Karp, R. M. (1973). An $n^{frac52}$ algorithm for maximum matchings in bipartite graphs. *SIAM Journal on Computing, 4*, 225–231.

Hopcroft, J., & Ullman, J. (1979). *Introduction to automata theory, languages and computation*. Reading: Addison-Wesley.

Horn, W. A. (1973). Minimizing average flow time with parallel machines. *Operations Research, 21*, 846–847.

Huo, Y., Leung, J. Y.-T., & Zhao, H. (2007a). Bi-criteria scheduling problems: Number of tardy jobs and maximum weighted tardiness. *European Journal of Operational Research, 177*, 116–134.

Huo, Y., Leung, J. Y.-T., & Zhao, H. (2007b). Complexity of two dual criteria scheduling problems. *Operations Research Letters, 35*, 211–220.

Jackson, J. R. (1955). Scheduling a production line to minimize maximum tardiness. In *Management Science Research* (Vol. 43). Los Angeles: University of California.

Johnson, S. M. (1954). Optimal two and three-stage production schedules with setup times included. *Naval Research Logistic Quarterly, 1*, 61–67.

Johnson, D. (1982). The NP-completeness column: An ongoing guide. *Journal of Algorithms, 2*, 393–405.

Johnson, D. S. (1990). A catalog of complexity classes. In J. van Leeuwen (Ed.), *Handbook of theoretical computer science: Algorithms and complexity* (pp. 67–161). Elsevier/MIT: Amsterdam/Cambridge.

Jozefowska, J. (2007). *Just-in-time scheduling: Models and algorithms for computer and manufacturing systems*. Berlin: Springer.

Karp, R. M. (1972). Reducibility among combinatorial problems. In R. E. Miller & J. W. Thatcher (Eds.), *Complexity of computer computations* (pp. 85–104). New York: Plenum Press.

Kellerer, H., & Strusevich, V. A. (2010). Fully polynomial approximation schemes for a symmetric quadratic knapsack problem and its scheduling applications. *Algorithmica, 57*, 769–795.

Khowala, K., Fowler, J., Keha, A., & Balasubramanian, H. (2009). Single machine scheduling with interfering job sets. In *Multidisciplinary international conference on scheduling: Theory and applications (MISTA 2009)*, 10–12 Aug 2009, Dublin (pp. 357–365).

Knotts, G., Dror, M., & Hartman, B. C. (2000). Agent-based project scheduling. *IIE Transactions, 32*, 387–401.

Knuth, D. E. (1967–1969). *The art of computer programming* (Vols. 1–3). Reading: Addison-Wesley.

Kononov, A. (1997). Scheduling problems with linear increasing processing times. In *Operations research September 3–6, 1996*, Braunschweig (pp. 208–212). Springer.

Kononov, A. (1998). Single machine scheduling problems with processing times proportional to an arbitrary function. *Discrete Analysis and Operations Research, 5*, 17–37.

Kononov, A., & Gawiejnowicz, S. (2001). NP-hard cases in scheduling deteriorating jobs on dedicated machines. *Journal of the Operational Research Society, 52*, 708–718.

Kovalyov, M. Y., Oulamara, A., & Soukhal, A. (2012). Two-agent scheduling on an unbounded serial batching machine. *Lecture Notes in Computer Science, 7422 LNCS*, 427–438.

Kovalyov, M. Y., Oulamara, A., & Soukhal, A. (2012b). Two-agent scheduling with agent specific batches on an unbounded serial batching machine. In *The 2nd international symposium on combinatorial optimization, ISCO 2012: Vol. 7422. Lecture Notes in Computer Science*, Athens.

Laumanns, M., Thiele, L., & Zitzler, E. (2006). An efficient, adaptive parameter variation scheme for metaheuristics based on the epsilon-constraint method. *European Journal of Operational Research, 169*(3), 932–942.

Lawler, E. L. (1973). Optimal sequencing of a single machine subject to precedence constraints. *Management Science, 19*(8), 544–546.

Lawler, E. L. (1977). A pseudopolynomial algorithm for sequencing jobs to minimize total tardiness. *Annals of Discrete Mathematics, 1*, 331–342.

Lawler, E. L. (1982). *Scheduling a single machine to minimize the number of late jobs* (Vol. 1, pp. 331–342). Berkeley: Computer Science Division, University of California. (preprint)

Lawler, E. L. (1990). A dynamic programming algorithm for preemptive scheduling of a single machine to minimize the number of late jobs. *Annals of Operations Research, 26*, 125–133.

Lawler, E. L., & Moore, J. (1969). A functional equation and its application to resource allocation and sequencing problems. *Management Science, 16*(1), 77–84.

Lee, C. (1991). Parallel machines scheduling with nonsimultaneous machine available time. *Discrete Applied Mathematics, 20*, 53–61.

Lee, C. Y., & Vairaktarakis, G. (1993). Complexity of single machine hierarchical scheduling: A survey. In P. M. Pardalos (Ed.), *Complexity in numerical optimization* (pp. 269–298). Singapore: World Scientific.

Lee, K., Choi, B.-C., Leung, J. Y.-T., & Pinedo, M. L. (2009). Approximation algorithms for multi-agent scheduling to minimize total weighted completion time. *Information Processing Letters, 109*, 913–917.

Lee, W. C., Wang, W. J., Shiau, Y. R., & Wu, C. C. (2010). A single-machine scheduling problem with two-agent and deteriorating jobs. *Applied Mathematical Modelling, 34*(10), 3098–3107.

Lee, W. C., Chung, Y., & Hu, M. (2012). Genetic algorithms for a two-agent single-machine problem with release time. *Applied Soft Computing, 12*, 3580–3589.

Lenstra, J. K., Rinnooy Kan, A. H. G., & Brucker, P. (1977). Complexity of machine scheduling problems. *Annals of Discrete Mathematics, 1*, 343–362.

Leung, J. Y.-T., & Young, G. H. (1989). Minimizing schedule length subject to minimum flow time. *SIAM Journal on Computing, 18*(2), 314–326.

Leung, J. Y.-T., Yu, V. K. M., & Wei, W.-D. (1994). Minimizing the weighted number of tardy task units. *Discrete Applied Mathematics, 51*, 307–316.

Leung, J. Y.-T., Pinedo, M. L., & Wan, G. (2010). Competitive two-agent scheduling and its applications. *Operations Research, 58*, 458–469.

Levin, A., & Woeginger, G. J. (2006). The constrained minimum weighted sum of job completion times problem. *Mathematical Programming Series A, 108*, 115–126.

Lew, A., & Mauch, H. (2007). *Dynamic programming: A computational tool*. Berlin/Heidelberg: Springer.

Lewis, H. R., & Papadimitriou, C. H. (1998). *Elements of the theory of computation* (2nd ed.). Upper Saddle River: Prentice-Hall.

Li, D. C., & Hsu, P. H. (2012). Solving a two-agent single-machine scheduling problem considering learning effect. *Computers and Operations Research, 39*, 1644–1651.

Li, S., & Yuan, J. (2012). Unbounded parallel-batching scheduling with two competitive agents. *Journal of Scheduling, 15*, 629–640.

Liu, P., & Tang, L. (2008). Two-agent scheduling with linear deteriorating jobs on a single machine. *Lecture Notes in Computer Science, 5092*, 642–650.

Liu, P., Tang, L., & Zhou, X. (2010a). Two-agent group scheduling with deteriorating jobs on a single machine. *International Journal of Advanced Manufacturing Technology, 47*, 657–664.

Liu, P., Zhou, X., & Tang, L. (2010b). Two-agent group single-machine scheduling with position-dependent processing times. *International Journal of Advanced Manufacturing Technology, 48*, 325–331.

Liu, P., Yi, N., & Zhou, X. Y. (2011). Two-agent single-machine scheduling problems under increasing linear deterioration. *Applied Mathematical Modelling, 35*, 2290–2296.

Liu, P., Yi, N., Zhou, X., & Gong, H. (2013). Scheduling two agents with sum-of-processing-times-based deterioration on a single machine. *Applied Mathematics and Computation, 219*, 8848–8855.

Manne, A. S. (1960). On the job-shop scheduling problem. *Operations Research, 8*, 219–223.

Mavrotas, G. (2009). Effective implementation of the epsilon-constraint method in multi-objective mathematical programming problems. *Applied Mathematics and Computation, 213*(2), 455–465.

Mc Naughton, R. (1959). Scheduling with deadlines and loss functions. *Management Science, 6*, 1–12.

Meiners, C. R., & Torng, E. (2007). Mixed criteria packet scheduling. In M. Y. Kao & X.-Y. Li (Eds.), *AAIM 2007: Vol. 4508. Lecture Notes on Computer Science* (pp. 120–133). Berlin/Heidelberg: Springer.

Mohri, S., Masuda, T., & Ishii, H. (1999). Bi-criteria scheduling problem on three identical parallel machines. *International Journal of Production Economics, 60–61*, 529–536.

Moore, J. M. (1968). An n job, one machine sequencing algorithm for minimizing the number of late jobs. *Management Science, 15*, 102–109.

Mor, B., & Mosheiov, G. (2010). Scheduling problems with two competing agents to minimize minmax and minsum earliness measures. *European Journal of Operational Research, 206*(3), 540–546.

Mor, B., & Mosheiov, G. (2011). Single machine batch scheduling with two competing agents to minimize total flowtime. *European Journal of Operational Research, 215*(3), 524–531.

Mosheiov, G. (1994). Scheduling jobs under simple linear deterioration. *Computers and Operations Research, 21*, 653–659.

Mosheiov, G. (2002). Complexity analysis of job-shop scheduling with deteriorating jobs. *Discrete Applied Mathematics, 117*, 195–209.

Nagar, A., Haddock, J., & Heragu, S. (1995). Multiple and bicriteria scheduling: A literature survey. *European Journal of the Operational Research, 81*, 88–104.

Ng, C. T., Cheng, T. C. E., & Yuan, J. J. (2006). A note on the complexity of the problem of two-agent scheduling on a single machine. *Journal of Combinatorial Optimization, 12*, 387–394.

Nong, Q., Ng, C., & Cheng, T. (2008). The bounded single-machine parallel-batching scheduling problem with family jobs and release dates to minimize makespan. *Operations Research Letters, 36*(1), 61–66.

Nong, Q., Cheng, T., & Ng, C. (2011). Two-agent scheduling to minimize the total cost. *European Journal of Operational Research, 215*, 39–44.

Nowicki, E., & Zdrzalka, S. (1990). A survey of results for sequencing problems with controllable processing times. *Discrete Applied Mathematics, 26*, 271–287.

Oulamara, A., Kovalyov, M. Y., & Finke, G. (2005). Scheduling a no-wait flowshop with unbounded batching machines. *IIE Transactions on Scheduling and Logistics, 37*, 685–696.

Oulamara, A., Finke, G., & Kuiten, A. K. (2009). Flowshop scheduling problem with batching machine and task compatibilities. *Computers & Operations Research, 36*, 391–401.

Papadimitriou, C. M. (1994). *Computational complexity*. Reading: Addison Wesley.

Papadimitriou, C. H., & Steiglitz, K. (1982). *Combinatorial optimization: Algorithms and complexity*. Englewood Cliffs: Prentice-Hall.

Peha, J. M. (1995). Heterogeneous-criteria scheduling: Minimizing weighted number of tardy jobs and weighted completion time. *Journal of Computers and Operations Research, 22*, 1089–1100.

Pessan, C., Bouquard, J.-L., & Neron, E. (2008). An unrelated parallelmachines model for an industrial production resetting problem. *European Journal of Industrial Engineering, 2*, 153–171.

Pinedo, M. (2008). *Scheduling: Theory, algorithms, and systems* (3rd ed.). Berlin: Springer.

Potts, C., & Kovalyov, M. (2000). Scheduling with batching: A review. *European Journal of Operational Research, 120*(2), 228–249.

Potts, C., Strusevich, V., & Tautenhahn, T. (2001). Scheduling batches with simultaneous job processing for two-machine shop problems. *Journal of Scheduling, 4*(1), 25–51.

Qi, F., Yuan, J. J., Liu, H., & He, C. (2013). A note on two-agent scheduling on an unbounded parallel-batching machine with makespan and maximum lateness objectives. *Applied Mathematical Modelling, 37*, 7071–7076.

Queyranne, M. (1993). Structure of a simple scheduling polyhedron. *Mathematical Programming, 58*, 263–285.

Rustogi, K., & Strusevich, V. A. (2012). Simple matching vs linear assignment in scheduling models with positional effects: A critical review. *European Journal of Operational Research, 222*, 393–407.

Ruzika, S., & Wiecek, M. M. (2005). Approximation methods in multiobjective programming. *Journal of Optimization Theory and Applications, 126*(3), 473–501.

Sabouni, M. Y., & Jolai, F. (2010). Optimal methods for batch processing problem with makespan and maximum lateness objectives. *Applied Mathematical Modelling, 34*(2), 314–324.

Sadi, F., Soukhal, A., & Billaut, J.-C. (2013, to appear). Solving multi-agent scheduling problems on parallel machines with a global objective function. *RAIRO Operations Research.*

Saule, E., & Trystram, D. (2009). Multi-users scheduling in parallel systems. In *Proceedings of the 23rd international symposium on parallel & distributed computing 2009*, Rome (pp. 1–9). IEEE Computer Society.

Schuurman, P., & Woeginger, G. J. (2011). Approximation schemes – A tutorial. In R. H. Mohring, C. N. Potts, A. S. Schulz, G. J. Woeginger, & L. A. Wolsey (Eds.), *Lectures on scheduling*.

Sedeño-Noda, A., Alcaide, D., & González-Martín, C. (2006). Network flow approaches to preemptive open-shop scheduling problems with time-windows. *European Journal of Operational Research, 174*(3), 1501–1518.

Shabtay, D., & Steiner, G. (2007). A survey of scheduling with controllable processing times. *Discrete Applied Mathematics, 155*, 1643–1666.

Smith, W. E. (1956). Various optimizer for single-stage production. *Naval Research Logistics Quarterly, 3*, 59–66.

Su, L.-H. (2009). Scheduling on identical parallel machines to minimize total completion time with deadline and machine eligibility constraints. *The International Journal of Advanced Manufacturing Technology, 40*, 572–581.

Tan, Q., Chen, H.-P., Du, B., & Li, X.-L. (2011). Two-agent scheduling on a single batch processing machine with non-identical job sizes. In *Proceedings of the 2nd international conference on artificial intelligence, management science and electronic commerce, AIMSEC 2011*, Art. No. 6009883 (pp. 7431–7435).

T'kindt, D. E. V. (2012, in press). Two-agent scheduling on uniform parallel machines with min-max criteria. *Annals of Operations Research*, 1–16.

T'Kindt, V., & Billaut, J.-C. (2006). *Multicriteria scheduling: Theory, models and algorithms* (2nd ed.). Berlin/Heildelberg/New York: Springer.

Tuong, N. H. (2009). *Complexité et Algorithmes pour l'Ordonnancement Multicritere de Travaux Indépendants: Problèmes Juste-À-Temps et Travaux Interférants* (in French). PhD thesis, Université François-Rabelais de Tours, Tours.

Tuong, N. H., Soukhal, A., & Billaut, J.-C. (2012). Single-machine multi-agent scheduling problems with a global objective function. *Journal of Scheduling, 15*, 311–321.

Tuzikov, A., Makhaniok, M., & Manner, R. (1998). Bicriterion scheduling of identical processing time jobs by uniform processors. *Computers and Operations Research, 25*, 31–35.

Uzsoy, R., & Yang, Y. (1997). Minimizing total weighted completion time on a single batch processing machine. *Production and Operations Management, 6*, 57–73.

Van de Velde, S. (1991). *Machine scheduling and Lagrangian relaxation*. PhD thesis, CWI Amsterdam.

Van Wassenhove, L. N., & Gelders, L. F. (1980). Solving a bicriterion problem. *European Journal of Operational Research, 4*(1), 42–48.

Vazirani, V. V. (2003). *Approximation algorithms* (2nd ed.). Berlin/Heidelberg: Springer.

Vickson, R. G. (1980a). Choosing the job sequence and processing times to minimize total processing plus flow cost on a single machine. *Operations Research, 28*, 1155–1167.

Vickson, R. G. (1980b). Two single machine sequencing problems involving controllable job processing times. *AIIE Transactions, 12*, 258–262.

Wagner, H. M. (1959). An integer linear programming model for machine scheduling. *Naval Research Logistic Quarterly, 6*, 131–140.

Walukiewicz, S. (1991). *Integer programming*. Warszawa: Polish Scientific Publishers.

Wan, G., Yen, B. P. C., & Li, C. L. (2001). Single machine scheduling to minimize total compression plus weighted flow cost is NP-hard. *Information Processing Letters, 79*, 273–280.

Wan, G., Leung, J.-Y., & Pinedo, M. (2010). Scheduling two agents with controllable processing times. *European Journal of Operational Research, 205*, 528–539.

Wan, L., Yuan, J., & Geng, Z. (2013, to appear). A note on the preemptive scheduling to minimize total completion time with release and deadline constraints. *Journal of Scheduling*.

Webster, S., & Baker, K. (1995). Scheduling groups of jobs on a single machine. *Operations Research, 43*, 692–704.

Woeginger, G. J. (2003). Exact algorithms for NP-hard problems: A survey. *Lecture Notes in Computer Science, 2570*, 187–205.

Wu, W. H. (2013). An exact and meta-heuristic approach for two-agent single-machine scheduling problem. *Journal of Marine Science and Technology, 21*, 215–221.

Wu, C. C., Huang, S. K., & Lee, W. C. (2011). Two-agent scheduling with learning consideration. *Computers and Industrial Engineering, 61*, 1324–1335.

Wu, W. H., Cheng, S. R., Wu, C. C., & Yin, Y. Q. (2012). Ant colony algorithms for a two-agent scheduling with sum-of processing times-based learning and deteriorating considerations. *Journal of Intelligent Manufacturing, 23*, 1985–1993.

Wu, C.-C., Wu, W.-H., Chen, J.-C., Yin, Y., & Wu, W.-H. (2013a). A study of the single-machine two-agent scheduling problem with release times. *Applied Soft Computing, 13*, 998–1006.

Wu, W. H., Xu, J., Wu, W., Yin, Y., Cheng, I., & Wu, C. C. (2013b). A tabu method for a two-agent single-machine scheduling with deterioration jobs. *Computers & Operations Research, 40*, 2116–2127.

Yin, Y. Q., Cheng, S. R., Cheng, T., Wu, C. C., & Wu, W.-H. (2012a). Two-agent single-machine scheduling with assignable due dates. *Applied Mathematics and Computation, 219*, 1674–1685.

Yin, Y. Q., Cheng, S. R., & Wu, C. C. (2012b). Scheduling problems with two agents and a linear non-increasing deterioration to minimize earliness penalties. *Information Sciences, 189*, 282–292.

Yin, Y. Q., Wu, W., Cheng, S. R., & Wu, C. C. (2012c). An investigation on a two-agent single-machine scheduling problem with unequal release dates. *Computers & Operations Research, 39*, 3062–3073.

Yuan, J. J., Shang, W. P., & Feng, Q. (2005). A note on the scheduling with two families of jobs. *Journal of Scheduling, 8*, 537–542.

Zhao, K., & Lu, X. (2013). Approximation schemes for two-agent scheduling on parallel machines. *Theoretical Computer Science, 468*, 114–121.

Zitzler, E., Knowles, J., & Thiele, L. (2008). Quality assessment of Pareto set approximations. *Lecture Notes in Computer Science, 5252 LNCS*, 373–404.

# Index



A. Agnetis et al., *Multiagent Scheduling*, DOI 10.1007/978-3-642-41880-8,

MIX
Papier aus verantwortungsvollen Quellen
Paper from responsible sources
FSC® C105338

If you have any concerns about our products,
you can contact us on
**ProductSafety@springernature.com**

In case Publisher is established outside the EU,
the EU authorized representative is:
**Springer Nature Customer Service Center GmbH**
**Europaplatz 3, 69115 Heidelberg, Germany**

Printed by Libri Plureos GmbH
in Hamburg, Germany